The Selected Writings Of Benjamin Rush

OSMANIA UNIVERSITY LIBRARY

Call No. 814-21/R895 Accession No. 29434

Author Runs, D.D.

Title Selected Writings of Benjamin Rush

This book should be returned on or before the date last marked below.

The Selected Writings of Benjamin Rush

ECCE HOMO!

The Selected Writings of Benjamin Rush

EDITED BY
DAGOBERT D RUNES

PHILOSOPHICAL LIBRARY
NEW YORK

COPYRIGHT, 1947, BY
THE PHILOSOPHICAL LIBRARY, INC.
15 East 40th Street
New York 16, N. Y

PRINTED IN THE UNITED STATES OF AMERICA

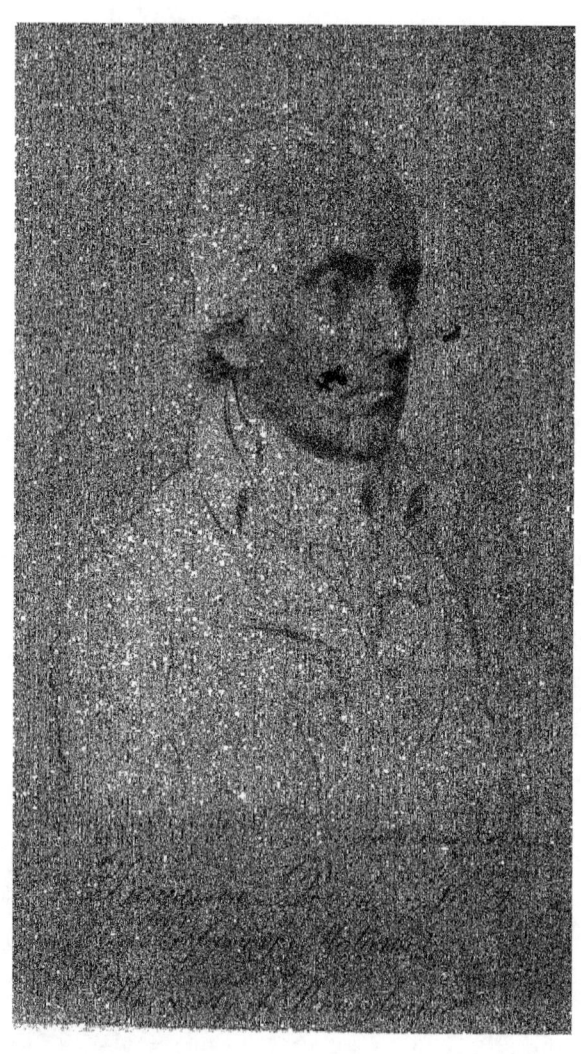

ORIGINAL AT THE AMERICAN PHILOSOPHICAL SOCIETY,
IN PHILADELPHIA.

EDITOR'S PREFACE

"IF A GREAT MAN DIES, there is a hole in the world." Time may do much to fill that hole; on the two hundredth anniversary of the birth of Benjamin Rush, for example, few memorials echoed his name in this great land. Yet few were as fiery as he, or more influential, in the vehemence of protest that brought this country into being; and few held the standards of its early learning and culture as high as he held them.

Only Thomas Paine—a close friend—could match Benjamin Rush in uncompromising revolutionary spirit. Rush, incidentally, suggested the title for Paine's historic pamphlet, "Common Sense." * Together, they ploughed the field for revolution in Colonial America. And only Benjamin Franklin, in the young United States, had the humane versatility, the many-sided interests, the wide learning, of Benjamin Rush.

The interests of Dr. Rush were varied, but their direction was unwaveringly toward the betterment of mankind. His scientific and medical investigations, as well as his social studies and endeavors, were interfused with deeply religious and ethical feeling. In science and medicine, he sought along the frontiers of knowledge. In the quest for social and political justice, he fought on the side of the weak. [Alexander Hamilton blocked his appointment to the medical faculty of Columbia College, on the ground of his "too radical beliefs."]

He was considered by many *the* great physician of his country and time. Perhaps he was not. Medicine, in his day, was still groping in the dark. The bacterial nature of diseases was as yet unknown; as yet undiscovered was the application of anaesthesia, the door to surgery.

Yet Benjamin Rush was the first in America to employ oc-

* See frontispiece (facsimile of *Diary*).

cupational therapy in the treatment of mental ills, and to encourage—anticipating modern methods—analytical *conversation with* the patient.

There can be no doubt as to the depth of Rush's burning patriotism, his hatred of the British oppression, of all tyranny. His signature on the Declaration of Independence was by no means a merely formal one. It signified not only his people's fight against British domination, but his continuing resolve to battle tyranny, intolerance, and suppression in his native America.

Benjamin Rush's pamphlets, articles, letters, and speeches mount into the thousands. He pleaded for the abolition of slavery. He urged the removal of the death penalty. He argued for the amelioration of the lot of civil prisoners, who, often jailed for no worse crime than debt, were sent to labor in city streets chained down with heavy iron balls. He advocated the establishment of special hospitals for the insane, then confined in vermin-infested stables, at the mercy of ignorant and brutal guards. There was no current cause worthy of support that did not benefit from the warm heart, the outstretched hand, and the uplifted voice of Benjamin Rush.

It was inevitable that so staunch a fighter should rally around him many friends and supporters, but also unite against him many who preferred or profited by the status quo. Conscious of the great opportunities of the new country, Rush was equally aware of its failings and insufficiencies. In his national pride and his forthright directness, he became the conscience of the new-born republic.

Even before the birth of the new nation, during the events that led up to and that marked the American Revolution, this keen conscience of Benjamin Rush was a goad to his fellows. It must be remembered that a considerable body of business men and of politicians was at first entirely opposed to a War for Independence, and during the War clamored for a policy of appeasement. In this struggle Benjamin Rush, along with his friend, Thomas Paine, was enlisted in the determined left. So strong were his political integrity and fervor, so rigid his devotion to the principles of political and social democracy, that he came into conflict with a number of the leaders of the day. Even George Washington—who, incidentally, Thomas Paine complained, deserted him during his imprisonment at the time of the French Revolution—was brought into opposition by Rush's refusal to grant the merest iota of compromise. Such men as he, holding steadfast to the ideal, point to the peaks toward which civilization must painfully and tardily climb. In later years, Rush removed from his papers most of the references to these conflicts. We may never resolve some of the controversies of their mystery; but we may be confident that Benjamin Rush, though not always practical, was always in the right.

* * *

Benjamin Rush was born on December 24, 1745, on his father's farm north of Philadelphia. At an early age he was sent to the Academy of his uncle, the Rev. Samuel Finley. Here he imbibed a deeply religious spirit. In 1759, he entered Princeton College, receiving the bachelor's degree before he had reached the age of fifteen.

For the next six years, he devoted himself to the study of medicine, under the direction of Dr. Redman of Philadelphia. He then enrolled at the University of Edinburgh where, in 1768, he was awarded the degree of Doctor of Medicine.

After his graduation, following a brief trip to France, Benjamin Rush returned to Philadelphia. In 1769 he was appointed Professor of Chemistry in the College of Philadelphia, the first medical school in America. When, in 1791, the College was expanded into a University, Rush was appointed Professor of the Institutes and Practices of Medicine.

In the meantime had come the struggle for independence, upon which Benjamin Rush embarked with equal energy and devotion. He was a member of the Revolutionary Congress, which in 1776 passed the Declaration of Independence. He served in the War as Military Surgeon. Having little taste for routine politics or for professional politicians, Rush later sought to withdraw from political activity. In 1799, however, President Adams honored him with the appointment as Treasurer of the National Mint. He held this office for his remaining fourteen years.

The medical and social concerns of Benjamin Rush had never lapsed. One of his basic characteristics as teacher and physician was his deep-set conviction that medical science was in its infancy. Although the great bacteriological discoveries in medicine did not bring their far-reaching changes until two generations later, Rush was outstanding for his rejection of medical orthodoxy, for his emphasis on continuing sober research. His self-denial and personal fortitude during the Philadelphia yellow fever epidemic of 1795 belong to the annals of medical heroism.

Benjamin Rush was an indefatigable student of natural science. He was rarely without a book in hand. Even at mealtimes, he was in one way or another preoccupied with study, research, or practice. In truly Socratic manner, he interrogated persons in all stations of life, and he frequently declared that he had received valuable information from laymen, quacks, even madmen. "The student," he said, "should always, like a plant, be in an absorbing state. Even his dreams should not be permitted to sport themselves idly in his brain."

The writings of Rush show a wide range of interest and knowledge, embracing agriculture and the mechanical arts, chemistry and medicine, political science and theology. Numerous are the letters and articles he wrote, anonymously as well as under his own name, in his constant endeavor to dispel prejudice, to fight oppression, to elevate the lot of the lowly.

Rush was continually active in the support of institutions and organizations for the advancement of human learning. Not only was he instrumental in establishing colleges and other schools of higher learning in his own state of Pennsylvania, but he advocated establishment of free public schools in every township, in order to create unified systems of state education. He wanted his beloved American Republic to grow into one great and enlightened family.

In the field of public welfare, Rush was the founder of the Philadelphia Dispensary, the first institution of its kind in the

EDITOR'S PREFACE

United States. He also made searching examinations of the methods of punishment of criminals. He protested against the viciousness of a penal law that chained convicts to wheelbarrows, dragging them through public streets on road jobs, dressed in conspicuous convict clothes, with shaven heads as a symbol of infamy. He vehemently maintained that such a system tended only to harden the criminals, not to improve them. In this field of penology, too, Rush was one of America's earliest reformers.

Benjamin Rush's lifework in the social and scientific fields places him clearly at the head of the early American fighters for a more wholesome, a more secure, a happier way of living. He stands also among the early patriots who with clear eye and unflagging zeal saw, and worked to achieve, the goals of human freedom. He himself sums up this aspect of his being: "My reading, observations, and reflections have tended more and more to show the absurdity of hereditary power and to prove that no form of government can be rational, but that which is derived from the suffrages of the people who are the subjects of it."

CONTENTS

	PAGE
EDITOR'S INTRODUCTION	v

ON GOOD GOVERNMENT

ON SLAVE-KEEPING [1773]	3
A PLAN OF A PEACE-OFFICE FOR THE UNITED STATES [1799]	19
ON HELPING THE AFRICANS [date unknown]	24
ON THE DEFECTS OF THE CONFEDERATION [1787]	26
ON SECURITIES FOR LIBERTY [1792]	32
ON PUNISHING MURDER BY DEATH [1792]	35
OBSERVATIONS ON THE GOVERNMENT OF PENNSYLVANIA [1777]	54

ON EDUCATION

OF THE MODE OF EDUCATION PROPER IN A REPUBLIC [1798]	87
EDUCATION AGREEABLE TO A REPUBLICAN FORM OF GOVERNMENT [1786]	97
PLAN OF A FEDERAL UNIVERSITY [1788]	101
THE AMUSEMENTS AND PUNISHMENTS WHICH ARE PROPER FOR SCHOOLS [1790]	106
THE BIBLE AS A SCHOOL BOOK [1791]	117

ON NATURAL AND MEDICAL SCIENCES

LECTURES ON ANIMAL LIFE [1799]	133
THE INFLUENCE OF PHYSICAL CAUSES UPON THE MORAL FACULTY [1786]	181

CONTENTS

	PAGE
ON THE DIFFERENT SPECIES OF MANIA [date unknown]	212
ON THE DIFFERENT SPECIES OF PHOBIA [date unknown]	220
THE PROGRESS OF MEDICINE [1801]	227
OBSERVATIONS AND REASONING IN MEDICINE [1791]	245
MEDICINE AMONG THE INDIANS OF NORTH AMERICA [1774]	254
THE VICES AND VIRTUES OF PHYSICIANS [1801]	293
DUTIES OF A PHYSICIAN [1789]	308

ON MISCELLANEOUS THINGS

INFLUENCE OF THE AMERICAN REVOLUTION [1789]	325
THE EFFECTS OF ARDENT SPIRITS UPON MAN [1805]	334
ON OLD AGE [1789]	342
SERMON ON EXERCISE [1772]	358
ON MANNERS [1769]	373
DIRECTIONS FOR CONDUCTING A NEWSPAPER [1788]	396
THE BENEFITS OF CHARITY [1788]	399
THE YELLOW FEVER [1792]	404

APPENDIX

LIST OF WRITINGS PUBLISHED DURING LIFETIME	419
SELECTED BIBLIOGRAPHY	423
INDEX	425

ON GOOD GOVERNMENT

ON SLAVE-KEEPING

So MUCH hath been said upon the subject of Slave-keeping, that an apology may be required for this paper. The only one I shall offer is, that the evil still continues. This may in part be owing to the great attachment we have to our own interest, and in part to the subject not being fully exhausted. The design of the following paper is to sum up the leading arguments against it, several of which have not been urged by any of those authors who have written upon it.

Without entering into the history of the facts which relate to the slave-trade, I shall proceed immediately to combat the principal arguments which are used to support it.

And here I need hardly say any thing in favor of the Intellects of the Negroes, or of their capacities for virtue and happiness, although these have been supposed by some to be inferior to those of the inhabitants of Europe. The accounts which travellers give us of their ingenuity, humanity, and strong attachment to their parents, relations, friends and country, show us that they are equal to the Europeans, when we allow for the diversity of temper and genius which is occasioned by climate. We have many well attested anecdotes of as sublime and disinterested virtue among them as ever adorned a Roman or a Christian character.* But we are to distinguish between an African in his own

---

* See SPECTATOR, Vol. I. No. 11.
There is now in the town of Boston a Free Negro Girl, about 18 years of age, who has been but 9 years in the country, whose singular genius and accomplishments are such as not only do honor to her sex, but to human nature. Several of her poems have been printed, and read with pleasure by the public.

country, and an African in a state of slavery in America. Slavery is so foreign to the human mind, that the moral faculties, as well as those of the understanding are debased, and rendered torpid by it. All the vices which are charged upon the Negroes in the southern colonies and the West-Indies, such as Idleness, Treachery, Theft, and the like, are the genuine offspring of slavery, and serve as an argument to prove that they were not intended, by Providence for it.

Nor let it be said, in the present Age, that their black color (as it is commonly called), either subjects them to, or qualifies them for slavery.* The vulgar notion of their being descended from Cain, who was supposed to have been marked with this color, is too absurd to need a refutation.—Without enquiring into the Cause of this blackness, I shall only add upon this subject, that so far from being a curse, it subjects the Negroes to no inconveniencies, but on the contrary qualifies them for that part of the Globe in which providence has placed them. The ravages of heat, diseases and time, appear less in their faces than in a white one; and when we exclude variety of color from our ideas of

---

*Montesquieu, in his Spirit of Laws, treats this argument with the ridicule it deserves.

"Were I to vindicate our right to make slaves of the Negroes, these should be my arguments.

The Europeans having extirpated the American Indians, were obliged to make slaves of the Africans, for clearing such vast tracts of land.

Sugar would be too dear, if the plants which produce it were cultivated by any other than slaves.

These creatures are all over black, and with such a flat nose, that they can scarcely be pitied.

It is hardly to be believed that God, who is a wise being, should place a soul, especially a good soul, in such a black ugly body.

The Negroes prefer a glass necklace to that gold, which polite nations so highly value: can there be a greater proof of their wanting common sense.

It is impossible for us to suppose these creatures to be men, because, allowing them to be men, a suspicion would follow, that we ourselves are not Christians."

BOOK XV. CHAP. V.

Beauty, they may be said to possess every thing necessary to constitute it in common with the white people.†

It has been urged by the inhabitants of the Sugar Islands and South Carolina, that it would be impossible to carry on the manufactories of Sugar, Rice, and Indigo, without Negro slaves. No manufactory can ever be of consequence enough to society, to admit the least violation of the laws of justice or humanity. But I am far from thinking the arguments used in favor of employing Negroes for the cultivation of these articles, should have any weight.

M. Le Poivre, late envoy from the king of France, to the king of Cochin-China, and now intendant of the isles of Bourbon and Mauritius, in his observations upon the manners and arts of the various nations in Africa and Asia, speaking of the culture of sugar in Cochin-China, has the following remarks—"It is worthy observation too, that the sugar cane is there cultivated by freemen, and all the process of preparation and refining, the work of free hands. Compare then the price of the Cochin-Chinese production with the same commodity which is cultivated and prepared by the wretched slaves of our European colonies, and judge if, to procure sugar from our colonies, it was necessary to authorize by law the slavery of the unhappy Africans transported to America. From what I have observed at Cochin-China, I cannot entertain a doubt, but that our West-India colonies, had they been distributed without reservation amongst a free people, would have produced double the quantity that it now procured from the labor of the unfortunate Negroes.

What advantage, then, has accrued to Europe, civilized as it is, and thoroughly versed in the laws of nature, and the rights

---

† "Quamvis ille niger, quamvis tu candidus esses.
————Nimium ne crede colori.
Alba Ligustra cadunt; Vaccinia nigra leguntur."
VIRGIL.
"I am black,——but *comely*."
SONG OF SOLOMON.

of mankind, by legally authorizing in our colonies, the daily outrages against human nature, permitting them to debase man almost below the level of the beasts of the field? These slavish laws have proved as opposite to its interest, as they are to its honor, and to the laws of humanity. This remark I have often made.

Liberty and property form the basis of abundance, and good agriculture: I never observed it to flourish where those rights of mankind were not firmly established. The earth which multiplies her productions with a kind of profusion, under the hands of the free-born laborer seems to shrink into barrenness under the sweat of the slave. Such is the will of the great Author of our Nature, who has created man free, and assigned to him the earth, that he might cultivate his possession with the sweat of his brow; but still should enjoy his Liberty.

Now if the plantations in the islands and the southern colonies were more limited, and freemen only employed in working them, the general product would be greater, although the profits to individuals would be less,—a circumstance this, which by diminishing opulence in a few, would suppress luxury and vice, and promote that equal distribution of property, which appears best calculated to promote the welfare of society.——* I know it has been said by some, that none but the natives of warm climates could undergo the excessive heat and labor of the West-India islands. But this argument is founded upon an error; for the reverse of this is true. I have been informed by good authority, that one European who escapes the first or second year,

---

* From this account of Le Poivre's, we may learn the futility of the argument, that the number of vessels in the sugar trade, serve as a nursery for seamen, and that the Negroes consume a large quantity of the manufactures of Great Britain. If freemen only were employed in the islands, a double quantity of sugar would be made, and of course twice the number of vessels and seamen would be made use of in the trade. One freeman consumes yearly four times the quantity of British goods that a Negro does. Slaves multiply in all countries slowly. Freemen multiply in proportion as slavery is discouraged. It is to be hoped therefore that motives of policy will at last induce Britons to give up a trade, which those of justice and humanity cannot prevail upon them to relinquish.

will do twice the work, and live twice the number of years that an ordinary Negro will do. nor need we be surprised at this, when we hear that such is the natural fertility of the soil, and so numerous the spontaneous fruits of the earth in the interior parts of Africa, that the natives live in plenty at the expence of little or no labor, which, in warm climates, has ever been found to be incompatible with long life and happiness. Future ages, therefore, when they read the accounts of the Slave Trade (—if they do not regard them as fabulous)——will be at a loss which to condemn most, our folly or our guilt, in abetting this direct violation of the laws of nature and religion.

But there are some who have gone so far as to say that slavery is not repugnant to the genius of Christianity, and that it is not forbidden in any part of the Scriptures. Natural and revealed Religion always speak the same things, although the latter delivers its precepts with a louder, and more distinct voice than the former. If it could be proved that no testimony was to be found in the Bible against a practice so pregnant with evils of the most destructive tendency to society, it would be sufficient to overthrow its divine original. We read it is true of Abraham's having slaves born in his house; and we have reason to believe, that part of the riches of the patriarchs consisted in them: but we can no more infer the lawfulness of the practice, from the short account which the Jewish historian gives us of these facts, than we can vindicate telling a lie, because Rahab is not condemned for it in the account which is given of her deceiving the king of Jericho.* We read that some of the same

---

*3 And the king of Jericho sent unto Rahab, saying, Bring forth the men that are come to thee, which are entered into thine house· for they be come to search out all the country.

4 And the woman took the two men, and hid them, and said thus, There came men unto me, but I wist not whence they *were*.

5 And it came to pass *about the time* of shutting of the gate, when it was dark, that the men went out: whither the men went, I wot not: pursue after them quickly, for ye shall overtake them.

6 But she brought them up to the roof of the house, and hid them with the stalks of flax, which she had laid in order upon the roof.

JOSHUA, Chap. II.

men indulged themselves in a plurality of wives, without any strictures being made upon their conduct for it; and yet no one will pretend to say, that this is not forbidden in many parts of the Old Testament.† But we are told the Jews kept the heathens in perpetual bondage.‡ The design of providence in permitting this evil, was probably to prevent the Jews from marrying among strangers, to which their intercourse with them upon any other footing than that of slaves, would naturally have inclined them.* Had this taken place—their Natural Religion would have been corrupted—they would have contracted all their vices,** and the intention of providence in keeping them a distinct people, in order to accomplish the promise made to Abraham, that "in his Seed all the Nations of the earth should be blessed," would have been defeated; so that the descent of the MESSIAH from ABRAHAM, could not have been traced, and the divine commission of the Son of God, would have wanted one of its most powerful arguments to support it. But with regard to their own countrymen, it is plain, perpetual slavery was not tolerated. Hence, at the end of seven years or in the year of the jubilee, all the

---

† Prov. v. 18, 19, 20.
‡ Levit. xxv. 44, 45, 46.
* That marriage with strangers was looked upon as a crime among the Jews, we learn from Ezra ix. 1 to 6, also from the whole of Chapter x.
** May not this be the reason why swine's flesh was forbidden to the Jews, lest they should be tempted to eat with their heathen neighbours, who used it in diet? This appears more probable than the opinion of Doctor MEAD, who supposes that it has a physical tendency to produce the leprosy; or that of VOLTAIRE, who asserts that the Jews learned to abstain from this flesh from the Egyptians, who valued the Hog almost to a degree of idolatry for its great usefulness in rooting up the Ground. What makes this conjecture the more probable is, that the Jews abstained from several other kinds of flesh used by their heathen neighbours, which have never been accused of bringing on diseases of the skin, and which were used constantly in diet by the Egyptians. The account which Tacitus gives of the diet and custom of the Jews, is directly to our purpose—

"Bos quoque immolantur, quem Ægyptii apin colunt. Ægyptii pleraque animalia, Effigiesque compositas venerantur, Judæi mente sola, unumque numen intelligunt, Separati Epulis, discreti Cubilibus, Alienarum Concubitu Abstinent."

HISTOR. LIB. V.

Hebrew slaves were set at liberty,* and it was held unlawful to detain them in servitude longer than that time, except by their own consent.† But if, in the partial revelation which GOD made, of his will to the Jews, we find such testimonies against slavery, what may we not expect from the Gospel, the design of which was to abolish all distinctions of name and country. While the Jews thought they complied with the precepts of the law, in confining the love of their neighbour "to the children of their own people," Christ commands us to look upon all mankind even our enemies ‡ as our neighbours and brethren, and "in all things, to do unto them whatever we would wish they should do unto us." He tells us further that his "Kingdom is not of this World," and therefore constantly avoids saying any thing that might interfere directly with the Roman or Jewish governments: so that altho' he does not call upon masters to emancipate their slaves, or upon slaves to assert that liberty wherewith God and nature had made them free, yet there is scarcely a parable or a sermon in the whole history of his life, but what contains the strongest arguments against slavery. Every prohibition of covetousness—intemperance—pride—uncleanness—theft—and murder, which he delivered,—every lesson of meekness, humility, forbearance, charity, self-denial, and brotherly-love which he taught, are levelled against this evil;—for slavery, while it includes all the former vices, necessarily excludes the practice of all the latter virtues, both from the master and the slave.—Let such, therefore, who vindicate the traffic of buying and selling souls, seek some modern system of religion to support it, and not presume to sanctify their crimes by attempting to reconcile it to the sublime and perfect Religion of the Great Author of Christianity.**

---

* Deuteronomy xxiv. 7.
† Deut. xv. 12.
‡ This is strongly inculcated in the story of the good Samaritan, Luke x.*
** The influence of Christianity in putting a stop to slavery, appears in the first Christian emperor Constantine, who commanded, under the severest penalties, all such as had slaves, to set them at liberty. He after-

There are some amongst us who cannot help allowing the force of our last argument, but plead as a motive for importing and keeping slaves, that they become acquainted with the principles of the religion of our country.—This is like justifying a highway robbery because part of the money acquired in this manner was appropriated to some religious use.—Christianity will never be propagated by any other methods than those employed by Christ and his apostles. Slavery is an engine as little fitted for that purpose as fire or the sword. A Christian slave is a contradiction in terms.* But if we enquire into the methods

---

wards contrived to render the manumission of them much easier than formerly, for instead of recurring to the forms prescribed by the Roman laws, which were attended with great difficulties and a considerable expence, he gave leave to masters to infranchise their slaves in the presence of a bishop, or a minister and a Christian assembly.
Universal History, vol. xv. p. 574, 577.

Dr. ROBERTSON, in treating of those causes which weakened the feudal system, and finally abolished slavery in Europe, in the 14th century, has the following observations——

"The gentle spirit of the Christian religion, together with the doctrines which it teaches, concerning the original equality of mankind, as well as the impartial eye with which the almighty regards men of every condition, and admits them to a participation of his benefits, are inconsistent with servitude. But in this, as in many other instances, considerations of interest and the maxims of false policy, led men to a conduct inconsistent with their principles. They were so sensible, however, of the inconsistency, that to set their fellow Christians at liberty from servitude was deemed an act of piety highly meritorious, and acceptable to Heaven. The humane spirit of the Christian religion, struggled with the maxims and manners of the world, and contributed more than any other circumstance, to introduce the practice of manumission. The formality of manumission was executed in a church or a religious assembly.—The person to be set free, was led round the great altar, with a torch in his hand, he took hold of the horns of the altar, and there the solemn words conferring liberty, were pronounced."
CHARLES V. Historical Illustrations. Note xx.

* St. Paul's letter to Philemon, in behalf of Onesimus, is said by some to contradict this assertion, but, if viewed properly, will rather support it. He desires Philemon to receive him "not as a servant, but as a brother beloved," "as his son—and part of himself." In other parts of his writings, he obliquely hints at the impossibility of uniting the duties of a Chris-

ON GOOD GOVERNMENT

employed for converting the Negroes to Christianity, we shall find the means suited to the end proposed. In many places Sunday is appropriated to work for themselves. Reading and writing are discouraged among them. A belief is even inculcated among some, that they have no souls. In a word,—Every attempt to instruct or convert them, has been constantly opposed by their masters. Nor has the example of their Christian masters any tendency to prejudice them in favor of our religion. How often do they betray, in their sudden transports of anger and resentment (against which there is no restraint provided towards their Negroes) the most violent degrees of passion and fury!—— What luxury—what ingratitude to the supreme being—what impiety in their ordinary conversation do some of them discover in the presence of their slaves; I say nothing of the dissolution of marriage vows, or the entire abolition of matrimony, which the frequent sale of them introduces, and which are directly contrary to the law of nature and the principles of Christianity. Would to heaven I could here conceal the shocking violations of chastity, which some of them are obliged to undergo without daring to complain. Husbands have been forced to prostitute their wives, and mothers their daughters, to gratify the brutal lust of a master. This—all—this is practised—blush—ye impure and hardened monsters, while I repeat it——by men who call themselves Christians!

But further——It has been said that we do a kindness to the Negroes by bringing them to America, as we thereby save their lives, which had been forfeited by their being conquered in war.*

---

tian, with the offices of a slave. "Ye are bought with a price, be not therefore the servants of men." 1 Corinth. vii. 23. Had he lived to see Christianity established by Law, in the countries where he preached, with what a torrent of Christian eloquence may we not suppose he would have declaimed against slavery!

* "From the right of killing in case of conquest, politicians have drawn that of reducing to slavery; a consequence as ill grounded as the principle.

There is no such thing as a right of reducing people to slavery, but when it becomes necessary for the preservation of the conquest. Preserva-

Let such as prefer or inflict slavery rather than death, disown their being descended from or connected with our mother countries.—But it will be found, upon enquiry, that many are stolen or seduced from their friends, who have never been conquered; and it is plain, from the testimony of historians and travellers, that wars were uncommon among them, until the Christians who began the slave trade, stirred up the different nations to fight against each other. Sooner let them imbrue their hands in each others blood, or condemn one another to perpetual slavery, than the name of one Christian, or one American be stained by the perpetuation of such enormous crimes. Nor let it be urged that by treating slaves well, we render their situation happier in this country than it was in their own.——slavery and vice are connected together, and the latter is always a source of misery. Besides, by the greatest humanity we can show them, we only lessen, but do not remove the crime, for the injustice of it continues the same. The laws of retribution are so strongly inculcated by the moral governor of the world, that even the ox is entitled to his reward for "treading the corn." How great then must be the amount of that injustice which deprives so many of our fellow creatures of the *just* reward of their labor! *

---

tion, but not servitude, is the end of conquest; though servitude may happen sometimes to be a necessary means of preservation.

Even in that case it is contrary to the nature of things, that the slavery should be perpetual. The people enslaved ought to be rendered capable of becoming subjects."

Montesquieu's Spirit of Laws, Book x. Chap. 3

"Servi autem ex eo appellati sunt, quod Imperatores captivos vendere, ac per hoc servare, nec occidere solent. Servitus est constitutio *Juris Gentium*, qua quis Dominio alieno CONTRA NATURAM subjicitur.——

Justinian. Institut. L. i. Tit. 3.

* The debt of a master to a Negro man whose work is valued at ten pounds sterling a year, deducting forty shillings a year, which is the most that is laid out for their clothing in the West-Indies, amounts, in the course of 20 years, to £. 160 sterling. The victuals are included in the above wages. These consist chiefly of vegetables, and are very cheap.

But it will be asked here, What steps shall we take to remedy this evil, and what shall we do with those slaves we have already in this country? This is indeed a most difficult question. But let every man contrive to answer it for himself. If you possessed an estate which was bequeathed to you by your ancestors, and were afterwards convinced that it was the just property of another man, would you think it right to continue in the possession of it? would you not give it up immediately to the lawful owner? The voice of all mankind would mark him for a villain who would refuse to comply with this demand of justice. And is not keeping a slave after you are convinced of the unlawfulness of it—a crime of the same nature? All the money you save, or acquire by their labor is stolen from them; and however plausible the excuse may be that you form to reconcile it to your consciences, yet be assured that your crime stands registered in the court of Heaven as a breach of the eighth commandment.

The first step to be taken to put a stop to slavery in this country, is to leave off importing slaves. For this purpose let our assemblies unite in petitioning the King and Parliament to dissolve the African Company.* It is by this incorporated band of robbers that the trade has been chiefly carried on to America. We have the more reason to expect relief from an application at this juncture, as, by a late decision in favor of a Virginia slave, at Westminster-Hall, the clamors of the whole nation are raised against them. Let such of our countrymen as engage in the slave trade, be shunned as the greatest enemies to our country, and, let the vessels which bring the slaves to us, be avoided as if they bore in them the seeds of that forbidden fruit, whose baneful taste destroyed both the natural and moral world.——As for the Negroes among us, who, from having acquired all the low vices of slavery, or who, from age or infirmities are unfit to be set at

---

* The Virginia Assembly, which had the honor of being first on the continent in opposing the American Stamp Act by their Resolves, have lately set another laudable example to the colonies in being the first in petitioning for a redress of this grievance.

liberty, I would propose, for the good of society, that they should continue the property of those with whom they grew old, or from whom they contracted those vices and infirmities. But let the young Negroes be educated in the principles of virtue and religion—let them be taught to read and write——and afterwards instructed in some business, whereby they may be able to maintain themselves. Let laws be made to limit the time of their servitude, and to entitle them to all the privileges of free-born British subjects. At any rate let retribution be done to God and to society.*

---

* A worthy friend of mine has favored me with the following Extract of a letter from GRANVILLE SHARP, Esq; of London.

"I am told of some regulations that have taken place in the Spanish Colonies, which do the Spaniards much honor, and are certainly worthy our imitation, in case we should not be so happy as to obtain an entire abolition of slavery and probably you wou'd find many American subjects that wou'd be willing to promote such regulations, tho' the same people wou'd strenuously oppose the scheme of a total abolition of slavery. I have never seen an account of the Spanish regulations in writing, but I understand that they are to the following effect: As soon as a slave is landed, his name, price, &c. are register'd in a public office, and the master is obliged to allow him one working day in every week to himself, besides Sundays, so that if the slave chuses to work for his master on that day, he receives the wages of a freeman for it, and whatever he gains by his labor on that day, is so secured to him by law, that the master cannot deprive him of it This is certainly a considerable step towards the abolishing absolute slavery. As soon as the slave is able to purchase another working day, the master is obliged to sell it to him at a proportionable price, viz 1-fifth part of his original cost. and so likewise the remaining 4 days at the same rate, as soon as the slave is able to redeem them, after which he is absolutely free. This is such an encouragement to industry, that even the most indolent are tempted to exert themselves. Men who have thus worked out their freedom are inured to the labor of the country and are certainly the most useful subjects that a colony can acquire. Regulations might be formed upon the same plan to encourage the industry of slaves that are already imported into the colonies, which would teach them how to maintain themselves and be as useful, as well as less expensive to the planter. They would by such means become members of society and have an interest in the welfare of the community, which would add greatly to the strength and security of each colony; whereas, at present, many of the planters are in continual danger of being cut off by their slaves,—a fate which, they but too justly deserve!"

And now my countrymen, What shall I add more to rouse up your indignation against slave-keeping. Consider the many complicated crimes it involves in it. Think of the bloody wars which are fomented by it, among the African nations, or if these are too common to affect you, think of the pangs which attend the dissolution of the ties of nature in those who are stolen from their relations. Think of the many thousands who perish by sickness, melancholy and suicide, in their voyages to America. Pursue the poor devoted victims to one of the West India islands, and see them exposed there to public sale. Hear their cries, and see their looks of tenderness at each other upon being separated.—Mothers are torn from their daughters, and brothers from brothers, without the liberty of a parting embrace. Their master's name is now marked upon their breasts with a red hot iron. But let us pursue them into a sugar field, and behold a scene still more affecting than this———See! the poor wretches with what reluctance they take their instruments of labor into their hands.—Some of them, overcome with heat and sickness, seek to refresh themselves by a little rest,———But, behold an overseer approaches them.—In vain they sue for pity.———He lifts up his whip, while streams of blood follow every stroke. Neither age nor sex are spared.—Methinks one of them is a woman far advanced in her pregnancy.—At a little distance from these behold a man, who from his countenance and deportment appears as if he was descended from illustrious ancestors.———Yes.—He is the son of a prince, and was torn, by a stratagem, from an amiable wife and two young children— Mark his sullen looks!—now he bids defiance to the tyranny of his master, and in an instant plunges a knife into his heart.— But, let us return from this Scene, and see the various modes of arbitrary punishments inflicted upon them by their masters. Behold one covered with stripes, into which melted wax is poured—another tied down to a block or a stake—a third suspended in the air by his thumbs—a fourth obliged to set or stand upon red hot iron———a fifth,———I cannot relate it.———
Where now is law or justice?———Let us fly to them to step in

for their relief.————Alas!——The one is silent, and the other denounces more terrible punishments upon them. Let us attend the place appointed for inflicting the penalties of the law. See here one without a limb, whose only crime was an attempt to regain his liberty—another led to a gallows for eating a morsel of bread, to which his labor gave him a better title than his master—a third famishing on a gibbet——a fourth, in a flame of fire!—his shrieks pierce the heavens.————O! God! Where is thy vengeance!————O! humanity—justice—liberty—religion!——Where,—where are ye fled.————

This is no exaggerated picture. It is taken from real life.—— Before I conclude I shall take the liberty of addressing several classes of my countrymen in behalf of our brethren (for by that name may we now call them) who are in a state of slavery among us.

In the first place let MAGISTRATES both supreme and inferior, exert the authority they are invested with, in suppressing this evil. Let them discountenance it by their example, and show a readiness to concur in every measure proposed to remedy it.

Let LEGISLATORS, reflect upon the trust reposed in them. Let their laws be made after the spirit of religion—liberty—and our most excellent English Constitution. You cannot show your attachment to your King or your love to your country better than by suppressing an evil which endangers the dominions of the former, and will in time destroy the liberty of the latter.* Population, and the accession of strangers, in which the riches of all countries consist, can only flourish in proportion as slavery is discouraged. Extend the privileges we enjoy, to every human creature born among us, and let not the journals of our assemblies

---

* By a late calculation, it appears that there are eight hundred and fifty thousand Negro slaves in the British colonies and islands. From the number and burden of ships which are sent from England to Africa for slaves, we can with a good deal of certainty, conclude, that there are not less than one hundred thousand of them imported into America every year. By particular enquiry it was found, that one hundred and four thousand were imported in the year 1768.

"In moderate governments, it is a point of the highest importance,

be disgraced with the records of laws, which allow exclusive privileges to men of one color in preference to another.*

Ye men of sense and virtue———Ye advocates for American liberty, rouse up and espouse the cause of humanity and general liberty. Bear a testimony against a vice which degrades human nature, and dissolves that universal tie of benevolence which should connect all the children of men together in one great family.——The plant of liberty is of so tender a nature, that it cannot thrive long in the neighbourhood of slavery. Remember the eyes of all Europe are fixed upon you, to preserve an asylum for freedom in this country, after the last pillars of it are fallen in every other quarter of the globe.

But chiefly——ye ministers of the gospel, whose dominion over the principles and actions of men is so universally acknowledged and felt,——Ye who estimate the worth of your fellow creatures by their immortality, and therefore must look upon all mankind as equal;—let your zeal keep pace with your opportunities to put a stop to slavery. While you inforce the duties of "tithe and cummin," neglect not the weightier laws of justice and humanity. Slavery is an Hydra sin, and includes in it every violation of the precepts of the Law and the Gospel. In vain will you command your flocks to offer up the incense of faith and

---

that there should not be a great number of slaves. The political liberty of those states adds to the value of civil liberty; and he who is deprived of the latter, is also deprived of the former. He sees the happiness of a society, of which he is not so much as a member; he sees the security of others fenced by laws, himself without so much protection. He sees his master has a soul, that can enlarge itself; while his own is constrained to submit to almost continual depression. Nothing more assimilates a man to a beast, than living among freemen, himself a slave. Such people as these are the natural enemies of a society, and their number must be dangerous."

Spirit of Laws, Book xv. Chap. 12.

* The alterations in the laws in favour of Negroes, should be gradual, —'till the evil habits they have acquired by slavery, are eradicated. There are several privileges, however, which might be extended to them immediately, without the least risk to society, in particular that inestimable one of trial by juries.

charity, while they continue to mingle the sweat and blood of Negro slaves with their sacrifices.——If the blood of Abel cried aloud for vengeance,—If, under the Jewish dispensation, cities of refuge could not screen the deliberate murderer—if even manslaughter required sacrifices to expiate it,—and if a single murder so seldom escapes with impunity in any civilized country, what may you not say against that trade, or those manufactures—or laws,* which destroy the lives of so many thousands of our fellow-creatures every year?——If in the Old Testament "God swears by his holiness, and by the excellency of Jacob, that the earth shall tremble, and every one mourn that dwelleth therein for the iniquity of those who oppress the poor and crush the needy," "who buy the poor with silver, and the needy with a pair of shoes,"† what judgments may you not denounce upon those who continue to perpetrate these crimes, after the more full discovery which God has made of the law of equity in the New Testament. Put them in mind of the rod which was held over them a few years ago in the Stamp and Revenue Acts. Remember that national crimes require national punishments, and without declaring what punishment awaits this evil, you may venture to assure them, that it cannot pass with impunity, unless God shall cease to be just or merciful.

---

* "If any Negro or other slave under punishment by his master, or his order for running away, or any other crimes or misdemeanors towards his said master, unfortunately shall suffer in life or member, no person whatever shall be liable to any fine, But if any man shall of wantonness, or only of bloody mindedness, or cruel intention, wilfully kill a Negro, or other slave of his own, he shall deliver into the public treasury fifteen pounds sterling, and not be liable to any other punishment, or forfeiture for the same."

Laws of Barbadoes, Act 329.

† Amos iv. 1, 2.——viii. 6, 7.

A PLAN OF A PEACE-OFFICE FOR THE UNITED STATES

AMONG THE defects which have been pointed out in the Federal Constitution by its antifederal enemies, it is much to be lamented that no person has taken notice of its total silence upon the subject of an office of the utmost importance to the welfare of the United States, that is, an *office* for promoting and preserving perpetual *peace* in our country.

It is to be hoped that no objection will be made to the establishment of such an office, while we are engaged in a war with the Indians, for as the *War-Office* of the United States was established in the *time of peace*, it is equally reasonable that a *Peace-Office* should be established in the *time of war*.

The plan of this office is as follows:

I. Let a Secretary of the Peace be appointed to preside in this office, who shall be perfectly free from all the present absurd and vulgar European prejudices upon the subject of government, let him be a genuine republican and a sincere Christian, for the principles of republicanism and Christianity are no less friendly to universal and perpetual peace, than they are to universal and equal liberty.

II. Let a power be given to this Secretary to establish and maintain free-schools in every city, village and township of the United States; and let him be made responsible for the talents, principles, and morals, of all his schoolmasters. Let the youth of our country be carefully instructed in reading, writing, arithmetic, and in the doctrines of a religion of some kind: the Christian religion should be preferred to all others; for it belongs to this religion exclusively to teach us not only to cultivate peace with men, but to forgive, nay more—to love our very enemies. It belongs to it further to teach us that the Supreme Being alone possesses a power to take away human life, and that we rebel against his laws, whenever we undertake to execute death in any way whatever upon any of his creatures.

III. Let every family in the United States be furnished at the public expense, by the Secretary of this office, with a copy of an American edition of the BIBLE. This measure has become the more necessary in our country, since the banishment of the bible, as a school-book, from most of the schools in the United States. Unless the price of this book be paid for by the public, there is reason to fear that in a few years it will be met with only in courts of justice or in magistrates' offices; and should the absurd mode of establishing truth by kissing this sacred book fall into disuse, it may probably, in the course of the next generation, be seen only as a curiosity on a shelf in a public museum.

IV. Let the following sentence be inscribed in letters of gold over the doors of every State and Court house in the United States.

THE SON OF MAN CAME INTO THE WORLD, NOT TO DESTROY MEN'S LIVES, BUT TO SAVE THEM.

V. To inspire a veneration for human life, and an horror at the shedding of human blood, let all those laws be repealed which authorise juries, judges, sheriffs, or hangmen to assume the resentments of individuals and to commit murder in cold blood in any case whatever. Until this reformation in our code of penal jurisprudence takes place, it will be in vain to attempt to introduce universal and perpetual peace in our country.

VI. To subdue that passion for war, which education, added to human depravity, have made universal, a familiarity with the instruments of death, as well as all military shows, should be carefully avoided. For which reason, militia laws should every where be repealed, and military dresses and military titles should be laid aside: reviews tend to lessen the horrors of a battle by connecting them with the charms of order; militia laws generate idleness and vice, and thereby produce the wars they are said to prevent; military dresses fascinate the minds of young men, and lead them from serious and useful professions; were there no *uniforms*, there would probably be no armies; lastly, military titles feed vanity, and keep up ideas in the mind which lessen a sense of the folly and miseries of war.

VII. In the last place, let a large room, adjoining the federal hall, be appropriated for transacting the business and preserving all the records of this *office*. Over the door of this room let there be a sign, on which the figures of a LAMB, a DOVE and an OLIVE BRANCH should be painted, together with the following inscriptions in letters of gold:

PEACE ON EARTH—GOOD-WILL TO MAN.
AH! WHY WILL MEN FORGET THAT THEY ARE BRETHREN?

Within this apartment let there be a collection of ploughshares and pruning-hooks made out of swords and spears; and on each of the walls of the apartment, the following pictures as large as the life:

1. A lion eating straw with an ox, and an adder playing upon the lips of a child.

2. An Indian boiling his venison in the same pot with a citizen of Kentucky.

3. Lord Cornwallis and Tippoo Saib, under the shade of a sycamore-tree in the East Indies, drinking Madeira wine together out of the same decanter.

4. A group of French and Austrian soldiers dancing arm and arm, under a bower erected in the neighbourhood of Mons.

5. A St. Domingo planter, a man of color, and a native of Africa, legislating together in the same colonial assembly.*

To complete the entertainment of this delightful apartment, let a group of young ladies, clad in white robes, assemble every day at a certain hour, in a gallery to be erected for the purpose, and sing odes, and hymns, and anthems in praise of the blessings of peace.

One of these songs should consist of the following lines.

> Peace o'er the world her olive wand extends,
> And white-rob'd innocence from heaven descends,
> All crimes shall cease, and ancient frauds shall fail,
> Returning justice lifts aloft her scale.

In order more deeply to affect the minds of the citizens of the United States with the blessings of peace, by *contrasting* them with the evils of war, let the following inscriptions be painted upon the sign, which is placed over the door of the War Office.

1. An office for butchering the human species.
2. A Widow and Orphan making office.
3. A broken bone making office.
4. A Wooden leg making office.
5. An office for creating public and private vices.
6. An office for creating a public debt.
7. An office for creating speculators, stock jobbers, and bankrupts.
8. An office for creating famine.
9. An office for creating pestilential diseases.
10. An office for creating poverty, and the destruction of liberty, and national happiness.

In the lobby of this office let there be painted representations

---

* At the time of writing this, there existed wars between the United States and the American Indians, between the British nation and Tippoo Saib, between the planters of St Domingo and their African slaves, and between the French nation and the emperor of Germany.

of all the common military instruments of death, also human skulls, broken bones, unburied and putrefying dead bodies, hospitals crowded with sick and wounded soldiers, villages on fire, mothers in besieged towns eating the flesh of their children, ships sinking in the ocean, rivers dyed with blood, and extensive plains without a tree or fence, or any other object, but the ruins of deserted farm houses.

Above this group of woeful figures,—let the following words be inserted, in red characters to represent human blood,

"NATIONAL GLORY."

ON HELPING THE AFRICANS
From a Letter to Granville Sharp

SINCE OUR correspondence began, in the year 1771, what wonderful things have come to pass in favor of our friends the poor Africans!—In Pennsylvania our laws have exterminated domestic Slavery, and in Philadelphia the free blacks now compose near 3,000 souls. Their men are chiefly waiters—day-labourers—and traders in a small way. Their women are chiefly cooks and washer-women. Such is their integrity, and quiet deportment, that they are universally preferred to white people of similar occupations. But under these circumstances they are still in a state of depression, arising chiefly from their being deprived of the means of regular education, and religious instruction. To remedy these inconveniences, a few gentlemen in this city have assisted in forming them into a church, to be called *The African Church of Philadelphia*. As they consist of the scattered appendages of most of the churches in the city, they have formed articles and a plan of church government so general as to embrace all, and yet so orthodox in cardinal points as to offend none. They have already been assisted in purchasing a valuable lot, in a centrical part of our city, on which they propose this fall to build a frame school-house, and in the spring (if they are further assisted) they wish to erect a plain brick church. They have already began to worship God in a borrowed school-house, where they assemble on Sundays. Two or three of their own colour conduct the worship, by reading the Scriptures, praying, singing, and occasionally exhorting. Hereafter they propose to have a regular minister:—in the meanwhile, the Rev. Mr. Pilmore, a worthy episcopal minister of this city, has promised to officiate for them occasionally. Much good may be expected from this institution. Indeed much good has already arisen from it; for it has produced a degree of order, and a spirit of inquiry and thoughtfulness in religion never evinced by them before.

I come now to the design of this long letter, which is to solicit your influence, among the friends of the Blacks in London, in obtaining a small contribution towards building the proposed African Church in our city. It may produce consequences far beyond our present expectations, or even comprehensions.

It is true the Blacks are not of *your* country. But what then? You have pleaded the cause of the Africans in their native country.—By helping them here, you will only change the *place*, but not the *objects* of your benevolence. The favor I now solicit for them is more substantial than even freedom itself. It will place them in a condition to make their freedom a blessing to them here, and prepare them for happiness beyond the grave.

In spreading the blessings of liberty, and religion, our Divine Master forbids us, in many of his parables and precepts, to have either friends or country. The globe is the native country, and the whole human race, the fellow-citizens of a Christian. This sentiment, I am sure, will accord with the feelings of your heart —for you have long exemplified it by your life and conversation.

From, my dear friend,
Your affectionate fellow-labourer,
And sincere friend and servant,
BENJAMIN RUSH.

ON THE DEFECTS OF THE CONFEDERATION

THERE IS nothing more common than to confound the terms of the American Revolution with those of the late American War. The American War is over: but this is far from being the case with the American Revolution. On the contrary, nothing but the first act of the great drama is closed. It remains yet to establish and perfect our new forms of government; and to prepare the principles, morals, and manners of our citizens, for these forms of government, after they are established and brought to perfection.

The Confederation, together with most of our state constitutions, were formed under very unfavorable circumstances. We had just emerged from a corrupted monarchy. Although we understood perfectly the principles of liberty, yet most of us were ignorant of the forms and combinations of power in republics. Add to this, the British army was in the heart of our country, spreading desolation wherever it went: our resentments, of course, were awakened. We detested the British name, and unfortunately refused to copy some things in the administration of justice and power, in the British government, which have made it the admiration and envy of the world. In our opposition to monarchy, we forgot that the temple of tyranny has two doors. We bolted one of them by proper restraints but we left the other open, by neglecting to guard against the effects of our own ignorance and licentiousness.

Most of the present difficulties of this country arise from the weakness and other defects of our governments.

My business at present shall be only to suggest the defects of the Confederation. These consist, 1st, In the deficiency of coercive power. 2d, In a defect of exclusive power to issue paper money, and regulate commerce. 3d, In vesting the sovereign power of the United States in a single legislature: and 4th, In the too frequent rotation of its members.

A convention is to sit soon* for the purpose of devising means of obviating part of the two first defects that have been mentioned. But I wish they may add to their recommendations to each state, to surrender up to Congress their power of emitting money. In this way, uniform currency will be produced, that will facilitate trade, and help to bind the states together. Nor will the states be deprived of large sums of money by this means when sudden emergencies require it: for they may always borrow them as they did during the war, out of the treasury of Congress. Even a loan-office may be better instituted in this way in each state, than in any other.

The two last defects that have been mentioned, are not of less magnitude than the first. Indeed, the single legislature of Congress will become more dangerous from an increase of power than ever. To remedy this, let the supreme federal power be divided, like the legislatures of most of our states, into two distinct, independent branches. Let one of them be styled the Council of the States, and the other the Assembly of the States. Let the first consist of a single delegate,—and the second, of two, three, or four delegates, chosen annually by each state. Let the president be chosen annually by the joint ballots of both houses, and let him possess certain powers in conjunction with a privy council, especially the power of appointing most of the officers of the United States. The officers will not only be better when appointed this way, but one of the principal causes of faction will be thereby removed from congress. I

---

* May 1787, in Philadelphia.

apprehend this division of the power of Congress will become more necessary, as soon as they are invested with more ample powers of levying and expending public money.

The custom of turning men out of power or office, as soon as they are qualified for it, has been found to be as absurd in practice, as it is virtuous in speculation. It contradicts our habits and opinions in every other transaction of life. Do we dismiss a general—a physician—or even a domestic as soon as they have acquired knowledge enough to be useful to us, for the sake of increasing the number of able generals—skilful physicians—and faithful servants? We do not. Government is a science; and can never be perfected in America, until we encourage men to devote not only three years, but their whole lives to it. I believe the principal reason why so many men of abilities object to serving in Congress, is owing to their not thinking it worth while to spend three years in acquiring a profession which their country immediately afterwards forbids them to follow.

There are two errors or prejudices on the subject of government in America, which lead to the most dangerous consequences.

It is often said that "the sovereign and all other power is seated *in* the people." This idea is unhappily expressed. It should be—"all power is derived *from* the people." They possess it only on the days of their elections. After this, it is the property of their rulers, nor can they exercise or resume it, unless it is abused. It is of importance to circulate this idea, as it leads to order and good government.

The people of America have mistaken the meaning of the word sovereignty: hence each state pretends to be sovereign. In Europe it is applied only to those states which possess the power of making war and peace—of forming treaties, and the like. As this power belongs only to Congress, they are the only sovereign power in the United States.

We commit a similar mistake in our ideas of the word independent.—No individual state as such has any claim to independence. She is independent only in a union with her sister states in Congress.

To conform the principles, morals, and manners of our citizens to our republican forms of government, it is absolutely necessary that knowledge of every kind, should be disseminated through every part of the United States.

For this purpose, let Congress, instead of laying out half a million of dollars in building a federal town, appropriate only a fourth part of that sum, in founding a federal university. In this university, let every thing connected with government, such as history—the law of nature and nations—the civil law—the municipal laws of our country—and the principles of commerce, be taught by competent professors. Let masters be employed likewise to teach gunnery—fortification—and every thing connected with defensive and offensive war.—Above all, let a professor, of what is called in the European universities, economy, be established in this federal seminary. His business should be to unfold the principles and practice of agriculture and manufactures of all kinds; and to enable him to make his lectures more extensively useful, Congress should support a travelling correspondent for him, who should visit all the nations of Europe, and transmit to him, from time to time, all the discoveries and improvements that are made in agriculture and manufactures. To this seminary young men should be encouraged to repair, after completing their academical studies in the colleges of their respective states. The honors and offices of the United States should, after a while, be confined to persons who had imbibed federal and republican ideas in this university.

For the purpose of diffusing knowledge, as well as extending the living principle of government to every part of the United States; every state—city—county—village—and township in the union, should be tied together by means of the post-office.—This is the true non-electric wire of government. It is the only means of conveying heat and light to every individual in the federal commonwealth. Sweden lost her liberties, says the Abbé Raynal, because her citizens were so scattered, that they had no means of acting in concert with each other. It should be a constant injunction to the postmasters to convey newspapers free of all charge for postage.—They are not only the vehicles of knowledge and intelligence, but the sentinels of the liberties of our country.

The conduct of some of those strangers who have visited our country, since the peace, and who fill the British papers with accounts of our distresses, shows as great a want of good sense, as it does of good nature. They fear nothing; but the foundations and walls of the temple of liberty, and yet they undertake to judge of the whole fabric.

Our own citizens act a still more absurd part, when they cry out, after the experience of three or four years, that we are not proper materials for republican government. Remember, we assumed these forms of government in a hurry, before we were prepared for them. Let every man exert himself in promoting virtue and knowledge in our country, and we shall soon become good republicans. Look at the steps by which governments have been changed or rendered stable in Europe. Read the history of Great Britain. Her boasted government has risen out of wars—and rebellions that lasted above sixty years. The United States are travelling peaceably into order and good government. They know no strife—but what arises from the collision of opinions. and in three years, they have advanced further in the road to stability and happiness, than most of the nations in Europe have done, in as many centuries.

There is but one path that can lead the United States to destruction, and that is their extent of territory. It was probably to effect this, that Great Britain ceded to us so much waste land. But even this path may be avoided. Let but one new state be exposed to sale at a time; and let the land office be shut up till every part of this new state is settled.

I am extremely sorry to find a passion for retirement so universal among the patriots and heroes of the war. They resemble skilful mariners, who, after exerting themselves to preserve a ship from sinking in a storm, in the middle of the ocean, drop asleep as soon as the waves subside, and leave the care of their lives and property, during the remainder of the voyage to sailors without knowledge or experience. Every man in a republic is public property. His time and talents—his youth—his manhood —his old age—nay more, life, all, belong to his country.

Patriots of 1774, 1775, 1776,—heroes of 1778, 1779, 1780! come forward! your country demands your services.—Philosophers and friends to mankind, come forward! your country demands your studies and speculations! Lovers of peace and order, who declined taking part in the late war, come forward! your country forgives your timidity, and demands your influence and advice!—Hear her proclaiming in sighs and groans, in her governments, in her finances, in her trade, in her manufactures, in her morals, and in her manners, *"The revolution is not over!"*

ON SECURITIES FOR LIBERTY

Letter from Dr. Rush, to Dr. Ramsay

Dear Sir,

I presume, before this time, you have heard, and rejoiced in the auspicious event of the ratification of the Federal Government by six of the United States.

The objections, which have been urged against the Federal Constitution, from its wanting a Bill of Rights, have been reasoned and ridiculed out of credit in every state that has adopted it. There can be only two securities for liberty in any government, viz. representation and checks. By the first, the rights of the people, and by the second, the rights of representation are effectually secured. Every part of a free constitution hangs upon these two points; and these form the two capital features of the proposed Constitution of the United States. Without them, a volume of rights would avail nothing; and with them, a declaration of rights is absurd and unnecessary: for the people, where their liberties are committed to an equal representation, and to a compound legislature, such as we observe in the new government, will always be the sovereigns of their rulers, and hold all their rights in their own hands. To hold them at the mercy of their servants, is disgraceful to the dignity of freemen. Men, who call for a Bill of Rights, have not recovered from the habits they acquired under the monarchical government of Great Britain.

I have the same opinion with the Antifederalists, of the danger of trusting arbitrary power to any single body of men: but no such power will be committed to our new rulers. Neither the

House of Representatives, the Senate, or the President, can perform a single legislative act by themselves. An hundred principles in man will lead them to watch, to check, and to oppose each other, should an attempt be made by either of them upon the liberties of the people. If we may judge of their conduct, by what we have so often observed in all the state-governments, the members of the Federal legislature will much oftener injure their constituents, by voting agreeably to their inclinations, than against them.

But are we to consider men entrusted with power, as the receptacles of all the depravity of human nature? by no means. The people do not part with their full proportions of it. Reason and revelation both deceive us, if they are all wise and virtuous. Is not history as full of the vices of the people, as it is of the crimes of the kings? what is the present moral character of the citizens of the United States? I need not describe it. It proves too plainly that the people are as much disposed to vice as their rulers; and that nothing but a vigorous and efficient government can prevent their degenerating into savages, or devouring each other like beasts of prey.

A simple democracy has been very aptly compared by Mr. Ames, of Massachusetts, to a volcano that contained within its bowels the fiery materials of its own destruction. A citizen of one of the cantons of Switzerland, in the year 1776, refused in my presence to drink "the commonwealth of America" as a toast, and gave as a reason for it, "that a simple democracy was the devil's own government." The experience of the American states, under the present Confederation, has, in too many instances, justified these two accounts of a simple popular government.

It would have been a truth, if Mr. Locke had not said it, that where there is no law, there can be no liberty; and nothing deserves the name of law but that which is certain, and universal in its operation, upon all the members of the community.

To look up to a government that establishes justice, insures order, cherishes virtue, secures property, and protects from every species of violence, affords a pleasure that can only be exceeded by looking up, in all circumstances, to an over-ruling Providence. Such a pleasure, I hope, is before us and our posterity, under the influence of the new government.

The dimensions of the human mind are apt to be regulated by the extent and objects of the government under which it is formed. Think then, my friend, of the expansion and dignity the American mind will acquire, by having its powers transferred from the contracted objects of a state, to the more unbounded objects of a national government?—A citizen and a legislator of the free and United States of America, will be one of the first characters in the world.

I would not have you suppose, after what I have written, that I believe the new government to be without fault. I can see them—yet not in any of the writings or speeches of the persons who are opposed to it. But who ever saw any thing perfect come from the hands of man? it realises, notwithstanding, in a great degree, every wish I ever entertained, in every stage of the Revolution, for the happiness of my country; for you know, that I have acquired no new opinions or principles, upon the subject of republics, by the sorrowful events we have lately witnessed in America. In the year 1776, I lost the confidence of the people of Pennsylvania, by openly exposing the dangers of a simple democracy, and declaring myself an advocate for a government composed of three legislative branches.

ON PUNISHING MURDER BY DEATH

IN AN ESSAY upon the effects of public punishments upon criminals and upon society, published in the second volume of the *American Museum*, I hinted, in a short paragraph, at the injustice of punishing murder by death. I shall attempt in the following essay, to support that opinion, and to answer all the objections that have been urged against it.

I. Every man possesses an absolute power over his own liberty and property, but not over his own life. When he becomes a member of political society, he commits the disposal of his liberty and property to his fellow citizens; but as he has no right to dispose of his life, he cannot commit the power over it to any body of men. To take away life, therefore, for any crime, is a violation of the first political compact.

II. The punishment of murder by death, is contrary to reason, and to the order and happiness of society.

1. It lessens the horror of taking away human life, and thereby tends to multiply murders.

2. It produces murder, by its influence upon people who are tired of life, and who, from a supposition, that murder is a less crime than suicide, destroy a life (and often that of a near connexion) and afterwards deliver themselves up to justice, that they may escape from their misery by means of a halter.

3. The punishment of murder by death, multiplies murders, from the difficulty it creates of convicting persons who are guilty of it. Humanity, revolting at the idea of the severity and certainty

of a capital punishment, often steps in, and collects such evidence in favour of a murderer, as screens him from justice altogether, or palliates his crime into manslaughter. If the punishment of murder consisted in long confinement, and hard labor, it would be proportioned by the measure of our feelings of justice, and every member of society would be a watchman or a magistrate, to apprehend a destroyer of human life, and to bring him to punishment.

4. The punishment of murder by death, checks the operations of universal justice, by preventing the punishment of every species of murder. Quack doctors—frauds of various kinds—and a licentious press, often destroy life, and sometimes with malice of the most propense nature. If murder were punished by confinement and hard labour, the authors of the numerous murders that have been mentioned, would be dragged forth, and punished according to their deserts. How much order and happiness would arise to society from such a change in human affairs! But who will attempt to define these species of murder, or to prosecute offenders of this stamp, if death is to be the punishment of the crime after it is admitted, and proved to be wilful murder?— only alter the punishment of murder, and these crimes will soon assume their proper names, and probably soon become as rare as murder from common acts of violence.

5. The punishment of murder by death, has been proved to be contrary to the order and happiness of society by the experiments of some of the wisest legislators in Europe. The Empress of Russia, the King of Sweden, and the Duke of Tuscany, have nearly extirpated murder from their dominions, by converting its punishment into the means of benefiting society, and reforming the criminals who perpetrate it.

III. The punishment of murder by death, is contrary to divine revelation. A religion which commands us to forgive and even to do good to our enemies, can never authorise the punishment of murder by death. "Vengeance is mine," said the Lord; "I will repay." It is to no purpose to say here, that this vengeance is taken out of the hands of an individual, and directed against the criminal by the hand of government. It is equally an usurpation of the prerogative of heaven, whether it be inflicted by a single person, or by a whole community.

Here I expect to meet with an appeal from the letter and spirit of the gospel, to the law of Moses, which declares, that "he that killeth a man shall surely be put to death." Forgive, indulgent heaven! the ignorance and cruelty of man, which by the misapplication of this text of scripture, has so long and so often stained the religion of Jesus Christ with folly and revenge.

The following considerations, I hope, will prove that no argument can be deduced from this law, to justify the punishment of murder by death. On the contrary, that several arguments against it, may be derived from a just and rational explanation of that part of the levitical institutions.

1. There are many things in scripture *above*, but nothing *contrary* to reason. Now, the punishment of murder by death, is *contrary* to reason. It cannot, therefore, be agreeable to the will of God.

2. The order and happiness of society cannot fail of being agreeable to the will of God. But the punishment of murder by death, destroys the order and happiness of society. It must therefore be contrary to the will of God.

3. Many of the laws given by Moses, were accommodated to the ignorance and "hardness of heart" of the ancient Jews. Hence their divine legislator expressly says, "I gave them statutes that were *not good,* and judgments whereby *they should not live.*" Of this, the law which respects divorces, and the law of retaliation, which required "an eye for an eye, and a tooth for a tooth," are remarkable instances.

But we are told, that the punishment of murder by death, is founded not only on the law of Moses, but upon a positive precept given to Noah and his posterity, that "whoso sheddeth man's blood, by man shall his blood be shed." In order to show that this text does not militate against my proposition, I shall beg leave to transcribe a passage from an essay on crimes and punishments, published by the Reverend Mr. Turner, in the second volume of the Manchester memoirs. "I hope," says this ingenious author, "that I shall not offend any one, by taking the liberty to put my own sense upon this celebrated passage, and to inquire, why it should be deemed a precept at all. To me, I confess, it appears to contain nothing more than a declaration of what will generally happen; and in this view, to stand exactly upon the same ground with such passages as the following: "He that leadeth into captivity shall go into captivity." "He that taketh up the sword, shall perish by the sword." *— The form of expression is exactly the same in each of the texts; why, then, may they not all be interpreted in the same manner, and considered, not as commands, but as denunciations, and if so, the magistrate will be no more bound by the text in Genesis, to punish murder with death, than he will by the text in the Revelations, to sell every Guinea captain to our West India planters; and yet, however just and proper such a proceeding might be, I suppose no one will assert that the magistrate is bound to it by that, or any other text in the scriptures, or that that alone would be admitted as a sufficient reason for so extraordinary a measure."

If this explanation of the precept given to Noah, be not satisfactory, I shall mention another. Soon after the flood, the infancy and weakness of society rendered it impossible to punish murder by *confinement*. There was therefore no medium between inflicting death upon a murderer, and suffering him to escape with impunity, and thereby to perpetrate more acts of violence against his fellow creatures. It pleased God in this condition of the world to permit a *less* in order to prevent a *greater* evil. He therefore commits *for a while* his exclusive power over human life, to his creatures for the safety and preservation of an infant society, which might otherwise have perished, and with it, the only stock of the human race. The command indirectly implies that the crime of murder was not punished by death in the mature state of society which existed before the flood. Nor is this the only instance upon record in the scriptures

---
* Rev. xv, 10.

in which God has delegated his power over human life to his creatures. Abraham expresses no surprise at the command which God gave him to sacrifice his son He submits to it as a precept founded in reason and natural justice, for nothing could be more obvious than that the giver of life had a right to claim it *when* and in *such manner* as he pleased. 'Till men are able to give life, it becomes them to tremble at the thought of *taking it* away. Will a man rob God?—Yes—he robs him of what is infinitely dear to him—of his darling attribute of *mercy*, every time he deprives a fellow creature of life.

4. If the Mosaic law with respect to murder, be obligatory upon Christians, it follows that it is equally obligatory upon them to punish adultery, blasphemy, and other capital crimes that are mentioned in the levitical law, by death. Nor is this all: it justifies the extirpation of the Indians, and the enslaving of the Africans, for the command to the Jews to destroy the Canaanites, and to make slaves of their heathen neighbours, is as positive as the command which declares, "that he that killeth a man, shall surely be put to death."

5. Every part of the levitical law, is full of types of the Messiah. May not the punishment of death, inflicted by it, be intended to represent the demerit and consequences of sin, as the cities of refuge were the offices of the Messiah?

6. The imperfection and severity of these laws were probably intended farther—to illustrate the perfection and mildness of the gospel dispensation. It is in this manner that God has manifested himself in many of his acts. He created darkness first, to illustrate by comparison the beauty of light; and he permits sin, misery, and death in the moral world, that he may hereafter display more illustriously the transcendent glories of righteousness, happiness, and immortal life. This opinion is favoured by St. Paul, who says, "the law made nothing perfect," and that "it was a shadow of good things to come."

How delightful to discover such an exact harmony between the dictates of reason, the order and happiness of society, and the precepts of the gospel! There is a perfect unity in truth.

Upon all subjects—in all ages—and in all countries—truths of every kind agree with each other.

It has been said, that the common sense of all nations, and particularly of savages, is in favour of punishing murder by death.

The common sense of all nations is in favor of the commerce and slavery of their fellow creatures. But this does not take away from their immorality. Could it be proved that the Indians punish murder by death, it would not establish the right of man over the life of a fellow creature, for revenge we know in its utmost extent is the universal and darling passion of all savage nations. The practice moreover, (if it exist) must have originated in *necessity;* for a people who have no settled place of residence, and who are averse from all labour, could restrain murder in no other way. But I am disposed to doubt whether the Indians punish murder by death among their own tribes. In all those cases where a life is taken away by an Indian of a *foreign* tribe, they always demand the satisfaction of *life* for *life*. But this practice is founded on a desire of preserving a balance in their numbers and power; for among nations which consist of only a few warriors, the loss of an individual often destroys this balance, and thereby exposes them to war or extermination. It is for the same purpose of keeping up an equality in numbers and power, that they often adopt captive children into their nations and families. What makes this explanation of the practice of punishing murder by death among the Indians more probable, is, that we find the same bloody and vindictive satisfaction is required of a foreign nation, whether the person lost, be killed by an accident, or by premeditated violence. Many facts might be mentioned from travellers to prove that the Indians do not punish murder by death within the jurisdiction of their own tribes. I shall mention only one which is taken from the Rev. Mr. John Megapolensis's account of the Mohawk Indians, lately published in Mr. Hazard's historical collection of state papers.— "There is no punishment, (says our author) here for murder, but every one is his own avenger. The friends of the deceased revenge themselves upon the murderer until peace is made with the next akin. But although they are so cruel, yet there are not half so many murders committed among them as among Christians, notwithstanding their severe laws, and heavy penalties."

It has been said, that the horrors of a guilty conscience proclaim the justice and necessity of death, as a punishment for murder. I draw an argument of another nature from this fact. Are the horrors of conscience the punishment that God inflicts upon murder? why, then, should we shorten or destroy them by death, especially as we are taught to direct the most atrocious murderers to expect pardon in the future world? no, let us not counteract the government of God in the human breast: let the murderer live—but let it be to suffer the reproaches of a guilty conscience: let him live, to make compensation to society for the injury he has done it, by robbing it of a citizen: let him live to maintain the family of the man whom he has murdered: let him live, that the punishment of his crime may become universal: and lastly let him live—that murder may be extirpated from the list of human crimes!

Let us examine the conduct of the moral ruler of the world towards the first murderer: see Cain returning from his field, with his hands reeking with the blood of his brother! Do the heavens gather blackness, and does a flash of lightning blast him to the earth? no. Does his father Adam, the natural legislator and judge of the world, inflict upon him the punishment of death?—No; the infinitely wise God becomes his judge and executioner. He expels him from the society of which he was a member. He fixes in his conscience a never-dying worm. He subjects him to the necessity of labor; and to secure a duration of his punishment, proportioned to his crime, he puts a mark or prohibition upon him, to prevent his being put to death, by weak and angry men; declaring, at the same time, that "whosoever slayeth Cain, vengeance shall be taken on him sevenfold."

Judges, attorneys, witnesses, juries and sheriffs, whose office it is to punish murder by death, I beseech you to pause, and listen to the voice of reason and religion, before you convict or execute another fellow-creature for murder!

But I despair of making such an impression upon the present citizens of the United States, as shall abolish the absurd and un-Christian practice. From the connection of this essay with the valuable documents of the late revolution contained in the American Museum, it will probably descend to posterity. To you, therefore, the unborn generations of the next century, I consecrate this humble tribute to justice. You will enjoy in point of knowledge, the meridian of a day, of which we only perceive the twilight. You will often review with equal contempt and horror, the indolence, ignorance and cruelty of your ancestors. The grossest crimes shall not exclude the perpetrators of them from your pity. You will *fully* comprehend the extent of the discoveries and precepts of the gospel, and you will be actuated, I hope, by its gentle and forgiving spirit. You will see many modern opinions in religion and government turned upside downwards, and many new connexions established between cause and effect. From the importance and destiny of every human soul, you will acquire new ideas of the dignity of human nature, and of the infinite value of every act of benevolence that has for its object, the bodies, the souls, and the lives of your fellow-creatures. You will love the whole human race, for you will perceive that you have a common Father, and you will learn to imitate him by converting those punishments to which their folly or wickedness have exposed them, into the means of their reformation and happiness.

Soon after the above enquiry was published in the American Museum, a reply to it made its appearance in the Pennsylvania Mercury, *under the signature of* Philochoras; *which produced the following answer. The principal arguments in favour of punishing murder by death, contained in the reply, are mentioned in the answer, for which reason it was not thought necessary to re-publish the whole of the reply in the order in which it appeared in the news paper.*

ON GOOD GOVERNMENT

I have read a reply subscribed Philochoras, to an enquiry into the justice and policy of punishing murder by death, published some time ago in the Museum. The author of it has attempted to justify public and capital punishments, as well as war, by the precepts of the gospel.—Let not my readers suppose that this author is a sceptic—or a heathen—or that he is in any degree unfriendly to Christianity. Far from it—he is a minister of the gospel—and a man of a worthy private as well as public character.

Our author begins his reply by asserting, that the objection to the punishment of death for murder, proceeded originally from the socinian objection to the great doctrine of the atonement. Here I must acknowledge my obligations to our author for having furnished me with a new argument in favor of my principles. I believe in the doctrine of the atonement, not only because it is clearly revealed in the Old and New Testaments, but because it is agreeable to nature, and reason. Life is the product of death, throughout every part of the animal creation. Reason likewise establishes the necessity of the atonement, for it has lately taught us in the writings of the Marquis of Beccaria, that in a perfect human government there should be *no pardoning power:* and experience has taught us that where *certainty* has taken the place of *severity* of punishment, crimes have evidently and rapidly diminished in every country The demands of the divine law which made the shedding of blood necessary to the remission of sin, is a sublime illustration of the perfection of the divine government, and of the love of the Supreme Being to his intelligent creatures. But in the demand *of life* for disobedience, let the divine law stand alone. Men stand in a very different relation to each other, from that which God sustains to men. They are all fallible, and deficient in a thousand duties which they owe to each other. They are bound, therefore, by the precept of doing to others, as they would have them do them, to *forgive*, without a satisfaction, inasmuch as they constantly require the same *forgiveness* to be exercised towards themselves. To punish murder, therefore, or any other crime, by death, under the gospel dispensation, is to exalt the angry and vindictive passions of men to an equality with the perfect law of God. It is to place imperfect individuals and corrupted human governments, upon the throne of the righteous judge of the universe. nay, more—it is to make the death of Christ of no effect; for every time we punish murder by death, we practically deny that it was a full expiation for every sin, and thereby exclude ourselves from deriving any benefit from it, for he has made the forgiveness of injuries, without any exceptions, whether committed against us in our private capacities, or as members of a community, the *express condition* of our title to the forgiveness which he has purchased for us by his death.

The arguments against the punishment of murder by death, from *reason*, remain on an immoveable foundation. Our author has *contradicted*—but has not *refuted* one of them. I affirmed in my former essay, that the punishment of murder by death had been abolished in several of the European nations. I wish for the honor of our author's profession, he had doubted of this assertion with more of the meek and gentle spirit of a Christian. To satisfy him upon this subject, I shall subjoin the following extracts from authorities which are now before me.—In the instructions to the commissioners appointed to frame a new code of laws for the Russian Empire, by Catharine II. the present empress of Russia, I find the following passage. I take great pleasure in transcribing it, as the sentiments it contains do so much honor not only to the female understanding, but to the human mind.

"Proofs from facts demonstrate to us, that the frequent use of capital punishments, never mended the morals of a people. Therefore, if I prove the death of a citizen to be neither *useful* nor *necessary* to society in general, I shall confute those who rise up against humanity. In a reign of peace and tranquillity, under a government established with the united wishes of a whole people, in a state well fortified against external enemies, and protected within by strong supports; that is, by its own internal strength, and virtuous sentiments, rooted in the minds of the citizens, there can be *no necessity* for *taking away the life* of a citizen. It is not the *excess* of severity, nor the *destruction* of the human species, that produces a powerful effect upon the hearts of the citizens, but the *continued duration* of the punishment. The death of a malefactor is not so efficacious a method of deterring from wickedness, as the example continually remaining, of a man who is deprived of his liberty, that he might repair, during a life of labour, the injury he has done to the community. The terror of death excited by the imagination may be more *strong*, but has not force enough to resist that *oblivion* which is so natural to mankind. It is a general rule, that rapid and violent impressions upon the human mind, disturb and *give pain*, but do not operate long upon the memory. That a punishment, therefore, might be conformable with justice, it ought to have such a degree of severity as might be sufficient to deter people from committing the crime. Hence I presume to affirm, that there is no man who, upon the least degree of reflexion, would put the *greatest possible* advantages, he might flatter himself from a crime, on the *one side*, into the balance against a life *protracted* under a *total* privation of liberty, *on the other*."

In a British review for the present year, I find a short account of the code of penal laws lately enacted by the emperor of Germany. This enlightened monarch has divided imprisonment into *mild—severe—*and *rigorous*. For the crime of murder, he inflicts the punishment of rigorous imprisonment—which from its duration, and other terrifying circumstances that attend it, is calculated to produce more beneficial effects in preventing murders, than all the executions that have ever taken place in any age or country.

I derived my information of the abolition of capital punishment in Sweden and Tuscany, from two foreigners of distinction, who lately visited the United States. The one was an Italian nobleman, the other was a captain in the Swedish navy—both of whom commanded every where respect and attachment for their abilities and virtues.

It is true, this happy revolution in favour of justice and humanity, in the instances that have been mentioned, did not originate in a convocation or a synod. It may either be ascribed to the light of the gospel shining in "darkness, which comprehended it not"—or to the influence of sound and cultivated reason—for reason and religion have the same objects. They are in no one instance opposed to each other. On the contrary, reason is nothing but imperfect religion, and religion is nothing but perfect reason.

It becomes Christians to beware how far they condemn the popular virtue of humanity, because it is recommended by Deists, or by persons who do not profess to be bound by the strict obligations of Christianity.—Voltaire first taught the princes of Europe the duty of religious toleration. The Duke of Sully has demonstrated the extreme folly of war, and has proved that when it has been conducted with the most glory, it never added an atom to national happiness. The Marquis of Beccaria has established a connexion between the abolition of capital punishments, and the order and happiness of society. Should any thing be found in the Scriptures, *contrary* to these discoveries, it is easy to foresee that the principles of the deists and the laws of modern legislators will soon have a *just* preference to the principles and precepts of the gospel.

Our author attempts to support his sanguinary tenets by an appeal to revelation. And here I shall make two preliminary remarks.

1. There is no opinion so absurd or impious, that may not be supported by *solitary* texts of scripture. To collect the *sense* of the bible upon any subject, we must be governed by its *whole* spirit and tenor.

2. The design of Christianity at its first promulgation was to reform the world by its *spirit* rather than by its positive precepts.

Our Saviour does not forbid slavery in direct terms—but he indirectly bears a testimony against it, by commanding us to do to others what we would have them in like circumstances to do to us. He did not aim to produce a sudden revolution in the affairs of men. He knew too well the power and efficacy of his religion for that purpose. It was unnecessary, therefore, to subject it to additional opposition, by a direct attack upon the prejudices and interests of mankind, both of which were closely interwoven with the texture of their civil governments.

After these remarks, I shall only add, that the declaration of St. Paul before Festus, respecting the punishment of death * and the speech of the dying thief on the cross,† only prove that the punishment of death was agreeable to the Roman law, but they by no means prove that they were sanctioned by the gospel.— Human life was extremely cheap under the Roman government. Of this we need no further proof than the head of John the Baptist forming a part of a royal entertainment. From the frequency of public executions, among those people, the *sword* was considered as an emblem of public justice—but to suppose from this appeal to a sign of justice, or from our Saviour's parable of the destruction of the husbandmen, that capital punishments are approved of in the New Testament, is as absurd as it would be to suppose that horseracing was a Christian exercise, from St. Paul's frequent allusions to the Olympic games.

The declaration of the barbarians upon seeing the snake fasten upon St. Paul's hand proves nothing but the ignorance of those uncivilized people. I deny the consent of all nations to the punishment of death for murder—but if it were true—it only proves the universality of the ignorance and depravity of man. Revenge, dissimulation, and even theft, prevail among all the nations in the world,—and yet who will dare to assert, that these vices are just, or necessary to the order or happiness of society.

Our author does not distinguish between the sense of justice so universal among all nations, and an approbation of death as a punishment for murder. The former is written by the finger

---

* "For if I be an offender, and have committed any thing worthy of death, I refuse not to die." Acts 25 and 11.

† "We indeed" suffer "*justly*, for we receive the due reward of our deeds." Luke 23 and 41.

of God upon every human heart, but like his own attribute of justice, it has the happiness of individuals and of society for its objects. It is always misled, when it seeks for satisfaction in punishments that are injurious to society, or that are disproportioned to crimes. The satisfaction of this universal sense of justice by the punishments of imprisonment and labor, would far exceed that which is derived from the punishment of death; for it would be of longer duration, and it would more frequently occur, for, upon a principle laid down in the first essay upon this subject, scarcely any species of murder would escape with impunity.*

The conduct and discourses of our Saviour should outweigh every argument that has been or can be offered in favour of capital punishment for any crime. When the woman caught in adultery was brought to him, he evaded inflicting the bloody sentence of the Jewish law upon her. Even the *maiming* of the body appears to be offensive in his sight, for when Peter drew his sword and smote off the ear of the servant of the high priest, he replaced it by miracle, and at the same time declared, that "all they who take the sword, shall perish with the sword." He forgave the crime of murder, on his cross; and after his resurrection, he commanded his disciples to preach the gospel of forgiveness *first* at Jerusalem, where he well knew his murderers still resided. These striking facts are recorded for our imitation, and seem intended to show that the Son of God died, not only to reconcile God to man, but to reconcile men to each other. There is one passage more, in the history of our Saviour's life, which would of itself overset the justice of the punishment of death for murder, if every other part of the Bible had been silent

---

* A scale of punishments by means of imprisonment and labor might easily be contrived, so as to be accommodated to the different degrees of atrocity in murder. For example—for the first or highest degree of guilt, let the punishment be solitude and darkness, and a total *want* of employment. For the second, solitude and labour, with the benefit of light. For the third, confinement and labor. The *duration* of these punishments should likewise be governed by the atrocity of the murder, and by the signs of contrition and amendment in the criminal.

upon the subject. When two of his disciples, actuated by the spirit of vindictive legislators, requested permission of him to call down fire from heaven to consume the inhospitable Samaritans, he answered them "the Son of Man is not come to *destroy* men's *lives*, but to *save* them." I wish these words composed the motto of the arms of every nation upon the face of the earth. They inculcate every duty that is calculated to preserve—restore —or prolong human life. They militate alike against war—and capital punishments—the objects of which are the unprofitable destruction of the lives of men. How precious does a human life appear from these words, in the sight of heaven! Pause, legislators, when you give your votes for inflicting the punishment of death for any crime. You frustrate, in one instance, the design of the mission of the Son of God into the world, and thereby either deny his appearance in the flesh, or reject the truth of his gospel. You moreover strengthen by your conduct the arguments of the Deists and Socinians against the particular doctrines of the Christian revelation. You do more—you preserve a bloody fragment of the ancient institution. "The Son of Man came not to *destroy* men's lives, but to *save* them." Excellent words! I require no others to satisfy me of the truth and divine original of the Christian religion, and while I am able to place a finger upon this text of scripture, I will not believe an angel from heaven, should he declare that the punishment of death for *any* crime was inculcated, or permitted by the spirit of the gospel.

It has been said, that a man who has committed a murder, has discovered a malignity of heart, that renders him ever afterwards unfit to live in human society. This is by no means true in many, and perhaps in most of the cases of murder. It is most frequently the effect of a sudden gust of passion, and has sometimes been the only stain of a well spent or inoffensive life. There are many crimes which unfit a man much more for human society, than a single murder, and there have been instances of murderers who have escaped or bribed the laws of their country, who have afterwards become peaceable, and useful members of society. Let it not be supposed that I wish to palliate by this remark, the enormity of murder. Far from it. It is only because I view murder with such superlative horror, that I wish to deprive our laws of the power of perpetrating and encouraging it.

Our author has furnished us with a number of tales to show that the providence of God is concerned in a peculiar manner in detecting murder, and that the confessions of murderers have in many instances sanctified the justice of their punishment. I do not wish to lessen the influence of such vulgar errors as tend to prevent crimes, but I will venture to declare, that many more murderers escape discovery, than are detected, or punished. Were I not afraid of trespassing upon the patience of my readers, I might mention a number of facts, in which circumstances of the most trifling nature have become the means of detecting theft and forgery, from which I could draw as strong proofs of the watchfulness of providence over the property of individuals, and the order of society, as our author has drawn from the detection of murder. I might mention instances, likewise, of persons in whom conscience has produced restitution for stolen goods, or confession of the justice of the punishment which was inflicted for theft. Conscience and knowledge always keep pace with each other, both with respect to divine and human laws. A party of soldiers in the Duke of Alva's army, murdered a man and his wife with six children. They roasted the youngest child, and dined upon it. One of them after dinner clapped his hands together, and with great agitation of mind cried out "good God—what have I done?"—What? said one of his companions—"why" said the other "I have eaten flesh in Lent time." Here conscience kept pace with his degrees of knowledge. The same thing occurs upon different occasions every day. The acquiescence of murderers in the justice of their execution, is the effect of prejudice and education. It cannot flow from a conscience acting in concert with reason or religion—for they both speak a very different language.

The world has certainly undergone a material change for the better within the last two hundred years. This change has been produced chiefly, by the secret and unacknowledged influence of Christianity upon the hearts of men. It is agreeable to trace the effects of the Christian religion in the extirpation of slavery—in the diminution of the number of capital punishments, and in the mitigation of the horrors of war. There was a time when masters possessed a power over the lives of their slaves. But Christianity has deposed this power, and mankind begins to see every where that slavery is alike contrary to the interests of society, and the spirit of the gospel. There was a time when torture was part of the punishment of death, and when the number of capital crimes amounted to one hundred and sixty-one. Christianity has abolished the former, and reduced the latter to not more than six or seven. It has done more. It has confined in some instances capital punishments to the crime of murder only—and in some countries it has abolished it altogether. The influence of Christianity upon the modes of war has been still more remarkable. It is agreeable to trace its progress.

1st. In rescuing women and children from being the objects of the desolations of war in common with men.

2dly. In preventing the destruction of captives taken in battle, in cold blood.

3dly. In protecting the peaceable husbandman from sharing in the carnage of war.

4thly. In producing an exchange of prisoners, instead of dooming them to perpetual slavery.

5thly. In avoiding the invasion or destruction, in certain cases, of private property.

6thly. In declaring all wars to be unlawful but such as are purely *defensive*.

This is the only tenure by which war now holds its place among Christians. It requires but little ingenuity to prove that a defensive war cannot be carried on successfully without offensive operations. If this be true, then this last degree of it, upon our author's principles, must be contrary to the spirit of the gospel. Already the princes and nations of the world discover the struggles of opinion or conscience in their preparations for war. Witness, the many national disputes which have been lately terminated in Europe by negotiation, or mediation. Witness, too, the establishment of the Constitution of the United States without force or bloodshed. These events indicate an improving state of human affairs. They lead us to look forward with expectation to the time, when the weapons of war shall be changed into implements of husbandry, and when rapine and violence shall be no more. These events are the promised fruits of the gospel. If they do not come to pass, the prophets have deceived us. But if they do—war must be as contrary to the spirit of the gospel, as fraud, or murder, or any other of the vices which are reproved or extirpated by it.*

I cannot take leave of this subject without remarking that capital punishments are the natural offspring of monarchical governments. Kings believe that they possess their crowns by a *divine* right: no wonder, therefore, they assume the divine power of taking away human life. Kings consider their subjects as their property: no wonder, therefore, they shed their blood with as little emotion as men shed the blood of their sheep or cattle. But the principles of republican governments speak a very different language. They teach us the absurdity of the divine origin of kingly power. They approximate the extreme ranks of men to each other. They restore man to his God—to society—and to himself. They revive and establish the relations of fellow-citizen, friend, and brother. They appreciate human life, and increase public and private obligations to preserve it. They consider human sacrifices as no less offensive to the sovereignty of the people, than they are to the majesty of heaven. They view the attributes of government, like the attributes of the Deity, as infinitely more honoured by destroying evil by means of *merciful* than by exterminating punishments. The United States have

---

* The spirit of Christianity which our author describes as a vulgar deistical species of humanity, has found its way into schools and families, and has abolished, in both, corporal and ignominious punishments. In the instructions to the masters and mistresses of the sundry schools, I observe with great pleasure a direction "to use corporal punishments as seldom as possible."

adopted these peaceful and benevolent forms of government. It becomes them therefore to adopt their mild and benevolent principles. An execution in a republic is like a human sacrifice in religion. It is an offering to monarchy, and to that malignant being, who has been styled a murderer from the beginning, and who delights equally in murder, whether it be perpetrated by the cold, but vindictive arm of the law, or by the angry hand of private revenge.

OBSERVATIONS ON THE GOVERNMENT OF PENNSYLVANIA

Letter I

EVERY FREE government should consist of three parts, viz. I. A BILL OF RIGHTS. II A CONSTITUTION And III. LAWS.

I. The BILL OF RIGHTS should contain the great principles of *natural* and *civil liberty*. It should be unalterable by any human power.

II. The CONSTITUTION is the executive part of the Bill of Rights. It should contain the division and distribution of the power of the people.—The modes and forms of making laws, of executing justice, and of transacting business. Also the limitation of power, as to time and jurisdiction. It should be unalterable by the legislature, and should be changed only by a representation of the people, chosen for that purpose.

III. LAWS are the executive part of a constitution. They cease to be binding whenever they transgress the principles of Liberty, as laid down in the Constitution and Bill of Rights.

Let us now apply these principles to the Bill of Rights, Constitution and Laws of Pennsylvania. But previous to my entering upon this task, I beg leave to declare, that I am not led to it by a single party or personal prejudice; on the contrary, I honour most of the friends of the present government as the warmest Whigs among us, and I am proud of numbering several of the gentlemen who were concerned in making, and in attempting to execute the government, among my particular friends.

I. The Bill of Rights has confounded *natural* and *civil* rights in such a manner as to produce endless confusion in society.

II. The Constitution in the gross is exceptionable in the following particulars:

1. No regard is paid in it to the ancient habits and customs of the people of Pennsylvania in the distribution of the supreme power of the state, nor in the forms of business, or in the style of the Constitution. The suddenness of the late revolution, the attachment of a large body of the people to the old Constitution of the state, and the general principles of human nature made an attention to ancient forms and prejudices a matter of the utmost importance to this state in the present controversy with Great Britain. Of so much consequence did the wise Athenians view the force of ancient habits and customs in their laws and government, that they punished all *strangers* with death who interfered in their politics. They well knew the effects of novelty upon the minds of the people, and that a more fatal stab could not be given to the peace and safety of their state than by exposing its laws and government to frequent or *unnecessary* innovations.

2. The Constitution is wholly repugnant to the principles of action in man, and has a direct tendency to check the progress of genius and virtue in human nature. It supposes perfect equality, and an equal distribution of property, wisdom and virtue, among the inhabitants of the state.

3. It comprehends many things which belong to a Bill of Rights, and to Laws, and which form no part of a Constitution.

4. It is contrary, in an important article, to the Bill of Rights. By the second article of the Bill of Rights, "no man can be abridged of any *civil* right, who acknowledges the being of a GOD;" but by the Constitution, no man can take his seat in the Assembly, who does not "acknowledge the Scriptures of the Old and New Testament to be given by divine inspiration."

5. It is deficient in point of perspicuity and method. Instead of reducing the legislative, executive and judicial parts of the constitution, with their several powers and forms of business,

to distinct heads, the whole of them are jumbled together in a most unsystematic manner.

6. It fixes all these imperfections upon the people for seven years, by precluding them from the exercise of their own power to remove them at any other time, or in any other manner than by a septennial convention, called by a Council of Censors.

III. The laws and proceedings of the Assembly of Pennsylvania are in many particulars contrary to the Constitution. Only one half of the Members took the oath of allegiance, prescribed in the tenth section of the Constitution. The Speaker of the House issued writs for the election of Members of Assembly and of Counsellors, notwithstanding this power is lodged, by the 19th section of the Constitution, *only* in the President and Council. Two gentlemen were appointed Members of Congress, who held offices under the Congress, which is expressly forbidden in the 11th section of the Constitution. The Constitution requires further in the 40th section, that every military officer should take the oath of allegiance, before he enters upon the execution of his office; but the Assembly have dispensed with this oath in their Militia Law. The 15th section of the Constitution declares, that no law shall be passed, unless it be previously published for the consideration of the People; but the Assembly passed all the laws of their late session, without giving the People an opportunity of seeing them, till they were called upon to obey them. These proceedings of the Assembly lead to one, and perhaps to all the three following conclusions: First, That the Assembly have violated the principles of the Constitution; secondly, that the Constitution is so formed, that it could not be executed by the Assembly, consistent with the safety of the State; lastly, that none of their laws are binding, inasmuch as they are contrary to the superior and radical laws of the Constitution. These considerations are all of a most alarming nature. Farewell to Liberty, when the sacred bulwarks of a Constitution can be invaded by a legislature! And if the Constitution cannot be executed in all its parts, without endangering the safety of the State, and if all our late laws must be set aside in a court of justice, because they were not assented to by the People, previous to their being enacted, is it not high time for the People to unite and form a more effectual, and more practicable system of government? . . .

If strict justice should poise the scale in the trial of Tory property, I can easily foresee from the virtue of the People, on which side the beam would turn; but it becomes us to reflect, that all trials for forfeited property must be held in courts of *written* law, and the flaws of our Constitution and laws are so wide, that the most gigantic Tory criminal might escape through them.

Letter II

I shall now proceed to say a few words upon particular parts of the Constitution.

In the second section, "the supreme legislature is vested in a '*single*' House of Representatives of the Freemen of the Commonwealth." By this section we find, that the supreme, absolute, and uncontrolled power of the whole State is lodged in the hands of *one body* of men. Had it been lodged in the hands of one man, it would have been less dangerous to the safety and liberties of the community. Absolute power should never be trusted to man. It has perverted the wisest heads, and corrupted the best hearts in the world. I should be afraid to commit my property, liberty and life to a body of angels for one whole year. The Supreme Being alone is qualified to possess supreme power over his creatures. It requires the wisdom and goodness of a Deity to control, and direct it properly.

In order to show the extreme danger of trusting all the legislative power of a State to a single representation, I shall beg leave to transcribe a few sentences from a letter, written by Mr. JOHN ADAMS, to one of his friends in North Carolina, who requested him to favour him with a plan of government for that State above a twelve-month ago. This illustrious Citizen, who is second to no man in America, in an inflexible attachment to the liberties of this country, and to republican forms of government, writes as follows,

"I think a people cannot be *long free*, nor *ever* happy, whose government is in one Assembly. My reasons for this opinion are as follow,

1. "A single Assembly is liable to all the vices, follies and frailties of an individual,—subject to fits of humour,—starts of passions,* flights of enthusiasm,—partialities of prejudice, and consequently productive of hasty results and absurd judgments. All these errors ought to be corrected, and defects supplied by some controlling power.

2. "A single Assembly is apt to be avaricious, and in time will not scruple to exempt itself from burdens, which it will lay, without compunction, upon its constituents.

3. "A single Assembly is apt to grow ambitious, and after a time will not hesitate to vote itself perpetual. This was one fault of the Long Parliament, but more remarkably of Holland, whose Assembly first voted themselves from *annual* to *septennial*, then for *life*, and after a course of years, that all vacancies happening by death or otherwise, should be filled by *themselves*, without any application to constituents at all.

4. "Because a single Assembly possessed of all the powers of government would make arbitrary laws for their own interest, and adjudge all controversies in their own favor." †

If any thing could be necessary upon this subject, after such an authority, I might here add, that Montesquieu—Harrington

---

* A Committee of the Convention, which formed the Constitution of Pennsylvania, published in the Pennsylvania Packet of October 15, 1776, as an apology for one of their Ordinances, that was thought to be arbitrary and unjust, that it was passed when "the minds of the Convention were agitated, and their passions inflamed."

† These reasons are given by our author for not lodging all power legislative, executive and judicial, in one body of men. This has been done, as will be shown hereafter in the Constitution of Pennsylvania. But, supposing it had been otherwise, our author adds, "shall the *whole* power of *legislation* rest in one Assembly? Most of the foregoing reasons (one is omitted) apply *equally* to prove, that the whole legislative power ought to be more *complex*."

—Milton—Addison—Price—Bolingbroke, and others, the wisest statesmen, and the greatest friends to Liberty in the world, have left testimonies upon record of the extreme folly and danger of a people's being governed by a single legislature. I shall content myself with the following extract from the last of those authors. The sentiments correspond exactly with those of our countryman before-mentioned.

"By simple forms of government, I mean such as lodge the whole supreme power, absolutely and without control, either in a single person, or in the principal persons of the community, or in the whole body of the people. Such governments are governments of arbitrary will, and therefore of all imaginable absurdities the most absurd. They stand in direct opposition to the sole motive of submission to any government whatsoever; for if men quit the State, and renounce the rights of nature, (one of which is, to be sure, that of being governed by their own will) they do this, that they may not remain exposed to the arbitrary will of other men, the weakest to that of the strongest, the few to that of the many. Now, in submitting to any single form of government whatever, they establish what they mean to avoid, and for fear of being exposed to arbitrary will sometimes, they choose to be governed by it always. These governments do not only degenerate into tyranny; they are tyranny in their very institution; and they who submit to them, are slaves, not subjects, however the supreme power may be exercised; for tyranny and slavery do not so properly consist in the stripes that are given and received, as in the power of giving them at pleasure, and the necessity of receiving them, whenever and for whatever they are inflicted."

I might go on further and show, that all the dissentions of Athens and Rome, so dreadful in their nature, and so fatal in their consequences, originated in single Assemblies possessing all the power of those commonwealths; but this would be the business of a volume, and not of a single essay.—I shall therefore pass on, to answer the various arguments that have been used in Pennsylvania, in support of a single legislature.

1. We are told, that the perfection of every thing consists in its simplicity,—that all mixtures in government are impurities, and that a single legislature is perfect, because it is simple.—To this I answer, that we should distinguish between simplicity in principles, and simplicity in the application of principles to practice. What can be more simple than the principles of mechanics, and yet into how many thousand forms have they been tortured by the ingenuity of man. A few simple elementary bodies compose all the matter of the universe, and yet how infinitely are they combined in the various forms and substances which they assume in the animal, vegetable, and mineral kingdoms. In like manner a few simple principles enter into the composition of all free governments. These principles are perfect security for property, liberty and life; but these principles admit of extensive combinations, when reduced to practice:—Nay more, they require them. A despotic government is the most simple government in the world, but instead of affording security to property, liberty or life, it obliges us to hold them all on the simple will of a capricious sovereign. I maintain therefore, that all governments are safe and free in proportion as they are compounded in a certain degree, and on the contrary, that all governments are dangerous and tyrannical in proportion as they approach to simplicity.

2. We are told by the friends of a single legislature, that there can be no danger of their becoming tyrannical, since they must partake of all the burdens they lay upon their constituents. Here we forget the changes that are made upon the head and heart by arbitrary power, and the cases that are recorded in history of *annual* Assemblies having refused to share with their constituents in the burdens which they had imposed upon them. If every elector in Pennsylvania is capable of being elected an assembly-man, then agreeably to the sixth section of the Constitution, it is possible for an Assembly to exist who do not possess a single foot of property in the State, and who can give no other evidence of a common interest in, or attachment to, the community than having paid "public taxes," which may mean

poor-taxes. Should this be the case, (and there is no obstacle in the Constitution to prevent it) surely it will be in the power of such an Assembly to draw from the State the whole of its wealth in a few years, without contributing any thing further towards it than their proportion of the trifling tax necessary to support the poor.—But I shall show in another place equal dangers from another class of men, becoming a majority in the Assembly.

3. We are told of instances of the House of Lords, in England, checking the most salutary laws, after they had passed the House of Commons, as a proof of the inconvenience of a compound legislature. I believed the fact to be true, but I deny its application in the present controversy. The House of Lords, in England, possess privileges and interests, which do not belong to the House of Commons. Moreover they derive their power from the crown and not from the people. No wonder therefore they consult their own interests, in preference to those of the People. In the State of Pennsylvania we wish for a council, with *no one* exclusive privilege, and we disclaim every idea of their possessing the smallest degree of power, but what is derived from the *annual* suffrages of the People. A body thus chosen could have no object in view but the happiness of their constituents. It is remarkable in Connecticut, that the legislative council of that State has in no one instance made amendments, or put a negative upon the acts of their Assembly, in the course of above one hundred years, in which both have not appeared to the people in a few months to have been calculated to promote their liberty and happiness.

4. We are told, that the Congress is a single legislature, therefore a single legislature is to be preferred to a compound one.— The objects of legislation in the Congress relate only to peace and war, alliances, trade, the Post-Office, and the government of the army and navy. They never touch the liberty, property, nor life of the individuals of any State in their resolutions, and even in their ordinary subjects of legislation, they are liable to be checked by *each* of the Thirteen States.

5. We have been told, that a legislative council or governor lays the foundation for aristocratical and monarchical power in a community. However ridiculous this objection to a compound legislature may appear, I have more than once heard it mentioned by the advocates for a single Assembly. Who would believe, that the same fountain of pure water should send forth, at the same time, wholesome and deadly streams? Are not the Council and Assembly both formed alike by the *annual* breath of the people? But I will suppose, that a legislative Council aspired after the honors of hereditary titles and power, would they not be *effectually* checked by the Assembly?

I cannot help commending the zeal that appears in my countrymen against the power of a King or a House of Lords. I concur with them in all their prejudices against hereditary titles, honour and power. History is little else than a recital of the follies and vices of kings and noblemen, and it is because I dread so much from them, that I wish to exclude them for ever from Pennsylvania, for notwithstanding our government has been called a simple democracy, I maintain, that a foundation is laid in it for the most complete aristocracy that ever existed in the world.

In order to prove this assertion, I shall premise two propositions, which have never been controverted: First, where there is wealth, there will be power; and, secondly, the rich have always been an over-match for the poor in all contests for power.

These truths being admitted, I desire to know what can prevent our single representation being filled, in the course of a few years, with a majority of rich men? Say not, the people will not choose such men to represent them. The influence of wealth at elections is irresistible. It has been seen and felt in Pennsylvania, and I am obliged in justice to my subject to say, that there are poor men among us as prepared to be influenced, as the rich are prepared to influence them. The fault must be laid in both cases upon human nature. The consequence of a majority of rich men getting into the legislature is plain. Their wealth will administer fuel to the love of arbitrary power that is common to all men. The present Assembly have furnished them with precedents for breaking the Constitution. Farewell now to annual elections! Public emergencies will sanctify the most daring measures. The clamours of their constituents will be silenced with offices, bribes or punishments. An aristocracy will be established, and Pennsylvania will be inhabited like most of the countries in Europe, with only two sorts of animals, tyrants and slaves.

It has often been said, that there is but one rank of men in America, and therefore, that there should be only one representation of them in a government. I agree, that we have no artificial distinctions of men into noblemen and commoners among us, but it ought to be remarked, that superior degrees of industry and capacity, and above all, commerce, have introduced inequality of property among us, and these have introduced natural distinctions of rank in Pennsylvania, as certain and general as the artificial distinctions of men in Europe. This will ever be the case while commerce exists in this country. The men of middling property and poor men can never be safe in a mixed representation with the men of over-grown property. Their liberties can only be secured by having exact bounds prescribed to their power, in the fundamental principles of the Constitution. By a representation of the men of middling fortunes in one house, their *whole* strength is collected against the influence of wealth. Without such a representation, the most violent efforts of individuals to oppose it would be divided and broken, and would want that system, which alone would enable them to check that lust for dominion which is always connected with opulence. The government of Pennsylvania therefore has been called most improperly a government for poor men. It carries in every part of it a poison to their liberties. It is impossible to form a government more suited to the passions and interests of rich men.

6. But says the advocate for a single legislature, if one of the advantages of having a Legislative Council arises from the Counsellors possessing more wisdom than the Assembly, why may not

the members of the Council be thrown into the Assembly, in order to instruct and enlighten them? If sound reasoning always prevailed in popular Assemblies, this objection to a Legislative Council might have some weight. The danger in this case would be, that the Counsellors would partake of the passions and prejudices of the Assembly, by taking part in their debates; or, if they did not, that they would be so inconsiderable in point of numbers, that they would be constantly out-voted by the members of the Assembly.

7. But would you suffer twenty or thirty men in a Legislative Council to control seventy or eighty in an Assembly? Yes, and that for two reasons: First, I shall suppose that they will consist of men of the most knowledge and experience in the State: Secondly, that their obligations to wisdom and integrity will be much stronger than the Assembly's can be, because fewer men will be answerable for unjust or improper proceedings at the bar of the public. But I beg pardon of my readers for introducing an answer to an objection to a small number of men controlling the proceedings of a greater. The friends of the present Constitution of Pennsylvania cannot urge this objection with any force, for in the 47th section of the Constitution I find twenty-four men called a COUNCIL of CENSORS, invested with a supreme and *uncontrolled* power to revise and to censure all the laws and proceedings of not a single Assembly, but of all the Assemblies that shall exist for seven years, which Assemblies may contain the united wisdom of five hundred and four Assembly-men. They are moreover, invested with more wisdom than the Convention that is to be chosen by their recommendation; for this Convention, which is to consist of seventy-two men, is to make no *one* alteration in the Constitution but what was suggested to them by the Council of Censors. I can easily conceive that two houses consisting of an unequal number of members, both viewing objects through the same medium of time and place, may agree in every thing essential, and disagree in matters only of doubtful issue to the welfare of the state; but I am sure, a body of twenty-four men sitting in judgment upon the pro-

ON GOOD GOVERNMENT

ceedings of a body of men defunct in their public capacity seven years before them, cannot fail of committing the most egregious mistakes from the obscurity which time, and their ignorance of a thousand facts and reasonings must throw upon all their deliberations. But more of the arbitrary power of the Censors hereafter.

8. We are told that the State of Pennsylvania has always been governed by a single legislature, and therefore, that part of our Constitution is not an innovation. There is a short way of confuting this assertion by pronouncing it without any foundation. The Governor always had a negative power upon our laws, and was a distinct branch of our legislature. It is true, he sometimes exercised his power to the disadvantage of the people; for he was the servant of a King who possessed an interest distinct from that of his people, and in some cases the Governor himself possessed an interest incompatible with the rights of the people. God forbid that ever we should see a resurrection of his power in Pennsylvania, but I am obliged to own, that I have known instances in which the *whole* state have thanked him for the interposition of his negative and amendments upon the acts of the Assembly. Even the Assembly-men themselves have acknowledged the justice of his conduct upon these occasions, by condemning in their cooler hours their own hasty, and ill-digested resolutions.

9. But why all these arguments in favor of checks for the Assembly. The Constitution (says the single legislative-man) has provided no less than four for them. First, Elections will be annual. Secondly, The doors of the Assembly are to be always open. Thirdly, All laws are to be published for the consideration and assent of the people: And, Fourthly, The Council of Censors will punish, by their censures, all violations of the Constitution, and the authors of bad laws. I shall examine the efficacy of each of these checks separately.

I hope, for the peace of the state, that we shall never see a body of men in power more attached to the present Constitution than the present Assembly, and if, with all their affection for it, they have broken it in many articles, it is reasonable to suppose that future Assemblies will use the same freedoms with it. They may, if they chuse, abolish annual elections.‡ They may tell their constituents that elections draw off the minds of the people from necessary labour; or, if a war should exist, they may show the impossibility of holding elections when there is a chance of the militia being called into the field to oppose a common enemy: Or lastly, they may fetter elections with oaths in such a manner as to exclude nine-tenths of the electors from voting. Such stratagems for perpetual power will never want men nor a *society* of men to support them; for the Assembly possesses such a plenitude of power from the influence of the many offices of profit and honour * that are in their gift, that they may always promise themselves support from a great part of the state. But I will suppose that no infringement is ever made upon annual elections. In the course of even one year a single Assembly may do the most irreparable mischief to a state. Socrates and Barnevelt were both put to death by Assemblies that held their powers at the election of the people. The same Assemblies would have shed oceans of tears to have recalled those illustrious citizens to life again, in less than half a year after they imbrued their hands in their blood.

I am highly pleased with having the doors of our Assembly kept constantly open, but how can this check the proceedings of the Assembly, when none but a few citizens of the town or county, where the Assembly sits, or a few travelling strangers, can ever attend or watch them?

‡ The late Convention was chosen for the *sole* purpose of making a government, and was composed of honest, well-meaning men, and yet, I have good authority to say, that several of them proposed to their friends forming themselves into an Assembly, to execute the government.

* The President is appointed chiefly by the Assembly. His salary, together with the salaries of the Judges, are fixed by the Assembly. Delegates in Congress, the Lieutenants and Sub-Lieutenants of counties, Protonotaries, Registers of Wills, Money-Signers, &c. &c. are all appointed solely by the Assembly. Each of these officers brings with him the influence of his friends and family-connections. When collected together, they make a little army of placemen.

I shall take no notice of the delays of business, which must arise from publishing all laws for the consideration and assent of the people; but I beg to be informed *how long* they must be published before they are passed? For I take it for granted, that each county has a right to equal degrees of time to consider of the laws. In what manner are they to be circulated? How are the sentiments of the people, scattered over a county fifty or sixty miles in extent, to be collected? Whether by ballot, or by voting in a tumultuary manner? These are insurmountable difficulties in the way of the people at *large* acting as a check upon the Assembly. But supposing an attempt should be made to restrain the single legislature in this manner, are we sure the disapprobation of the people would be sufficient to put a negative upon improper or arbitrary laws? Would not the Assembly, from their partiality to their own proceedings, be apt to pass over the complaints of the people in silence? to neglect or refuse to enter their petitions or remonstrances upon their Journals? or to raise the hue and cry of a fostered junto upon them, as "*Tories,*" or "*apostate Whigs,*" or "*an aristocratic faction?*"

To talk of the Councils of Censors, as a check upon the Assembly, is to forget that a man or a body of men may deceive, rob, and enslave the public for seven years, and then may escape the intended efficacy of the censures of the Council by death, or by flying into a neighbouring state.

10. We are informed that a single legislature was supported in the Convention by Dr. Franklin, and assented to by Mr. Rittenhouse; gentlemen distinguished for their uncommon abilities, and deservedly dear for their virtues to every lover of human nature. The only answer, after what has been said, that I shall give to this argument, is, that Divine Providence seems to have permitted them to *err* upon this subject, in order to console the world for the very great superiority they both possess over the rest of mankind in every thing else, except the science of government.

Thus have I answered all the arguments that ever I have heard offered in favour of a single legislature, and I hope, silenced all the objections that have been made to a double representation of the people. I might here appeal further to the practice of our courts of law in favour of repeated deliberations and divisions. In a free government, the most inconsiderable portion of our liberty and property cannot be taken from us, without the judgment of two or three courts; but, by the Constitution of Pennsylvania, the whole of our liberty and property, and even our lives, may be taken from us, by the hasty and passionate decision of a single Assembly.

I shall conclude my observations upon this part of the Constitution, by summing up the advantages of a compound or double legislature.

1. There is the utmost *freedom* in a compound legislature. The decisions of two legislative bodies cannot fail of coinciding with the wills of a great majority of the community.

2. There is *safety* in such a government, in as much as each body possesses a free and independent power, so that they mutually check ambition and usurpation in each other.

3. There is the greatest *wisdom* in such a government. Every act being obliged to undergo the revision and amendments of two bodies of men, is necessarily strained of every mixture of folly, passion, and prejudice.†

4. There is the longest *duration* of freedom in such a government.*

5. There is the most *order* in such a government. By order, I mean obedience to laws, subordination to magistrates, civility

---

† The Militia Law of the Delaware State received twenty-four amendments from the Council after it had had three readings in the Assembly; all of which were adopted at once by the Assembly. I grant, the wisdom of men collected in any way that can be devised, cannot make a *perfect* law; but I am sure a Legislative Council would not have overlooked many inaccuracies in the laws passed in the last session of the present Assembly of Pennsylvania.

* Sparta, which possessed a compound legislature, preserved her liberties above five hundred years. The fatal dissentions of Athens and Rome ceased as soon as their Senates, which were filled only with rich men, were checked by another Representation of the people.

and decency of behaviour, and the contrary of every thing like mobs and factions.

6. Compound governments are most agreeable to *human nature*, inasmuch as they afford the greatest scope for the expansion of the powers and virtues of the mind. Wisdom, learning, experience, with the most extensive benevolence, the most unshaken firmness, and the utmost elevation of soul, are all called into exercise by the opposite and different duties of the different representations of the people.

Letter III

The powers of government have been very justly divided into legislative, executive and judicial. Having discussed the legislative power of the government of Pennsylvania, I shall proceed now to consider the executive and judicial.

It is agreed on all hands that the executive and judicial powers of government should be *wholly independant* of the legislative. The authors of the Pennsylvania Constitution *seem* to have given their sanction to this opinion, by separating those powers from the powers of the Assembly.—It becomes us to enquire whether they have made them so independant of the Assembly as to give them the free exercise of their own judgments.

The insignificant figure the President and Council make in the Constitution from not having a negative upon the laws of the Assembly, alone would soon have destroyed their authority and influence in the State. But the authors of the Constitution have taken pains to throw the whole power of the Council at once into the hands of the Assembly, by rendering the former dependant upon the latter in the two following particulars.

1. The President is chosen by the joint ballot of the Assembly and Council. The Assembly being to the Council, in point of numbers, as five are to one, of course chuse the President. Each member will expect in his turn to fill the first chair in the State, and hence the whole Council will yield themselves up to the will of the Assembly.

2. The salaries of the President and of each of the Counsellors

are fixed by the Assembly. This will necessarily render them dependant upon them. It is worthy of notice here, that a rotation is established in the 19th section of the Constitution, to "prevent the danger of an inconvenient aristocracy."—From what abuse of power can this aristocracy arise? Are they not the creatures of the Assembly? But there is a magic terror in the sound of a Counsellor. Call a man an Assemblyman, or a Censor, and he becomes an innocent creature, though you invest him with the despotism of an Eastern monarch. If the Council are dependant upon the Assembly, it follows of course that the Judges, who are appointed by the Council, are likewise dependant upon them. But in order more fully to secure their dependance upon the will of the Assembly, they are obliged to hold their salaries upon the tenure of their will. In vain do they hold their commissions for seven years. This is but the shadow of independance. They cannot live upon the air, and their absolute dependance upon the Assembly gives that body a transcendent influence over all the courts of law in the State. Here then we have discovered the legislative, executive and judicial powers of the State all blended together.—The liberty, the property and life of every individual in the State are laid prostrate by the Constitution at the feet of the Assembly. This combination of powers in one body has in all ages been pronounced a tyranny. To live by one man's will became the cause of all men's misery; but better, far better, would it be to live by the will of one man, than to live, or rather to die, by the will of a body of men. Unhappy Pennsylvania! Methinks I see the scales of justice broken in thy courts.—I see the dowry of the widow and the portion of the orphans unjustly taken from them, in order to gratify the avarice of some demagogue who rules the Assembly by his eloquence and arts.—I see the scaffolds streaming with the blood of the wisest and best men in the State.—I see the offices of government . . . But the prospect is too painful, I shall proceed to take notice of some other parts of the Constitution.

It was not sufficient to contaminate justice at its fountain, but its smallest streams are made to partake of impurity by the Convention. In the 30th section of the Constitution "all Justices of the Peace are to be elected by the freeholders of each city and county." The best observations that can be made on this part of the Constitution is to inform the public, that not above one half the people of the State chose magistrates agreeable to the laws of the Assembly for that purpose; that more than one half of those that were chosen have refused to accept of commissions, and that many of those who act are totally disqualified from the want of education or leisure for the office.—It has been said often, and I wish the saying was engraven over the doors of every statehouse on the Continent, that "all power is *derived* from the people," but it has never yet been said that all power is *seated* in the people. Government supposes and requires a delegation of power: It cannot exist without it. And the idea of making the people at large judges of the qualifications necessary for magistrates, or judges of laws, or checks for Assemblies proceeds upon the supposition that mankind are all alike wise, and just, and have equal leisure. It moreover destroys the necessity for all government. What man ever made himself his own attorney? And yet this would not be more absurd than for the people at *large* to pretend to give up their power to a set of rulers, and afterwards reserve the right of making and of judging of all their laws themselves. Such a government is a monster in nature. It contains as many Governors, Assemblymen, Judges and Magistrates as there are freemen in the State, all exercising the same powers and at the same time. Happy would it be for us, if this monster was remarkable only for his absurdity; but, alas! he contains a tyrant in his bowels. All history shows us that the people soon grow weary of the folly and tyranny of one another. They prefer one to many masters, and stability to instability of slavery. They prefer a Julius Cæsar to a Senate, and a Cromwell to a perpetual Parliament.

I cannot help thinking a mistake lays rather in words than ideas when we talk of the rights of the people. Where is the difference between my choosing a Justice of Peace, and my choosing an Assemblyman and a Counsellor, by whose joint suffrages a Governor is chosen, who appoints a Justice for me? I am still the first link of the sacred chain of the power of the State. But are there no cases in which I may be bound by acts of a single, or of a body of magistrates in the State, whom I have had no hand in choosing? Yes, there are. Here then I am bound contrary to the principles of liberty (which consist in a man being governed by men chosen by himself), whereas if all the magistrates in the State were appointed by the Governor, or executive part of the State, it would be impossible for me to appear before the bar of a magistrate any where who did not derive his power *originally* from me.

By the 5th section all militia officers below the rank of a Brigadier General are to be chosen by the people. Most of the objections that have been mentioned against magistrates being chosen by the people, apply with equal force against the people's choosing their military officers. By the militia law of this State we find the soldier ceases to be commanded by the officer of his choice as soon as he comes in the field. He might as well be commanded by an officer of another State as by one of his own States, for whom he did not vote. Had he been appointed by the executive power of the government, he might have looked upon him originally as the creature of his own power, and might have claimed his care in the camp, from his influence at elections, in moving those springs in government, from which he derived his commission. But the unsuitableness of this part of the Constitution to the genius of the people of Pennsylvania, will appear in the strongest point of light, from attending to the two following facts: 1st: Most of the irregularities committed by the militia, that were in service last year, were occasioned by that laxity of discipline, which was introduced and kept up by officers holding their commissions by the breath of the people: And 2dly, Above one half of the State have refused or neglected to choose officers, agreeably to the recommendation of the Assembly.—And even in many of those places, where elections for officers have been held, Colonels have been chosen by forty and Captains and Subalterns by only four or five votes.

In the 22d section of the Constitution it is said, "every officer of the state, whether judicial or executive, shall be liable to be impeached by the General Assembly, before the President and Council, either when in office or after his resignation or removal for maladministration." Why is a man in this case to be deprived of a trial by jury? and what is the reason that no *time* is *fixed* for the commencement of this impeachment after resignation or removal for maladministration? A judicial or military officer may be innocent, and yet, from the delay of his trial for six or seven years, he may be deprived by death or other ways of the vouchers of his innocence. Woe to the man that ever holds one of the high offices of the State of Pennsylvania! He must ever, after his resignation, hold his life at the pleasure of the orator who rules the Assembly. The least mark of disrespect shown to him, or to any of the Assembly, rouses the Constitution and laws of his country against him; and perhaps, after an interval of twenty or thirty years conscious integrity, his grey hairs are dragged with sorrow to the grave. Let not this be thought to be too high a picture of this part of the Constitution of Pennsylvania. It is a picture of human nature in similar circumstances, in every age and country. Men possessed of unlimited and uncontrolled power are beasts of prey.

But is there no power lodged in the Constitution to alter these imperfections? Has our Convention monopolized all the wisdom of succeeding years, so as to preclude any improvements being made in the infant science of government? Must we groan away our lives in a patient submission to all the evils in the Constitution which have been described? Let the 47th and last section of the Constitution answer these questions. By this section it is declared, that after the expiration of seven years, there shall "be chosen two men from each city and county, (a majority of whom shall be a quorum in every case, except as to *calling a Convention*) who shall be called a Council of Censors, and who shall have power to call a Convention within two years after their sitting, if there appears to them an absolute necessity of amending any article of the Constitution which may be defective, explaining such as may be thought not clearly expressed, and of adding such as are necessary for the preservation of the rights and happiness of the people." From this paragraph it is evident, that the Constitution was thought to be the perfection of human wisdom, and that the authors of it intended that it should last for ever. Every section of the Constitution, I believe, was determined by a *majority* of the Members of the Convention, and in the 12th section of the Constitution we find, that if only two-thirds of the people concur in the execution of it, the members of Assembly chosen by them, are to "possess all the powers of the General Assembly as fully and amply as if the whole were present." This is strictly agreeable to the principles of good government, but, why are these principles to be trampled upon, when the great question is to be agitated, whether the Constitution shall be altered? For, unless every county and city in the State concur in electing Censors, and unless *two thirds* of them agree in calling a Convention, there is no possibility of obtaining an alteration of a single article of the Constitution. If the Assembly had not taught us that it was neither treason nor perjury to break the Constitution, I am sure it would have remained inviolate for ever; for I am persuaded that several of the counties would have refused to have chosen Censors. But suppose they had, if only one short of *two thirds* of them refused to agree in the measure, we could have no Convention. The minority would give laws to a majority. A solecism in government! But there is no end to the tyranny and absurdity of our Constitution.

But the Council of Censors have not yet finished their business. They are empowered by the Constitution "to enquire, whether the *Constitution* has been preserved *inviolate* in *every* part? and whether the legislative and executive branches of government have performed their duty, as guardians of the people; or assumed to themselves, or exercised *other* or greater powers than they are entitled to by the Constitution: They are also to enquire, whether the public taxes have been justly laid and collected in all parts of this commonwealth;—in what manner the public monies have been disposed of, and whether the laws have been duly executed: For these purposes they shall have power to send for persons, papers and records; they shall have authority to pass public censures, and to recommend to the legislature, the repealing such laws as appear to them to have been enacted contrary to the principles of the Constitution: These powers they shall continue to have for, and during the space of one year, from the day of their election, and no longer."

Is this the commission of the Grand Turk? or is it an extract from an act of the British Parliament, teeming with vengeance against the liberties of America?—No.—It is an epitome of the powers of the Council of Censors established by the late Convention of Pennsylvania. Innocence has nothing to fear from justice, when it flows through the regular channels of law, but where is the man who can ensure himself a moment's safety from a body of men invested with absolute power for one whole year to censure and condemn, without judge or jury, every individual in the State. I shall suppose the Council to consist of a majority of those Members of Assembly, who took the oath of allegiance to the Constitution, and who voted, that no officer should be excused from taking it, who accepted of a militia-commission under the authority of this State. I shall suppose them assembled for the business of their office. The work of an age is to be performed in a single year.—Methinks I see such of those worthy gentlemen as are living, who, for the sake of union, consented to dispense with the oath of allegiance to the Constitution, led like criminals to their bar.—I hear peals of wrath denounced against them. I see those virtuous gentlemen, who composed the Executive Council in the year 1777, summoned to appear at their tribunal, to answer for their having abdicated the duties of their office, by an adjournment, at a time when the State was threatened with an invasion. In vain they plead, that the Constitution had invested them with no power for the defence of the State. Their names and their families are branded with infamy by a "public censure." I see hundreds and thousands coming, one after another, before the Council, to be censured for refusing to choose magistrates and militia-officers, agreeably to the laws of the Assembly. But who are they who are dragged with so much violence to the inquisitorial tribunal? They are a number of citizens who prayed for some alterations to be made in the Constitution. In vain they plead the obligations of reason and conscience against submitting to the government. In vain they plead their zeal and services in the common cause of America. It is all to no purpose. They recommend to the Assembly to impeach them for high treason. They are condemned as traitors, and the streets swim with their blood.—Good heavens! where was the mild genius of Pennsylvania, when this part of the Constitution obtained the assent of the Convention? . . . Spirit of liberty, whither wast thou fled? . . .

But perhaps the Constitution has provided a remedy for its defects, without the aid of the Council of Censors? No—this cannot be done; for every Member of Assembly, before he takes his seat, is obliged, by the 10th section of the Constitution, to swear that he will not "do nor consent to any act whatever, that shall have a tendency to lessen or abridge their rights and privileges as declared *in the Constitution of this State*," as also, "that he will not directly or indirectly do or consent to any act or thing prejudicial or injurious to the Constitution or Government thereof, as *established by the Convention*," agreeably to the 40th section of the Constitution. These oaths of infallibility and passive obedience to the form of the Constitution, effectually preclude every man, who holds an office under it, from attempting to procure the least amendment in any part of it.* It is a mere quibble upon words to say, that a man may mend the Constitu-

---

* That it was the design of the Convention, that the Constitution should not be touched by any power but a Convention to be called by the Council of Censors, appears from the oath contained in the 40th section, being required by one of their ordinances as the only condition upon which an Elector could vote for an Assemblyman. Strange! that men should call God to witness their determination to support a government, which a majority of them had not seen, and which even the minority of them did not understand or disliked! But, for the honour of the State it should be recorded, that not above 1500 of the 2500, who voted for the Assembly, took the oath required by the ordinance of the Convention.

tion, without "doing any thing prejudicial or injurious to it." The Convention did not intend any such construction to be put upon their oaths, and hence we find in the introduction to the Constitution, they "declare the frame of government to be the Constitution of this commonwealth, and to remain in force therein *forever, unaltered,* except in such articles as shall hereafter, upon experience, be found to require improvement, and which shall, by the same authority of the people fairly delegated, as this *frame of government* directs, be amended and improved." Now we know, that the frame of government forbids the least amendment being made in the Constitution in any other than by the recommendation of a Council of Censors.

Had the Constitution appeared to me to have been unexceptionable in every part, and had it been the result of the united wisdom of men and angels, I would not have taken an oath of passive obedience to it, for seven or nine years. The constant changes in human affairs, and in the dispositions of a people, might render occasional alterations, in that time, necessary in the most perfect Constitution. But to take an oath of allegiance to a Constitution,—full of experiments,—a Constitution that was indeed a new thing under the sun,—that had never been tried in some of its parts in *any* country,—and that had produced misery in other of its parts in *every* country.—I say to swear to support or even to submit, for seven or nine years, to such a Constitution, is to trifle with all morality, and to dishonour the sacred name of God himself.

What would you think of a man, who would consent to shut his eyes, and swallow a quantity of food that had never before been tasted by a human creature, and swear at the same time, that if it should disorder him in ever so great a degree, he would take nothing to relieve him for eight and forty hours? Such a man would be wise, compared with the man who takes an oath of allegiance to the Constitution of Pennsylvania.

It is to no purpose to talk here of the many excellent articles in the Bill of Rights; such as religious toleration,—the habeas corpus act,—trials by juries,—the rotation of office, &c. None of them can flourish long in the neighbourhood of a single Assembly, and a Council of Censors possessing all the powers of the State. . . . These inestimable privileges in the Constitution of Pennsylvania resemble a tree loaded with the most luscious fruit, but surrounded with thorns, in such a manner, as to be for ever inaccessible to the hungry traveller.

Perhaps, while the government is upon its good behaviour, and while the passions of the State are directed against a cruel and common enemy, we may not experience all the calamities that have been demonstrated to flow from the Constitution. . . . But the revolution of a few years, and the return of peace, will most certainly render Pennsylvania, under her present Constitution, the most miserable spot upon the surface of the globe.

I believe all the Members of the late Convention were true Whigs, and aimed sincerely at forming a free and happy government. But, I am sure, that if Filmar and Hobbes had sat among them, they could not have formed a government more destructive of human happiness, nor could Lord North or General Howe have formed one more destructive of union and vigour, in our public affairs, than the present Constitution of Pennsylvania.

It is one thing to understand the *principles*, and another thing to understand the *forms* of government. The former are simple; the latter are difficult and complicated. There is the same difference between principles and forms in all other sciences. Who understood the principles of mechanics and optics better than Sir Isaac Newton? and yet Sir Isaac could not for his life have made a watch or a microscope. Mr. Locke is an oracle as to the *principles*, Harrington and Montesquieu are oracles as to the *forms* of government.

Letter IV

A question very naturally arises from taking a review of the tyranny of the government of Pennsylvania, What measures

ON GOOD GOVERNMENT

shall be taken to amend them? There can be but two answers to this question. 1st. To submit to the Constitution for the present, till a peace with Great Britain will give us leisure to make a better; or, 2dly, to call a Convention immediately for the purpose of making a new Constitution. I believe the State is divided only about these two things; for the party who believe the government to be a *good* one, is too inconsiderable to be noticed in this place.

I. I beg leave to offer a few objections to our *submitting* to the Constitution, and shall endeavour, II. to obviate the objections that have been made to the immediate calling of a Convention, for the purpose of altering and amending it.

There is the utmost danger to the State of Pennsylvania in a temporary submission to the Constitution from the following causes, 1. The government is a tyranny. The moment we submit to it we become slaves. We hold every thing dear to us in society upon the tenure of the will of a single man in a single Assembly. Perhaps the mark of the beast may not be fixed immediately upon us, but the contract is made, and we are sold, together with our posterity, to be hewers of wood and drawers of water for ever. 2. The Constitution cannot be executed in part without being *broken*. Now there cannot be a more dangerous precedent in a free country, than a legislature violating in a single article even the *forms* of a Constitution. 3. The present government will not draw forth the wisdom nor strength of the State, nor afford that assistance to our Sister States which is expected from us in the present contest with Great Britain. Wise and good men every where decline to accept of the first offices in the government. The militia law is only partially executed. We have no courts of justice open for the sequestration or confiscation of Tory property; and, lastly, we shall never be able under the present government to contribute our share towards sinking the Continental debt by taxes. There is not force enough in the *whole* State to draw taxes from a *single* county against their consent.† Alas! we are on the brink of ruin. Our State has lifted a knife to her throat, and is about to undo herself by a hasty and ill-judged exercise of her own power. Our enemies are exulting, and our friends are weeping over our alarming situation. Our ancestors look down, and our posterity look up to us for a happier Constitution. We are engaged with our Sister States in a bloody and expensive war. The liberty of the whole world is the price for which we fight. Human nature looks to us to avenge the mighty ills she has suffered from the tyrants of the old world. She has already dropped a tear of joy upon the prospect of recovering among us her first and original dignity. A *good government* is an engine not less necessary to ensure us success in these glorious purposes than ammunition and *fire-arms*. The way of duty is plain. Let a Convention be chosen, to alter and amend the government. This measure alone will restore vigor and union to Pennsylvania. Say not, my dear countrymen, that this is not the time, the enemy are at our gates, let us first repel them. Look at our militia on a field day—see the attempts of the friends to the Constitution to open our courts—hear the complaints and murmurs of the people. They all proclaim that NOW is the time for altering our Constitution. No confusion can arise from it. The gentlemen in the opposition declare their determination to support the present Assembly in the execution of every law necessary

---

† The gentlemen in the opposition to the government have constantly prayed, that the Constitution might be referred to the arbitration of a Convention, and have declared their willingness to submit to, or concur in the execution of it, if it should be confirmed by a representation of the people *fairly* chosen. I am sorry to find upon the Journals of the Assembly, an address from a battalion of militia in Chester county, to the Honourable House, assuring them, that "they will support the present government with their lives and fortunes." Such addresses indicated the weakness, and foreboded the present contemptible situation of the court of Britain. They were presented in times similar to our own, viz. when the American colonies were upon their knees to the throne, praying to be governed by their own representatives, and to be delivered from impending slavery. But it is characteristic of the present Constitution, that, in the first year of its execution, the journals of our rulers were stained with threats of bloodshed, against men who only petitioned for a redress of grievances.

for the safety and defence of the State, and above all in the execution of the militia and test laws. They have no interest unconnected with yours. They see with the same distress as you do the Tories triumphing in our disunion. Be not deceived. The Tories are not enemies to the present government; they enjoy the benefits of its weakness, and there is good authority to say they have *secretly* helped to carry it into execution. Let us beware of being imposed upon by the popular cry of the *necessity of the times*. When the Dissenters in Virginia and South Carolina prayed for the abolition of the Episcopal establishment in those States, the High Churchmen acknowledged that their demands were just, but said, that *this was not the time* for attending to them, and that such a change in the government would throw all things into confusion. The demands were notwithstanding complied with, and an union unparalleled in former times was immediately produced in those States. When a declaration of independence last summer appeared to be the only measure that could save America, the Tories and moderate men acknowledged the justice of our separation from Great Britain, but said, "This is not the time." The event showed that the time was come, for, exclusive of the advantages we have gained from it in foreign Courts, it served to precipitate the timid, the doubtful and the disaffected characters from their mixture with the real Whigs, and although it lessened the numbers in the opposition, it added to their strength by producing union and decision among them. To delay justice (has been emphatically said) is to deny it. In like manner to *delay* liberty is to *take* it away.

The Convention of New York formed their government within the reach of the thunder of the enemy's cannon, and while one half of their State was in their possession. Is our situation more dangerous than it was last year? The members of the late Convention were chosen on a day when the Associators of the whole State were in motion. The Constitution was made while above 5000 of them were in the field. The sense of the people was not *asked* upon the subject of the Constitution; but it was *given* in the most public manner. No more than 1500 freemen voted for its being executed, for that number only took the oath of allegiance to the Constitution at the election in October. Let us talk no more then of the *"necessity of the times."* This is the State apology at St. James's for all the crimes of the present reign and for all the ravages and bloodshed we have witnessed in America. The State of Massachusetts Bay are preparing for an invasion; they expect General Burgoyne every hour in their harbours with a powerful army, and yet in a Boston paper, of the 5th of May, I find the following resolution of their Assembly and Council,

STATE OF *MASSACHUSETTS BAY.*
In the HOUSE of REPRESENTATIVES, May 5, 1777.

"Resolved, That it be, and hereby is recommended to the several towns and places in this State, impowered by the laws thereof, to send Members to the General Assembly, that, at their next election of a Member or Members to represent them, they make choice of men, in whose integrity and abilities they can place the greatest confidence; and, in addition to the common and ordinary powers of representation, instruct them in one Body with the Council, to form such a Constitution of Government, as they shall judge best calculated to promote the happiness of this State, and when completed, to cause the same to be printed in all the *Boston* News-Papers, and also in Hand-Bills, one of which to be transmitted to the Selectmen of each town, or the Committee of each plantation, to be by them laid before their respective towns or plantations, at a regular meeting of the inhabitants thereof, to be called for that purpose; in order to its being, by each town and plantation, duly considered. And a return of their approbation or disapprobation to be made into the Secretary's Office of this State, at a reasonable time to be fixed on by the General Court, specifying the numbers present in such meeting, voting for, and those voting against the same: And if, upon a fair examination of the said returns by the Gen-

eral Court, or such Committee as they shall appoint for that purpose, it shall appear, that the said Form of Government is approved of by at least two thirds of those who are free, and twenty one years of age, belonging to this State, and present in the several meetings, then the General Court shall be impowered to establish the same as the Constitution and Form of Government of the State of *Massachusetts Bay*, according to which the inhabitants thereof shall be governed in all succeeding generations, unless the same shall be altered by their own express direction, or that of at least two thirds of them. And it is further recommended to the Selectmen of the several towns, in the return of their precepts for the choice of Representatives, to signify their having considered this Resolve, and their doings thereon."

But further, recollect, my dear countrymen, our conduct upon reading the resolution of the Honourable Congress of the 15th of May, 1776. We seized it as a Warrant that proclaimed liberty to us and our posterity for ever. It was said by some people at that time, "Let the Assembly execute that resolution;" but we spurned the advice, and we acted like men. We said, that the "Assembly was not chosen by a majority of votes in the State," owing to the inequality of our representation, and that they wanted the "confidence of the people." We thought nothing then of the loss of time occasioned by the meeting of a Conference of Committees, to settle the mode and time of choosing a Convention. The delay of months, the distractions of the State, and the danger of an invasion, were thought to be trifling when compared with the prospect of a good Constitution, that should *immediately* collect and exert the Whig strength of the state.

Thus have I finished my observations upon the Constitution of Pennsylvania. I have taken notice only of its most essential defects, and have aimed to discuss them with candor. The occasional remarks upon the proceedings of the Assembly, are to be charged entirely to the faults of the Constitution.—I believe the gentlemen in power have nothing in view but the freedom and independance of the State; and such has been the zeal and integrity of many of them in the pursuit of those great objects, that it gives me pain to reflect, that I have been obliged to differ from them in the best means of obtaining them.

With this declaration I shall close my letters to the people of Pennsylvania. Accept thou dear asylum of my ancestors, nurse of my infancy, protectress of my childhood, and generous rewarder of the toils of my youth, accept of these humble efforts to restore thee to freedom and happiness! If I have laboured in vain, I shall henceforth mourn in secret only over my beloved country, and lament the day that I was born a Pennsylvanian.

ON EDUCATION

OF THE MODE OF EDUCATION PROPER IN A REPUBLIC

THE BUSINESS of education has acquired a new complexion by the independence of our country. The form of government we have assumed, has created a new class of duties to every American. It becomes us, therefore, to examine our former habits upon this subject, and in laying the foundations for nurseries of wise and good men, to adapt our modes of teaching to the peculiar form of our government.

The first remark that I shall make upon this subject is, that an education in our own, is to be preferred to an education in a foreign country. The principle of patriotism stands in need of the reinforcement of prejudice, and it is well known that our strongest prejudices in favour of our country are formed in the first one and twenty years of our lives. The policy of the Lacedemonians is well worthy of our imitation. When Antipater demanded fifty of their children as hostages for the fulfillment of a distant engagement, those wise republicans refused to comply with his demand, but readily offered him double the number of their adult citizens, whose habits and prejudices could not be shaken by residing in a foreign country. Passing by, in this place, the advantages to the community from the early attachment of youth to the laws and constitution of their country, I shall only remark, that young men who have trodden the paths of science together, or have joined in the same sports, whether of swimming, skating, fishing, or hunting, generally feel, thro' life, such ties to each other, as add greatly to the obligations of mutual benevolence.

I conceive the education of our youth in this country to be peculiarly necessary in Pennsylvania, while our citizens are composed of the natives of so many different kingdoms in Europe. Our schools of learning, by producing one general, and uniform system of education, will render the mass of the people more homogeneous, and thereby fit them more easily for uniform and peaceable government.

I proceed in the next place, to enquire, what mode of education we shall adopt so as to secure to the state all the advantages that are to be derived from the proper instruction of youth; and here I beg leave to remark, that the only foundation for a useful education in a republic is to be laid in Religion. Without this there can be no virtue, and without virtue there can be no liberty, and liberty is the object and life of all republican governments.

Such is my veneration for every religion that reveals the attributes of the Deity, or a future state of rewards and punishments, that I had rather see the opinions of Confucius or Mahomed inculcated upon our youth, than see them grow up wholly devoid of a system of religious principles. But the religion I mean to recommend in this place, is that of the New Testament.

It is foreign to my purpose to hint at the arguments which establish the truth of the Christian revelation. My only business is to declare, that all its doctrines and precepts are calculated to promote the happiness of society, and the safety and well being of civil government. A Christian cannot fail of being a republican. The history of the creation of man, and of the relation of our species to each other by birth, which is recorded in the Old Testament, is the best refutation that can be given to the divine right of kings, and the strongest argument that can be used in favor of the original and natural equality of all mankind. A Christian, I say again, cannot fail of being a republican, for every precept of the Gospel inculcates those degrees of humility, self-denial, and brotherly kindness, which are directly opposed to the pride of monarchy and the pageantry of a court. A Christian cannot fail of being useful to the republic, for his religion teacheth him, that no man "liveth to himself." And lastly, a Christian cannot fail of being wholly inoffensive, for his religion teacheth him, in all things to do to others what he would wish, in like circumstances, they should do to him.

I am aware that I dissent from one of those paradoxical opinions with which modern times abound; and that it is improper to fill the minds of youth with religious prejudices of any kind, and that they should be left to choose their own principles, after they have arrived at an age in which they are capable of judging for themselves. Could we preserve the mind in childhood and youth a perfect blank, this plan of education would have more to recommend it, but this we know to be impossible. The human mind runs as naturally into principles as it does after facts. It submits with difficulty to those restraints or partial discoveries which are imposed upon it in the infancy of reason. Hence the impatience of children to be informed upon all subjects that relate to the invisible world. But I beg leave to ask, why should we pursue a different plan of education with respect to religion, from that which we pursue in teaching the arts and sciences? Do we leave our youth to acquire systems of geography, philosophy, or politics, till they have arrived at an age in which they are capable of judging for themselves? We do not. I claim no more then for religion, than for the other sciences, and I add further, that if our youth are disposed after they are of age to think for themselves, a knowledge of one system, will be the best means of conducting them in a free enquiry into other systems of religion, just as an acquaintance with one system of philosophy is the best introduction to the study of all the other systems in the world.

Next to the duty which young men owe to their Creator, I wish to see a regard to their country, inculcated upon them. When the Duke of Sully became prime minister to Henry the IVth of France, the first thing he did, he tells us, "Was to subdue and forget his own heart." The same duty is incumbent upon every citizen of a republic. Our country includes family, friends and property, and should be preferred to them all. Let our pupil be taught that he does not belong to himself, but that he is public property. Let him be taught to love his family, but let him be taught, at the same time, that he must forsake, and even forget them, when the welfare of his country requires it. He must watch for the state, as if its liberties depended upon his vigilance alone, but he must do this in such a manner as not to defraud his creditors, or neglect his family. He must love private life, but he must decline no station, however public or responsible it may be, when called to it by the suffrages of his fellow citizens. He must love popularity, but he must despise it when set in competition with the dictates of his judgement, or the real interest of his country. He must love character, and have a due sense of injuries, but he must be taught to appeal only to the laws of the state, to defend the one, and punish the other. He must love family honor, but he must be taught that neither the rank nor antiquity of his ancestors, can command respect, without personal merit. He must avoid neutrality in all questions that divide the state, but he must shun the rage, and acrimony of party spirit. He must be taught to love his fellow creatures in every part of the world, but he must cherish with a more intense and peculiar affection, the citizens of Pennsylvania and of the United States. I do not wish to see our youth educated with a single prejudice against any nation or country; but we impose a task upon human nature, repugnant alike to reason, revelation and the ordinary dimensions of the human heart, when we require him to embrace, with equal affection, the whole family of mankind. He must be taught to amass wealth, but it must be only to encrease his power of contributing to the wants and demands of the state. He must be indulged occasionally in amusements, but he must be taught that study and business should be his principal pursuits in life. Above all he must love life, and endeavour to acquire as many of its conveniences as possible by industry and economy, but he must be taught that this life "is not his own," when the safety of his country requires it. These are practicable lessons, and the history of the commonwealths of Greece and Rome show, that human nature, without the aids of Christianity, has attained these degrees of perfection.

While we inculcate these republican duties upon our pupil, we must not neglect, at the same time, to inspire him with republican principles. He must be taught that there can be no durable liberty but in a republic, and that government, like all other sciences, is of a progressive nature. The chains which have bound this science in Europe are happily unloosed in America. Here it is open to investigation and improvement. While philosophy has protected us by its discoveries from a thousand natural evils, government has unhappily followed with an unequal pace. It would be to dishonor human genius, only to name the many defects which still exist in the best systems of legislation. We daily see matter of a perishable nature rendered durable by certain chemical operations. In like manner, I conceive, that it is possible to combine power in such a way as not only to encrease the happiness, but to promote the duration of republican forms of government far beyond the terms limited for them by history, or the common opinions of mankind.

To assist in rendering religious, moral and political instruction more effectual upon the minds of our youth, it will be necessary to subject their bodies to physical discipline. To obviate the inconveniences of their studious and sedentary mode of life, they should live upon a temperate diet, consisting chiefly of broths, milk and vegetables. The black broth of Sparta, and the barley broth of Scotland, have been alike celebrated for their beneficial effects upon the minds of young people. They should avoid tasting spirituous liquors. They should also be accustomed occasionally to work with their hands, in the intervals of study, and in the busy seasons of the year in the country. Moderate sleep, silence, occasional solitude and cleanliness, should be inculcated upon them, and the utmost advantage should be taken of a proper direction of those great principles in human conduct,—sensibility, habit, imitations and association.

The influence of these physical causes will be powerful upon the intellects, as well as upon the principles and morals of young people.

To those who have studied human nature, it will not appear paradoxical to recommend, in this essay, a particular attention to vocal music. Its mechanical effects in civilizing the mind, and thereby preparing it for the influence of religion and government, have been so often felt and recorded, that it will be unnecessary to mention facts in favour of its usefulness, in order to excite a proper attention to it.

I cannot help bearing a testimony, in this place, against the custom, which prevails in some parts of America, (but which is daily falling into disuse in Europe) of crowding boys together under one roof for the purpose of education. The practice is the gloomy remains of monkish ignorance, and is as unfavorable to the improvements of the mind in useful learning, as monasteries are to the spirit of religion. I grant this mode of secluding boys from the intercourse of private families, has a tendency to make them scholars, but our business is to make them men, citizens and Christians. The vices of young people are generally learned from each other. The vices of adults seldom infect them. By separating them from each other, therefore, in their hours of relaxation from study, we secure their morals from a principal source of corruption, while we improve their manners, by subjecting them to those restraints which the difference of age and sex, naturally produce in private families.

From the observations that have been made it is plain, that I consider it is possible to convert men into republican machines. This must be done, if we expect them to perform their parts properly, in the great machine of the government of the state. That republic is sophisticated with monarchy or aristocracy that does not revolve upon the wills of the people, and these must be fitted to each other by means of education before they can be made to produce regularity and unison in government.

Having pointed out those general principles, which should be inculcated alike in all the schools of the state, I proceed now to make a few remarks upon the method of conducting, what is commonly called, a liberal or learned education in a republic.

I shall begin this part of my subject, by bearing a testimony against the common practice of attempting to teach boys the learned languages, and the arts and sciences too early in life. The first twelve years of life are barely sufficient to instruct a boy in reading, writing and arithmetic. With these, he may be taught those modern languages which are necessary for him to speak. The state of the memory, in early life, is favorable to the acquisition of languages, especially when they are conveyed to the mind, through the ear. It is, moreover, in early life only, that the organs of speech yield in such a manner as to favour the just pronunciation of foreign languages.

Too much pains cannot be taken to teach our youth to read and write our American language with propriety and elegance. The study of the Greek language constituted a material part of the literature of the Athenians, hence the sublimity, purity and immortality of so many of their writings. The advantages of a perfect knowledge of our language to young men intended for the professions of law, physic, or divinity are too obvious to be mentioned, but in a state which boasts of the first commercial city in America, I wish to see it cultivated by young men, who are intended for the compting house, for many such, I hope, will be educated in our colleges. The time is past when an academical education was thought to be unnecessary to qualify a young man for merchandize. I conceive no profession is capable of receiving more embellishments from it. The French and German languages should likewise be carefully taught in all our colleges. They abound with useful books upon all subjects. So important and necessary are those languages, that a degree should never be conferred upon a young man who cannot speak or translate them.

Connected with the study of languages is the study of eloquence. It is well known how great a part it constituted of the

Roman education. It is the first accomplishment in a republic, and often sets the whole machine of government in motion. Let our youth, therefore, be instructed in this art. We do not extol it too highly when we attribute as much to the power of eloquence as to the sword, in bringing about the American Revolution.

With the usual arts and sciences that are taught in our American colleges, I wish to see a regular course of lectures given upon History and Chronology. The science of government, whether it relates to constitutions or laws, can only be advanced by a careful selection of facts, and these are to be found chiefly in history. Above all, let our youth be instructed in the history of the ancient republics, and the progress of liberty and tyranny in the different states of Europe. I wish likewise to see the numerous facts that relate to the origin and present state of commerce, together with the nature and principles of money, reduced to such a system, as to be intelligible and agreeable to a young man. If we consider the commerce of our metropolis only as the avenue of the wealth of the state, the study of it merits a place in a young man's education, but, I consider commerce in a much higher light when I recommend the study of it in republican seminaries. I view it as the best security against the influence of hereditary monopolies of land, and, therefore, the surest protection against aristocracy. I consider its effects as next to those of religion in humanizing mankind, and lastly, I view it as the means of uniting the different nations of the world together by the ties of mutual wants and obligations.

Chemistry by unfolding to us the effects of heat and mixture, enlarges our acquaintance with the wonders of nature and the mysteries of art; hence it has become, in most of the universities of Europe, a necessary branch of a gentleman's education. In a young country, where improvements in agriculture and manufactures are so much to be desired, the cultivation of this science, which explains the principles of both of them, should be considered as an object of the utmost importance.

Again, let your youth be instructed in all the means of promoting national prosperity and independence, whether they relate to improvements in agriculture, manufactures, or inland navigation. Let him be instructed further in the general principles of legislation, whether they relate to revenue, or to the preservation of life, liberty or property. Let him be directed frequently to attend the courts of justice, where he will have the best opportunities of acquiring habits of comparing, and arranging his ideas by observing the discovery of truth, in the examination of witnesses, and where he will hear the laws of the state explained, with all the advantages of that species of eloquence which belongs to the bar. Of so much importance do I conceive it to be, to a young man, to attend occasionally to the decisions of our courts of law, that I wish to see our colleges established, only in county towns.

But further, considering the nature of our connection with the United States, it will be necessary to make our pupil acquainted with all the prerogatives of the national government. He must be instructed in the nature and variety of treaties. He must know the difference in the powers and duties of the several species of ambassadors. He must be taught wherein the obligations of individuals and of states are the same, and wherein they differ. In short, he must acquire a general knowledge of all those laws and forms, which unite the sovereigns of the earth, or separate them from each other.

I beg pardon for having delayed so long to say any thing of the separate and peculiar mode of education proper for women in a republic. I am sensible that they must concur in all our plans of education for young men, or no laws will ever render them effectual. To qualify our women for this purpose, they should not only be instructed in the usual branches of female education, but they should be taught the principles of liberty and government; and the obligations of patriotism should be inculcated upon them. The opinions and conduct of men are often regulated by the women in the most arduous enterprizes of life; and their approbation is frequently the principal reward of the hero's dangers, and the patriot's toils. Besides, the first impressions upon the minds of children are generally derived from the women. Of how much consequence, therefore, is it in a republic, that they should think justly upon the great subject of liberty and government!

The complaints that have been made against religion, liberty and learning, have been, against each of them in a separate state. Perhaps like certain liquors, they should only be used in a state of mixture. They mutually assist in correcting the abuses, and in improving the good effects of each other. From the combined and reciprocal influence of religion, liberty and learning upon the morals, manners and knowledge of individuals, of these, upon government, and of government, upon individuals, it is impossible to measure the degrees of happiness and perfection to which mankind may be raised. For my part, I can form no ideas of the golden age, so much celebrated by the poets, more delightful, than the contemplation of that happiness which it is now in the power of the legislature of Pennsylvania to confer upon her citizens, by establishing proper modes and places of education in every part of the state.

EDUCATION AGREEABLE TO A REPUBLICAN FORM OF GOVERNMENT

Before I proceed to the subject of this essay, I shall point out, in a few words, the influence and advantages of learning upon mankind.

I. It is friendly to religion, inasmuch as it assists in removing prejudice, superstition and enthusiasm, in promoting just notions of the Deity, and in enlarging our knowledge of his works.

II. It is favourable to liberty. Freedom can exist only in the society of knowledge. Without learning, men are incapable of knowing their rights, and where learning is confined to a few people, liberty can be neither equal nor universal.

III. It promotes just ideas of laws and government. "When the clouds of ignorance are dispelled (says the Marquis of Beccaria) by the radiance of knowledge, power trembles, but the authority of laws remains immovable."

IV. It is friendly to manners. Learning in all countries, promotes civilization, and the pleasures of society and conversation.

V. It promotes agriculture, the great basis of national wealth and happiness. Agriculture is as much a science as hydraulics, or optics, and has been equally indebted to the experiments and researches of learned men. The highly cultivated state, and the immense profits of the farms in England, are derived wholly from the patronage which agriculture has received in that country, from learned men and learned societies.

VI. Manufactures of all kinds owe their perfection chiefly to learning—hence the nations of Europe advance in manufactures, knowledge, and commerce, only in proportion as they cultivate the arts and sciences.

For the purpose of diffusing knowledge through every part of the state, I beg leave to propose the following simple plan.

I. Let there be one university in the state, and let this be established in the capital. Let law, physic, divinity, the law of nature and nations, economy, &c. be taught in it by public lectures in the winter season, after the manner of the European universities, and let the professors receive such salaries from the state as will enable them to deliver their lectures at a moderate price.

II. Let there be four colleges. One in Philadelphia, one at Carlisle; a third, for the benefit of our German fellow citizens, at Lancaster; and a fourth, some years hence at Pittsburgh. In these colleges, let young men be instructed in mathematics and in the higher branches of science, in the same manner that they are now taught in our American colleges. After they have received a testimonial from one of these colleges, let them, if they can afford it, complete their studies by spending a season or two in attending the lectures in the university. I prefer four colleges in the state to one or two, for there is a certain size of colleges as there is of towns and armies, that is most favourable to morals and good government. Oxford and Cambridge in England are the seats of dissipation, while the more numerous, and less crowded universities and colleges in Scotland, are remarkable for the order, diligence, and decent behaviour of their students.

II. Let there be free schools established in every township, or in districts consisting of one hundred families. In these schools let children be taught to read and write the English and German languages, and the use of figures. Such of them as have parents that can afford to send them from home, and are disposed to extend their educations, may remove their children from the free school to one of the colleges.

By this plan the whole state will be tied together by one

system of education. The university will in time furnish masters for the colleges, and the colleges will furnish masters for the free schools, while the free schools, in their turns, will supply the colleges and the university with scholars, students and pupils. The same systems of grammar, oratory and philosophy, will be taught in every part of the state, and the literary features of Pennsylvania will thus designate one great, and equally enlightened family.

But, how shall we bear the expense of these literary institutions?—I answer—These institutions will *lessen* our taxes. They will enlighten us in the great business of finance—they will teach us to increase the ability of the state to support government, by increasing the profits of agriculture, and by promoting manufactures. They will teach us all the modern improvements and advantages of inland navigation. They will defend us from hasty and expensive experiments in government, by unfolding to us the experience and folly of past ages, and thus, instead of adding to our taxes and debts, they will furnish us with the true secret of lessening and discharging both of them.

But, shall the estates of orphans, bachelors and persons who have no children, be taxed to pay for the support of schools from which they can derive no benefit? I answer in the affirmative, to the first part of the objection, and I deny the truth of the latter part of it. Every member of the community is interested in the propagation of virtue and knowledge in the state. But I will go further, and add, it will be true economy in individuals to support public schools. The bachelor will in time save his tax for this purpose, by being able to sleep with fewer bolts and locks to his doors—the estates of orphans will in time be benefited, by being protected from the ravages of unprincipled and idle boys, and the children of wealthy parents will be less tempted, by bad company, to extravagance. Fewer pillories and whipping posts, and smaller gaols, with their usual expenses and taxes, will be necessary when our youth are properly educated, than at present; I believe it could be proved, that the expenses of confining, trying and executing criminals, amount every year, in most of the counties, to more money than would be sufficient to maintain all the schools that would be necessary in each county. The confessions of these criminals generally show us, that their vices and punishments are the fatal consequences of the want of a proper education in early life.

I submit these detached hints to the consideration of the legislature and of the citizens of Pennsylvania. The plan for the free schools is taken chiefly from the plans which have long been used with success in Scotland, and in the eastern states * of America, where the influence of learning, in promoting religion, morals, manners and good government, has never been exceeded in any country.

The manner in which these schools should be supported and governed—the modes of determining the characters and qualifications of schoolmasters, and the arrangement of families in each district, so that children of the same religious sect and nation, may be educated as much as possible together, will form a proper part of a law for the establishment of schools, and therefore does not come within the limits of this plan.

---

* There are 600 of these schools in the small state of Connecticut, which at this time have in them 25,000 scholars.

PLAN OF A FEDERAL UNIVERSITY

"Your government cannot be executed. It is too extensive for a republic. It is contrary to the habits of the people," say the enemies of the Constitution of the United States.—However opposite to the opinions and wishes of a majority of the citizens of the United States, these declarations and predictions may be, they will certainly come to pass, unless the people are prepared for our new form of government by an education adapted to the new and peculiar situation of our country. To effect this great and necessary work, let one of the first acts of the new Congress be, to establish within the district to be allotted for them, a federal university, into which the youth of the United States shall be received after they have finished their studies, and taken their degrees in the colleges of their respective states. In this University, let those branches of literature only be taught, which are calculated to prepare our youth for civil and public life. These branches should be taught by means of lectures, and the following arts and sciences should be the subjects of them.

1. The principles and forms of government, applied in a particular manner to the explanation of every part of the Constitution and laws of the United States, together with the laws of nature and nations, which last should include every thing that relates to peace, war, treaties, ambassadors, and the like.
2. History both ancient and modern, and chronology.
3. Agriculture in all its numerous and extensive branches.
4. The principles and practice of manufactures.
5. The history, principles, objects and channels of commerce.

6. Those parts of mathematics which are necessary to the division of property, to finance, and to the principles and practice of war, for there is too much reason to fear that war will continue, for some time to come, to be the unChristian mode of deciding disputes between Christian nations.

7. Those parts of natural philosophy and chemistry, which admit of an application to agriculture, manufactures, commerce and war.

8. Natural history, which includes the history of animals, vegetables and fossils. To render instruction in these branches of science easy, it will be necessary to establish a museum, as also a garden, in which not only all the shrubs, &c. but all the forest trees of the United States should be cultivated. The great Linnæus of Upsal enlarged the commerce of Sweden, by his discoveries in natural history. He once saved the Swedish navy by finding out the time in which a worm laid its eggs, and recommending the immersion of the timber, of which the ships were built, at that season wholly under water So great were the services this illustrious naturalist rendered his country by the application of his knowledge to agriculture, manufactures and commerce, that the present king of Sweden pronounced an eulogium upon him from his throne, soon after his death.

9. Philology which should include, besides rhetoric and criticism, lectures upon the construction and pronunciation of the English language. Instruction in this branch of literature will become the more necessary in America, as our intercourse must soon cease with the bar, the stage and the pulpits of Great Britain, from whence we received our knowledge of the pronunciation of the English language. Even modern English books should cease to be the models of style in the United States. The present is the age of simplicity in writing in America. The turgid style of Johnson—the purple glare of Gibbon, and even the studied and thick set metaphors of Junius, are all equally unnatural, and should not be admitted into our country. . . . The cultivation and perfection of our language becomes a matter of consequence when viewed in another light. It will probably be spoken by more

people in the course of two or three centuries, than ever spoke any one language at one time since the creation of the world. When we consider the influence which the prevalence of only *two* languages, viz. the English and the Spanish, in the extensive regions of North and South America, will have upon manners, commerce, knowledge and civilization, scenes of human happiness and glory open before us, which elude from their magnitude the utmost grasp of the human understanding.

10. The German and French languages should be taught in this University. The many excellent books which are written in both these languages upon all subjects, more especially upon those which relate to the advancement of national improvements of all kinds, will render a knowledge of them an essential part of the education of a legislator of the United States.

11. All those athletic and manly exercises should likewise be taught in the University, which are calculated to impart health, strength, and elegance to the human body.

To render the instruction of our youth as easy and extensive as possible in several of the above mentioned branches of literature, let four young men of good education and active minds be sent abroad at the public expense, to collect and transmit to the professors of the said branches all the improvements that are daily made in Europe, in agriculture, manufactures and commerce, and in the art of war and practical government. This measure is rendered the more necessary from the distance of the United States from Europe, by which means the rays of knowledge strike the United States so partially, that they can be brought to a useful focus, only by employing suitable persons to collect and transmit them to our country. It is in this manner that the northern nations of Europe have imported so much knowledge from their southern neighbours, that the history of agriculture, manufactures, commerce, revenues and military arts of *one* of these nations will soon be alike applicable to all of them.

Besides sending four young men abroad to collect and transmit knowledge for the benefit of our country, *two* young men of suitable capacities should be employed at the public expense in exploring the vegetable, mineral and animal productions of our country, in procuring histories and samples of each of them, and in transmitting them to the professor of natural history. It is in consequence of the discoveries made by young gentlemen employed for these purposes, that Sweden, Denmark and Russia have extended their manufactures and commerce, so as to rival in both the oldest nations in Europe.

Let the Congress allow a liberal salary to the Principal of this university. Let it be his business to govern the students, and to inspire them by his conversation, and by occasional public discourses, with federal and patriotic sentiments. Let this Principal be a man of extensive education, liberal manners and dignified deportment.

Let the Professors of each of the branches that have been mentioned, have a moderate salary of 150*l.* or 200*l.* a year, and let them depend upon the number of their pupils to supply the deficiency of their maintenance from their salaries. Let each pupil pay for each course of lectures two or three guineas.

Let the degrees conferred in this university receive a new name, that shall designate the design of an education for civil and public life.

In thirty years after this university is established, let an act of Congress be passed to prevent any person being chosen or appointed into power or office, who has not taken a degree in the federal university. We require certain qualifications in lawyers, physicians and clergymen, before we commit our property, our lives or our souls to their care. We even refuse to commit the charge of a ship to a pilot, who cannot produce a certificate of his education and knowledge in his business. Why then should we commit our country, which includes liberty, property, life, wives and children, to men who cannot produce vouchers of their qualifications for the important trust? We are restrained from injuring ourselves by employing quacks in law; why should we not be restrained in like manner, by law, from employing quacks in government?

Should this plan of a federal university or one like it be

adopted, then will begin the golden age of the United States. While the business of education in Europe consists in lectures upon the ruins of Palmyra and the antiquities of Herculaneum, or in disputes about Hebrew points, Greek particles, or the accent and quantity of the Roman language, the youth of America will be employed in acquiring those branches of knowledge which increase the conveniences of life, lessen human misery, improve our country, promote population, exalt the human understanding, and establish domestic, social and political happiness.

Let it not be said, "that this is not the *time* for such a literary and political establishment. Let us first restore public credit, by funding or paying our debts, let us regulate our militia, let us build a navy, and let us protect and extend our commerce. After this, we shall have leisure and money to establish a University for the purposes that have been mentioned." This is false reasoning. We shall never restore public credit, regulate our militia, build a navy, or revive our commerce, until we remove the ignorance and prejudices, and change the habits of our citizens, and this can never be done 'till we inspire them with federal principles, which can only be effected by our young men meeting and spending two or three years together in a national University, and afterwards disseminating their knowledge and principles through every county, township and village of the United States. 'Till this is done—Senators and Representatives of the United States, you will undertake to make bricks without straw. Your supposed union in Congress will be a rope of sand. The inhabitants of Massachusetts began the business of government by establishing the University of Cambridge, and the wisest Kings in Europe have always found their literary institutions the surest means of establishing their power as well as of promoting the prosperity of their people.

These hints for establishing the Constitution and happiness of the United States upon a permanent foundation, are submitted to the friends of the federal government in each of the states, by a private

CITIZEN OF PENNSYLVANIA.

THE AMUSEMENTS AND PUNISHMENTS WHICH ARE PROPER FOR SCHOOLS

Addressed to George Clymer, Esq.

DEAR SIR,

The last time I had the pleasure of being in your company, you did me the honour to request my opinion upon the AMUSE-MENTS and PUNISHMENTS which are proper for schools. The subjects are of a very opposite nature, but I shall endeavour to comply with your wishes, by sending you a few thoughts upon each of them. I am sure you will not reject my opinions because they are contrary to received practices, for I know that you are accustomed to think for yourself, and that every proposition that has for its objects the interests of humanity and your country, will be treated by you with attention and candor.

I shall begin with the subjects of AMUSEMENTS. Montesquieu informs us that the exercises of the last day of the life of Epaminondas, were the same as his amusements in his youth. Herein we have an epitome of the perfection of education. The amusements of Epaminondas were of a military nature; but as the profession of arms is the business of only a small part of mankind, and happily much less necessary in the United States than in ancient Greece, I would propose that the amusements of our youth, at school, should consist of such exercises as will be most subservient to their future employments in life. These are; 1. agriculture; 2. mechanical occupations; and 3. the business of the learned professions.

I. There is a variety in the employments of agriculture which may readily be suited to the genius, taste, and strength of young people. An experiment has been made of the efficacy of these employments, as amusements, in the Methodist College at Abington, in Maryland; and, I have been informed, with the happiest effects. A large lot is divided between the scholars, and premiums are adjudged to those of them who produce the most vegetables from their grounds, or who keep them in the best order.

II. As the employments of agriculture cannot afford amusement at all seasons of the year, or in cities I would propose, that children should be allured to seek amusements in such of the mechanical arts as are suited to their strength and capacities. Where is the boy who does not delight in the use of a hammer—a chisel—or a saw? and who has not enjoyed a high degree of pleasure in his youth, in constructing a miniature house?

III. To train the youth who are intended for the learned professions or for merchandize, to the duties of their future employments, by means of useful amusements, which are *related* to those employments, will be impracticable; but their amusements may be derived from cultivating a spot of ground; for where is the lawyer, the physician, the divine, or the merchant, who has not indulged or felt a passion, in some part of his life, for rural improvements?—Indeed I conceive the seeds of knowledge in agriculture will be most productive, when they are planted in the minds of this class of scholars.

I have only to add under this head, that the common amusements of children have no connection with their future occupations. Many of them injure their clothes, some of them waste their strength, and impair their health, and all of them prove more or less, the means of producing noise, or of exciting angry passions, both of which are calculated to beget vulgar manners. The Methodists have wisely banished every species of play from their college. Even the healthy and pleasurable exercise of swimming, is not permitted to their scholars, except in the presence of one of their masters.

Do not think me too strict if I here exclude *gunning* from

the amusements of young men. My objections to it are as follows.

1. It hardens the heart, by inflicting unnecessary pain and death upon animals.

2. It is unnecessary in civilized society, where animal food may be obtained from domestic animals, with greater facility.

3. It consumes a great deal of time, and thus creates habits of idleness.

4. It frequently leads young men into low, and bad company.

5. By imposing long abstinence from food, it leads to intemperance in eating, which naturally leads to intemperance in drinking.

6. It exposes to fevers, and accidents. The newspapers are occasionally filled with melancholy accounts of the latter, and every physician must have met with frequent and dangerous instances of the former, in the course of his practice.

I know the early use of a gun is recommended in our country, to teach our young men the use of firearms, and thereby to prepare them for war and battle. But why should we inspire our youth, by such exercises, with hostile ideas towards their fellow creatures?—Let us rather instill into their minds sentiments of universal benevolence to men of all nations and colours. Wars originate in error and vice. Let us eradicate these, by proper modes of education, and wars will cease to be necessary in our country. The divine author and lover of peace "will then suffer no man to do us wrong, yea, he will reprove kings for our sake, saying, touch not my anointed and do my people no harm." Should the nations with whom war is a trade, approach our coasts, they will retire from us, as Satan did from our Saviour, when he came to assault him, and for the same reason, because they will "find nothing in us" congenial to their malignant dispositions; for the flames of war can be spread from one nation to another, only by the conducting mediums of vice and error.

I have hinted at the injury which is done to the health of young people by some of their amusements; but there is a practice

ON EDUCATION

common in all our schools, which does more harm to their bodies than all the amusements that can be named, and that is, obliging them to sit too long in *one place*, or crowding too many of them together *in one room*. By means of the former, the growth and shape of the body have been impaired; and by means of the latter, the seeds of fevers have often been engendered in schools. In the course of my business, I have been called to many hundred children who have been seized with indispositions in school, which evidently arose from the action of morbid effluvia, produced by the confined breath and perspiration of too great a number of children in one room. To obviate these evils, children should be permitted, after they have said their lessons, to amuse themselves in the open air, in some of the useful and agreeable exercises which have been mentioned. Their minds will be strengthened, as well as their bodies relieved by them. To oblige a sprightly boy to sit *seven* hours in a day, with his little arms pinioned to his sides, and his neck unnaturally bent towards his book; and for *no crime!*—what cruelty and folly are manifested, by such an absurd mode of instructing or governing young people!

I come next to say a few words upon the subject of PUNISHMENTS which are proper in schools.

In barbarous ages every thing partook of the complexion of the times Civil, ecclesiastical, military, and domestic punishments were all of a cruel nature. With the progress of reason and Christianity, punishments of all kinds have become less severe. Solitude and labor are now substituted in many countries, with success, in the room of the whipping-post and the gallows.—The innocent infirmities of human nature are no longer proscribed, and punished by the church. Discipline, consisting in the vigilance of officers, has lessened the supposed necessity of military executions; and husbands—fathers—and masters now blush at the history of the times, when wives, children, and servants, were governed only by force. But unfortunately this spirit of humanity and civilization has not reached our schools. The rod is yet the principal instrument of governing them, and a school-master remains the only despot now known in free countries. Perhaps it is because the little subjects of their arbitrary and capricious power have not been in a condition to complain. I shall endeavour therefore to plead their cause, and to prove that corporal punishments (except to children under four or five years of age) are never necessary, and always hurtful, in schools.— The following arguments I hope will be sufficient to establish this proposition.

1. Children are seldom sent to school before they are capable of feeling the force of rational or moral obligation. They may therefore be deterred from committing offences, by motives less disgraceful than the fear of corporal punishments.

2. By correcting children for ignorance and negligence in school, their ideas of *improper* and *immoral* actions are confounded, and hence the moral faculty becomes weakened in after life. It would not be more cruel or absurd to inflict the punishment of the whipping-post upon a man, for not dressing fashionably or neatly, than it is to ferule a boy for blotting his copy book, or mis-spelling a word.

3. If the natural affection of a parent is sometimes insufficient, to restrain the violent effects of a sudden gust of anger upon a child, how dangerous must the power of correcting children be when lodged in the hands of a school-master, in whose anger there is no mixture of parental affection! Perhaps those parents act most wisely, who never trust themselves to inflict corporal punishments upon their children, after they are four or five years old, but endeavour to punish, and reclaim them, by confinement, or by abridging them of some of their usual gratifications, in dress, food or amusements.

4. Injuries are sometimes done to the bodies, and sometimes to the intellects of children, by corporal punishments. I recollect, when a boy, to have lost a school-mate, who was said to have died in consequence of a severe whipping he received in school. At that time I did not believe it possible, but from what I now know of the disproportion between the violent emotions of the mind, and the strength of the body in children, I am disposed

to believe, that not only sickness, but that even *death* may be induced, by the convulsions of a youthful mind, worked up to a high sense of shame and resentment.

The effects of thumping the head, boxing the ears, and pulling the hair, in impairing the intellects, by means of injuries done to the brain, are too obvious to be mentioned.

5. Where there is *shame*, says Dr. Johnson, there may be *virtue*. But corporal punishments, inflicted at school, have a tendency to destroy the sense of shame, and thereby to destroy all moral sensibility. The boy that has been often publicly whipped at school, is under great obligations to his maker, and his parents, if he afterwards escape the whipping-post or the gallows.

6. Corporal punishments, inflicted at school, tend to beget a spirit of violence in boys towards each other, which often follows them through life; but they more certainly beget a spirit of hatred, or revenge, towards their masters, which too often becomes a ferment of the same baneful passions towards other people. The celebrated Dr. afterwards Baron Haller declared, that he never saw, without horror, during the remaining part of his life, a school-master, who had treated him with unmerited severity, when he was only ten years old. A similar anecdote is related of the famous M de Condamine. I think I have known several instances of this vindictive, or indignant spirit, to continue towards a cruel and tyrannical school-master, in persons who were advanced in life, and who were otherwise of gentle and forgiving dispositions.

7. Corporal punishments, inflicted at schools, beget a hatred to instruction in young people. I have sometimes suspected that the Devil, who knows how great an enemy knowledge is to his kingdom, has had the address to make the world believe that *feruling, pulling* and *boxing ears, cudgelling, horsing*, &c. and, in boarding-schools, a *little starving*, are all absolutely necessary for the government of young people, on purpose that he might make both schools, and school-masters odious, and thereby keep our world in ignorance; for ignorance is the best means the

Devil ever contrived, to keep up the number of his subjects in our world.

8. Corporal punishments are not only hurtful, but altogether unnecessary, in schools. Some of the most celebrated and successful school-masters, that I have known, never made use of them.

9. The fear of corporal punishments, by debilitating the body, produces a corresponding debility in the mind, which contracts its capacity of acquiring knowledge. This capacity is enlarged by the tone which the mind acquires from the action of hope, love, and confidence upon it; and all these passions might easily be cherished, by a prudent and enlightened schoolmaster.

10. As there should always be a certain ratio between the strength of a remedy, and the excitability of the body in diseases, so there should be a similar ratio between the force employed in the government of a school, and the capacities and tempers of children. A kind rebuke, like fresh air in a fainting fit, is calculated to act upon a young mind with more effect, than stimulants of the greatest power; but corporal punishments level all capacities and tempers, as quack-medicines do, all constitutions and diseases. They dishonour and degrade our species; for they suppose a total absence of all moral and intellectual feeling from the mind. Have we not often seen dull children suddenly improve, by changing their schools? The reason is obvious. The successful teacher only accommodated his manner and discipline to the capacities of his scholars.

11. I conceive corporal punishments, inflicted in an arbitrary manner, to be contrary to the spirit of liberty, and that they should not be tolerated in a free government. Why should not children be protected from violence and injuries, as well as white and black servants?—Had I influence enough in our legislature to obtain only a single law, it should be to make the punishment for striking a school boy, the same as for assaulting and beating an adult member of society.

To all these arguments I know some well disposed people

ON EDUCATION

will reply, that the *rod* has received a divine commission from the sacred scriptures, as the instrument of correcting children. To this I answer that the *rod*, in the Old Testament, by a very common figure in rhetoric, stands for punishments of *any* kind, just as the *sword*, in the New Testament, stands for the faithful and general administration of justice, in such a way as is most calculated to reform criminals, and to prevent crimes.

The following method of governing a school, I apprehend, would be attended with much better effects, than that which I have endeavoured to show to be contrary to reason, humanity, religion, liberty, and the experience of the wisest and best teachers in the world.

Let a school-master endeavour, in the first place, to acquire the confidence of his scholars, by a prudent deportment. Let him learn to command his passions and temper, at all times, in his school,—Let him treat the name of the Supreme Being with reverence, as often as it occurs in books, or in conversation with his scholars.—Let him exact a respectful behaviour towards himself, in his school; but in the intervals of school hours, let him treat his scholars with gentleness and familiarity. If he should even join in their amusements, he would not lose, by his condescension, any part of his authority over them. But to secure their affection and respect more perfectly, let him, once or twice a year, lay out a small sum of money in pen-knives, and books, and distribute them among his scholars, as rewards for proficiency in learning, and for good behaviour. If these prudent and popular measures should fail of preventing offences at school, then let the following modes of punishment be adopted.

1. *Private* admonition. By this mode of rebuking, we imitate the conduct of the divine Being towards his offending creatures, for his *first* punishment is always inflicted *privately*, by means of the *still* voice of conscience.

2. Confinement after school-hours are ended; but with the knowledge of the parents of the children.

3. Holding a small sign of disgrace, of any kind, in the middle of the floor, in the presence of a whole school.

If these punishments fail of reclaiming a bad boy, he should be dismissed from school, to prevent his corrupting his school-mates. It is the business of parents, and not of school-masters, to use the last means for eradicating idleness and vice from their children.

The world was created in love. It is sustained by love. Nations and families that are happy, are made so only by love. Let us extend this divine principle, to those little communities which we call schools. Children are capable of loving in a high degree. They may therefore be governed by love.

The occupation of a school-master is truly dignified. He is, next to mothers, the most important member of civil society. Why then is there so little rank connected with that occupation? Why do we treat it with so much neglect or contempt? It is because the voice of reason, in the human heart, associates with it the idea of despotism and violence. Let school-masters cease to be tyrants, and they will soon enjoy the respect and rank, which are naturally connected with their profession.

We are grossly mistaken in looking up wholly to our governments, and even to ministers of the gospel, to promote public and private order in society. Mothers and school-masters plant the seeds of nearly all the good and evil which exist in our world. Its reformation must therefore be begun in nurseries and in schools. If the habits we acquire there, were to have no influence upon our future happiness, yet the influence they have upon our governments, is a sufficient reason why we ought to introduce new modes, as well as new objects of education into our country.

You have lately been employed in an attempt to perpetuate our existence as a free people, by establishing the means of national credit and defense;* but these are feeble bulwarks against slavery, compared with habits of labor and virtue, disseminated among our young people. Let us establish schools for this purpose, in every township in the United States, and con-

---

* Mr. Clymer was one of the Representatives of Pennsylvania, in the first Congress of the United States which met in New York, in the year 1789.

form them to reason, humanity, and the present state of society in America. Then, Sir, will the generations who are to follow us, realize the precious ideas of the dignity and excellence of republican forms of government, which I well recollect you cherished with so much ardor, in the beginning of the American Revolution, and which you have manifested ever since, both by your public and private conduct.

We suffer so much from traditional error of various kinds, in education, morals, and government, that I have been led to wish, that it were possible for us to have schools established, in the United States, for teaching *the art of forgetting*. I think three-fourths of all our school-masters, divines, and legislators would profit very much, by spending two or three years in such useful institutions.

An apology may seem necessary, not only for the length of this letter, but for some of the opinions contained in it. I know how apt mankind are to brand every proposition for innovation, as visionary and Utopian. But good men should not be discouraged, by such epithets, from their attempts to combat vice and error. There never was an improvement, in any art or science, nor even a proposal for meliorating the condition of man, in any age or country, that has not been considered in the light of what has been called, since Sir Thomas More's time, an *Utopian scheme*. The application of the magnet to navigation, and of steam to mechanical purposes, have both been branded as Utopian projects. The great idea in the mind of Columbus, of exploring a new world, was long viewed, in most of the courts of Europe, as the dream of a visionary sailor. But why do we go to ancient times, for proofs of important innovations in human affairs having been treated as Utopian schemes. You and I recollect the time, when the abolition of Negro slavery in our state, as also when the independence of the United States, and the present wise and happy confederacy of our republics, were all considered by many of our sober prudent men, as subjects of an Utopian nature.

If those benefactors of mankind, who have levelled mountains in the great road of human life, by the discoveries or labors which have been mentioned, have been stigmatized with obloquy, as visionary projectors, why should an individual be afraid of similar treatment, who has only attempted to give to that road, from its beginning, a straight direction.

If but a dozen men like yourself, approve of my opinions, it will overbalance the most illiberal opposition they may meet with, from all the learned vulgar of the United States.

For the benefit of those persons who consider opinions as improved, like certain liquids, by time, and who are opposed to innovations, only because they did not occur to their ancestors, I shall conclude my letter with an anecdote of a minister in London, who, after employing a long sermon, in controverting what he supposed to be an heretical opinion, concluded it with the following words, "I tell you, I tell you my brethren,—I tell you again,—that an old error is better than a new truth."

THE BIBLE AS A SCHOOL BOOK
Addressed to the Rev. Jeremy Belknap, of Boston

Dear Sir,

It is now several months, since I promised to give you my reasons for preferring the Bible as a school book, to all other compositions. I shall not trouble you with an apology for my delaying so long to comply with my promise, but shall proceed immediately to the subject of my letter.

Before I state my arguments in favour of teaching children to read by means of the Bible, I shall assume the five following propositions.

I. That Christianity is the only true and perfect religion, and that in proportion as mankind adopt its principles, and obey its precepts, they will be wise, and happy.

II. That a better knowledge of this religion is to be acquired by reading the bible, than in any other way.

III. That the bible contains more knowledge necessary to man in his present state, than any other book in the world.

IV. That knowledge is most durable, and religious instruction most useful, when imparted in early life,

V. That the Bible, when not read in schools, is seldom read in any subsequent period of life.

My arguments in favor of the use of the Bible as a school book are founded, I. In the constitution of the human mind.

1. The memory is the first faculty which opens in the minds of children. Of how much consequence, then, must it be, to

impress it with the great truths of Christianity, before it is preoccupied with less interesting subjects! As all the liquors, which are poured into a cup, generally taste of that which first filled it, so all the knowledge, which is added to that which is treasured up in the memory from the Bible, generally receives an agreeable and useful tincture from it.

2. There is a peculiar aptitude in the minds of children for religious knowledge. I have constantly found them in the first six or seven years of their lives, more inquisitive upon religious subjects, than upon any others· and an ingenious instructor of youth has informed me, that he has found young children more capable of receiving just ideas upon the most difficult tenets of religion, than upon the most simple branches of human knowledge. It would be strange if it were otherwise; for God creates all his means to suit all his ends. There must of course be a fitness between the human mind, and the truths which are essential to its happiness.

3. The influence of *prejudice* is derived from the impressions, which are made upon the mind in early life; prejudices are of two kinds, true and false. In a world where *false* prejudices do so much mischief, it would discover great weakness not to oppose them, by such as are *true*.

I grant that many men have rejected the prejudices derived from the Bible: but I believe no man ever did so, without having been made *wiser* or *better*, by the early operation of these prejudices upon his mind. Every just principle that is to be found in the writings of Voltaire, is borrowed from the Bible: and the morality of the Deists, which has been so much admired and praised, is, I believe, in most cases, the effect of habits, produced by early instruction in the principles of Christianity.

4. We are subject, by a general law in our natures, to what is called *habit*. Now if the study of the scriptures be necessary to our happiness at any time of our lives, the sooner we begin to read them, the more we shall be attached to them; for it is peculiar to all the acts of habit, to become easy, strong and agreeable by repetition.

5. It is a law in our natures, that we remember *longest* the knowledge we acquire by the greatest number of our senses. Now a knowledge of the contents of the Bible, is acquired in school by the aid of the *eyes* and the *ears*; for children after getting their lessons, always say them to their masters in an audible voice; of course there is a presumption, that this knowledge will be retained much longer than if it had been acquired in any other way.

6. The interesting events and characters, recorded and described in the Old and New Testaments, are accommodated above all others to seize upon all the faculties of the minds of children. The understanding, the memory, the imagination, the passions, and the moral powers, are all occasionally addressed by the various incidents which are contained in those divine books, insomuch that not to be delighted with them, is to be devoid of every principle of pleasure that exists in a sound mind.

7. There is a native love of *truth* in the human mind. Lord Shaftesbury says, that "truth is so congenial to our minds, that we love even the *shadow* of it:" and Horace, in his rules for composing an epic poem, establishes the same law in our natures, by advising the "fictions in poetry to resemble truth." Now the Bible contains more truths than any other book in the world: so true is the testimony that it bears of God in his works of creation, providence, and redemption, that it is called *truth* itself, by way of pre-eminence above things that are only simply true. How forcibly are we struck with the evidences of truth, in the history of the Jews, above what we discover in the history of other nations? Where do we find a hero, or an historian record his own faults or vices except in the Old Testament? Indeed, my friend, from some accounts which I have read of the American Revolution, I begin to grow sceptical to all history except to that which is contained in the Bible. Now if this book be known to contain nothing but what is materially true, the mind will naturally acquire a love for it from this circumstance: and from this affection for the truths of the Bible, it will acquire a dis-

cernment of truth in other books, and a preference of it in all the transactions of life.

VIII. There is a wonderful property in the *memory*, which enables it in old age, to *recover* the knowledge it had acquired in early life, after it had been apparently forgotten for forty or fifty years. Of how much consequence, then, must it be, to fill the mind with that species of knowledge, in childhood and youth, which, when *recalled* in the decline of life, will support the soul under the infirmities of age, and smooth the avenues of approaching death? The Bible is the only book which is capable of affording this support to old age, and it is for this reason that we find it resorted to with so much diligence and pleasure by such old people as have read it in early life. I can recollect many instances of this kind in persons who discovered no attachment to the Bible, in the meridian of their lives, who have notwithstanding, spent the evening of them, in reading no other book. The late Sir John Pringle, Physician to the Queen of Great Britain, after passing a long life in camps and at court, closed it by studying the scriptures. So anxious was he to increase his knowledge in them, that he wrote to Dr. Michaelis, a learned professor of divinity in Germany, for an explanation of a difficult text of scripture, a short time before his death.

IX. My second argument in favour of the use of the Bible in schools, is founded upon an implied command of God, and upon the practice of several of the wisest nations of the world.—In the 6th chapter of Deuteronomy, we find the following words, which are directly to my purpose, "And thou shalt love the Lord thy God, with all thy heart and with all thy soul, and with all thy might. And these words which I command thee this day shall be in thine heart. And thou *shalt teach them diligently unto thy children,* and shalt talk of them when thou sittest in thine house, and when thou walkest by the way, and when thou liest down, and when thou risest up."

It appears, moreover, from the history of the Jews, that they flourished as a nation, in proportion as they honored and read the books of Moses, which contained, a written revelation of the will of God, to the children of men. The law was not only neglected, but lost during the general profligacy of manners which accompanied the long and wicked reign of Manassah. But the discovery of it, in the rubbish of the temple, by Josiah, and its subsequent general use, were followed by a return of national virtue and prosperity. We read further, of the wonderful effects which the reading of the law by Ezra, after his return from his captivity in Babylon, had upon the Jews. They hung upon his lips with tears, and showed the sincerity of their repentance, by their general reformation.

The learning of the Jews, for many years consisted in nothing but a knowledge of the scriptures. These were the text books of all the instruction that was given in the schools of their prophets. It was by means of this general knowledge of their law, that those Jews that wandered from Judea into our countries, carried with them and propagated certain ideas of the true God among all the civilized nations upon the face of the earth. And it was from the attachment they retained to the old Testament, that they procured a translation of it into the Greek language, after they lost the Hebrew tongue, by their long absence from their native country. The utility of this translation, commonly called the Septuagint, in facilitating the progress of the gospel, is well known to all who are acquainted with the history of the first age of the Christian church.

But the benefits of an early and general acquaintance with the Bible, were not confined only to the Jewish nations. They have appeared in many countries in Europe, since the reformation. The industry, and habits of order, which distinguish many of the German nations, are derived from their early instruction in the principles of Christianity, by means of the Bible. The moral and enlightened character of the inhabitants of Scotland, and of the New England states, appears to be derived from the same cause. If we descend from nations to sects, we shall find them wise and prosperous in proportion as they become early acquainted with the scriptures. The bible is still used as a school book among the

Quakers. The morality of this sect of Christians is universally acknowledged. Nor is this all,—their prudence in the management of their private affairs, is as much a mark of their society, as their sober manners.

I wish to be excused for repeating here, that if the Bible did not convey a single direction for the attainment of future happiness, it should be read in our schools in preference to all other books, from, its containing the greatest portion of that kind of knowledge which is calculated to produce private and public temporal happiness.

We err not only in human affairs, but in religion likewise, *only* because "we do not know the scriptures." The opposite systems of the numerous sects of Christians arise chiefly from their being more instructed in catechism, creeds, and confessions of faith, than in the scriptures. Immense truths, I believe, are concealed in them. The time, I have no doubt, will come, when posterity will view and pity our ignorance of these truths, as much as we do the ignorance of the disciples of our Saviour, who knew nothing of the meaning of those plain passages in the Old Testament which were daily fulfilling before their eyes. Whenever that time shall arrive, those truths which have escaped our notice, or, if discovered, have been thought to be opposed to each other, or to be inconsistent with themselves, will then like the stones of Solomon's temple, be found so exactly to accord with each other, that they shall be cemented without noise or force, into one simple and sublime system of religion.

But further, we err, not only in religion but in philosophy likewise, because we "do not know or *believe* the scriptures." The sciences have been compared to a circle of which religion composes a part. To understand any one of them perfectly it is necessary to have some knowledge of them all. Bacon, Boyle, and Newton included the scriptures in the inquiries to which their universal geniuses disposed them, and their philosophy was aided by their knowledge in them. A striking agreement has been lately discovered between the history of certain events recorded in the Bible and some of the operations and productions of nature, particularly those which are related in Whitehurst's observations on the deluge—in Smith's account of the origin of the variety of color in the human species, and in Bruce's travels. It remains yet to be shown how many other events, related in the Bible, accord with some late important discoveries in the principles of medicine. The events, and the principles alluded to, mutually establish the truth of each other. From the discoveries of the Christian philosophers, whose names have been last mentioned, I have been led to question whether most harm has been done to revelation, by those divines who have unduly multiplied the objects of faith, or by those deists who have unduly multiplied the objects of reason, in explaining the scriptures.

I shall now proceed to answer some of the objections which have been made to the use of the Bible as a school book.

I. We are told, that the familiar use of the Bible in our schools, has a tendency to lessen a due reverence for it. This objection, by proving too much, proves nothing at all. If familiarity lessens respect for divine things, then all those precepts of our religion, which enjoin the daily or weekly worship of the Deity, are improper. The bible was not intended to represent a Jewish ark; and it is an antichristian idea, to suppose that it can be profaned, by being carried into a school house, or by being handled by children. But where will the Bible be read by young people with more reverence than in a school? Not in most private families; for I believe there are few parents, who preserve so much order in their houses, as is kept up in our common English schools.

II. We are told, that there are many passages in the Old Testament, that are improper to be read by children, and that the greatest part of it is no way interesting to mankind under the present dispensation of the gospel. There are I grant, several chapters, and many verses in the Old Testament, which in their present unfortunate translation, should be passed over by children. But I deny that any of the books of the Old Testament are not interesting to mankind, under the gospel dispensation.

Most of the characters, events, and ceremonies, mentioned in them, are personal, providential, or instituted types of the Messiah: All of which have been, or remain yet to be, fulfilled by him It is from an ignorance or neglect of these types, that we have so many deists in Christendom, for so irrefragably do they prove the truth of Christianity, that I am sure a young man who had been regularly instructed in their meaning, could never doubt afterwards of the truth of any of its principles. If any obscurity appears in these principles, it is only (to use the words of the poet) because *they are dark, with excessive bright.*

I know there is an objection among many people to teach children doctrines of any kind, because they are liable to be controverted. But where will this objection lead us?—The being of a God, and the obligations of morality, have both been controverted; and yet who has objected to our teaching these doctrines to our children?

The curiosity and capacities of young people for the mysteries of religion, awaken much sooner than is generally supposed. Of this we have two remarkable proofs in the Old Testament. The first is mentioned in the twelfth chapter of Exodus. "And it shall come when your *children* shall say unto you, "*What mean you by this service?*" that ye shall say, "It is the sacrifice of the Lord's passover, who passed over the houses of the children of Israel in Egypt, when he smote the Egyptians, and delivered our houses. And the children of Israel went away, and did as the Lord had commanded Moses and Aaron." A second proof of the desire of children to be instructed in the mysteries of religion, is to be found in the sixth chapter of Deuteronomy. "And when thy son *asketh* thee in the time to come saying, "What mean the testimonies—and the statutes—and the judgments which the Lord our God hath commanded you?" Then thou shalt say unto thy son, "We were Pharaoh's bondmen in Egypt, and the Lord our God brought us out of Egypt with a mighty hand." These enquiries from the mouths of children are perfectly natural; for where is the parent who has not had similar questions proposed to him by his children upon their being first conducted to a place of worship, or upon their beholding, for the first time, either of the sacraments of our religion?

Let us not be wiser than our Maker. If moral precepts alone could have reformed mankind, the mission of the Son of God into our world, would have been unnecessary. He came to promulgate a system of *doctrines*, as well as a system of morals. The perfect morality of the gospel rests upon a *doctrine*, which though often controverted, has never been refuted, I mean the vicarious life and death of the Son of God. This sublime and ineffable doctrine delivers us from the absurd hypotheses of modern philosophers, concerning the foundation of moral obligation, and fixes it upon the eternal and self moving principle of LOVE. It concentrates a whole system of ethics in a single text of scripture. *"A new commandment I give unto you, that ye love one another, even as I have loved you."* By withholding the knowledge of this doctrine from children, we deprive ourselves of the best means of awakening moral sensibility in their minds. We do more, we furnish an argument, for withholding from them a knowledge of the morality of the gospel likewise; for this, in many instances, is as supernatural, and therefore as liable to be controverted, as any of the doctrines or miracles which are mentioned in the New Testament. The miraculous conception of the saviour of the world by a virgin, is not more opposed to the ordinary course of natural events, nor is the doctrine of the atonement more above human reason, than those moral precepts, which command us to love our enemies, or to die for our friends.

III. It has been said, that the division of the Bible into chapters and verses, renders it more difficult to be read, by children than many other books.

By a little care in a master, this difficulty may be obviated, and even an advantage derived from it. It may serve to transfer the attention of the scholar to the *sense* of a subject; and no person will ever read well, who is guided by any thing else, in his stops, emphasis, or accents. The division of the Bible into chapters and verses, is not a greater obstacle to its being read with ease, than the bad punctuation of most other books. I deliver this stricture upon other books, from the authority of Mr. Rice, the celebrated author of the art of speaking, whom I heard declare in a large company in London, that he had never seen a book properly pointed in the English Language. He exemplified, notwithstanding, by reading to the same company a passage from Milton, his perfect knowledge of the art of reading.

Some people, I know, have proposed to introduce extracts from the Bible, into our schools, instead of the Bible itself. Many excellent works of this kind, are in print, but if we admit any one of them, we shall have the same inundation of them that we have had of grammars, spelling books, and lessons for children, many of which are published for the benefit of the authors only, and all of them have tended greatly to increase the expence of education. Besides, these extracts or abridgements of the Bible, often contain the tenets of particular sects or persons, and therefore, may be improper for schools composed of the children of different sects of Christians. The Bible is a cheap book, and is to be had in every bookstore. It is, moreover, esteemed and preferred by all sects; because each finds its peculiar doctrines in it. It should therefore be used in preference to any abridgements of it, or histories extracted from it.

I have heard it proposed that a portion of the Bible should be read every day by the master, as a means of instructing children in it: But this is a poor substitute for obliging children to read it as a school book; for by this means we insensibly *engrave*, as it were, its contents upon their minds: and it has been remarked that children, instructed in this way in the scriptures, seldom forget any part of them. They have the same advantage over those persons, who have only heard the scriptures read by a master, that a man who has worked with the tools of a mechanical employment for several years, has over the man who has only stood a few hours in a work shop and seen the same business carried on by other people.

In this defence of the use of the Bible as a school book, I beg you would not think that I suppose the Bible to contain the only revelation which God has made to man. I believe in an internal revelation, or a moral principle, which God has implanted in the heart of every man, as the precursor of his final dominion over the whole human race. How much this internal revelation accords with the external, remains yet to be explored by philosophers. I am disposed to believe, that most of the doctrines of Christianity revealed in the Bible might be discovered by a close examination of all the principles of action in man: But who is equal to such an enquiry? It certainly does not suit the natural indolence, or laborious employments of a great majority of mankind. The internal revelation of the gospel may be compared to the straight line which is made through a wilderness by the assistance of a compass, to a distant country, which few are able to discover, while the Bible resembles a public road to the same country, which is wide, plain, and easily found. "And a highway shall be there, and it shall be called the way of holiness. The way faring men, though fools, shall not err therein."

Neither let me in this place exclude the Revelation which God has made of himself to man in the works of creation. I am far from wishing to lessen the influence of this species of Revelation upon mankind. But the knowledge of God obtained from this source, is obscure and feeble in its operation, compared with that which is derived from the Bible. The visible creation speaks of the Deity in hieroglyphics, while the Bible describes all his attributes and perfections in such plain, and familiar language that "he who runs may read."

How kindly has our maker dealt with his creatures, in providing three different cords to draw them to himself! But how weakly do some men act, who suspend their faith, and hopes upon only one of them! By laying hold of them all, they would approach more speedily and certainly to the centre of all happiness.

To the arguments I have mentioned in favour of the use of the Bible as a school book, I shall add a few reflections.

The present fashionable practice of rejecting the Bible from our schools, I suspect has originated with the deists. They discover great ingenuity in this new mode of attacking Christianity. If they proceed in it, they will do more in half a century, in extirpating our religion, than Bolingbroke or Voltaire could have effected in a thousand years. I am not writing to this class of people. I despair of changing the opinions of any of them. I wish only to alter the opinions and conduct of those lukewarm, or superstitious Christians, who have been misled by the deists upon this subject. On the ground of the good old custom, of using the Bible as a school book, it becomes us to entrench our religion. It is the last bulwark the deists have left it; for they have rendered instruction in the principles of Christianity by the pulpit and the press, so unfashionable, that little good for many years seems to have been done by either of them.

The effects of the disuse of the Bible, as a school book have appeared of late in the neglect and even contempt with which scripture names are treated by many people. It is because parents have not been early taught to know or respect the characters and exploits of the Old and New Testament worthies, that their names are exchanged for those of the modern kings of Europe, or of the principal characters in novels and romances. I conceive there may be some advantage in bearing scripture names It may lead the persons who bear them, to study that part of the scriptures, in which their names are mentioned, with uncommon attention, and perhaps it may excite a desire in them to possess the talents of virtues of their ancient namesakes. This remark first occurred to me, upon hearing a pious woman whose name was Mary, say, that the first passages of the Bible, which made a serious impression on her mind, were those interesting chapters and verses in which the name of Mary is mentioned in the New Testament.

It is a singular fact, that while the names of the kings and emperors of Rome, are now given chiefly to *horses* and *dogs,* scripture names have hitherto been confined only to the human species. Let the enemies and contemners of those names take care, lest the names of more modern kings be given hereafter only to the same animals, and lest the names of the modern heroines of romances be given to animals of an inferior species.

It is with great pleasure, that I have observed the Bible to be the only book read in the Sunday schools in England. We have adopted the same practice in the Sunday schools, lately established in this city. This will give our religion (humanly speaking) the chance of a longer life in our country. We hear much of the persons educated in free schools in England, turning out well in the various walks of life. I have enquired into the cause of it, and have satisfied myself, that it is wholly to be ascribed to the general use of the Bible in those schools, for it seems the children of poor people are of too little consequence to be guarded from the supposed evils of reading the scriptures in early life, or in an unconsecrated school house.

However great the benefits of reading the scriptures in schools have been, I cannot help remarking, that these benefits might be much greater, did schoolmasters take more pains to explain them to their scholars. Did they demonstrate the divine original of the Bible from the purity, consistency, and benevolence of its doctrines and precepts—did they explain the meaning of the levitical institutions, and show their application to the numerous and successive gospel dispensations—did they inform their pupils that the gross and abominable vices of the Jews were recorded *only* as proofs of the depravity of human nature, and of the insufficiency of the law, to produce moral virtue and thereby to establish the necessity and perfection of the gospel system—and above all, did they often enforce the discourses of our Saviour, as the best rule of life, and the surest guide to happiness, how great would be the influence of our schools upon the order and prosperity of our country! Such a mode of instructing children in the Christian religion, would convey knowledge into their *understandings*, and would therefore be preferable to teaching them creeds, and catechisms, which too often convey, not knowledge, but *words* only, into their *memories*. I think I am not too sanguine in believing, that education, conducted in this manner, would, in the course of two generations, eradicate infidelity from among us, and render civil government scarcely necessary in our country.

In contemplating the political institutions of the United States, I lament, that we waste so much time and money in punishing crimes, and take so little pains to prevent them. We profess to be republicans, and yet we neglect the only means of establishing and perpetuating our republican forms of goverment, that is, the universal education of our youth in the principles of Christianity, by means of the Bible; for this divine book, above all others, favours that equality among mankind, that respect for just laws, and all those sober and frugal virtues, which constitute the soul of republicanism.

I have now only to apologize for having addressed this letter to you, after having been assured by you, that your opinion, respecting the use of the Bible as a school book, coincided with mine. My excuse for what I have done is, that I knew you were qualified by your knowledge, and disposed by your zeal in the cause of truth, to correct all the errors you would discover in my letter. Perhaps a further apology may be necessary for my having presumed to write upon a subject so much above my ordinary studies. My excuse for it is, that I thought a single mite from a member of a profession, which has been frequently charged with scepticism in religion, might attract the notice of persons who had often overlooked the more ample contributions upon this subject, of gentlemen of other professions.

*ON NATURAL AND MEDICAL
SCIENCES*

LECTURES ON ANIMAL LIFE

LECTURE I

GENTLEMEN,

My business in this chair is to teach the institutes of medicine. They have been divided into Physiology, Pathology, and Therapeutics. The objects of the first are, the laws of the human body in its healthy state. The second includes the history of the causes, and seats of diseases. The subjects of the third, are the remedies for those diseases. In entering upon the first part of our course, I am met by a remark delivered by Dr. Hunter in his introductory lectures to his course of anatomy. "In our branch (says the Doctor) those teachers who study to captivate young minds with ingenious speculations, will not leave a reputation behind them that will outlive them, half a century. When they cease from their labours, their labours will be buried along with them. There never was a man more followed, and admired in physiology, than Dr. Boerhaave. I remember the veneration in which he was held And now, in the space of forty years,———his physiology is ——————————— it shocks me to think, in what a light it appears." * Painful as this premonition may be to the teachers of physiology, it should not deter them from speculating upon physiological subjects. Simple anatomy is a mass of dead matter. It is physiology which infuses life into it. A knowledge of the structure of the human body, occupies only the memory. Physiology introduces it to the higher, and more noble faculties of the mind. The component parts of the body, may be

---
* Lect. xi. p. 98.

compared to the materials of a house, lying without order in a yard. It is physiology, like a skilful architect, which connects them together, so as to form from them an elegant, and useful building. The writers against physiology, resemble in one particular, the writers against luxury. They forget that the functions they know, and describe, belong to the science of physiology; just as the declaimers against luxury, forget that all the conveniences which they enjoy beyond what are possessed in the most simple stage of society, belong to the luxuries of life. The anatomist who describes the circulation of the blood, acts the part of a physiologist, as much as he does, who attempts to explain the functions of the brain. In this respect Dr. Hunter did honor to our science; for few men ever explained that subject, and many others equally physiological, with more perspicuity and eloquence, than that illustrious anatomist. Upon all new and difficult subjects, there must be pioneers. It has been my lot to be called to this office of hazard, and drudgery; and if in discharging its duties, I should meet the fate of my predecessors, in this branch of medicine, I shall not perish in vain. My errors, like the bodies of those who fall in forcing a breach, will serve to compose a bridge for those who shall come after me, in our present difficult enterprise. This consideration, aided by just views of the nature, and extent of moral obligation, will overbalance the evils anticipated by Dr. Hunter, from the loss of posthumous fame. Had a prophetic voice whispered in the ear of Dr. Boerhaave in the evening of his life, that in the short period of forty years, the memory of his physiological works would perish from the earth; I am satisfied, from the knowledge we have of his elevated genius and piety, he would have treated the prediction with the same indifference, that he would have done, had he been told, that in the same time, his name should be erased from a pane of glass, in a noisy and vulgar country tavern.

The subjects of the lectures I am about to deliver, you will find in a syllabus which I have prepared, and published, for the purpose of giving you a succinct view of the extent, and connection of our course. Some of these subjects will be new in lectures upon the institutes of medicine, particularly those which relate to morals, metaphysicks, and theology. However thorny these questions may appear, we must approach and handle them; for they are intimately connected with the history of the faculties, and operations of the human mind; and these form an essential part of the animal economy. Perhaps it is because physicians have hitherto been restrained from investigating, and deciding upon these subjects, by an erroneous belief that they belong exclusively to another profession; that physiology has so long been an obscure, and conjectural science.

In beholding the human body, the first thing that strikes us, is its LIFE. This, of course should be the first object of our inquiries. It is a most important subject; for the end of all the studies of a physician is to preserve life; and this cannot be perfectly done, until we know in what it consists.

I include in animal life as applied to the human body, *motion* —*sensation*—and *thought*. These three, when united, compose perfect life. It may exist without thought, or sensation; but neither sensation, nor thought, can exist without motion. The lowest grade of life, probably exists in the absence of even motion, as I shall mention hereafter. I have preferred the term *motion* to those of oscillation, or vibration which have been employed by Dr. Hartley in explaining the laws of animal matter; because I conceived it to be more simple, and better adapted to common apprehension.

In treating upon this subject, I shall first consider animal life as it appears in the waking, and sleeping states in a healthy adult, and shall afterwards inquire into the modification of its causes, in the foetal, infant, youthful, and middle states of life, in certain diseases, in different states of society, in different climates, and in different animals.

I shall begin, by delivering three general propositions.

I. Every part of the human body (the nails and hair excepted) is endowed with sensibility, or excitability, or with both of them. By sensibility is meant the power of having sensation excited by the action of impressions. Excitability denotes that property in the human body, by which motion is excited by means of impressions. This property has been called by several other names, such as, irritability, contractility, mobility, and stimulability. I shall make use of the term excitability, for the most part, in preference to either of them. I mean by it, a capacity of imperceptible, as well as obvious motion.—It is of no consequence to our present inquiries, whether, this excitability be a quality of animal matter, or a substance. The latter opinion has been maintained by Dr. Girtanner, and has some probability in its favor.

II. The whole human body is so formed, and connected, that impressions made in the healthy state upon one part, excite motion, or sensation, or both, in every other part of the body. From this view, it appears to be an unit, or a simple and indivisible quality, or substance. Its capacity for receiving motion, and sensation, is variously modified by means of what are called, the senses. It is external, and internal. The impressions which act upon it, shall be enumerated in order.

III. Life is the EFFECT of certain stimuli acting upon the sensibility, and excitability which are extended in different degrees, over every external, and internal part of the body. These stimuli are as necessary to its existence, as air is to flame. Animal life is truly (to use the words of Dr. Brown) "a forced state." I have said, the *words* of Dr. Brown, for the opinion was delivered by Dr. Cullen in the University of Edinburgh in the year 1766, and was detailed by me in this school, many years before the name of Dr. Brown was known as a teacher of medicine. It is true, Dr. Cullen afterwards deserted it; but it is equally true, I never did; and the belief of it, has been the foundation of many of the principles, and modes of practice in medicine which I have since adopted. In a lecture which I delivered in the year 1771, I find the following words, which are taken from a manuscript copy of lectures given by Dr. Cullen upon the institutes of medicine. "The human body is not an automaton, or self-moving machine; but is kept alive, and in motion by the constant action of stimuli upon it." In thus ascribing the discovery of the cause of life which I shall endeavour to establish, to Dr. Cullen; let it not be supposed, I mean to detract from the genius, and merit of Dr. Brown. To his intrepidity in reviving, and propagating it, as well as for the many other truths contained in his system of medicine posterity, I have no doubt, will do him ample justice, after the errors that are blended with them, have been corrected, by their unsuccessful application to the cure of diseases.

Agreeably to our last proposition, I proceed to remark, that the action of the brain, the diastole, and systole of the heart, the pulsation of the arteries, the contraction of the muscles, the peristaltic motion of the bowels, the absorbing power of the lymphatics, secretion, excretion, hearing, seeing, smelling, taste, and the sense of touch, nay more, thought itself, are all the effects of stimuli acting upon the organs of sense and motion. These stimuli have been divided into external, and internal. The external are light, sound, odors, air, heat, exercise, and the pleasures of the senses. The internal stimuli are food, drinks, chyle, the blood, a certain tension of the glands, which contain secreted liquors, and the exercises of the faculties of the mind; each of which I shall treat in the order, in which they have been mentioned.

Of external stimuli The first of these is light. It is remarkable that the progenitor of the human race was not brought into existence until all the luminaries of heaven were created. The first impulse of life, was probably imparted to his body by means of light. It acts chiefly through the medium of the organs of vision. Its influence upon animal life is feeble, compared with some other stimuli to be mentioned hereafter; but it has its proportion of force.—Sleep has been said to be a tendency to death, now the absence of light we know invites to sleep, and the return of it excites the waking state. The late Mr. Rittenhouse informed me, that for many years he had constantly awoke with the first dawn of the morning light, both in summer and winter. Its influence upon the animal spirits strongly demonstrates its connection with animal life, and hence we find a cheerful and a depressed state of mind in many people, and more especially in invalids, to be intimately connected with the presence or absence of the rays of the sun. The well known pedestrian traveller Mr. Stewart in one of his visits to this city informed me, that he had spent a summer in Lapland in the latitude of 69° during the greatest part of which time the sun was seldom out of sight. He enjoyed he said during this period, uncommon health and spirits, both of which he ascribed to the long duration, and invigorating influence of light. These facts will surprise us less when we attend to the effects of light upon vegetables. Some of them lose their colour by being deprived of it; many of them discover a partiality to it in the direction of their flowers; and all of them discharge their pure air only while they are exposed to it.*

Sound has an extensive influence upon human life. Its numerous artificial and natural sources need not be mentioned. I shall only take notice, that the currents of winds, the passage of insects through the air, and even the growth of vegetables, are all attended with an emission of sound; and although they become imperceptible from habit; yet there is reason to believe they all act upon the body, through the mediums of the ears. The existence of these sounds, is established by the reports of persons who have ascended two or three miles from earth in a Balloon. They tell us that the silence which prevails in those regions of the air is so new and complete, as to produce an awful solemnity in their minds. It is not necessary that these sounds should excite sensation, or perception in order to their exerting a degree of stimulus upon the body. There are a hundred impressions daily made upon it, which from habit, are not followed by sensation. The stimulus of aliment upon the stomach, and of blood upon

---

* "Organization, sensation, spontaneous motion and life, exist only at the surface of the earth, and in places exposed to *light*. We might affirm the flame of Prometheus's torch was the expression of a philosophical truth that did not escape the ancients. Without light, nature was lifeless, inanimate and dead. A benevolent God by producing life has spread organization, sensation and thought over the surface of the earth." Lavoissier.

the heart and arteries, probably cease to be felt, only from the influence of habit. The exercise of walking, which was originally the result of a deliberate act of the will, is performed from habit without the least degree of consciousness. It is unfortunate for this, and many other parts of physiology, that we forget what passed in our minds the first two or three years of our lives. Could we recollect the manner in which we acquired our first ideas, and the progress of our knowledge with the evolution of our senses, and faculties; it would relieve us from many difficulties, and controversies upon this subject. Perhaps this forgetfulness by children, of the origin and progress of their knowledge, might be remedied by our attending more closely to the first effects of impressions, sensation, and perception upon them as discovered by their little actions; all of which probably have a meaning, as determined as any of the actions of men or women.

The influence of sounds of a certain kind in producing excitement, and thereby increasing life, cannot be denied. Fear produces debility which is a tendency to death —Sound obviates this debility, and thus restores the system to the natural, and healthy grade of life. The school boy and the clown, invigorate their feeble and trembling limbs, by whistling or singing as they pass by a country church yard, and the soldier feels his departing life recalled in the onset of a battle by the noise of the fife, and of the poet's "spirit stirring drum." Intoxication is frequently attended with a higher degree of life than is natural. Now sound we know will produce this with a very moderate portion of fermented liquor; hence we find men are more easily and highly excited by it at public entertainments where there is music, loud talking, and hallooing, than in private companies where there is no auxiliary stimulus added to that of the wine. I wish these effects of sound upon animal life to be remembered; for I shall mention it hereafter as a remedy for the weak state of life in many diseases, and shall relate an instance in which a scream suddenly extorted by grief, proved the means of resuscitating a person, who was supposed to be dead, and who had exhibited the usual recent marks of the extinction of life.

I shall conclude this head by remarking that persons, who are destitute of hearing and seeing, possess life in a more languid state than other people, and hence arise the dulness, and want of spirits which they discover in their intercourse with the world.

3. Odors have a sensible effect in promoting animal life. The greater healthiness of the country, than cities, is derived in part from the effluvia of odoriferous plants which float in the atmosphere in the spring and summer months, acting upon the system, through the medium of the sense of smelling. The effects of odors, upon animal life, appear still more obvious in the sudden revival of it, which they produce in cases of fainting. Here the smell of a few drops of hartshorn, or even of a burnt feather, has frequently in a few minutes restored the system, from a state of weakness bordering upon death, to an equable and regular degree of excitement.

4. Air acts as a powerful stimulus upon the system through the medium of the lungs. The component parts of this fluid, and its decomposition in the lungs, will be considered in another place. I shall only remark here, that the circulation of the blood has been ascribed by Dr. Goodwin exclusively to the action of air upon the lungs and heart. Does the external air act upon any other part of the body besides those which have been mentioned? It is probable it does, and that we lose our sensation and consciousness of it, by habit. It is certain children cry, for the most part, as soon as they come into the world. May not this be the effect of the sudden impression of air upon the tender surface of their bodies? And may not the red color of their skins, be occasioned by an irritation excited on them by the stimulus of the air? It is certain it acts powerfully upon dinudated animal fibres; for who has not observed a sore, and even the skin when deprived of its cuticle, to be affected, when long exposed to the air, with pain, and inflammation?— The stimulus of air, in promoting the natural actions of the alimentary canal, cannot be doubted. A certain portion of it seems to be necessarily present in the bowels in a healthy state.

5. Heat is an uniform and active stimulus in promoting life.

It is derived, in certain seasons and countries, in part from the sun; but its principal source is from the lungs, in which it appears to be generated by the decomposition of pure air, and from whence it is conveyed by means of the circulation, to every part of the body. The extensive influence of heat upon animal life, is evident from its decay and suspension during the winter in certain animals, and from its revival upon the approach and action of the vernal sun. It is true, life is diminished much less in man, from the distance and absence of the sun, than in other animals, but this must be ascribed to his possessing reason in so high a degree, as to enable him to supply the abstraction of heat, by the action of other stimuli upon his system.

6. Exercise acts as a stimulus upon the body in various ways. Its first impression is upon the muscles. These act upon the blood vessels, and they upon the nerves and brain The necessity of exercise to animal life is indicated, by its being kindly imposed upon man in paradise. The change which the human body underwent by the fall, rendered the same salutary stimulus necessary to its life, in the more active form of labor. But we are not to suppose, that motion is excited in the body by exercise or labor alone. It is constantly stimulated by the positions of standing, sitting, and lying upon the sides, all of which act more or less upon muscular fibres, and by their means, upon every part of the system.

7. The pleasures we derive from our senses have a powerful and extensive influence upon human life. The number of these pleasures, and their proximate cause, will form an agreeable subject for two or three future lectures.

We proceed next to consider the internal stimuli which produce animal life. These are

I. FOOD. This acts in the following ways. 1. Upon the tongue. Such are the sensibility and excitability of this organ, and so intimate is its connection with every other part of the body; that the whole system is invigorated by aliment, as soon as it comes in contact with it. 2. By mastication. This moves a number of muscles and blood vessels situated near the brain and heart, and of course imparts impressions to them. 3. By deglutition, which acts upon similar parts, and with the same effect. 4. By its presence in the stomach, in which it acts by its quantity and quality. Food, by distending the stomach, stimulates the contiguous parts of the body. A moderate degree of distention of the stomach and bowels is essential to a healthy excitement of the system. Vegetable aliment, and drinks, which contain less nourishment than animal food, serve this purpose in the human body. Hay acts in the same manner in a horse. Sixteen pounds, of this light food, are necessary to keep up such a degree of distention in the stomach and bowels of this animal, as to impart to him his natural grade of strength and life. The *quality* of food, when of a stimulating nature, supplies the place of distention from its quantity. A single onion will support a lounging Highlander on the hills of Scotland for four and twenty hours. A moderate quantity of salted meat, or a few ounces of sugar, have supplied the place of pounds of less stimulating food. Even indigestible substances, which remain for days, or perhaps weeks in the stomach, exert a stimulus there, which has an influence upon animal life. It is in this way the tops of briars, and the twigs of trees, devoid not only of nourishing matter, but of juices, support the camel in his journeys through the deserts of the Eastern countries. Chips of cedar posts, moistened with water, have supported horses for two or three weeks, during a long voyage from Boston to Surinam; and the indigestible cover of an old Bible, preserved the life of a dog, accidentally confined in a room at New Castle upon Tyne, for twenty days. 5. Food stimulates the whole body by means of the process of digestion which goes forward in the stomach. This animal function is carried on in part by fermentation, in which there is an extrication of heat, and air. Now both these, it has been remarked, exert a stimulus in promoting animal life.

Drinks when they consist of fermented or distilled liquors, stimulate from their quality; but when they consist of water, either in its simple state, or impregnated with any sapid substance, they act principally by distention.

II. The chyle acts upon the lacteals, mesenteric glands, and thoracic duct, in its passage through them; and it is highly probable, its first mixture with the blood in the subclavian vein, and its first action on the heart, are attended with considerable stimulating effects.

III. The blood is a very important internal stimulus. It has been disputed whether it acts by its quality, or only by distending the blood vessels. It appears to act in both ways. I believe with Dr. Whytt, that the blood stimulates the heart and arteries by a specific action. But if this be not admitted, its influence in distending the blood vessels in every part of the body, and thereby imparting extensive and uniform impressions to every animal fibre, cannot be denied.—In support of this assertion it has been remarked, that in those persons who die of hunger, there is no diminution of the quantity of blood in the large blood vessels.

IV. A certain TENSION of the glands, and of other parts of the body, contributes to support animal life. This is evident in the vigor which is imparted to the system, by the fulness of the seminal vesicle and gall bladder, and by the distention of the uterus in pregnancy. This distention is so great, in some instances, as to prevent sleep for many days and even weeks before delivery. It serves the valuable purpose of rendering the female system less liable to death during its continuance, than at any other time. By increasing the quantity of life in the body, it often suspends the fatal issue of pulmonary consumption, and ensures a temporary victory over the plague and other malignant fevers; for death, from those diseases, seldom takes place until the stimulus, from the distention of the uterus, is removed by parturition.

V. The exercises of the faculties of the mind have a wonderful influence in increasing the quantity of human life. They all act by *reflection* only, after having been previously excited into action by impressions made upon the body. This view, of the *reaction* of the mind upon the body, accords with the simplicity of other operations in the animal economy. It is thus the brain repays the heart for the blood it conveys to it, by reacting upon its muscular fibres.—The influence of the different faculties of the mind is felt in the pulse, in the stomach, and in the liver, and is seen in the face, and other external parts of the body. Those which act most unequivocally in promoting life, are the understanding, the imagination, and the passions. Thinking belongs to the understanding, and is attended with an obvious influence upon the degree and duration of life. Intense study has often rendered the body insensible to the debilitating effects of cold, and hunger. Men of great and active understandings, who blend with their studies, temperance and exercise, are generally long lived. In support of this assertion, a hundred names might be added to those of Newton and Franklin. Its truth will be more fully established by attending to the state of human life in persons of an opposite intellectual character. The Cretins, a race of idiots in Valais in Switzerland, travellers tell us, are all short lived. Common language justifies the opinion of the stimulus of the understanding upon the brain, hence it is common to say of dull men, that they have scarcely ideas enough to keep themselves awake.

The imagination acts with great force upon the body, whether its numerous associations produce pleasure or pain. But the passions pour a constant stream upon the wheels of life. They have been subdivided into emotions and passions properly so called. The former have for their objects present, the latter, future good and evil. All the objects of the passions are accompanied with desire or aversion. To the former belong chiefly, hope, love, ambition, and avarice; to the latter—fear, hatred, malice, envy and the like. Joy, anger, and terror, belong to the class of emotions. The passions and emotions have been further divided into stimulating and sedative Our business at present is to consider their first effect only upon the body. In the original constitution of human nature, we were made to be stimulated by such passions and emotions only as have moral good for their objects. Man was designed to be always under the influence of hope, love, and joy. By the loss of his innocence, he has subjected himself to the dominion of passions and emotions of a malignant nature; but they possess, in common with such as are good, a stimulus which renders them subservient to the purpose of promoting animal life. It is true, they are like the stimulus of a dislocated bone in their operation upon the body, compared with the action of antagonist muscles stretched over bones, which gently move in their natural sockets. The effects of the good passions and emotions, in promoting health and longevity, have been taken notice of by many writers. They produce a flame, gentle and pleasant, like oil perfumed with frankincense in the lamp of life. There are instances likewise of persons who have derived strength, and long life from the influence of the evil passions and emotions that have been mentioned. Dr. Darwin relates the history of a man, who used to overcome the fatigue induced by travelling, by thinking of a person whom he hated. The debility induced by disease, is often removed by a sudden change in the temper. This is so common, that even nurses predict a recovery in persons as soon as they become peevish and ill-natured, after having been patient during the worst stage of their sickness. This peevishness acts as a gentle stimulus upon the system in its languid state, and thus turns the scale in favour of life and health. The famous Benjamin Lay of this state, who lived to be eighty years of age, was of a very irascible temper. Old Elwes was a prodigy of avarice, and every court in Europe furnishes instances of men who have attained to extreme old age, who have lived constantly under the dominion of ambition. In the course of a long inquiry, which I instituted some years ago into the state of the body and mind in old people, I did not find a single person above eighty, who had not possessed an active understanding, or active passions. Those different and opposite faculties of the mind, when in excess, happily supply the place of each other. Where they unite their forces, they extinguish the flame of life, before the oil which feeds it is consumed.

In another place I shall resume the influence of the faculties of the mind upon human life, as they discover themselves in the different pursuits of men.

I have only to add here, that I see no occasion to admit, with the followers of Dr. Brown, that the mind is active in sleep, in preserving the motions of life. I hope to establish hereafter the opinion of Mr. Locke, that the mind is always passive in sound sleep. It is true it acts in dreams, but these depend upon a morbid state of the brain, and therefore do not belong to the present stage of our subject; for I am now considering animal life only in the healthy states of the body. I shall say presently, that dreams are intended to supply the absence of some natural stimulus, and hence we find they occur in those persons most commonly, in whom there is a want of healthy action in the system induced by the excess, or deficiency of customary stimuli.

Life is in a languid state, in the morning. It acquires vigor by the gradual, and successive application of stimuli in the forenoon. It is in its most perfect state about midday, and remains stationary for some hours. From the diminution of the sensibility and contractility of the system to action of impressions, it lessens in the evening, and becomes again languid at bedtime. These facts will admit of an extensive application hereafter in our lectures upon the practice of physic.

LECTURE II

GENTLEMEN,

The stimuli which have been enumerated, when they act collectively, and within certain bounds, produce a healthy waking state. But they do not always act collectively, nor in the determined and regular manner that has been described. There is in many states of the system, a deficiency of some stimuli, and in some of its states, an apparent absence of them all. To account for the continuance of animal life under such circumstances, two things must be premised, before we proceed to take notice of the diminution, or absence of the stimuli which support it.

1. The healthy actions of the body in the waking state, consist in a proper degree of what has been called excitability, and excitement. The former is the medium on which stimuli act in producing the latter. In an exact proportion, and a due relation of both, diffused uniformly throughout every part of the body, consists good health. Disease is the reverse of this. It depends *in*

part upon a disproportion between excitement and excitability, and in a partial distribution of each of them. In thus distinguishing the different states of excitement and excitability in health and sickness, you see I dissent from Dr. Brown, who supposes them to be uniform and equable, in the morbid, as well as the healthy states of the body.

2. It is a law of the system, that the absence of one natural stimulus is generally supplied by the increased action of others. This is more certainly the case, where a natural stimulus is abstracted *suddenly;* for the excitability is thereby so instantly formed and accumulated, as to furnish a highly sensible and moveable surface for the remaining stimuli to act upon. Many proofs might be adduced in support of this proposition. The reduction of the excitement of the blood vessels, by means of cold, prepares the way for a full meal, or a warm bed, to excite in them the morbid actions which take place in a pleurisy or a rheumatism. A horse in a cold stable eats more than in a warm one; and thus counteracts the debility which would otherwise be induced upon his system, by the abstraction of the stimulus of warm air.

These two propositions being admitted, I proceed next to inquire into the different degrees and states of animal life. The first departure from its ordinary and perfect state, which strikes us, is in

I. Sleep: This is either natural or artificial. Natural sleep is induced by a diminution of the excitement, and excitability of the system by the continued application of the stimuli which act upon the body in its waking state. When these stimuli act in a determined degree, that is, when the same number of stimuli act with the same force, and for the same time, upon the system; sleep will be brought on at the same hour every night. But when they act with uncommon force, or for an unusual time, it is brought on at an earlier hour. Thus a long walk, or ride by persons accustomed to a sedentary life, unusual exercise of the understanding, the action of strong passions, or emotions, and the continual application of unusual sounds seldom fail of inducing premature sleep. It is recorded of Pope Ganganelli, that he slept more soundly, and longer than usual, the night after he was raised to the papal chair. The effects of unusual sounds in bringing on premature sleep, is further demonstrated by that constant inclination to retire to bed at an early hour, which country people discover the first and second days they spend in a city, exposed from morning till night to the noise of hammers, files and looms, or of drays, carts, waggons, and coaches rattling over pavements of stone.—Sleep is further hastened by the absence of light, the cessation of sounds, and labor, and the recumbent posture of the body on a soft bed.

Artificial sleep may be induced at any time by certain stimulating substances, particularly by opium. They act by carrying the system beyond the healthy grade of excitement, to a degree of indirect debility which Dr. Brown has happily called the sleeping point. The same point may be induced in the system at any time by the artificial abstraction of the usual stimuli of life. For example. Let a person shut himself up at mid-day in a dark room, remote from noise of all kinds, let him lie down on his back upon a soft bed in a temperate state of the atmosphere, and let him cease to think upon interesting subjects, or let him think only upon one subject, and he will soon fall asleep. Dr. Boerhaave relates an instance of a Dutch physician who having persuaded himself that waking was a violent state, and sleep the only natural one of the system; contrived by abstracting every kind of stimulus in the manner that has been mentioned, to sleep away whole days and nights, until at length he impaired his understanding, and finally perished in a public hospital in a state of idiotism.

In thus anticipating a view of the cause of sleep, I have said nothing of the effects of diseases of the brain in inducing it. These belong to another part of our course. The short explanation I have given of its cause, was necessary in order to render the history of animal life, in that state of the system, more intelligible.

At the usual hour of sleep there is an abstraction of the stimuli of light, sound and muscular motion. The stimuli which remain, and act with an increased force upon the body in sleep are,

1. The heat which is discharged from the body, and confined by means of bed clothes. It is most perceptible when exhaled from a bed fellow. Heat obtained in this way, has sometimes been employed to restore declining life to the bodies of old people. Witness the damsel who lay for this purpose in the bosom of the king of Israel. The advantage of this external heat will appear further, when we consider how impracticable, or imperfect sleep is, when we lie under too light covering in cold weather.

2. The air which is applied to the lungs during sleep probably acts with more force than in the waking state. I am disposed to believe that more air is phlogisticated in sleep than at any other time, for the smell of a close room in which a person has slept one night, we know, is much more disagreeable than that of a room under equal circumstances, in which half a dozen people have sat for the same number of hours in the day time.— The action of decomposed air on the lungs and heart was spoken of in a former lecture. An increase in its quantity must necessarily have a powerful influence upon animal life during the sleeping state.

3. Respiration is performed with a greater extension, and contraction of the muscles of the breast in sleep than in the waking state; and this cannot fail of increasing the impetus of the blood in its passage through the heart and blood vessels. The increase of the fulness and force of the pulse in sleep, is probably owing in part to the action of respiration upon it. In another place I hope to elevate the rank of the blood vessels in the animal economy, by shewing that they are the fountains of power in the body. They derive this preeminence from the protection and support they afford to every part of the system. They are the perpetual centinels of health and life; for they never partake in the repose which is enjoyed by the muscles and nerves. During sleep, their sensibility seems to be converted into contractility,

by which means their muscular fibres are more easily moved by the blood, than in the waking state. The diminution of sensibility in sleep is proved by many facts to be mentioned hereafter; and the change of sensibility into contractility will appear, when we come to consider the state of animal life in infancy and old age.

4. Aliment in the stomach acts more powerfully in sleep, than in the waking state. This is evident from digestion going on more rapidly when we are awake than when we sleep.—The more flow the digestion, the greater is the stimulus of the aliment in the stomach. Of this we have many proofs in daily life. Labourers object to milk as a breakfast; because it digests too soon, and often call for food in a morning, which they can feel all day in their stomachs. Sausages, fat pork, and onions are generally preferred by them for this purpose. A moderate supper is favourable to easy and sound sleep; and the want of it in persons who are accustomed to that meal, is often followed by a restless night. The absence of its stimulus is probably supplied by a full gall bladder (which always attends an empty stomach) in persons who are not in the habit of eating suppers.

5. The stimulus of the urine, accumulated in the bladder during sleep, has a perceptible influence upon animal life. It is often so considerable as to interrupt sleep; and it is one of the causes of our waking at a regular hour in the morning. It is moreover a frequent cause of the activity of the understanding and passions in dreams, and hence we dream more in our morning slumbers when the bladder is full, than we do in the beginning, or middle of the night.

6. The fæces exert a constant stimulus upon the bowels in sleep. This is so considerable as to render it less profound, when they have been accumulated for two or three days, or when they have been deposited in the extremity of the alimentary canal.

7. The partial and irregular exercises of the understanding and passions in dreams have an occasional influence in promoting

life. They occur only where there is a deficiency of other stimuli. Such is the force with which the mind acts upon the body in dreams, that Dr. Brambilla, physician to the emperor of Germany, informs us, that he has seen instances of wounds in soldiers being inflamed, and putting on a gangrenous appearance in consequence of the commotions excited in their bodies by irritating dreams. The stimulating passions act through the medium of the will, and the exercises of this faculty of the mind sometimes extend so far as to produce actions in the muscles of the limbs, and occasionally in the whole body, as we see in persons who walk in their sleep. The stimulus of lust often awakens us with pleasure or pain, according as we are disposed to respect, or disobey the precepts of our Maker. The angry and revengeful passions often deliver us in like manner, from the imaginary guilt of murder. Even the debilitating passions of grief, and fear, produce an indirect operation upon the system that is favourable to life in sleep, for they excite that distressing disease called the night mare, which prompts us to speak, or halloo, and by thus invigorating respiration, restores the languid circulation of the blood in the heart and brain. Do not complain then, gentlemen, when you are bestrode by this midnight hag. She is kindly sent to prevent your sudden death. Persons who go to bed in good health, and are found dead the succeeding morning, are said most commonly to die of this disease.

I cannot dismiss the subject of the stimulating effects of dreams, without taking notice of an opinion of Dr. Darwin which is connected with it. He supposes dreams are never attended with volition. The facts which have been mentioned, prove, that the will frequently acts with *more* force in them, than in the waking state.

I proceed now to inquire into the state of animal life in its different stages. I pass over for the present its history in generation. It will be sufficient only to remark in this place, that its first motion is produced by the stimulus of the male seed upon the female ovum. This opinion is not originally mine. You will find it in Dr. Haller.* The pungent taste which Mr. John Hunter discovered in the male seed, renders it peculiarly fit for this purpose. No sooner is the female ovum thus set in motion, and the foetus formed, than its capacity of life is supported,

1. By the stimulus of the heat which it derives from its connection with its mother in the womb.

2. By the stimulus of its own circulating blood.

3. By its constant motion in the womb after the third month of pregnancy. The absence of this motion for a few days, is always a sign of the indisposition or death of a foetus. Considering how early a child is accustomed to it, it is strange that a cradle should ever have been denied to it after it comes into the world.

II. In infants there is an absence of many of the stimuli which support life.—Their excretions are in a great measure deficient in acrimony, and their mental faculties are too weak to exert much influence upon their bodies. But the absence of stimulus from those causes, is amply supplied

1. By the very great excitability of their systems to those of light, sound, heat, and air. So powerfully do light and sound act upon them, that the author of nature has kindly defended their eyes and ears from an excess of their impressions by imperfect vision, and hearing, for several weeks after birth. The capacity of infants to be acted upon by moderate degrees of heat is evident from their suffering less from cold than grown people. This is so much the case, that we read in Mr. Umfreville's account of Hudson's Bay, of a child that was found alive upon the back of its mother after she was frozen to death. I before hinted at the action of the air upon the bodies of new born infants in producing the red color of their skins. It is highly probable, (from a fact formerly mentioned) that the first impression of the atmosphere which produces this redness is accompanied with pain, and this we know is a stimulus of a very active nature. By a kind law of sensation, impressions, that were originally

---

* "Novum foetum a seminis masculi *stimulo* vitam concepisse." Elementa Physiologiæ, vol. viii. p. 177.

ON NATURAL AND MEDICAL SCIENCES 153

painful, become pleasurable by repetition, or duration. This is remarkably evident in the impression now under consideration, and hence we find infants at a certain age, discover signs of an increase of life by their delightful gestures, when they are carried into the open air. Recollect further, gentlemen, what was said formerly, of excitability, predominating over sensibility in infants. We see it daily, not only in their patience of cold, but in the short time in which they cease to complain of the injuries they meet with from falls, cuts, and even severe surgical operations.

2. Animal life is supported in infants by their sucking, or feeding, nearly every hour in the day, and night when they are awake. I explained formerly the manner in which food stimulated the system. The action of sucking, supplies by the muscles employed in it, the stimulus of mastication.

3. Laughing and Crying, which are universal in infancy, have a considerable influence in promoting animal life, by their action upon respiration, and the circulation of the blood. Laughing exists under all circumstances, independently of education or imitation. The child of a negro slave born only to inherit the toils and misery of its parents, receives its master with a smile every time he enters his kitchen, or a negro-quarter. But laughing exists in infancy under circumstances still more unfavourable to it, an instance of which is related by Mr. Bruce. After a journey of several hundred miles across the sands of Nubia, he came to a spring of water shaded by a few scrubby trees. Here he intended to have rested during the night, but he had not slept long, before he was awakened by a noise which he perceived was made by a solitary Arab equally fatigued, and half famished with himself, who was preparing to murder and plunder him. Mr. Bruce rushed upon him, and made him his prisoner. The next morning he was joined by a half starved female companion, with an infant of six months old in her arms. In passing by this child, Mr. Bruce says it laughed and crowed in his face, and attempted to leap upon him. From this fact it would seem as if laughing was not only characteristic of our species, but that it

was early and intimately connected with human life. The child of these Arabs had probably never seen a smile upon the faces of its ferocious parents, and perhaps had never, (before the sight of Mr. Bruce), beheld any other human creature.

Crying has a considerable influence upon health and life in children. I have seen so many instances of its salutary effects, that I have satisfied myself that it is as possible for a child to "cry and be fat," as it is to "laugh and be fat."

4. As children advance in life, the constancy of their appetites for food, and their disposition to laugh, and cry, lessen, but the diminution of these stimuli is supplied by exercise. The limbs, and tongues of children are always in motion. They continue likewise to eat oftener than adults. A crust of bread is commonly the last thing they ask for at night, and the first thing they call for in the morning. It is now they begin to feel the energy of their mental faculties. This stimulus is assisted in its force, by the disposition to prattle which is so universal among children. This habit of converting their ideas into words as fast as they rise, follows them to their beds, where we often hear them talk themselves to sleep in a whisper, or to use less correct, but more striking terms, by *thinking aloud*.

5. Dreams act at an early period upon the bodies of children. Their smiles, startings, and occasional screams in their sleep appear to arise from them. After the third or fourth year of their lives, they sometimes confound them with things that are real. From observing the effects of this mistake upon the memory, a sensible woman whom I once knew, forbad her children to tell their dreams, lest they should contract habits of lying, by confounding imaginary, with real events.

6. New objects whether natural or artificial, are never seen by children without emotions of pleasure which act upon their capacity of life. The effects of novelty upon the tender bodies of children may easily be conceived, by its friendly influence upon the health of invalids who visit foreign countries, and who pass months, or years in a constant succession of new and agreeable impressions.

III. From the combination of all the stimuli that have been enumerated, human life is generally in excess from fifteen to thirty-five. It is during this period, the passions blow a perpetual storm. The most predominating of them is the love of pleasure. No sooner does the system become insensible to this stimulus, than ambition succeeds it in,

IV. The middle stage of life. Here we behold man in his most perfect physical state. The stimuli which now act upon him are so far regulated by prudence, that they are seldom excessive in their force. The habits of order the system acquires in this period, continue to produce good health for many years afterwards, and hence bills of mortality prove that fewer persons die between forty and fifty-seven; than in any other seventeen years of human life.

V. In OLD AGE the senses of seeing, hearing and touch are impaired. The venereal appetite is weakened, or entirely extinguished. The pulse becomes slow, and subject to frequent intermissions, from a decay in the force of the blood vessels; Exercise becomes impracticable, or irksome, and the operations of the understanding are performed with languor and difficulty. In this shattered and declining state of the system, the absence and diminution of all the stimuli which have been mentioned are supplied,

1. By an increase in the quantity, and by the peculiar quality of the food which is taken by old people. They generally eat twice as much as persons in middle life, and they bear with pain the usual intervals between meals. They moreover prefer that kind of food which is savoury and stimulating. The stomach of the celebrated Parr, who died in the one hundred and fiftieth year of his age, was found full of strong, nourishing aliment.

2. By the stimulus of the fæces which are frequently retained for five or six days in the bowels of old people.

3. By the stimulus of fluids rendered preternaturally acrid by age. The urine, sweat and even the tears of old people, possesses a peculiar acrimony. Their blood likewise loses part of the mildness which is natural to that fluid; and hence the difficulty with

which sores heal in old people; and hence too the reason why cancers are more common in the decline, than in any other period of human life.

4. By the uncommon activity of certain passions. These are either good or evil. To the former belong an increased vigor in the operations of those passions which have for their objects the Divine Being, or the whole family of mankind, or their own offspring, particularly their grand-children. To the latter passions belong, malice, a hatred of the manners and fashions of the rising generation, and above all, avarice. This passion knows no holidays. Its stimulus is constant, though varied daily by the numerous means which it has discovered of increasing, securing, and perpetuating property. It has been observed that weak mental impressions produce much greater effects in old people than in persons in middle life. A trifling indisposition in a grand-child, an inadvertent act of unkindness from a friend, or the fear of losing a few shillings, have in many instances produced in them a degree of wakefulness that has continued for two or three nights. It is to this highly excitable state of the system that Solomon probably alludes, when he describes the grasshopper as burdensome to old people.

5. By the passion for talking, which is so common, as to be one of the characteristics of old age. I mentioned formerly, the influence of this stimulus upon animal life. Perhaps it is more necessary in the female constitution than in the male; for it has long ago been remarked, that women who are very taciturn, are generally unhealthy.

6. By their wearing warmer clothes, and preferring warmer rooms, than in the former periods of their lives. This practice is so uniform, that it would not be difficult in many cases to tell a man's age by his dress, or by finding out at what degree of heat he found himself comfortable in a close room.

7. By dreams. These are universal among old people. They arise from their short and imperfect sleep.

8. It has been often said that "We are once men, and twice children." In speaking of the state of animal life in infancy, I

remarked that the contractility of the animal fibres, predominated over their sensibility in that stage of life. The same thing takes place in old people, and it is in consequence of the return of this infantile state of the system, that all the stimuli which have been mentioned act upon them with much more force than in middle life. This sameness, in the predominance of excitability over sensibility in children and old people, will account for the similarity of their habits with respect to eating, sleep, exercise, and the use of fermented or distilled liquors. It is from the increase of excitability in old people, that so small a quantity of strong drink intoxicates them; and it is from an ignorance of this change in their constitutions, that many of them become drunkards after passing the early and middle stages of life with sober characters.

Life is continued in a less imperfect state in old age, in women than in men. The former sew, and knit, and spin, after they lose the use of their ears and eyes; whereas the latter, after losing the use of those senses, frequently pass the evening of their lives in a torpid state in a chimney corner. It is from the influence of moderate and gently stimulating employments, upon the female constitution, that more women live to be old, than men, and that they rarely survive their usefulness in domestic life.

Hitherto the principles I am endeavouring to establish, have been applied to explain the cause of life in its more common forms. Let us next inquire, how far they will enable us to explain its continuance in certain morbid states of the body, in which there is a diminution of some, and an apparent abstraction of all the stimuli, which have been supposed to produce animal life.

I. We observe some people to be blind, or deaf and dumb from their birth. The same defects of sight, hearing, and speech, are sometimes brought on by diseases. Here animal life is deprived of all those numerous stimuli, which arise from light, colors, sounds, and speech. But the absence of these stimuli is supplied,

1. By increased sensibility and excitability in their remaining

senses. The ears, the nose, and the fingers, afford a surface for impressions in blind people which frequently overbalances the loss of their eyesight. There are two blind young men, brothers, in this city, of the name of Dutton, who can tell when they approach a post in walking across a street, by a peculiar sound which the ground under their feet emits in the neighbourhood of the post. Their sense of hearing is still more exquisite to sounds of another kind. They can tell the names of a number of tame pidgeons, with which they amuse themselves in a little garden, by only hearing them fly over their heads. The celebrated blind philosopher Dr. Moyse can distinguish a black dress on his friends, by its smell; and we read of many instances of blind persons who have been able to perceive colors by rubbing their fingers upon them. One of these persons mentioned by Mr. Boyle, has left upon record an account of the specific quality of each color as it affected his sense of touch. He says, black imparted the most, and blue, the least perceptible sense of asperity to his fingers.

2. By an increase of vigor in the exercises of the mental faculties. The poems of Homer, Milton and Blacklock, and the attainments of Sanderson in mathematical knowledge, all discover how much the energy of the mind is increased by the absence of impressions upon the organs of vision.

II. We sometimes behold life in idiots in whom there is not only an absence of the stimuli of the understanding and passions; but frequently from the weakness of their bodies, a deficiency of the locomotive powers. Here an inordinate appetite for food, or venereal pleasures, or a constant habit of laughing, or talking, or playing with their hands and feet, supply the place of the stimulating operations of the mind, and of general bodily exercise. Of the inordinate force of the venereal appetite in idiots we have many proofs. The Cretins are much addicted to venery; and Dr. Michaelis tells us that the idiot whom he saw at the Pesaiac falls in New Jersey, who had passed six and twenty years in a cradle, acknowledged that he had venereal desires, and wished to be married, for the Doctor adds, he had a sense of religion upon his fragment of mind, and of course did not wish to gratify that appetite in an unlawful manner.

III. How is animal life supported in persons who pass many days, and even weeks without food, and in some instances without drinks? Long fasting is usually the effect of disease, of necessity, or of a principle of religion. When it arises from the first cause, the actions of life are kept up by the stimulus of disease. The absence of food when accidental, or submitted to as a means of producing moral happiness, is supplied,

1. By the stimulus of a full gall bladder. This state of the receptacle of bile, has generally been found to accompany an empty stomach. The bile is sometimes absorbed, and imparts a yellow color to the skin of persons who suffer or die of famine.

2. By increased acrimony in all the secretions and excretions of the body. The saliva becomes so acrid by long fasting, as to excoriate the gums, and the breath acquires not only a fœtor, but a pungency so active, as to draw tears from the eyes of persons exposed to it.

3. By increased sensibility and excitability in the sense of touch. The blind man mentioned by Mr. Boyle who could distinguish colors by his fingers, possessed this talent only after fasting. Even a draught of any kind of liquor deprived him of it. I have taken notice in my account of the yellow fever in Philadelphia in the year 1793, of the effects of a diet bordering upon fasting for six weeks, in producing a quickness and correctness in my perceptions of the state of the pulse, which I had never experienced before.

4. By an increase of activity in the understanding and passions. Gamesters often improve the exercises of their minds when they are about to play for a large sum of money, by living for a day or two upon roasted apples and cold water. Where the passions are excited into preternatural action, the absence of the stimulus of food is scarcely felt. I shall hereafter mention the influence of the desire of life, upon its preservation under all circumstances. It acts with peculiar force when fasting is accidental. But when it is submitted to as a religious duty, it is accom-

panied by sentiments and feelings which more than balance the abstraction of aliment. The body of Moses was sustained, probably without a miracle, during an abstinence of forty days and forty nights, by the pleasure he derived from conversing with his Maker "Face to face, as a man speaking with his friend." *

I remarked formerly that the veins discover no deficiency of blood in persons who die of famine. Death from this cause seems to be less the effect of the want of food, than of the combined and excessive operation of the stimuli, which supply its place in the system.

IV. We come now to a difficult inquiry, and that is, how is life supported during the total abstraction of external and internal stimuli which takes place in asphixia, or in apparent death, from all its numerous causes?

I took notice in a former lecture, that ordinary life consisted in the excitement, and excitability of the different parts of the body; and that they were occasionally changed into each other. In apparent death from violent emotions of the mind, from the sudden impression of miasmata, or from drowning, there is a loss of excitement; but the excitability of the system remains for minutes, and in some instances for hours afterwards unimpaired, provided the accident which produced the loss of excitement has not been attended with such exertions as are calculated to waste it. If for example, a person should fall suddenly into the water, without bruising his body, and sink before his fears, or exertions had time to dissipate his excitability; his recovery from apparent death might be effected by the gentle action of heat, or frictions upon his body, so as to convert his accumulated excitability gradually into excitement. The same condition of the system takes place when apparent death occurs from freezing, and a recovery is accomplished by the same gentle application of stimuli, provided the organization of the body be not injured, or its excitability wasted, by violent exertions previously to its freezing. This excitability is the vehicle of motion, and motion

---

* Exodus xxxiii. 11. xxxiv. 28.

when continued long enough produces sensation, which is soon followed by thought; and in these, I said formerly, consists perfect life in the human body.

For this explanation of the manner in which life is suspended, and revived in persons apparently dead from cold, I am indebted to Mr. John Hunter, who supposes, if it were possible for the body to be *suddenly* frozen by an instantaneous abstraction of its heat, life might be continued for many years in a suspended state, and revived at pleasure; provided the body were preserved constantly in a temperature barely sufficient to prevent reanimation, and never so great, as to endanger the destruction of any organic part. The resuscitation of insects that have been in a torpid state for months, and perhaps years, in substances that have preserved their organization, should at least defend this bold proposition from being treated as chimerical. The effusions even of the imagination of such men as Mr. Hunter, are entitled to respect. They often become the germs of future discoveries.

In that state of suspended animation which occurs in acute diseases, and which has sometimes been denominated a *trance;* the system is nearly in the same excitable state that it is in apparent death from drowning, and freezing. Resuscitation in these cases is not the effect as in those which have been mentioned of artificial applications made to the body for that purpose. It appears to be spontaneous; but it is produced by impressions made upon the ears, and by the operations of the mind in dreams. Of the action of these stimuli upon the body in its apparently lifeless state, I have satisfied myself by many facts. I once attended a citizen of Philadelphia, who died of a pulmonary disease in the 80th year of his age. A few days before his death he begged that he might not be interred until one week after the usual signs of life had left his body, and gave as a reason for this request, that he had when a young man, died to all appearance of the yellow fever in one of the West-India islands.—In this situation he distinctly heard the persons who attended him, fix upon the time, and place, of burying him. The horror of being put under ground alive, produced such distressing emotions in his mind, as to diffuse motion throughout his body, and finally excited in him all the usual functions of life. In Dr. Creighton's essay upon mental derangement there is a history of a case nearly of a similar nature. "A young lady (says the Doctor) an attendant on the princess of ——, after having been confined to her bed for a great length of time, with a violent nervous disorder, was at last, to all appearance, deprived of life. Her lips were quite pale, her face resembled the countenance of a dead person, and her body grew cold. She was removed from the room in which *she died*, was laid in a coffin, and the day for her funeral was fixed on. The day arrived, and according to the custom of the country, funeral songs and hymns were sung before the door. Just as the people were about to nail on the lid of the coffin, a kind of perspiration was observed on the surface of her body. She recovered. The following is the account she gave of her sensations; she said, "It seemed to her as if in a dream, that she was really dead; yet she was perfectly conscious of all that happened around her. She distinctly heard her friends speaking and lamenting her death at the side of her coffin. She felt them pull on the dead clothes, and lay her in it. This feeling produced a mental anxiety which she could not describe. She tried to cry out, but her mind was without power, and could not act on her body. She had the contradictory feeling as if she were in her own body, and not in it, at the same time. It was equally impossible for her to stretch out her arm or open her eyes, as to cry, although she continually endeavoured to do so. The internal anguish of her mind was at its utmost height when the funeral hymns began to be sung, and when the lid of the coffin was about to be nailed on. The thought that she was to be buried alive was the first which gave activity to her mind, and enabled it to operate on her corporeal frame."

Where the ears lose their capacity of being acted upon by stimuli, the mind by its operations in dreams, becomes a source of impressions which again set the wheels of life in motion. There is an account published by Dr. Arnold in his observations upon insanity,* of a certain John Engelbreght a German, who was believed to be dead, and who was evidently resuscitated by the exercises of his mind upon subjects which were of a delightful and stimulating nature. This history shall be taken from Mr. Engelbreght's words. "It was on Thursday noon (says he) about 12 o'clock when I perceived that death was making his approaches upon me from the lower parts upwards, insomuch that my whole body became stiff. I had no feeling left in my hands and feet, neither in any other part of my whole body, nor was I at last able to speak or see, for my mouth now becoming very stiff, I was no longer able to open it, nor did I feel it any longer. My eyes also broke in my head in such a manner that I distinctly felt it. For all that, I understood what they said, when they were praying by me, and I distinctly heard them say, feel his legs, how stiff, and cold they have become. This I heard distinctly, but I had no perception of their touch. I heard the watchman cry 11 o'clock, but at 12 o'clock my hearing left me. After relating his passage from the body to heaven with the velocity of an arrow shot from a cross bow, he proceeds, and says that as he was twelve hours in dying, so he was twelve hours in returning to life. "As I died (says he) from beneath upwards, so I revived again the contrary way from above to beneath, or from top to toe. Being conveyed back from the heavenly glory, I began to hear again something of what they were praying for me, in the same room with me. Thus was my hearing, the *first* sense I recovered. After this I began to have a perception of my eyes, so that by little and little, my whole body became strong, and sprightly, and no sooner did I get a feeling of my legs and feet, than I arose and stood firm upon them with a firmness I had never enjoyed before. The heavenly joy I had experienced, invigorated me to such a degree, that people were astonished at my rapid, and almost instantaneous recovery."

The explanation, I have given of the cause of resuscitation in this man, will serve to refute a belief in a supposed migration

---

* Vol. ii. p. 298.

of the soul from the body in cases of apparent death. The imagination, it is true, usually conducts the whole mind to the abodes of happy or miserable spirits, but it acts here in the same way that it does when it transports it in common dreams, to numerous and distant parts of the world.

There is nothing supernatural in Mr. Engelbreght being invigorated by his supposed flight to heaven. Pleasant dreams always stimulate and strengthen the body, while dreams which are accompanied with distress, or labour debilitate, and fatigue it.

LECTURE III

GENTLEMEN,

Let us next take a view of the state of animal life in the different inhabitants of our globe, as varied by the circumstances of civilization, diet, situation and climate.

I. In the Indians of the northern latitudes of America, there is often a defect of the stimulus of aliment, and of the understanding and passions. Their vacant countenances, and their long and disgusting taciturnity, are the effects of the want of action in their brains from a deficiency of ideas, and their tranquillity under all the common circumstances of irritation, pleasure or grief, are the result of an absence of passion; for they hold it to be disgraceful to shew any outward signs of anger, joy, or even of domestic affection. This account of the Indian character, I know is contrary to that which is given by Rousseau, and several other writers, who have attempted to prove that man may become perfect and happy, without the aids of civilization and religion. This opinion is contradicted by the experience of all ages, and is rendered ridiculous by the facts which are well ascertained in the history of the customs and habits of our American savages. In a cold climate they are the most miserable beings upon the face of the earth. The greatest part of their time is spent in sleep, or under the alternate influence of hunger and gluttony. They moreover indulge in vices which are alike contrary to moral and physical happiness. It is in consequence of these habits, that they discover so early the marks of old age, and that so few of them are long-lived. The absence and diminution of many of the stimuli of life in these people is supplied in part, by the violent exertions with which they hunt, and carry on war, and by the extravagant manner with which they afterwards celebrate their exploits, in their savage dances and songs.

II. In the inhabitants of the torrid regions of Africa, there is a deficiency of labor; for the earth produces spontaneously nearly all the sustenance they require. Their understandings and passions are moreover in a torpid state. But the absence of bodily and mental stimuli in these people, is amply supplied by the constant heat of the sun, by the profuse use of spices in their diet, and by the passion for musical sounds which so universally characterises the African nations.

III. In Greenland the body is exposed during a long winter to such a degree of cold as to reduce the pulse to 40, or 50 strokes in a minute. But the effects of this cold in lessening the quantity of life, are obviated in part by the heat of close stove rooms, by warm clothing, and by the peculiar nature of the aliment of the Greenlanders, which consists chiefly of animal food, of dried fish, and of whale oil. They prefer the last of those articles in so rancid a state, that it imparts a fœtor to their perspiration which, Mr. Crantz says, renders even their churches offensive to strangers I need hardly add, that a diet possessed of such diffusible qualities, cannot fail of being highly stimulating. It is remarkable that the food of all the northern nations of Europe is composed of stimulating animal, or vegetable matters, and that the use of spiritous liquors is universal among them.

IV. Let us next turn our eyes to the miserable inhabitants of those eastern countries which compose the Ottoman empire. Here we behold life in its most feeble state, not only from the absence of physical, but of other stimuli which operate upon the inhabitants of other parts of the world. Among the poor people of Turkey there is a general deficiency of aliment. Mr. Volney in his travels tells us "That the diet of the Bedouins seldom exceeds six ounces a day, and that it consists of six or seven dates soaked in butter-milk, and afterwards mixed with a little sweet milk, or curds."—There is likewise a general deficiency among them of stimulus, from the operations of the mental faculties, for such is the despotism of the government in Turkey, that it weakens not only the understanding; but it annihilates all that immense source of stimuli which arises from the exercise of the domestic and public affections. A Turk lives wholly to himself. In point of time, he occupies only the moment in which he exists; for his futurity, as to life and property, belongs altogether to his master. Fear is the reigning principle of his actions, and hope and joy seldom add a single pulsation to his heart. Tyranny even imposes a restraint upon the stimulus which arises from conversation, for "They speak (says Mr. Volney) with a slow feeble voice, as if the lungs wanted strength to propel air enough through the glottis to form distinct articulate sounds." The same traveller adds, that "They are slow in all their motions, that their bodies are small, that they have small evacuations, and that their blood is so destitute of ferocity, that nothing but the greatest heat can preserve its fluidity." The deficiency of aliment, and the absence of mental stimuli in these people is supplied,

1. By the heat of their climate.
2. By their passion for musical sounds and fine clothes, and
3. By their general use of coffee and opium.

The more debilitated the body is, the more forcibly these stimuli act upon it. Hence according to Mr. Volney, the Bedouins, whose slender diet has been mentioned, enjoy good health; for this consists not in strength, but in an exact proportion being kept up between the excitability of the body, and the number and force of the stimuli which act upon it.

V. Many of the observations which have been made upon the inhabitants of Africa, and of the Turkish dominions, apply to the inhabitants of China, and the East Indies. They want in many instances the stimulus of animal food. Their minds are moreover in a state too languid to act with much force upon their bodies. The absence and deficiency of these stimuli are supplied by,

1. The heat of the climate in the southern parts of those countries.

2. By a vegetable diet abounding in nourishment, particularly rice and beans.

3. By the use of tea in China, and by a stimulating coffee made of the dried and toasted feeds of the datura stramonium, in the neighbourhood of the Indian coast. Some of these nations likewise chew stimulating substances, as too many of our citizens do tobacco.

Among the poor and depressed subjects of the governments of the middle and southern parts of Europe, the deficiency of the stimulus of wholesome food, of clothing, of fuel, and of liberty, is supplied in some countries by the invigorating influence of the Christian religion upon animal life; and in others, by the general use of tea, coffee, garlic, onions, opium, tobacco, malt liquors, and ardent spirits. The use of each of these stimuli seems to be regulated by the circumstances of climate. In cold countries where the earth yields its increase with reluctance, and where vegetable aliment is scarce, the want of the stimulus of distention which that species of food is principally calculated to produce, is sought for in that, of ardent spirits. To the southward of 40° a substitute for the distention from mild vegetable food is sought for, in onions, garlic and tobacco. But further, a uniform climate calls for more of these artificial stimuli than a climate that is exposed to the alternate action of heat and cold, winds and calms, and of wet and dry weather. Savages and ignorant people likewise require more of them than persons of civilized manners, and cultivated understandings It would seem from these facts that man cannot exist without *sensation* of some kind, and that when it is not derived from natural means, it will always be sought for in such as are artificial.

In no part of the human species, is animal life in a more perfect state than in the inhabitants of Great Britain,* and the United States of America. With all the natural stimuli that have

---

* Haller's Elementa Physiologiæ, vol. viii. p. 2. p. 107.

been mentioned, they are constantly under the invigorating influence of liberty. There is an indissoluble union between moral, political and physical happiness; and if it be true, that elective and representative governments are most favourable to individual, as well as national prosperity, it follows of course, that they are most favourable to animal life. But this opinion does not rest upon an induction derived from the relation, which truths upon all subjects bear to each other. Many facts prove, animal life to exist in a larger quantity and for a longer time, in the enlightened and happy state of Connecticut, in which republican liberty has existed above one hundred and fifty years, than in any other country upon the surface of the globe.

It remains now to mention certain mental stimuli which act nearly alike in the production of animal life, upon the individuals of all the nations in the world. They are,

1. The desire of life. This principle so deeply, and universally implanted in human nature, acts very powerfully in supporting our existence. It has been observed to prolong life. Sickly travellers by sea and land, often live under circumstances of the greatest weakness, till they reach their native country, and then expire in the bosom of their friends. This desire of life often turns the scale in favor of a recovery in acute diseases. Its influence will appear, from the difference in the periods in which death was induced in two persons, who were actuated by opposite passions with respect to life. Atticus, we are told, died of voluntary abstinence from food in five days. In Sir William Hamilton's account of the earthquake at Calabria, we read of a girl who lived eleven days without food, before she expired. In the former case, life was shortened by an aversion from it; in the latter, it was protracted by the desire of it. The late Mr. Brissot in his visit to this city, informed me that the application of animal magnetism (in which he was a believer) had in no instance cured a disease in a West India slave. Perhaps it was rendered inert by its not being accompanied by a strong desire of life; for this principle exists in a more feeble state in slaves than in freemen. It is possible likewise the wills and imaginations of these degraded

people may have become so paralytic by slavery, as to be incapable of being excited by the impression of this fanciful remedy.

2. The love of money sets the whole animal machine in motion. Hearts which are insensible to the stimuli of religion, patriotism, love, and even of the domestic affections, are excited into action by this passion. The city of Philadelphia between the 10th and 15th of August 1791, will long be remembered by contemplative men, for having furnished the most extraordinary proofs of the stimulus of the love of money upon the human body. A new scene of speculation was produced at that time by the scrip of the bank of the United States. It excited febrile diseases in three persons who became my patients. In one of them, the acquisition of twelve thousand dollars in a few minutes by a lucky sale, brought on madness which terminated in death in a few days.* The whole city felt the impulse of this paroxysm of avarice. The slow and ordinary means of earning money were deserted, and men of every profession and trade, were seen in all our streets hastening to the coffee house, where the agitation of countenance, and the desultory manners, of all the persons who were interested in this species of gaming, exhibited a truer picture of a bedlam, than of a place appropriated to the transaction of mercantile business. But further, the love of money discovers its stimulus upon the body in a peculiar manner in the games of cards and dice. I have heard of a gentleman in Virginia who passed two whole days and nights in succession at a card table, and it is related in the life of a noted gamester in Ireland, that when he was so ill as to be unable to rise from his chair, he would suddenly revive when brought to the hazard table, by hearing the rattling of the dice.

3. Public amusements of all kinds, such as a horse race, a cockpit, a chase, the theatre, the circus, masquerades, public dinners and tea parties, all exert an artificial stimulus upon the

---

* Dr. Mead relates upon the authority of Dr. Hales, that more of the successful speculators in the South Sea Scheme of 1720 became insane, than of those who had been ruined by it.

system, and thus supply the defect of the rational exercises of the mind.

4. The love of dress is not confined in its stimulating operation to persons in health. It acts perceptibly in some cases upon invalids. I have heard of a gentleman in South Carolina, who always relieved himself of a fit of low spirits by changing his dress; and I believe there are few people who do not feel themselves enlivened, by putting on a new suit of clothes.

5. Novelty is an immense source of agreeable stimuli. Companions, studies, pleasures, modes of business, prospects, and situations with respect to town, and country, or to different countries, that are *new*, all exert an invigorating influence upon health and life.

6. The love of fame acts in various ways; but its stimulus is most sensible and durable in military life. It counteracts in many instances the debilitating effects of hunger, cold and labor. It has sometimes done more, by removing the weakness which is connected with many diseases. In several instances it has assisted the hardships of a camp life, in curing pulmonary consumption.

7. The love of country is a deep seated principle of action in the human breast. Its stimulus is sometimes so excessive, as to induce disease in persons who recently migrate, and settle in foreign countries.—It appears in various forms, but exists most frequently in the solicitude, labors, attachments, and hatred of party spirit. All these act forcibly in supporting animal life. It is because newspapers are supposed to contain the measure of the happiness, or misery of our country, that they are so interesting to all classes of people. Those vehicles of intelligence, and of public pleasure or pain, are frequently desired with the impatience of a meal, and they often produce the same stimulating effects upon the body.

8. The different religions of the world, by the activity they excite in the mind, have a sensible influence upon human life. Atheism is the worst of sedatives to the understanding, and passions. It is the abstraction of thought from the most sublime,

ON NATURAL AND MEDICAL SCIENCES

and of love, from the most perfect of all possible objects. Man is as naturally a religious, as he is a social, and domestic animal; and the same violence is done to his mental faculties, by robbing him of a belief in a God, that is done, by dooming him to live in a cell, deprived of the objects and pleasures of social and domestic life. The necessary and immutable connection between the texture of the human mind, and the worship of an object of some kind, has lately been demonstrated by the atheists of Europe, who after rejecting the true God, have instituted the worship of nature, of fortune, and of human reason, and in some instances, with ceremonies of the most expensive and splendid kind. Religions are friendly to animal life, in proportion as they elevate the understanding, and act upon the passions of hope and love. It will readily occur to you, that Christianity when believed, and obeyed, according to its original consistency with itself, and with the divine attributes, is more calculated to produce those effects, than any other religion in the world.—Such is the salutary operation of its doctrines, and precepts upon health and life, that if its divine authority rested upon no other argument, this alone would be sufficient to recommend it to our belief. How long mankind may continue to prefer substituted pursuits and pleasures, to this invigorating stimulus, is uncertain; but the time we are assured will come, when the understanding shall be elevated from its present inferior objects, and the luxated passions be reduced to their original order.—This change in the mind of man, I believe, will be effected only by the influence of the Christian religion, after all the efforts of human reason to produce it, by means of civilization, philosophy, liberty, and government, have been exhausted to no purpose.

Thus far, gentlemen, we have considered animal life as it respects the human species; but the principles I am endeavouring to establish, require that we should take a view of it in animals of every species, in all of which we shall find it depends upon the same causes, as in the human body.

And here I shall begin by remarking, that if we should discover the stimuli which support life in certain animals, to be fewer in number, or weaker in force than those which support it in our species, we must resolve it into that attribute of the Deity which seems to have delighted in variety in all his works.

The following observations apply more or less, to all the animals upon our globe.

1. They all possess either hearts, lungs, brains, nerves, or muscular fibres. It is as yet a controversy among naturalists whether animal life can exist without a brain, but no one has denied, muscular fibres, and of course contractility, or excitability to belong to animal life in all its shapes.

2. They all require more or less air for their existence. Even the snail inhales it for seven months under ground, through a pellicle which it weaves out of slime, as a covering for its body. If this pellicle at any time become too thick to admit the air; the snail opens a passage in it for that purpose. Now air we know acts powerfully in supporting animal life.

3. Many of them possess heat equal to that of the human body. Birds possess several degrees beyond it. Now heat, it was said formerly, acts with great force, in the production of animal life.

4. They all feed upon substances more or less stimulating to their bodies. Even water itself, chemistry has taught us, affords an aliment not only stimulating, but nourishing to many animals.

5. Many of them possess senses, more acute and excitable, than the same organs in the human species. These expose surfaces for the action of external impressions, that supply the absence, or deficiency of mental faculties.

6. Such of them as are devoid of sensibility, possess an uncommon portion of contractility, or simple excitability. This is most evident in the Polypus. When cut to pieces, it appears to feel little or no pain.

7. They all possess locomotive powers in a greater or less degree, and of course are acted upon by the stimulus of muscular motion.

8. Most of them appear to feel a stimulus, from the gratifica-

tion of their appetites for food, and for venereal pleasures, far more powerful than that which is felt by our species from the same causes. I shall hereafter mention some facts from Spalanzani upon the subject of generation, that will prove the stimulus, from venery, to be strongest in those animals, in which other stimuli act with the least force. Thus the male frog during its long connection with its female, suffers its limbs to be amputated, without discovering the least mark of pain, and without relaxing its hold of the object of its embraces.

9. In many animals we behold evident marks of understanding, and passion. The elephant, the fox and the ant, exhibit strong proofs of thought; and where is the school boy that cannot bear testimony to the anger of the bee, and the wasp?

10. But what shall we say of those animals, which pass long winters in a state in which there is an apparent absence of the stimuli of heat, exercise and the motion of the blood. Life in these animals is probably supported,

1. By such an accumulation of excitability, as to yield to impressions, which to us are imperceptible.

2. By the stimulus of aliment in a state of digestion in the stomach, or by the stimulus of aliment restrained from digestion by means of cold; for Mr. John Hunter has proved by an experiment on a frog, that cold below a certain degree, checks that animal process.

3. By the constant action of air upon their bodies.

It is possible life may exist in these animals, during their hybernation, in the total absence of impression and motion of every kind. This may be the case where the torpor from cold, has been *suddenly* brought upon their bodies. Excitability here, is in an accumulated, but quiescent state.

11. It remains only under this head to inquire; in what manner is life supported in those animals which live in a cold element, and whose blood is sometimes but a little above the freezing point? It will be a sufficient answer to this question to remark, that heat and cold are relative terms, and that different animals according to their organization, require very different degrees

of heat for their existence. Thirty-two degrees of it are probably as stimulating to some of these cold blooded animals (as they are called) as 70°, or 80° are to the human body.

It might afford additional support to the doctrine of animal life, which I have delivered, to point out the manner in which life and growth are produced in vegetables of all kinds. But this subject belongs to the professor of botany, and natural history,* who is amply qualified to do it justice. I shall only remark, that vegetable life is as much the offspring of stimuli as animal, and that skill in agriculture consists chiefly in the proper application of them. The seed of a plant, like an animal body, has no principle of life within itself. If preserved for years in a drawer, or in earth below the stimulating influence of heat, air and water, it discovers no sign of vegetation. It grows, like an animal, only in consequence of stimuli acting upon its *capacity* of life.

From a review of what has been said of animal life in all its numerous forms and modifications; we see that it is as much an effect of impressions upon a peculiar species of matter, as sound is of the stroke of a hammer upon a bell, or music, of the motion of the bow upon the strings of a violin. I exclude therefore the intelligent principle of Whytt, the medical mind of Stahl, the healing powers of Cullen, and the vital principle of John Hunter, as much from the body, as I do an intelligent principle from air, fire, and water.

It is no uncommon thing for the simplicity of causes, to be lost in the magnitude of their effects. By contemplating the wonderful functions of life, we have strangely overlooked the numerous and obscure circumstances which produce it. Thus the humble but true origin of power in the people, is often forgotten in the splendor and pride of governments. It is not necessary to be acquainted with the precise nature of that form of matter, which is capable of producing life, from impressions made upon it. It is sufficient for our purpose, to know the fact. It is immaterial moreover whether this matter derive its power

---

* Dr. Barton.

of being acted upon wholly from the brain, or whether it be in part inherent in animal fibres. The inferences are the same in favour of life being the effect of stimuli, and of its being as truly mechanical, as the movements of a clock from the pressure of its weights, or the passage of a ship in the water, from the impulse of winds, and tide.

The infinity of effects from similar causes, has often been taken notice of in the works of the Creator. It would seem as if they had all been made after one pattern. The late discovery of the cause of combustion, has thrown great light upon our subject. Wood and coal are no longer believed to contain a principle of fire. The heat and flames they emit, are derived from an agent altogether external to them. They are produced by a matter which is absorbed from the air, by means of its decomposition. This matter acts upon the predisposition of the fuel to receive it, in the same way that stimuli act upon the human body. The two agents differ only in their effects. The former produces the destruction of the bodies upon which it acts; while the latter excite the more gentle, and durable motions of life. Common language in expressing these effects is correct, as far as it relates to their cause. We speak of a coal of fire being *alive*, and of the *flame* of life.

The causes of life which I have delivered, will receive considerable support, by contrasting them with the causes of death. This catastrophe of the body consists in such a change induced on it by disease, or old age, as to prevent its exhibiting the phænomena of life. It is brought on,

1. By the abstraction of all the stimuli which support life. Death, from this cause, is produced by the same mechanical means that the emission of sound from a violin is prevented by the abstraction of the bow from its strings.

2. By the excessive force of stimuli of all kinds. No more occurs here than happens from too much pressure upon the strings of a violin preventing its emitting musical tones.

3. By too much relaxation, or too weak a texture of the matter which composes the human body. No more occurs here than is

observed in the extinction of sound by the total relaxation, or slender combination of the strings of a violin.

4. By an error in the place of certain fluid, or solid parts of the body. No more occurs here, than would happen from fixing the strings of a violin upon its body, instead of elevating them upon its bridge.

5. By the action of poisonous exhalations, or of certain fluids vitiated in the body, upon parts which emit most forcibly the motions of life. No more happens here than occurs from enveloping the strings of a violin in a piece of wax.

6. By the solution of continuity by means of wounds in solid parts of the body. No more occurs in death from this cause, than takes place when the emission of sound from a violin is prevented by a rupture of its strings.

7. Death is produced by a preternatural rigidity, and in some instances by an ossification of the solid parts of the body in old age; in consequence of which they are incapable of receiving and emitting the motions of life. No more occurs here, than would happen if a stick, or pipe-stem were placed in the room of catgut, upon the bridges of the violin. But death may take place in old age without a change in the texture of animal matter, from the stimuli of life losing their effect by repetition, just as opium from the same cause, ceases to produce its usual effects upon the body.

Should it be asked, what is that peculiar organization of matter, which enables it to emit life, when acted upon by stimuli, I answer, I do not know. The great Creator has kindly established a witness of his unsearchable wisdom in every part of his works, in order to prevent our forgetting him, in the successful exercises of our reason. Mohammed once said "that he should believe himself to be a God, if he could bring down rain from the clouds, or give life to an animal." It belongs exclusively to the true God to endow matter with those singular properties, which enable it under certain circumstances, to exhibit the appearances of life.

I cannot conclude this subject, without taking notice of its extensive application to medicine, metaphysics, theology and morals.

The doctrine of animal life which has been taught, exhibits in the

First place, a new view of the nervous system, by discovering its origin in the extremities of the nerves on which impressions are made, and its termination in the brain. This idea is extended in an ingenious manner by Mr. Valli in his treatise upon animal electricity.

2. It discovers to us the true means of promoting health and longevity, by proportioning the number and force of stimuli to the age, climate, situation, habits and temperament of the human body.

3. It leads us to a knowledge of the causes of all diseases. These consist in excessive, or preternatural excitement in the whole, or a part of the human body, accompanied *generally* with irregular motions, and induced by natural, or artificial stimuli. The latter have been called very properly by Mr. Hunter *irritants*. The occasional absence of motion in acute diseases, is the effect only of the excess of impetus in their remote causes.

4. It discovers to us that the cure of all diseases depends simply upon the abstraction of stimuli from the whole, or from a part of the body, when the motions excited by them, are in excess, and in the increase of their number and force, when motions are of a moderate nature. For the former purpose, we employ a class of medicines known by the name of sedatives. For the latter, we make use of stimulants. Under these two extensive heads, are included all the numerous articles of the Materia Medica.

5. It enables us to reject the doctrine of innate ideas, and to ascribe all our knowledge of sensible objects to impressions acting upon an *innate* capacity to receive ideas. Were it possible for a child to grow up to manhood without the use of any of its senses, it would not possess a single idea of a material object; and as all human knowledge is compounded of simple ideas, this

person would be as destitute of knowledge of every kind, as the grossest portion of vegetable, or fossil matter.

6. The account which has been given of animal life, furnishes a striking illustration of the origin of human actions, by the impression of motives upon the will. As well might we admit an inherent principle of life in animal matter, as a self determining power in this faculty of the mind. Motives are necessary not only to constitute its *freedom*, but its *essence;* for without them, there could be no more a will than there could be vision without light, or hearing without sound. It is true, they are often so obscure as not to be perceived; and they sometimes become insensible from habit, but the same things have been remarked in the operation of stimuli; and yet we do not upon this account deny their agency in producing animal life. In thus deciding in favor of the necessity of motives, to produce actions, I cannot help bearing a testimony against the gloomy misapplication of this doctrine by some modern writers. When properly understood, it is calculated to produce the most comfortable views of the divine government, and the most beneficial effects upon morals, and human happiness.

7. There are errors of an impious nature, which sometimes obtain a currency, from being disguised by innocent names. The doctrine of animal life that has been delivered, is directly opposed to an error of this kind, which has had the most baneful influence upon morals and religion. To suppose a principle to reside necessarily, and constantly in the human body, which acted independently of external circumstances, is to ascribe to it an attribute, which I shall not connect, even in language, with the creature man. Self existence belongs only to God.

The best criterion of the truth of a philosophical opinion, is its tendency to produce exalted ideas, of the Divine Being, and humble views of ourselves. The doctrine of animal life which has been delivered, is calculated to produce these effects in an eminent degree, for

8. It does homage to the Supreme Being, as the governor of the universe, and establishes the certainty of his universal, and

ON NATURAL AND MEDICAL SCIENCES 179

particular providence. Admit a principle of life in the human body, and we open a door for the restoration of the old Epicurean or atheistical philosophy, which supposed the world to be governed by a principle called nature, and which was believed to be inherent in every kind of matter. The doctrine I have taught, cuts the sinews of this error, for by rendering the *continuance* of animal life, no less than its commencement, the effect of the constant operation of divine power and goodness, it leads us to believe that the whole creation is supported in the same manner.

9. The view that has been given of the dependent state of man for the blessing of life, leads us to contemplate with very opposite and inexpressible feelings, the sublime idea which is given of the Deity in the scriptures, as possessing life "within himself." This divine prerogative has never been imparted but to one being, and that is, the Son of God. This appears from the following declaration. "For as the Father hath life in himself, so hath he given to the Son to have life *within himself*." * To his plenitude of independent life, we are to ascribe his being called the "life of the world," "the prince of life," and "life" itself, in the New Testament. These divine epithets which are very properly, founded upon the manner of our Saviour's existence, exalt him infinitely above simple humanity, and establish his divine nature upon the basis of reason, as well as revelation.

10. We have heard that some of the stimuli which produce animal life, are derived from the moral, and physical evils of our world. From beholding these instruments of death thus converted by divine skill into the means of life, we are led to believe goodness to be the supreme attribute of the Deity, and that it will appear finally to predominate in all his works.

11. The doctrine which has been delivered, is calculated to humble the pride of man; by teaching him his constant dependence upon his Maker for his existence, and that he has no preeminence in his tenure of it, over the meanest insect that flutters

---

* John v. verse 26.

in the air, or the humblest plant that grows upon the earth. What an inspired writer says of the innumerable animals which inhabit the ocean, may with equal propriety be said of the whole human race. "Thou sendest forth thy spirit, and they are created. Thou takest away their breath—they die, and return to their dust."

12. Melancholy indeed would have been the issue of all our inquiries, did we take a final leave of the human body in its state of decomposition in the grave. Revelation furnishes us with an elevating, and comforable assurance that this will not be the case. The precise manner of its re-organization, and the new means of its future existence, are unknown to us. It is sufficient to believe, the event will take place, and that after it, the soul and body of man will be exalted in one respect, to an equality with their Creator. They will be immortal.

Here, gentlemen, we close the history of animal life. I feel as if I had waded across a rapid and dangerous stream. Whether I have gained the opposite shore with my head clean, or covered with mud and weeds, I leave wholly to your determination.

THE INFLUENCE OF PHYSICAL CAUSES UPON THE MORAL FACULTY

BY THE moral faculty I mean a capacity in the human mind of distinguishing and choosing good and evil, or, in other words, virtue and vice. It is a native principle, and though it be capable of improvement by experience and reflection, it is not derived from either of them. St. Paul and Cicero give us the most perfect account of it that is to be found in modern or ancient authors. "For when the Gentiles (says St Paul,) which have not the law, do by nature the things contained in the law, *these*, having not the law, are a *law* unto themselves, which show the works of the law written in their hearts, their consciences also, bearing witness, and their thoughts the mean while accusing, or else excusing, another."

The words of Cicero are as follow: "Est igitur hæc, judices, non scripta, sed nata lex, quam non didicimus, accepimus, legimus, verum ex natura ipsa arripuimus, hausimus, expressimus, ad quam non docti, sed facti, non instituti, sed imbuti sumus." † This faculty is often confounded with conscience, which is a distinct and independent capacity of the mind. This is evident from the passage quoted from the writings of St. Paul, in which conscience is said to be the witness that accuses or excuses us, of a breach of the law written in our hearts. The moral faculty is what the schoolmen call the "regula regulans;" the conscience is their "regula regulata;" or, to speak in more modern terms, the moral faculty performs the office of a lawgiver, while the

---
* Rom. i. 14, 15. † Oratio pro Milone.

business of conscience is to perform the duty of a judge. The moral faculty is to the conscience, what taste is to the judgment, and sensation to perception. It is quick in its operations, and like the sensitive plant, acts without reflection, while conscience follows with deliberate steps, and measures all her actions by the unerring square of right and wrong. The moral faculty exercises itself upon the actions of others. It approves, even in books, of the virtues of a Trajan, and disapproves of the vices of a Marius, while conscience confines its operations only to its own actions. These two capacities of the mind are generally in an exact ratio to each other, but they sometimes exist in different degrees in the same person. Hence we often find conscience in its full vigour, with a diminished tone, or total absence of the moral faculty.

It has long been a question among metaphysicians, whether the conscience be seated in the will or in the understanding. The controversy can only be settled by admitting the will to be the seat of the moral faculty, and the understanding to be the seat of the conscience. The mysterious nature of the union of those two moral principles with the will and understanding is a subject foreign to the business of the present inquiry.

As I consider virtue and vice to consist in *action*, and not in opinion, and as this action has its seat in the *will*, and not in the conscience, I shall confine my inquiries chiefly to the influence of physical causes upon that moral power of the mind, which is connected with volition, although many of these causes act likewise upon the conscience, as I shall show hereafter. The state of the moral faculty is visible in actions, which affect the well-being of society. The state of the conscience is invisible, and therefore removed beyond our investigation.

The moral faculty has received different names from different authors. It is the "moral sense" of Dr. Hutchison; "the sympathy" of Dr. Adam Smith; the "moral instinct" of Rousseau; and "the light that lighteth every man that cometh into the world" of St. John. I have adopted the term of moral faculty from Dr. Beattie, because I conceive it conveys, with the most perspicuity, the idea of a capacity in the mind of choosing good and evil.

Our books of medicine contain many records of the effects of physical causes upon the memory, the imagination, and the judgment. In some instances we behold their operation only on one, in others on two, and in many cases, upon the whole of these faculties. Their derangement has received different names, according to the number or nature of the faculties that are affected. The loss of memory has been called "amnesia;" false judgment upon one subject has been called "melancholia;" false judgment upon all subjects has been called "mania;" and a defect of all the three intellectual faculties that have been mentioned has received the name of "amentia." Persons who labour under the derangement, or want, of these faculties of the mind, are considered, very properly, as subjects of medicine; and there are many cases upon record, that prove that their diseases have yielded to the healing art.

In order to illustrate the effects of physical causes upon the moral faculty, it will be necessary *first* to show their effects upon the memory, the imagination, and the judgment, and at the same time to point out the analogy between their operation upon the intellectual faculties of the mind and the moral faculty.

1. Do we observe a connection between the intellectual faculties and the degrees of consistency and firmness of the brain in infancy and childhood? The same connection has been observed between the strength, as well as the progress, of the moral faculty in children.

2. Do we observe a certain size of the brain, and a peculiar cast of features, such as the prominent eye, and the aquiline nose, to be connected with extraordinary portions of genius? We observe a similar connection between the figure and temperament of the body and certain moral qualities. Hence we often ascribe good temper and benevolence to corpulency, and irascibility to sanguineous habits. Cæsar thought himself safe in the friendship of the "sleek-headed" Anthony and Dolabella, but was afraid to trust to the professions of the slender Cassius.

3. Do we observe certain degrees of the intellectual faculties to be hereditary in certain families? The same observation has been frequently extended to moral qualities. Hence we often find certain virtues and vices as peculiar to families, through all their degrees of consanguinity and duration, as a peculiarity of voice, complexion, or shape.

4. Do we observe instances of a total want of memory, imagination, and judgment, either from an original defect in the stamina of the brain, or from the influence of physical causes? The same unnatural defect is sometimes observed, and probably from the same causes, of a moral faculty. The celebrated Servin, whose character is drawn by the Duke of Sully, in his Memoirs, appears to be an instance of the total absence of the moral faculty, while the chasm produced by this defect, seems to have been filled up by a more than common extension of every other power of his mind. I beg leave to repeat the history of this prodigy of vice and knowledge. "Let the reader represent to himself a man of a genius so lively, and of an understanding so extensive, as rendered him scarce ignorant of any thing that could be known; of so vast and ready a comprehension, that he immediately made himself master of whatever he attempted; and of so prodigious a memory, that he never forgot what he once learned. He possessed all parts of philosophy, and the mathematics, particularly fortification and drawing Even in theology he was so well skilled, that he was an excellent preacher, whenever he had a mind to exert that talent, and an able disputant for and against the reformed religion, indifferently. He not only understood Greek, Hebrew, and all the languages which we call learned, but also all the different jargons, or modern dialects. He accented and pronounced them so naturally, and so perfectly imitated the gestures and manners both of the several nations of Europe, and the particular provinces of France, that he might have been taken for a native of all, or any, of these countries: and this quality he applied to counterfeit all sorts of persons, wherein he succeeded wonderfully. He was, moreover, the best comedian, and the greatest droll that perhaps ever appeared. He had a

genius for poetry, and had wrote many verses. He played upon almost all instruments, was a perfect master of music, and sang most agreeably and justly. He likewise could say mass, for he was of a disposition to do, as well as to know, all things. His body was perfectly well suited to his mind. He was light, nimble, and dexterous, and fit for all exercises. He could ride well, and in dancing, wrestling, and leaping, he was admired. There are not any recreative games that he did not know, and he was skilled in almost all mechanic arts. But now for the reverse of the medal. Here it appeared, that he was treacherous, cruel, cowardly, deceitful, a liar, a cheat, a drunkard, and a glutton, a sharper in play, immersed in every species of vice, a blasphemer, an atheist. In a word, in him might be found all the vices that are contrary to nature, honour, religion, and society, the truth of which he himself evinced with his latest breath; for he died in the flower of his age, in a common brothel, perfectly corrupted by his debaucheries, and expired with the glass, in his hand, cursing and denying God." *

It was probably a state of the human mind such as has been described, that our Saviour alluded to in the disciple who was about to betray him, when he called him "a devil." Perhaps the essence of depravity, in infernal spirits, consists in their being wholly devoid of a moral faculty. In them the will has probably lost the power of choosing,† as well as the capacity of enjoying moral good. It is true, we read of their trembling in a belief of the existence of a God, and of their anticipating future punishment, by asking whether they were to be tormented before their time: but this is the effect of conscience, and hence arises another argument in favour of this judicial power of the mind being distinct from the moral faculty. It would seem as if the Supreme Being had preserved the moral faculty in man from the ruins of

---

* Vol. iii. p. 216, 217.

† Milton seems to have been of this opinion. Hence, after ascribing repentance to Satan, he makes him declare,

"Farewell remorse; all good to me is lost,
Evil, be thou my good."————
PARADISE LOST, Book IV.

his fall, on purpose to guide him back again to Paradise, and at the same time had constituted the conscience, both in men and fallen spirits, a kind of royalty in his moral empire, on purpose to show his property in all intelligent creatures, and their original resemblance to himself. Perhaps the essence of moral depravity in man consists in a total, but temporary, suspension of the power of conscience. Persons in this situation are emphatically said in the Scriptures to "be past feeling," and to have their consciences seared with a "hot iron;" they are likewise said to be "twice dead," that is, the same torpor, or moral insensibility, has seized both the moral faculty and the conscience.

5. Do we ever observe instances of the existence of only *one* of the three intellectual powers of the mind that have been named, in the absence of the other two? We observe something of the same kind with respect to the moral faculty. I once knew a man, who discovered no one mark of reason, who possessed the moral sense or faculty in so high a degree, that he spent his whole life in acts of benevolence. He was not only inoffensive (which is not always the case with idiots), but he was kind and affectionate to every body. He had no ideas of time, but what were suggested to him by the returns of the stated periods for public worship, in which he appeared to take great delight. He spent several hours of every day in devotion, in which he was so careful to be private, that he was once found in the most improbable place in the world for that purpose, viz. in an oven.

6. Do we observe the memory, the imagination, and the judgment to be affected by diseases, particularly by madness? Where is the physician, who has not seen the moral faculty affected from the same causes! How often do we see the temper wholly changed by a fit of sickness! And how often do we hear persons of the most delicate virtue utter speeches, in the delirium of a fever, that are offensive to decency or good manners! I have heard a well-attested history of a clergyman of the most exemplary moral character, who spent the last moments of a fever, which deprived him both of his reason and his life, in profane cursing and swearing. I once attended a young woman in a

nervous fever, who discovered, after her recovery, a loss of her former habit of veracity. Her memory (a defect of which might be suspected of being the cause of this vice), was in every respect as perfect as it was before the attack of the fever.* The instances of immorality in maniacs, who were formerly distinguished for the opposite character, are so numerous, and well known, that it will not be necessary to select any cases, to establish the truth of the proposition contained under this head.

7. Do we observe any of the three intellectual faculties that have been named enlarged by diseases? Patients in the delirium of a fever, often discover extraordinary flights of imagination, and madmen often astonish us with their wonderful acts of memory. The same enlargement, sometimes, appears in the operations of the moral faculty. I have more than once heard the most sublime discourses of morality in the cell of a hospital, and who has not seen instances of patients in acute diseases discovering degrees of benevolence and integrity, that were not natural to them in the ordinary course of their lives? †

8. Do we ever observe a partial insanity, or false perception on one subject, while the judgment is sound and correct, upon all others? We perceive, in some instances, a similar defect in the moral faculty. There are persons who are moral in the highest degree as to certain duties, who nevertheless live under the influence of some one vice. I knew an instance of a woman, who was exemplary in her obedience to every command of the moral law, except one. She could not refrain from stealing. What made this vice the more remarkable was, that she was in easy circumstances, and not addicted to extravagance in any thing. Such was her propensity to this vice, that when she could lay her hands upon nothing more valuable, she would often, at the table

---

* I have selected this case from many others which have come under my notice, in which the moral faculty appeared to be impaired by diseases, particularly by the typhus of Dr. Cullen, and by those species of palsy which affect the brain.

† Xenophon makes Cyrus declare, in his last moments, "That the soul of man, at the hour of death, appears *most divine,* and then foresees something of future events."

of a friend, fill her pockets secretly with bread As a proof that her judgment was not affected by this defect in her moral faculty, she would both confess and lament her crime, when detected in it.

9. Do we observe the imagination in many instances to be affected with apprehensions of dangers that have no existence? In like manner we observe the moral faculty to discover a sensibility to vice, that is by no means proportioned to its degrees of depravity. How often do we see persons labouring under this morbid sensibility of the moral faculty refuse to give a direct answer to a plain question, that related perhaps only to the weather, or to the hour of the day, lest they should wound the peace of their minds by telling a falsehood!

10. Do dreams affect the memory, the imagination, and the judgment? Dreams are nothing but incoherent ideas, occasioned by partial or imperfect sleep. There is a variety in the suspension of the faculties and operations of the mind in this state of the system. In some cases the imagination only is deranged in dreams, in others the memory is affected, and in others the judgment. But there are cases in which the change that is produced in the state of the brain, by means of sleep, affects the moral faculty likewise; hence we sometimes dream of doing and saying things, when asleep, which we shudder at, as soon as we awake. This supposed defection from virtue exists frequently in dreams, where the memory and judgment are scarcely impaired. It cannot therefore be ascribed to an absence of the exercises of those two powers of the mind.

11. Do we read, in the accounts of travellers, of men, who, in respect of intellectual capacity and enjoyments, are but a few degrees above brutes? We read likewise of a similar degradation of our species, in respect to moral capacity and feeling. Here it will be necessary to remark, that the low degrees of moral perception, that have been discovered in certain African and Russian tribes of men, no more invalidate our proposition of the universal and essential existence of a moral faculty in the human mind, than the low state of their intellects prove, that reason

is not natural to man. Their perceptions of good and evil are in exact proportion to their intellectual faculties. But I will go further, and admit, with Mr. Locke,* that some savage nations are totally devoid of the moral faculty, yet it will by no means follow, that this was the original constitution of their minds. The appetite for certain aliments is uniform among all mankind. Where is the nation and the individual, in their primitive state of health, to whom bread is not agreeable? But if we should find savages, or individuals, whose stomachs have been so disordered by intemperance as to refuse this simple and wholesome article of diet, shall we assert that this was the original constitution of their appetites? By no means. As well might we assert, because savages destroy their beauty by painting and cutting their faces, that the principles of taste do not exist naturally in the human mind. It is with virtue as with fire. It exists in the mind, as fire does in certain bodies, in a latent or quiescent state. As collision renders the one sensible, so education renders the other visible. It would be as absurd to maintain, because olives become agreeable to many people from habit, that we have no natural appetites for any other kind of food, as to assert that any part of the human species exist without a moral principle, because in some of them it has wanted causes to excite it into action, or has been perverted by example. There are appetites that are wholly artificial. There are tastes so entirely vitiated, as to perceive beauty in deformity. There are torpid and unnatural passions. Why, under certain unfavourable circumstances, may there not exist also a moral faculty, in a state of sleep, or subject to mistakes?

The only apology I shall make, for presuming to differ from that justly celebrated oracle,† who first unfolded to us a map of the intellectual world, shall be, that the eagle eye of genius often darts its views beyond the notice of facts, which are accommodated to the slender organs of perception of men, who possess no other talent than that of observation.

It is not surprising, that Mr. Locke has confounded this moral

---

* Essay concerning the Human Understanding, Book I. chap. 3.
† Mr. Locke.

principle with *reason,* or that Lord Shaftesbury has confounded it with *taste,* since all three of these faculties agree in the objects of their approbation, notwithstanding they exist in the mind independently of each other. The favourable influence, which the progress of science and taste has had upon the morals, can be ascribed to nothing else, but to the perfect union that subsists in nature between the dictates of reason, of taste, and of the moral faculty. Why has the spirit of humanity made such rapid progress for some years past in the courts of Europe? It is because kings and their ministers have been taught to *reason* upon philosophical subjects. Why have indecency and profanity been banished from the stage in London and Paris? It is because immorality is an offence against the highly cultivated *taste* of the French and English nations.

It must afford great pleasure to the lovers of virtue, to behold the depth and extent of this moral principle in the human mind. Happily for the human race, the intimations of duty and the road to happiness are not left to the slow operations or doubtful inductions of reason, nor to the precarious decisions of taste. Hence we often find the moral faculty in a state of vigour in persons, in whom reason and taste exist in a weak, or in an uncultivated state. It is worthy of notice, likewise, that while *second* thoughts are best in matters of judgment, *first* thoughts are always to be preferred in matters that relate to morality. *Second* thoughts, in these cases, are generally parlies between duty and corrupted inclinations. Hence Rousseau has justly said, that "a well regulated moral instinct is the surest guide to happiness."

It must afford equal pleasure to the lovers of virtue to behold, that our moral conduct and happiness are not committed to the determination of a single legislative power. The conscience, like a wise and faithful legislative council, performs the office of a check upon the moral faculty, and thus prevents the fatal consequences of immoral actions.

An objection, I foresee, will arise to the doctrine of the influence of physical causes upon the moral faculty, from its being supposed to favour the opinion of the *materiality* of the soul. But I do not see that this doctrine obliges us to decide upon the question of the nature of the soul, any more than the facts which prove the influence of physical causes upon the memory, the imagination, or the judgment. I shall, however, remark upon this subject, that the writers in favour of the *immortality* of the soul have done that truth great injury, by connecting it necessarily with its immateriality. The immortality of the soul depends upon the *will* of the Deity, and not upon the supposed properties of spirit. Matter is in its own nature as immortal as spirit. It is resolvable by heat and mixture into a variety of forms; but it requires the same Almighty hand to annihilate it, that it did to create it. I know of no arguments to prove the immortality of the soul, but such as are derived from the Christian revelation.* It would be as reasonable to assert that the basin of the ocean is immortal, from the greatness of its capacity to hold water; or that we are to live for ever in this world, because we are afraid of dying, as to maintain the immortality of the soul, from the greatness of its capacity for knowledge and happiness, or from its dread of annihilation.

I remarked, in the beginning of this discourse, that persons who are deprived of the just exercise of memory, imagination, or judgment, were proper subjects of medicine; and that there are many cases upon record which prove, that the diseases from the derangement of these faculties have yielded to the healing art.

It is perhaps only because the diseases of the moral faculty have not been traced to a connection with physical causes, that medical writers have neglected to give them a place in their systems of nosology, and that so few attempts have been hitherto made to lessen or remove them, by physical as well as rational and moral remedies.

I shall not attempt to derive any support to my opinions, from the analogy of the influence of physical causes upon the temper and conduct of brute animals. The facts which I shall

---

* "Life and immortality *are* brought to light *only* through the gospel."
2 Tim. i. 10.

produce in favour of the action of these causes upon morals in the human species, will, I hope, render unnecessary the arguments that might be drawn from that quarter.

I am aware, that in venturing upon this subject I step upon untrodden ground. I feel as Æneas did, when he was about to enter the gates of Avernus, but without a sybil to instruct me in the mysteries that are before me. I foresee, that men who have been educated in the mechanical habits of adopting popular or established opinions will revolt at the doctrine I am about to deliver, while men of sense and genius will hear my propositions with candour, and if they do not adopt them, will commend that boldness of inquiry, that prompted me to broach them.

I shall begin with an attempt to supply the defects of nosological writers, by naming the partial or weakened action of the moral faculty, MICRONOMIA. The total absence of this faculty I shall call ANOMIA. By the law, referred to in these new genera of vesaniæ, I mean the law of nature written in the human heart, and which I formerly quoted from the writings of St. Paul.

In treating of the effects of physical causes upon the moral faculty, it might help to extend our ideas upon this subject, to reduce virtues and vices to certain species, and to point out the effects of particular species of virtue and vice; but this would lead us into a field too extensive for the limits of the present inquiry. I shall only hint at a few cases, and have no doubt but the ingenuity of my auditors will supply my silence, by applying the rest.

It is immaterial, whether the physical causes that are to be enumerated act upon the moral faculty through the medium of the senses, the passions, the memory, or the imagination. Their influence is equally certain, whether they act as remote, predisposing, or occasional causes.

1. The effects of CLIMATE upon the moral faculty claim our first attention. Not only individuals, but nations, derive a considerable part of their moral, as well as intellectual character, from the different portions they enjoy of the rays of the sun.

Irascibility, levity, timidity, and indolence, tempered with occasional emotions of benevolence, are the moral qualities of the inhabitants of warm climates, while selfishness, tempered with sincerity and integrity, form the moral character of the inhabitants of cold countries. The state of the weather, and the seasons of the year also, have a visible effect upon moral sensibility. The month of November, in Great Britain, rendered gloomy by constant fogs and rains, has been thought to favour the perpetration of the worst species of murder, while the vernal sun, in middle latitudes, has been as generally remarked for producing gentleness and benevolence.

2. The effects of DIET upon the moral faculty are more certain, though less attended to, than the effects of climate. "Fullness of bread," we are told, was one of the predisposing causes of the vices of the Cities of the Plain. The fasts so often inculcated among the Jews were intended to lessen the incentives to vice, for pride, cruelty, and sensuality, are as much the natural consequences of luxury, as apoplexies and palsies. But the *quality* as well as the quantity of aliment has an influence upon morals; hence we find the moral diseases that have been mentioned are most frequently the offspring of animal food. The prophet Isaiah seems to have been sensible of this, when he ascribes such salutary effects to a temperate and vegetable diet. "Butter and honey shall he eat," says he, "*that* he may know to refuse the evil, and to choose the good." But we have many facts which prove the efficacy of a vegetable diet upon the passions. Dr. Arbuthnot assures us, that he cured several patients of irascible tempers, by nothing but a prescription of this simple and temperate regimen.

3. The effects of CERTAIN DRINKS upon the moral faculty are not less observable, than upon the intellectual powers of the mind. Fermented liquors, of a good quality, and taken in a moderate quantity, are favourable to the virtues of candour, benevolence, and generosity; but when they are taken in excess, or when they are of a bad quality, and taken even in a moderate quantity, they seldom fail of rousing every latent spark of vice into action. The last of these facts is so notorious, that when a

man is observed to be ill-natured or quarrelsome in Portugal, after drinking, it is common in that country to say, that "he has drunken bad wine." While occasional fits of intoxication produce ill-temper in many people, habitual drunkenness (which is generally produced by distilled spirits) never fails to eradicate veracity and integrity from the human mind. Perhaps this may be the reason why the Spaniards, in ancient times, never admitted a man's evidence in a court of justice, who had been convicted of drunkenness. Water is the universal sedative of turbulent passions; it not only promotes a general equanimity of temper, but it composes anger. I have heard several well-attested cases, of a draught of cold water having suddenly composed this violent passion, after the usual remedies of reason had been applied to no purpose.

4. EXTREME HUNGER produces the most unfriendly effects upon moral sensibility. It is immaterial, whether it act by inducing a relaxation of the solids, or an acrimony of the fluids, or by the combined operations of both those physical causes. The Indians in this country whet their appetites for that savage species of war, which is peculiar to them, by the stimulus of hunger; hence, we are told, they always return meagre and emaciated from their military excursions. In civilized life we often behold this sensation to overbalance the restraints of moral feeling; and perhaps this may be the reason why poverty, which is the most frequent parent of hunger, disposes so generally to theft; for the character of hunger is taken from that vice; it belongs to it "to break through stone walls." So much does this sensation predominate over reason and moral feeling, that Cardinal de Retz suggests to politicians, never to risk a motion in a popular assembly, however wise or just it may be, immediately before dinner. That temper must be uncommonly guarded, which is not disturbed by long abstinence from food. One of the worthiest men I ever knew, who made his breakfast his principal meal, was peevish and disagreeable to his friends and family, from the time he left his bed till he sat down to his morning

repast; after which, cheerfulness sparkled in his countenance, and he became the delight of all around him.

5. I hinted formerly, in proving the analogy between the effects of DISEASES upon the intellects, and upon the moral faculty, that the latter was frequently impaired by fevers and madness. I beg leave to add further upon this head, that not only madness, but the hysteria and hypochondriasis, as well as all those states of the body, whether idiopathic or symptomatic, which are accompanied with preternatural irritability—sensibility—torpor—stupor or mobility of the nervous system, dispose to vice, either of the body or of the mind. It is in vain to attack these vices with lectures upon morality. They are only to be cured by medicine,—particularly by exercise,—the cold bath,—and by a cold or warm atmosphere. The young woman, whose case I mentioned formerly, that lost her habit of veracity by a nervous fever, recovered this virtue, as soon as her system recovered its natural tone, from the cold weather which happily succeeded her fever.*

6. Idleness is the parent of every vice. It is mentioned in the Old Testament as another of the predisposing causes of the vices of the Cities of the Plain. Labor of all kinds favors and facilitates

---

* There is a morbid state of excitability in the body during the convalescence from fever, which is intimately connected with an undue propensity to venereal pleasures. I have met with several instances of it. The marriage of the celebrated Mr. Howard to a woman who was twice as old as himself, and very sickly, has been ascribed by his biographer, Dr. Aiken, to *gratitude* for her great attention to him in a fit of sickness. I am disposed to ascribe it to a sudden paroxysm of another passion, which as a religious man, he could not gratify in any other, than in a lawful way. I have heard of two young clergymen who married the women who had nursed them in fits of sickness. In both cases there was great inequality in their years, and condition in life. Their motive was, probably, the same as that which I have attributed to Mr. Howard. Dr. Patrick Russel takes notice of an uncommon degree of venereal excitability which followed attacks of the plague at Messina, in 1743, in all ranks of people. Marriages, he says, were more frequent after it than usual, and virgins were, in some instances violated, who died of that disease, by persons who had just recovered from it.

the practice of virtue. The country life is happy, chiefly because its laborious employments are favourable to virtue, and unfriendly to vice. It is a common practice, I have been told, for the planters in the southern states, to consign a house slave, who has become vicious from idleness, to the drudgery of the field, in order to reform him. The bridewells and workhouses of all civilized countries prove that LABOR is not only a very severe, but the most benevolent of all punishments, in as much as it is one of the most suitable means of reformation. Mr. Howard tells us in his History of Prisons, that in Holland it is a common saying, "Make men work and you will make them honest." And over the rasp and spin-house at Grœningen, this sentiment is expressed (he tells us) by a happy motto

"Vitiorum semina—otium—labore exhauriendum."

The effects of steady labour in early life, in creating virtuous habits, is still more remarkable. The late Anthony Benezet of this city, whose benevolence was the sentinel of the virtue, as well as of the happiness of his country, made it a constant rule in binding out poor children, to avoid putting them into wealthy families, but always preferred masters for them who worked themselves, and who obliged these children to work in their presence. If the habits of virtue, contracted by means of this apprenticeship to labour, are purely mechanical, their effects are, nevertheless, the same upon the happiness of society, as if they flowed from principle. The mind, moreover, when preserved by these means from weeds, becomes a more mellow soil afterwards, for moral and rational improvement.

7. The effects of EXCESSIVE SLEEP are intimately connected with the effects of idleness upon the moral faculty; hence we find that moderate, and even scanty portions of sleep, in every part of the world, have been found to be friendly, not only to health and long life, but in many instances to morality. The practice of the monks, who often sleep upon a floor, and who generally rise with the sun, for the sake of mortifying their

sensual appetites, is certainly founded in wisdom, and has often produced the most salutary moral effects.

8. The effects of BODILY PAIN upon the moral, are not less remarkable than upon the intellectual powers of the mind. The late Dr. Gregory, of the University of Edinburgh, used to tell his pupils, that he always found his perceptions quicker in a fit of the gout, than at any other time. The pangs which attend the dissolution of the body, are often accompanied with conceptions and expressions upon the most ordinary subjects, that discover an uncommon elevation of the intellectual powers. The effects of bodily pain are exactly the same in rousing and directing the moral faculty. Bodily pain, we find, was one of the remedies employed in the Old Testament, for extirpating vice and promoting virtue. and Mr. Howard tells us, that he saw it employed successfully as a means of reformation, in one of the prisons which he visited. If pain has a physical tendency to cure vice, I submit it to the consideration of parents and legislators, whether moderate degrees of corporal punishments, inflicted for a great length of time, would not be more medicinal in their effects, than the violent degrees of them, which are of short duration.

9. Too much cannot be said in favour of CLEANLINESS, as a physical means of promoting virtue. The writings of Moses have been called, by military men, the best "orderly book" in the world. In every part of them we find cleanliness inculcated with as much zeal, as if it was part of the moral, instead of the Levitical law. Now, it is well-known, that the principal design of every precept and rite of the ceremonial parts of the Jewish religion, was to prevent vice, and to promote virtue. All writers upon the leprosy, take notice of its connection with a certain vice. To this disease gross animal food, particularly swine's flesh, and a dirty skin, have been thought to be predisposing causes—hence the reason, probably, why pork was forbidden, and why ablutions of the body and limbs were so frequently inculcated by the Jewish law. Sir John Pringle's remarks, in his oration upon Captain Cook's Voyage, delivered before the Royal So-

ciety in London, are very pertinent to this part of our subject:—
"Cleanliness (says he) is conducive to health, but is it not obvious, that it also tends to good order and other virtues? Such (meaning the ship's crew) as were made more cleanly, became more sober, more orderly, and more attentive to duty." The benefit to be derived by parents and schoolmasters from attending to these facts, is too obvious to be mentioned.

10. I hope I shall be excused in placing SOLITUDE among the physical causes which influence the moral faculty, when I add, that I confine its effects to persons who are irreclaimable by rational or moral remedies. Mr. Howard informs us, that the chaplain of the prison at Liege in Germany assured him "that the most refractory and turbulent spirits, became tractable and submissive, by being closely confined for four or five days." In bodies that are predisposed to vice, the stimulus of cheerful, but much more of profane society and conversation, upon the animal spirits, becomes an exciting cause, and like the stroke of the flint upon the steel, renders the sparks of vice both active and visible. By removing men out of the reach of this exciting cause, they are often reformed, especially if they are confined long enough to produce a sufficient chasm in their habits of vice. Where the benefit of reflection, and instruction from books, can be added to solitude and confinement, their good effects are still more certain. To this philosophers and poets in every age have assented, by describing the life of a hermit as a life of passive virtue.

11. Connected with solitude, as a mechanical means of promoting virtue, SILENCE deserves to be mentioned in this place. The late Dr. Fothergill, in his plan of education for that benevolent institution at Ackworth, which was the last care of his useful life, says every thing that can be said in favour of this necessary discipline, in the following words: "To habituate children from their early infancy, to silence and attention, is of the greatest advantage to them, not only as a preparative to their advancement in a religious life, but as the groundwork of a well-cultivated understanding. To have the active minds of children put

under a kind of restraint—to be accustomed to turn their attention from external objects, and habituated to a degree of abstracted quiet, is a matter of great consequence, and lasting benefit to them. Although it cannot be supposed, that young and active minds are always engaged in silence as they ought to be, yet to be accustomed thus to quietness, is no small point gained towards fixing a habit of patience, and recollection, which seldom forsakes those who have been properly instructed in this entrance of the school of wisdom, during the residue of their days."

For the purpose of acquiring this branch of education, children cannot associate too early, nor too often with their parents, or with their superiors in age, rank, and wisdom.

12. The effects of music upon the moral faculty, have been felt and recorded in every country. Hence we are able to discover the virtues and vices of different nations, by their tunes, as certainly as by their laws. The effects of music, when simply mechanical, upon the passions, are powerful and extensive. But it remains yet to determine the degrees of moral ecstacy, that may be produced by an attack upon the ear, the reason, and the moral principle, at the same time, by the combined powers of music and eloquence.

13. The ELOQUENCE of the PULPIT is nearly allied to music in its effects upon the moral faculty. It is true, there can be no permanent change in the temper and moral conduct of a man, that is not derived from the understanding and the will; but we must remember that these two powers of the mind are most assailable, when they are attacked through the avenue of the passions; and these, we know, when agitated by the powers of eloquence, exert a mechanical action upon every power of the soul. Hence we find, in every age and country where Christianity has been propagated, the most accomplished orators have generally been the most successful reformers of mankind. There must be a defect of eloquence in a preacher, who, with the resources for oratory which are contained in the Old and New Testaments, does not produce in every man who hears him at

least a temporary love of virtue. I grant that the eloquence of the pulpit alone cannot change men into Christians, but it certainly possesses the power of changing brutes into men. Could the eloquence of the stage be properly directed, it is impossible to conceive the extent of its mechanical effects upon morals. The language and imagery of a Shakspeare, upon moral and religious subjects, poured upon the passions and the senses, in all the beauty and variety of dramatic representation; who could resist, or describe their effects?

14. ODOURS of various kinds have been observed to act in the most sensible manner upon the moral faculty. Brydone tells us, upon the authority of a celebrated philosopher in Italy, that the peculiar wickedness of the people who live in the neighbourhood of Ætna and Vesuvius is occasioned chiefly by the smell of the sulphur, and of the hot exhalations which are constantly discharging from those volcanoes. Agreeable odours seldom fail to inspire serenity, and to compose the angry spirits. Hence the pleasure, and one of the advantages, of a flower-garden. The smoke of tobacco is likewise of a composing nature, and tends not only to produce what is called a train in perception, but to hush the agitated passions into silence and order. Hence the practice of connecting the pipe or cigar and the bottle together, in public company.

15. It will be sufficient only to mention LIGHT and DARKNESS, to suggest facts in favour of the influence of each of them upon moral sensibility. How often do the peevish complaints of the night, in sickness, give way to the composing rays of the light of the morning? Othello cannot murder Desdemona by candlelight, and who has not felt the effects of a blazing fire upon the gentle passions? *

---

* The temperature of the air has a considerable influence upon moral feeling. Henry the Third of France was always ill-humoured, and sometimes cruel, in cold weather. There is a damp air which comes from the sea in Northumberland county in England, which is known by the name of the *seafret*, from its inducing fretfulness in the temper.

16. It is to be lamented, that no experiments have as yet been made, to determine the effects of all the different species of AIRS, which chemistry has lately discovered, upon the moral faculty. I have authority, from actual experiments, only to declare, that dephlogisticated air, when taken into the lungs, produces cheerfulness, gentleness, and serenity of mind.

17. What shall we say of the effects of MEDICINES upon the moral faculty? That many substances in the materia medica act upon the intellects is well known to physicians. Why should it be thought impossible for medicines to act in like manner upon the moral faculty? May not the earth contain, in its bowels, or upon its surface, antidotes? But I will not blend facts with conjectures. Clouds and darkness still hang upon this part of my subject.

Let it not be suspected, from any thing that I have delivered, that I suppose the influence of physical causes upon the moral faculty renders the agency of divine influence unnecessary to our moral happiness. I only maintain, that the operations of the divine government are carried on in the moral, as in the natural world, by the instrumentality of second causes. I have only trodden in the footsteps of the inspired writers; for most of the physical causes I have enumerated are connected with moral precepts, or have been used as the means of reformation from vice, in the Old and New Testaments. To the cases that have been mentioned, I shall only add, that Nebuchadnezzar was cured of his pride, by means of solitude and a vegetable diet. Saul was cured of his evil spirit, by means of David's harp, and St. Paul expressly says, "I keep my body under, and bring it into subjection, lest that by any means, when I have preached to others, I myself should be a cast-away." But I will go one step further, and add, in favour of divine influence upon the moral principle, that in those extraordinary cases, where bad men are suddenly reformed, without the instrumentality of physical, moral or rational causes, I believe that the organization of those parts of the body, in which the faculties of the mind are seated, undergoes a physical change;* and hence the expression of a "new creature," which is made use of in the Scriptures to denote this change, is proper in a literal, as well as a figurative sense. It is probably the beginning of that perfect renovation of the human body, which is predicted by St. Paul in the following words: "For our conversation is in heaven, from whence we look for the Saviour, who shall change our vile bodies, that they may be fashioned according to his own glorious body." I shall not pause to defend myself against the charge of enthusiasm in this place; for the age is at length arrived, so devoutly wished for by Dr. Cheyne, in which men will not be deterred in their researches after truth, by the terror of odious or unpopular names.

I cannot help remarking under this head, that if the conditions of those parts of the human body which are connected with the human soul influence morals, the same reason may be given for a virtuous education, that has been admitted for teaching music, and the pronunciation of foreign languages, in the early and yielding state of those organs which form the voice and speech. Such is the effect of a moral education, that we often see its fruits in advanced stages of life, after the religious principles which were connected with it have been renounced; just as we perceive the same care in a surgeon in his attendance upon patients, after the sympathy which first produced this care has ceased to operate upon his mind. The boasted morality of the deists is, I believe, in most cases, the offspring of habits, produced originally by the principles and precepts of christianity. Hence appears the wisdom of Solomon's advice, "Train up a child in the way he should go, and when he is old he will not," I had almost said, he cannot, "depart from it."

Thus have I enumerated the principal causes which act

---

* St. Paul was suddenly transformed from a persecutor into a man of a gentle and amiable spirit. The manner in which this change was effected upon his mind, he tells us in the following words· "Neither circumcision availeth any thing, nor uncircumcision, but a new creature. From henceforth let no man trouble me; for I bear in *my body* the *marks* of our Lord Jesus." Galatians vi. 15, 17.

mechanically upon morals. If, from the combined action of physical powers that are opposed to each other, the moral faculty should become stationary, or if the virtue or vice produced by them should form a neutral quality, composed of both of them, I hope it will not call in question the truth of our general propositions. I have only mentioned the effects of physical causes in a simple state.*

It might help to enlarge our ideas upon this subject, to take notice of the influence of the different stages of society, of agriculture and commerce, of soil and situation, of the different degrees of cultivation of taste, and of the intellectual powers, of the different forms of government, and lastly, of the different professions and occupations of mankind, upon the moral faculty; but as these act indirectly only, and by the intervention of causes that are unconnected with matter, I conceive they are foreign to the business of the present inquiry. If they should vary the action of the simple physical causes in any degree, I hope it will not call in question the truth of our general propositions, any more than the compound action of physical powers that are opposed to each other. There remain but a few more causes which are of a compound nature, but they are so nearly related to those which are purely mechanical, that I should beg leave to trespass upon your patience, by giving them a place in my oration.

The effects of imitation, habit, and association, upon morals, would furnish ample matter for investigation. Considering how much the shape, texture, and conditions of the human body influence morals, I submit it to the consideration of the ingenious, whether, in our endeavours to imitate moral examples, some advantage may not be derived, from our copying the features and external manners of the originals. What makes the success of this experiment probable is, that we generally find men, whose

---

* The doctrine of the influence of physical causes on morals is happily calculated to beget charity towards the failings of our fellow-creatures. Our duty to practise this virtue is enforced by motives drawn from science, as well as from the precepts of christianity.

faces resemble each other, have the same manners and dispositions. I infer the possibility of success in an attempt to imitate originals in a manner that has been mentioned, from the facility with which domestics acquire a resemblance to their masters and mistresses, not only in manners, but in countenance, in those cases where they are tied to them by respect and affection. Husbands and wives also, where they possess the same species of face, under circumstances of mutual attachment often acquire a resemblance to each other.

From the general detestation in which hypocrisy is held, both by good and bad men, the mechanical effects of habit upon virtue have not been sufficiently explored. There are, I am persuaded, many instances, where virtues have been assumed by accident or necessity, which have become real from habit, and afterwards derived their nourishment from the heart. Hence the propriety of Hamlet's advice to his mother:

> "Assume a virtue, if you have it not.
> That monster, Custom, who all sense doth eat
> Of habits evil, is angel yet in this,
> That to the use of actions fair and good
> He likewise gives a frock or livery,
> That aptly is put on. Refrain to-night,
> And that shall lend a kind of easiness
> To the next abstinence, the next more easy.
> For use can almost change the stamp of nature,
> And master even the devil, or throw him out,
> With wondrous potency."

The influence of ASSOCIATION upon morals opens an ample field for inquiry. It is from this principle, that we explain the reformation from theft and drunkenness in servants, which we sometimes see produced by a draught of spirits, in which tartar emetic had been secretly dissolved. The recollection of the pain and sickness excited by the emetic, naturally associates itself with the spirits, so as to render them both equally the objects of aversion. It is by calling in this principle only, that we can account for the conduct of Moses, in grinding the golden calf into a powder, and afterwards dissolving it (probably by means of hepar sulphuris,) in water, and compelling the children of Israel to drink of it, as a punishment for their idolatry. This mixture is bitter and nauseating in the highest degree. An inclination to idolatry, therefore, could not be felt, without being associated with the remembrance of this disagreeable mixture, and of course being rejected, with equal abhorrence. The benefit of corporal punishments, when they are of a short duration, depends in part upon their being connected, by time and place, with the crimes for which they are inflicted. Quick as the thunder follows the lightning, if it were possible, should punishments follow the crimes, and the advantage of association would be more certain, if the spot where they were committed were made the theatre of their expiation. It is from the effects of this association, probably, that the change of place and company, produced by exile and transportation, has so often reclaimed bad men, after moral, rational, and physical means of reformation had been used to no purpose.

As SENSIBILITY is the avenue to the moral faculty, every thing which tends to diminish it tends also to injure morals. The Romans owed much of their corruption to the sights of the contests of their gladiators, and of criminals, with wild beasts. For these reasons, executions should never be public. Indeed, I believe there are no public punishments of any kind, that do not harden the hearts of spectators, and thereby lessen the natural horror which all crimes at first excite in the human mind.

CRUELTY to brute animals is another means of destroying moral sensibility. The ferocity of savages has been ascribed in part to their peculiar mode of subsistence. Mr. Hogarth points out, in his ingenious prints, the connection between cruelty to brute animals in youth, and murder in manhood. The emperor Domitian prepared his mind, by the amusement of killing flies, for all those bloody crimes which afterwards disgraced his reign. I am so perfectly satisfied of the truth of a connection between morals and humanity to brutes, that I shall find it difficult to restrain my idolatry for that legislature, that shall first establish a system of laws to defend them from outrage and oppression.

In order to preserve the vigour of the moral faculty, it is of the utmost consequence to keep young people as ignorant as possible of those crimes that are generally thought most disgraceful to human nature. Suicide, I believe, is often propagated by means of newspapers. For this reason, I should be glad to see the proceedings of our courts kept from the public eye, when they expose or punish monstrous vices.

The last mechanical method of promoting morality that I shall mention, is to keep sensibility alive, by a familiarity with scenes of distress from poverty and disease. Compassion never awakens in the human bosom, without being accompanied by a train of sister virtues. Hence the wise man justly remarks, that "By the sadness of the countenance, the heart is made better."

A late French writer in his prediction of events that are to happen in the year 4000, says, "That mankind in that era shall be so far improved by religion and government, that the sick and the dying shall no longer be thrown, together with the dead, into splendid houses, but shall be relieved and protected in a connection with their families and society." For the honor of humanity, an institution,* destined for that distant period, has lately been founded in this city, that shall perpetuate the year 1786 in the history of Pennsylvania. Here the feeling heart, the tearful eye, and the charitable hand, may always be connected together, and the flame of sympathy, instead of being extinguished in taxes, or expiring in a solitary blaze by a single contribution, may be kept alive by constant exercise. There is a necessary connection between animal sympathy and good morals. The priest and the Levite, in the New Testament, would probably have relieved the poor man who fell among thieves, had accident brought them near enough to his wounds. The un-

---

* A public dispensary.

fortunate Mrs. Bellamy was rescued from the dreadful purpose of drowning herself, by nothing but the distress of a child, rending the air with its cries for bread. It is probably owing, in some measure, to the connection between good morals and sympathy, that the fair sex, in every age and country, have been more distinguished for virtue than men; for how seldom do we hear of a woman devoid of humanity?

Lastly, ATTRACTION, COMPOSITION, and DECOMPOSITION, belong to the passions as well as to matter. Vices of the same species attract each other with the most force—hence the bad consequences of crowding young men (whose propensities are generally the same) under one roof, in our modern plans of education. The effects of composition and decomposition upon vices, appear in the meanness of the school boy, being often cured by the prodigality of a military life, and by the precipitation of avarice, which is often produced by ambition and love.*

If physical causes influence morals in the manner we have described, may they not also influence religious principles and opinions?—I answer in the affirmative; and I have authority, from the records of physic, as well as from my own observations, to declare, that religious melancholy and madness, in all their variety of species, yield with more facility to medicine, than simply to polemical discourses, or to casuistical advice. But this subject is foreign to the business of the present inquiry.

From a review of our subject, we are led to contemplate with admiration, the curious structure of the human mind. How distinct are the number, and yet how united! How subordinate and yet how coequal are all its faculties! How wonderful is the action of the mind upon the body! Of the body upon the

---

* A citizen of Philadelphia had made many unsuccessful attempts to cure his wife of drinking ardent spirits. At length, despairing of her reformation, he purchased a hogshead of rum, and after tapping it, left the key in the door where he had placed it, as if he had forgotten it. His design was to give her an opportunity of destroying herself, by drinking as much as she pleased. The woman suspected this to be his design—and suddenly left off drinking. Anger here became the antidote of intemperance.

mind!—And of the divine spirit upon both! What a mystery is the mind of man to itself!——O! nature!——Or to speak more properly,——O! THOU GOD OF NATURE!——In vain do we attempt to scan THY immensity, or to comprehend THY various modes of existence, when a single particle of light issued from THYSELF, and kindled into intelligence in the bosom of man, thus dazzles and confounds our understandings!

The extent of the moral powers and habits in man is unknown. It is not improbable, but the human mind contains principles of virtue, which have never yet been excited into action. We behold with surprise the versatility of the human body in the exploits of tumblers and rope-dancers. Even the agility of a wild beast has been demonstrated in a girl of France, and an amphibious nature has been discovered in the human species, in a young man in Spain. We listen with astonishment to the accounts of the *memories* of Mithridates, Cyrus, and Servin. We feel a veneration bordering upon divine homage, in contemplating the stupendous *understandings* of Lord Verulam and Sir Isaac Newton, and our eyes grow dim, in attempting to pursue Shakspeare and Milton in their immeasurable flights of *imagination* And if the history of mankind does not furnish similar instances of the versatility and perfection of our species in virtue, it is because the moral faculty has been the subject of less culture and fewer experiments than the body, and the intellectual powers of the mind. From what has been said, the reason of this is obvious. Hitherto the cultivation of the moral faculty has been the business of parents, schoolmasters and divines.* But if the principles, we have laid down, be just, the improvement and extension of this principle should be equally

---

* The people commonly called Quakers, and the Methodists, make use of the greatest number of physical remedies in their religious and moral discipline, of any sects of Christians; and hence we find them every where distinguished for their good morals. There are several excellent *physical* institutions in other churches, and if they do not produce the same moral effects that we observe from physical institutions among those two modern sects, it must be ascribed to their being more neglected by the members of those churches.

the business of the legislator—the natural philosopher—and the physician, and a physical regimen should as necessarily accompany a moral precept, as directions with respect to the air—exercise—and diet, generally accompany prescriptions for the consumption and the gout. To encourage us to undertake experiments for the improvement of morals, let us recollect the success of philosophy in lessening the number, and mitigating the violence of incurable diseases. The intermitting fever, which proved fatal to two of the monarchs of Britain, is now under absolute subjection to medicine. Continual fevers are much less fatal than formerly. The small-pox is disarmed of its mortality by inoculation, and even the tetanus and the cancer have lately received a check in their ravages upon mankind. But medicine has done more. It has penetrated the deep and gloomy abyss of death, and acquired fresh honours in his cold embraces.—Witness the many hundred people who have lately been brought back to life, by the successful efforts of the humane societies, which are now established in many parts of Europe, and in some parts of America. Should the same industry and ingenuity, which have produced these triumphs of medicine over diseases and death, be applied to the moral science, it is highly probable, that most of those baneful vices, which deform the human breast, and convulse the nations of the earth, might be banished from the world. I am not so sanguine as to suppose, that it is possible for man to acquire so much perfection from science, religion, liberty and good government, as to cease to be mortal; but I am fully persuaded, that from the combined action of causes, which operate at once upon the reason, the moral faculty, the passions, the senses, the brain, the nerves, the blood and the heart, it is possible to produce such a change in his moral character, as shall raise him to a resemblance of angels—nay more, to the likeness of God himself. The state of Pennsylvania still deplores the loss of a man, in whom not only reason and revelation, but many of the physical causes that have been enumerated, concurred to produce such attainments in moral excellency, as have seldom appeared in a human being. This amiable citizen, considered his fellow-creature, man, as God's extract, from his own works, and, whether this image of himself, was cut out from ebony or copper—whether he spoke his own or a foreign language—or whether he worshipped his Maker with ceremonies, or without them, he still considered him as a brother, and equally the object of his benevolence. Poets and historians, who are to live hereafter, to you I commit his panegyric; and when you hear of a law for abolishing slavery in each of the American states, such as was passed in Pennsylvania, in the year 1780—when you hear of the kings and queens of Europe, publishing edicts for abolishing the trade in human souls—and lastly, when you hear of schools and churches with all the arts of civilized life, being established among the nations of Africa, then remember and record, that this revolution in favour of human happiness, was the effect of the labours—the publications—the private letters—and the prayers of ANTHONY BENEZET.*

I return from this digression, to address myself in a particular manner to you, VENERABLE SAGES and FELLOW-CITIZENS in the REPUBLIC OF LETTERS. The influence of philosophy, we have been told, has already been felt in course. To increase, and complete, this influence, there is nothing more necessary, than for the

---

* This worthy man was descended from an ancient and honourable family that flourished in the court of Louis XIV. With liberal prospects in life, he early devoted himself to teaching an English school; in which, for industry, capacity, and attention to the morals and principles of the youth committed to his care, he was without an equal. He published many excellent tracts against the African trade, against war, and the use of spirituous liquors, and one in favour of civilizing and christianizing the Indians. He wrote to the queen of Great Britain, and the queen of Portugal, to use their influence in their respective courts to abolish the African trade. He also wrote an affectionate letter to the king of Prussia, to dissuade him from making war. The history of his life affords a remarkable instance, how much it is possible for an individual to accomplish in the world, and that the most humble stations do not preclude good men from the most extensive usefulness. He bequeathed his estate (after the death of his widow), to the support of a school for the education of negro children, which he had founded and taught for several years before he died. He departed this life in May, 1784, in the seventy-first year of his age, in the meridian of his usefulness, universally lamented by persons of all ranks and denominations.

numerous literary societies in Europe and America to add the SCIENCE OF MORALS to their experiments and inquiries. The godlike scheme of Henry IV. of France, and of the illustrious queen Elizabeth, of England, for establishing a perpetual peace in Europe, may be accomplished without a system of jurisprudence, by a confederation of learned men and learned societies. It is in their power, by multiplying the objects of human reason, to bring the monarchs and rulers of the world under their subjection, and thereby to extirpate war, slavery, and capital punishments, from the list of human evils. Let it not be suspected that I detract, by this declaration, from the honour of the Christian religion. It is true, Christianity was propagated without the aid of human learning; but this was one of those miracles, which was necessary to establish it, and which, by repetition, would cease to be a miracle. They misrepresent the Christian religion, who suppose it to be wholly an internal revelation, and addressed only to the moral faculties of the mind. The truths of Christianity afford the greatest scope for the human understanding, and they will become intelligible to us, only in proportion as the human genius is stretched, by means of philosophy, to its utmost dimensions. Errors may be opposed to errors; but truths, upon all subjects, mutually support each other. And perhaps one reason why some parts of the Christian revelation are still involved in obscurity, may be occasioned by our imperfect knowledge of the phenomena and laws of nature. The truths of philosophy and Christianity dwell alike in the mind of the Deity, and reason and religion are equally the offspring of his goodness. They must, therefore, stand and fall together. By reason, in the present instance, I mean the power of judging of truth, as well as the power of comprehending it. Happy era! when the divine and the philosopher shall embrace each other, and unite their labours for the reformation and happiness of mankind!

ON THE DIFFERENT SPECIES OF MANIA

By the assistance of Dr. Cullen's nosology, I perceive that madness is divided into two genera. The one is called mania, which our author defines to be "universal madness." The other is called melancholia, which the doctor defines to be "partial madness." This partial madness includes six species.—But in this number, the learned professor is certainly too limited—for if false judgement or injudicious conduct upon any subject, constitutes madness, I am persuaded that that disease is the most frequent of any that occurs in the whole nomenclature of medicine.

To supply the defects of Dr. Cullen's nosology, I have set down a list of the different species of partial insanity, which have occurred to me in the course of my observations upon mankind —I shall deliver them in the language of our country, because I wish to be understood by men of all classes, and by both sexes, although it would be easy to clothe them in more technical and learned terms.

I shall define madness in the present instance to be *a want of perception, or an undue perception of truth, duty, or interest.*

I shall begin by naming some of those species of madness which at present prevail in America.

1. The Negro Mania. This disease, which formerly prevailed in the eastern and middle, is now confined chiefly to the southern states. The inhabitants of these states *mistake* their interest and happiness in supposing that their lands can be cul-

tivated only by Negro slaves. The Author of nature never destined the natives of Africa to hard labour, and hence he has made that part of the globe to yield almost spontaneously all that is necessary for the subsistence of man. There is no reason why rice and indigo may not be cultivated by white men, as well as wheat and indian corn. It is true, if the owners of the soil in the Carolinas and Georgia, cultivated their lands with their own hands, they would not be able to roll in coaches, or to squander thousands of pounds yearly in visiting all the cities of Europe, but they would enjoy more health and happiness in a competency acquired without violating the laws of nature and religion.

2. The LAND MANIA is a frequent disease in every part of America. It broke out with peculiar violence in most of the states immediately after the peace, and has continued to be more or less the epidemic of our country ever since. A room in a gaol, instead of a cell in an hospital, is the usual cure of this species of madness.

3. The HORSE MANIA. A race—a carriage—or riding horse is often an object of greater attachment with persons who are afflicted with this disorder, than a wife or a mistress. A gentleman once spent a long evening with a company of these maniacal gentlemen, soon after he had read the Roman history, and unfortunately, from not being interested in their conversation, fell into a reverie.—A debate about the pedigree of a race horse having been started, one of the disputants appealed to him by mistake, and said, "Say Tom—was not Jupiter the sire of Emperor?" "Which of the Roman emperors do you mean, Sir?" said the gentleman. "Poh, you fool," said his companion, "I mean Col. B——'s bay horse, Emperor."

4. THE LIBERTY MANIA. This disease shews itself in visionary ideas of liberty and government. It occupies the time and talents so constantly, as to lead men to neglect their families for the sake of taking care of the state. Such men expect liberty without law—government without power—sovereignty without a head —and wars without expense. They consider industry and its usual consequence, wealth, as the only evils of a state, and ascribe

Roman attainments in virtue to those men only, who, by consuming an undue proportion of their time in writing, talking, or debating upon politics, bequeath the maintenance of their families to their country.

5. The MONARCHICAL MANIA. All those people who believe that "a king can do no wrong," and who hold it to be criminal to depose tyrants, are affected with this mania. They are likewise affected with this species of mania, who suppose that wise and just government cannot be carried on without kings. A young Scotch officer discovered an extraordinary degree of this madness in a speech he made to an American prisoner during the late American war. "This is (said he) the strangest rebellion I ever heard of in au my life. Ye are au fighting, and yet ye have na king to fight for." He had no idea that men had any property in themselves, or that it was right for them to contend, by arms, for any thing, but the power or glory of a king.

6. THE REPUBLICAN MANIA. Every man, who attempts to introduce a republican form of government, where the people are not prepared for it by *virtue* and *knowledge,* is as much a madman as St. Anthony was, when he preached the Gospel to fishes. We have a remarkable instance of this species of madness in a member of the Rump Parliament, who objected to the word "King" of heaven, in an ordinance that was offered to the House, and proposed, as an amendment, that instead of the "King" of heaven, the phrase should be, the "parliament of heaven."

7. The DONATION MANIA. All those people who impoverish their families, by extravagant contributions to public undertakings, or who neglect their relations at their death, by bequeathing their estates to hospitals, colleges, and churches, are affected with this species of madness.

8. The MILITARY MANIA.—Young men are most afflicted with this madness, but we now and then meet with it in an old soldier, as in uncle Toby, in Tristram Shandy. It is impossible to understand a conversation with these gentlemen without the help of a military dictionary.—Counterscarps, morasses, fosses, glacis, ramparts, redoubts, abbatis, &c. form the beginning, mid-

dle, and end of every sentence. They remember nothing in history, but the detail of sieges and battles, and they consider men as made only to carry muskets. The adventurers in the holy wars, before the Reformation, were all infected with this species of military madness.

9. The DUELLING MANIA. There are some men, whose ideas of honour amount to madness; hence every attack upon their character, whether true or false, can be expiated only by a duel. The madness of this passion appears in this, that a good character stands in no need of a pistol or sword to defend it, nor can a bad character be supported by a whole park of artillery.

10. THE HUNTING MANIA. A mad man in England was ordered by his physician to use the cold bath. In returning one day from the bath, he stopped to converse with a servant, who was following his master to the place appointed for a fox-chase. The madman asked the servant how much it cost his master to maintain his horses and hounds? The servant replied £.500 a year. And how much does he sell his foxes for after he catches them?—"For nothing at all," said the servant.—"For nothing!" said the madman with astonishment—"I wish my physician could come across him—he would soon order him to use the cold bath."

11. The GAMING MANIA. This disorder seizes gentlemen in some instances before breakfast in the morning, and continues, with only short intervals for meals, till 11 o'clock at night. It affects some people in the night as well as the day, and on Sundays as well as week days. Its operation is not confined to the fire-side: it appears on the public roads—at courts—elections—and even at places of public worship. It is impossible for two gentlemen, afflicted with this madness, to meet on horseback, without laying a wager upon the gaits, whether of running, pacing, or trotting, of their respective horses. This madness is of a destructive tendency, and often conducts persons afflicted with it to poverty, imprisonment, and an ignominious death.

12. The MACHINE MANIA. This species includes all those maniacs, who have ruined themselves by castle-building, whether

the objects of their schemes have been perpetual motion, or princely fortunes, to be raised by a sudden exertion of the mechanical powers.

13. The ALCHEMICAL MANIA. The objects with the persons afflicted with this disorder are, the *art* of converting base metals into gold, and an *elixir*, the property of which shall be, to restore the duration of human life to its antediluvian extent. This species of madness has lessened within these thirty years, owing to the discoveries which have been made in the principles of general science, and particularly of chemistry. I once met with a man who charmed me with his profound and extensive learning upon every topic, till alchemy became the subject of conversation; when he suddenly broke out in praise of an elixir, discovered, he said, in India, which had preserved a Jew alive, above 1800 years. This Jew, he said, was present at the trial and crucifixion of the Saviour of the world. He was so confident of the truth of what he asserted, that he seemed offended at the cold manner in which I appeared to assent to his story.

14. The VIRTUOSO MANIA In this species of madness I include an extravagant fondness for the monstrous and rare productions of nature and art. It is widely different from a well-regulated passion for the objects of natural history. Distorted shells—petrified toads—Indian pipes—expensive coins, &c. &c. form the collections of this species of madmen. The English gentleman who gave one hundred guineas for the stopper of a vinegar cruet dug out of the Herculaneum, and the English Marquis who gave three hundred guineas for one of Queen Elizabeth's farthings, were deeply affected with this madness.

15. The RAMBLING MANIA. This species of madness includes all those people who are perpetually changing their country—houses—or occupations, and who are always praising the absent, and abusing the present good things of life. I have known several men afflicted with this disease, who have settled and unsettled themselves in half the kingdoms of Europe, and in one third of the states of America. These men are in general useless

to their families, and to society, and often end their days in dependence and poverty.

16. The ECCLESIASTICAL MANIA. This species of madness includes bigots of all denominations. The late Dr. Johnson was a striking example of Episcopal madness. The minister of the church of Scotland, who daily drank at his table the "glorious memory of Jenny Geddes, who threw the stool at the bishop," was likewise affected with it.

17. The NATIONAL MANIA. This disease is very common in Great Britain and France. The late Lord Chatham was affected with it. The very name of Bourbon quickened his pulse with resentment, and he fainted at the idea of American independence. The Antigallican society in London, is the offspring of this madness.

18. The LOVE MANIA. All marriages, without a visible or probable means of subsistence, are founded in madness. All premature attachments between the sexes which obstruct the pursuits of business, are likewise the offspring of the love mania. The expenses of a family, like a blistering plaster between the shoulders, never fail of curing this species of madness.

19. The PRIDE MANIA. Every man who values himself upon his birth—titles, or wealth, more than upon merit, is affected with this madness. It is a most loathsome disorder. I have heard of a nostrum which seldom fails of curing it, and that is, to treat it with contempt. Mordecai made Haman miserable in the sunshine of a court, only by refusing to pull off his hat to him.

20. The DRESS MANIA. Let not curiosity lead us to Bedlam or the cells of an hospital to see madmen or mad-women. Every place of public resort—nay, every street of our city is filled with them. A. B. demands a court of enquiry to prove the insanity of his sister, in order to sequester her estate. What has she done? says the court. Why look at her hat—her craw—and her bishop!—Do they not proclaim her madness? Nor is this all—To lessen the inconveniences of those articles of dress, she has altered her carriage—raised the doors of her chambers—and enlarged the bottoms of every chair in her house.—Do, good

gentlemen, issue a statute of lunacy against her, or she will come upon the township, or end her days in the bettering-house.

21. The PLEASURE MANIA. An attachment to balls—to the stage—or to feeding—dancing—sleighing—and card parties—or to any other amusement to the exclusion of business, or the injury of fortune or health, may justly be considered as a species of madness. I once saw a caricature of a young lady going in a sedan chair through a street in London. On one side of the chair a physician walked with a smelling bottle in his hand; on the other, a young macaroni with a fan in his hand. The young lady, upon seeing one of her acquaintances pass her, cried out, "I'm a going"—"yes, my dear," said her acquaintance, "you look as if you had not a day to live",—"you mistake me," said the sickly pleasure-worn lady, "I am going—not to my grave,—but to Ranelagh." Nor is this pleasure mania confined to the female sex. The gentleman in London, who left his wife in the last stage of a fever, and charged his servant not to send for him from a club, unless his mistress should die in his absence, certainly laboured under uncommon degrees of this species of madness.

22. The ROGUE MANIA. There are some men whose rage against oppression—fraud—and injustice of every kind, rises so high, as to constitute a species of madness. Such men often expose themselves to ridicule and injury, by attempting to detect and expose culprits—speculators—and public defaulters, without considering that such men are often the best supporters of parties, and in some instances of governments, from each of whom they will always be sure to meet with protection. I once knew a man who rose from table in a large company, and walked across the floor, stamping and swearing in a fit of insanity, upon hearing a gentleman say a few words in favour of the slave trade. His host, a sensible Scotchman, brought him to his senses by a very simple rebuke—"Hod hod man—you conno put the world to rights—come—tak your soup."

23. The HUMANE MANIA.—Strange!—that an excess of humanity should often produce those irregularities in behaviour

and conduct, which constitute madness! Dr. Goldsmith has, with great ingenuity, described this species of madness in his comedy of the good natured man. Persons afflicted with this madness, feel for every species of distress, and seem to pour forth tears upon some occasions, from every pore of their bodies. Their souls vibrate in unison with every touch of misery that affects any member of the great family of mankind. Gracious heaven! if ever I should be visited with this species of madness, however much it may expose me to ridicule or resentment, my constant prayer to the divine fountain of justice and pity—shall be, that I *may never be cured of it.*

To these species I might add,

24. The MUSICAL,

25. POETICAL, and

26. MATHEMATICAL MANIAS.—But these are so common and well known, that it will not be necessary to describe them.

Upon a review of this essay, it will appear, that every man is mad, according to Linnæus, upon some subject, or, to quote a higher authority, that "madness is in their hearts while they live, and after that, they go to the dead."

How great are our obligations to Christianity, which, by enlightening—directing—and regulating our judgments—wills—and passions, in the knowledge—choice—and pursuit of *duty*—*truth* and *interest*, restores us to what the apostle very emphatically calls "a sound mind."

ON THE DIFFERENT SPECIES
OF PHOBIA

~~~~~~~~~~~~~~~~~~~~~~~~~~~~~~~~

Dr. Cullen has divided the Hydrophobia into two species. The principal species that disease which is communicated by the bite of a mad animal, and which is accompanied with a dread of water. Without detracting from the merit of Dr Cullen, I cannot help thinking that the genus of the disease which he has named Hydrophobia, should have been Phobia, and that number, and names of the species, should have been taken from the names of the objects of fear or aversion. In conformity to this idea, I shall define Phobia to be "a fear of an imaginary evil, or an undue fear of a real one." The following species appear to belong to it.

1. The Cat Phobia. It will be unnecessary to mention instances of the prevalence of this distemper. I know several gentlemen of unquestionable courage, who have retreated a thousand times from the sight of a cat, and who have even discovered signs of fear and terror upon being confined in a room with a cat that was out of sight.

2. The Rat Phobia is a more common disease than the first species that has been mentioned. It is peculiar, in some measure, to the female sex. I know several ladies who never fail to discover their terror by screaming at the sight of a rat, and who cannot even sleep within the noise of that animal.

3. The Insect Phobia. This disease is peculiar to the female sex. A spider—a flea—or a mosquito alighting upon a lady's neck, has often produced an hysterical fit. To compensate for this defect, in the constitutions of certain ladies, nature has kindly

ON NATURAL AND MEDICAL SCIENCES

endowed them with the highest degree of courage, with respect to the great object of religious fear. They dare "provoke even Omnipotence to arms," by irreverently taking his name in vain in common conversation. Hence our ears are often grated by those ladies, with the exclamations of "Good God!"—"God preserve me!"—"O Lord!" &c. &c. upon the most trifling occasions. Dr. Young seems to have had this species of Insect Phobia in his eye, when he cries out,

> "Say, O! my Muse—say whence such boldness springs,—
> Such daring courage—in such tim'rous things?
> Start from a feather—from an *insect* fly—
> A match for nothing—but, the Deity!"

4. The ODOR PHOBIA is a very frequent disease with all classes of people. There are few men or women to whom smells of some kind are not disagreeable. Old cheese has often produced paleness and tremor in a full fed guest. There are odors from certain flowers that produce the same effects. hence it is not altogether a figure to say, that there are persons who "die of a rose in aromatic pain."

5. The DIRT PHOBIA. This disease is peculiar to certain ladies, especially to such as are of low Dutch extraction. They make every body miserable around them with their excessive cleanliness: the whole of their lives is one continued warfare with dirt—their rooms resound at all hours with the noise of scrubbing brushes, and their entries are obstructed three times a week, with tubs and buckets. I have heard of women, afflicted with this disease, who sat constantly in their kitchens, lest they should dirty their parlours. I once saw one of those women in New-Jersey, fall down upon her knees, with a house cloth in her hand, and wipe away such of the liquid parts of the food as fell upon the floor from a company of gentlemen, that dined in her house; muttering, at the same time, the most terrible complaints, in low Dutch of the beastly manners of her guests. I have heard of a woman in the same state, who never received a visit

from any persons who did not leave their shoes at her door in muddy weather. She always had a pair of slippers placed at the door, for her visitors to put on, till their shoes were cleaned by a servant.

6. The RUM PHOBIA is a very *rare* distemper. I have known only five instances of it in the course of my life. The smell of rum, and of spirituous liquors of all kinds, produced upon these persons, sickness and distress. If it were possible to communicate this distemper as we do the small-pox, by inoculation, what an immense revenue would be derived from it by physicians, provided every person in our country who is addicted to the intemperate use of spirits, were compelled to submit to that operation!

7. The WATER PHOBIA. This species includes not the dread of swallowing, but of *crossing* water. I have known some people, who sweat with terror in crossing an ordinary ferry. Peter the Great of Muscovy laboured under this disease in early life. As a variety of this species of Water Phobia, may be considered that aversion from drinking water, which we sometimes observe in some men, without being accompanied with a similar dislike to artificial liquors. I recollect once to have heard of a physician in this city, who told a gentleman that was afflicted with a dropsy, just before he tapped him, that he expected to draw off not less than three gallons of water from him—"Of *wine* you mean, doctor, said he, for I have not drank that quantity of *water* these twenty years."

8. The SOLO PHOBIA; by which I mean the dread of solitude. This distemper is peculiar to persons of vacant minds, and guilty consciences. Such people cannot bear to be alone, especially if the horror of sickness is added to the pain of attempting to *think*, or to the terror of *thinking*.

9. The POWER PHOBIA. This distemper belongs to certain demagogues. Persons afflicted with it, consider power as an evil— they abhor even the sight of an officer of government.

10. The FACTION PHOBIA. This disease is peculiar to persons of an opposite character to those who are afraid of power. It

discovers itself in undue fears of mobs, insurrections, and such other things as may affect the order and stability of governments.

11. The WANT PHOBIA. This disease is confined chiefly to old people. It is not the father of Tristram Shandy alone who wipes the sweat from his face, and examines both sides of a guinea every time he pays it away. There are few old men who part with money without feeling some of the symptoms of an intermitting fever. This distemper has arisen to such a height, as to furnish the most entertaining and ludicrous scenes in plays and novels. I have heard of an old gentleman in London, who had above £.20,000 in the funds, who sold a valuable library a year or two before he died; and gave as a reason for it, that he was afraid he should not have enough to bury him without making that addition to his fortune.

12. The DOCTOR PHOBIA. This distemper is often complicated with other diseases. It arises, in some instances, from the dread of taking physic, or of submitting to the remedies of bleeding and blistering. In some instances I have known it occasioned by a desire sick people feel of deceiving themselves, by being kept in ignorance of the danger of their disorders. It might be supposed, that, "the dread of a long bill" was one cause of the Doctor Phobia; but this excites terror in the minds of but few people: for who ever thinks of paying a doctor, while he can use his money to advantage in another way! It is remarkable this Doctor Phobia always goes off as soon as a patient is sensible of his danger. The doctor, then, becomes an object of respect and attachment, instead of horror.

13. The BLOOD PHOBIA. There is a native dread of the sight of blood in every human creature, implanted probably for the wise purpose of preventing our injuring or destroying ourselves, or others. Children cry oftener from seeing their blood, than from the pain occasioned by falls or blows. Valuable medicines are stamped with a disagreeable taste to prevent their becoming ineffectual from habit, by being used as condiments or articles of diet. In like manner, Blood-letting as a remedy, is defended from being used improperly, by the terror which accompanies

its use. This terror rises to such a degree as sometimes to produce paleness and faintness when it is prescribed as a remedy. However unpopular it may be, it is not contrary to nature, for she relieves herself when oppressed, by spontaneous discharges of blood from the nose, and other parts of the body. The objections to it therefore appear to be founded less in the judgments than in the *fears* of sick people.

14. The THUNDER PHOBIA. This species is common to all ages, and to both sexes. I have seen it produce the most distressing appearances and emotions upon many people. I know a man, whom the sight of a black cloud in the morning, in the season of thunder-gusts, never fails to make melancholy during the whole of the ensuing day.

15. The HOME PHOBIA. This disease belongs to all those men who prefer tavern, to domestic society, and to all those women who spend the principal part of their time in morning, and afternoon visits, or in long evening parties, at the theatre, or in tumultuous meetings of any kind.

16. The CHURCH PHOBIA. This disease has become epidemic in the city of Philadelphia: hence we find half the city flying in chariots, phaetons, chairs, and even stage-waggons, as well as on horse-back, from the churches, every Sunday in summer, as soon as they are opened for divine worship. In the winter, when it is more difficult to escape the horror of looking into an open church, we observe our citizens drowning their fear of the church, in plentiful entertainments. A short story will shew the prevalence of this distemper in Philadelphia. The Sunday after the inhabitants of Charleston arrived here, during the late war, they assembled to worship God in one of our churches. A young lady (one of the company) was surprised at seeing no faces but such as had been familiar to her in her own state, in the church, but very kindly ascribed it to the politeness of the ladies and gentlemen of Philadelphia, who had that day given up their seats to accommodate the Carolina strangers.

17. The GHOST PHOBIA. This distemper is most common among servants and children. It manifests itself chiefly in passing

by grave-yards, and old empty houses. I have heard of a few instances of grown people, and of men of cultivated understandings, who have been afflicted with this species of Phobia. Physicians who have sacrificed the lives of their patients through carelessness, rashness, or ignorance,—as also witnesses who have convicted by their evidence—judges who have condemned by their influence—and kings and governors who have executed by their power, innocent persons, through prejudice or resentment, are all deeply affected with the Ghost Phobia. Generals of armies and military butchers, who make war only to gratify ambition or avarice, are likewise subject to paroxysms of this disorder. The late King of Prussia, upon a certain occasion, abused his guards most intemperately, for conducting him from a review through a grave-yard. The reflection on the number of men whom his power and sword had consigned to the mansions of death, produced in his majesty, this Ghost Phobia in all its horrors.

18. The DEATH PHOBIA. The fear of death is natural to man—but there are degrees of it which constitute a *disease*. It prevails chiefly among the rich—the luxurious—and the profane. A man of pleasure in the city of New-York, used frequently to say in his convivial moments, that "this world would be a most delightful place to live in, if it were not for that cursed thing called death—it comes in and spoils all." The late King of Prussia always concealed his occasional indispositions from his subjects, lest he should be led after them to connect the idea of his sickness with that of his death. I have heard of a man, who possessed this Death Phobia in so high a degree, that he never would see his friends when they were sick—avoided seeing funerals—and, upon one occasion, threatened to kick a sexton of a church out of his house, for inviting him to the burial of one of his neighbours.——It is remarkable, that even old age, with all its infirmities, will not subdue this disease in some people. The late Dr. Johnson discovered the most unphilosophical as well as unChristian fear of dying, in the 73d year of his age. and the late Dr. P——, after having lived 84 years, went from Edinburgh

to Padua in Italy, in order, by exercise and a change of climate, to protract the hour of his dissolution.

For these maladies of the mind, there are two infallible remedies, viz. reason and religion. The former is the sure antidote of such of them as originate in folly,—while the latter is effectual in those species, which are derived from vice. "I fear God (said Pascal) and therefore I have no other fear."—A belief in God's providence, and a constant reliance upon his power and goodness, impart a composure and firmness to the mind which render it incapable of being moved by all the real, or imaginary evils of life.

THE PROGRESS OF MEDICINE
A Lecture

The imperfection of medicine is a common subject of complaint, by the enemies of our profession. It has been admitted by physicians. The design of this lecture is, to enumerate the causes which have retarded its progress, and to point out the means of promoting its certainty, and greater usefulness. The subject is an interesting one, and highly proper as an introduction to a course of lectures upon the institutes and practice of medicine. I shall begin by briefly enumerating the causes which have retarded the progress of our science.

1st. The first cause, that I shall mention is, connecting it with such branches of knowledge, as have but a slender relation to it. What affinity have the abstruse branches of mathematics with medicine? and yet, years have been spent in the study of that science by physicians, and volumes have been written to explain the functions of the body, by mathematical demonstrations.

2d. The neglect to cultivate those branches of science, which are most intimately connected with medicine. These are chiefly, Natural History, and Metaphysics. In the former, I include, not only botany, zoology, and fossiology, but comparative anatomy and physiology. In the latter, I include a simple history of the faculties and operations of the mind, unconnected with the ancient nomenclature of words and phrases, which once constituted the science of metaphysics.

3d. The publication of systems and discoveries in medicine

in the Latin language. Our science is interesting to all mankind; but by locking it up in a dead language, which is but partially known, we have prevented its associating with other sciences, and precluded it from attracting the notice and support of ingenious men of other professions. While the study of chemistry was confined exclusively to physicians, it was limited in its objects, and nearly destitute of principles. It was from the laboratories of private gentlemen, and particularly of Priestley, Cavendish, and Lavoisier, that those great discoveries have issued, which have exalted chemistry to its present rank and usefulness among the sciences. The same remark applied to agriculture and manufactures, while they were carried on by the daily labor of men who derived their subsistence from them. It is only since they have become a part of the studies and employment of speculative men of general knowledge, that they constitute the basis of individual and national prosperity and independence.

4th. An undue attachment to great names. Hippocrates, Galen, and Aræteus, among the ancients; Boerhaave, Cullen, and Brown, among the moderns, have all, in their turns, established a despotism in medicine, by the popularity of their names, which has imposed a restraint upon free inquiry, and thereby checked the progress of medicine, particularly in the ages and countries, in which they have lived.

5th. An undue attachment to unsuccessful, but fashionable, modes of practice. Where a medicine does not generally cure a disease, in its recent state, it is either an improper remedy, or it is given at an improper time, or in an improper quantity. In such cases, a mode of practice, directly opposed to the former one, has sometimes proved successful. This occurred in a remarkable manner, when cool air and cold drinks succeeded the hot regimen, in the treatment of the smallpox. The same happy effects have attended the use of bleeding in the inflammatory state of the dropsy, after stimulating medicines had been give to cure it, for many years to no purpose.

6th. Indolence and credulity in admitting things to be true, without sufficient examination. The acrid humors of Boerhaave would not have prevailed so long in our systems of pathology, had the blood been sooner subjected to a natural and chemical analysis, nor would a belief in the specific nature of the plague, or the competency of quarantines to prevent the importation of the yellow fever, have been so universal, in the beginning of the nineteenth century, had the facts, which are numerous and plain upon those subjects, received a faithful and candid investigation.

7th. Neglect in recording the rise, progress, and symptoms of epidemic diseases, and of certain circumstances essentially connected with them. The loss which our science has sustained from the want of regular and connected histories of epidemics, may be estimated by the value of the knowledge which it has gained from the writings of Ballonius and Riverius in France, and of Sydenham, Wintringham, and Huxham, in Great Britain. The yellow fever has prevailed, in this city, four times between the years 1699 and 1793, and yet no history of its origin, symptoms, or treatment, has been left to us by any of the physicians who witnessed it, nor is there any record but one, of the times of its appearance, to be found, except in the letter-books of merchants, and in ancient newspapers. Had our ancestors in medicine transmitted to us the history of that epidemic, with an account of the diseases which preceded it, and of the changes in the air, and in the animal and vegetable kingdoms, with which it was accompanied, it is probable, we might have predicted the malignant constitution of the atmosphere that produced the fevers of 1793, and of subsequent years, and by removing the filth of our cities, have thereby prevented them. Upon this subject, it may be added, that it is by studying diseases as they have appeared, in different countries, and in different years, that we shall be able to understand and cure them, much better than by reading abstract treatises upon them in systems of medicine, in which no notice is taken of their relations to time and place. Dr. Cleghorn's Account of the Diseases of Minorca, has outlived many hundred publications upon the diseases which he has described. Such excellent books owe their duration and fame to the difference which they mark in the symptoms and mode of cure of diseases in different countries, and in successive years. Even the signs of life and death, are varied by both those circumstances. In a malignant fever, which prevailed at Cuneum, in the years 1778, and 1784, a mortification in the extremity of the spine and buttocks, was always the sign of a recovery; while the same symptom as uniformly preceded death, in a fever which prevailed at Modena, in the year 1781.* I shall mention several other instances of the same signs being followed by an opposite issue in different years, in the late pestilential epidemic of our country.

8th. Neglect to record *minute* symptoms in the history of diseases. Hippocrates and Sydenham are justly exempted from this charge against our profession. Had their method of examining and describing diseases been generally followed, we should not, this day, complain of so much imperfection in our science. A disease is a lawless evil. To understand its nature from its symptoms, it should be inspected every hour of the day and night. It is, during the latter period, fevers most frequently have their exacerbations and remissions; and it is only by accommodating our remedies to them, that the practice of medicine can become regular and successful. How much is to be learned from sitting up with sick people, may be known from conversing with sensible nurses. I have profited by their remarks; and I have often imposed their duties upon my pupils, in order, among other things, to increase their knowledge of diseases.

9th. The neglect to discriminate between the remote and exciting causes of diseases. Under the influence of this negligence, the death of many persons from the miasmata which produce the yellow fever, has often been ascribed to the full meal, the intoxicating draught, the long walk, or the night air, which excited them into action.

10th. The neglect to ascertain the nature, and strength of

---

* Burserus, p. 497.

diseases by the pulse, or an exclusive reliance upon its frequency for that purpose, and that too only in morbid affections of the sanguiferous system.

11th. The neglect to employ the passions as remedies in the cure of diseases. An accidental paroxysm of joy, fear, or anger, has often induced a sudden and favourable crisis in cases of doubtful issue. Quacks owe a great deal of their occasional success, to their command over the feelings of their patients. The advantages to be derived from them might be an hundred times greater, were they properly directed by regular bred physicians.

12th. An undue reliance upon the powers of nature in curing diseases. I have elsewere endeavoured to expose this superstition in medicine, and shall in another place, mention some additional facts to show its extensive mischief in our science.

13th. The practice among physicians of waiting till diseases have evolved their specific characters before they prescribe for them, thus allowing them time to form those effusions, and obstructions, which frequently produce immediate death, or a train of chronic complaints.

14th. The great and unnecessary number of medicines which are used for the cure of diseases. Did we prescribe more for their state, and less for their name, a fourth part of the medicines now in use, would be sufficient for all the purposes intended by them. By thus limiting their number, we should acquire a more perfect knowledge of their virtues and doses, and thereby exhibit them with more success.

15th. The exhibition of medicines, without a due regard to the different stages of diseases. Bark, opium, and mercury, are remedies, or poisons, according as they are accommodated, or not, to the existing state of the system. The same may be said of many of the most simple articles in the materia medica. Bathing the feet in warm water, often prevents a fever in its forming state. The same remedy, when used after the fever is formed, often induces delirium, and other symptoms of a dangerous and alarming nature.

16th. An exclusive dependence upon some one medicine, or one class of remedies. Bleeding, purges, and vomits, sweating medicines, hot and cold water, ice and snow, baths of different kinds, opium and bark, crude quicksilver, and calomel, iron and copper, acids and alkalies, lime and tar water, fixed air and oxygen, have all been used separately by physicians, in diseases which required in their occasional changes, the successive application of many different medicines of opposite virtues, or a variety of the same class of medicines. This exclusive attachment to one set of remedies, has not been confined to individual physicians. Whole nations are as much distinguished by it, as they are by language and manners. In England, cordial and sweating medicines; in France, bleeding, injections, and diluting drinks; in Germany, alterative medicines; in Italy, cups and leeches, in Russia, hot and cold baths; and in China, frictions; constitute the predominating and fashionable remedies in all their respective diseases.

17th. The neglect to inquire after, and record, cures which have been performed by time, by accident, or by medicines, administered by quacks, or by the friends of sick people. By examining the precise condition of the system, and stage of diseases, in which such remedies have produced their salutary effects, and afterwards regulating them by principles, great additions might have been made to our stock of medical knowledge.

18th. The neglect to dissect, and examine, morbid bodies after death, and where this has been done, mistaking the effects, for the causes of diseases.

19th. The attempts which have been made to establish regular modes of practice in medicine, upon experience without reasoning, and upon reasoning without experience.

20th. The dependent state of physicians, upon public opinion for their subsistence. It is this which has checked innovation in the practice of medicine, and too often made physicians the apothecaries of their patients. To a dependence of our profession upon commerce, we are in part to ascribe the belief of the importation of pestilential diseases in nearly all the large cities in Europe and America.

21st. The interference of governments in prohibiting the use of certain remedies, and inforcing the use of others by law. The effect of this mistaken policy has been as hurtful to medicine, as a similar practice with respect to opinions, has been to the Christian religion.

22d. Conferring exclusive privileges upon bodies of physicians, and forbidding men, of equal talents and knowledge, under severe penalties, from practising medicine within certain districts of cities and countries. Such institutions, however sanctioned by ancient charters and names, are the bastiles of our science.

23d. The refusal in universities to tolerate any opinions, in the private or public exercises of candidates for degrees in medicine, which are not taught nor believed by their professors, thus restraining a spirit of inquiry in that period of life which is most distinguished for ardour and invention in our science It was from a view of the prevalence of this conduct, that Dr. Adam Smith, has called universities the "dull repositories of exploded opinions." I am happy in being able to exempt the university of Pennsylvania, from this charge. Candidates for degrees are here not only permitted to controvert the opinions of their teachers, but to publish their own, provided they discover learning and ingenuity in defending them.

24th. The last cause I shall mention, which has retarded the progress of medicine, is the division of diseases into genera and species by means of what has lately received the name of nosology. Upon this part of our subject, I shall be more particular than was necessary, under any of the former heads of our lecture, for no one of the causes, which have been assigned of the imperfection of our science, has operated with more effect than the nosological arrangement of diseases. To expose its unfriendly influence upon medicine, it will be proper first to repeat in part, what I have published in the fourth volume of my Inquiries and Observations, before I proceed to mention the manner of its operation.

1st. Nosology presupposes the characters of diseases to be as fixed as the characters of animals and plants: but this is far from being the case. Animals and plants are exactly the same in all their properties, that they were nearly six thousand years ago, but who can say the same thing of any one disease? They are all changed by time and still more by climate, and a great variety of accidental circumstances. But the same morbid state of the system often assumes in the course of a few days, all the symptoms of a dozen different genera of diseases. Thus a malignant fever frequently invades every part of the body, and is at once, or in succession, an epitome of the whole class of prexiæ in Dr. Cullen's Synopsis.

2d. The nosological arrangement of diseases has been attempted from their causes and seats. The remote causes of diseases all unite in producing but one effect, that is irritation and morbid excitement, and of course are incapable of division. The proximate cause of diseases, is an unit; for whether it appears in the form of convulsion, spasm, a prostration of action, heat, or itching, it is alike the effect of simple diseased excitement. The impracticability of dividing diseases into genera and species, from their seats, will appear when we consider the feeble state of sensibility in some of the internal organs, and the want of connexion between impression and sensation in others; by which means there is often a total absence of the sign of pain, or a deceitful and capricious translation of it to another part of the body, in many diseases. In the most acute stage of inflammation in the stomach, there is frequently no pain, vomiting, nor sickness. The liver in the East Indies, undergoes a general suppuration, and sometimes a partial destruction, without pain, or any of the common signs of local inflammation. Dr. Chisholm, in his essay upon the malignant West India fever, mentions its fatal issue in two sailors whom he dissected: in one of whom he discovered great marks of inflammation in the lungs, and in the other, a mortification of the right kidney; but in neither of them, he adds, was perceived the least sign of disease in those viscera, during their sickness.* Baglivi found a stone in the kidney of a man who had complained of a pain only in the kidney of the opposite side, during his life. I have lost two patients with abscesses in the lungs, who complained only of a pain in the head. Neither of them had a cough, and one of them had never felt any pain in his breast or sides. Many hundred facts of a similar nature, are to be met with in the records of medicine. Even in those cases where impression does not produce sensations in remote parts of the body, it is often so diffused by means of what has been happily called, by Dr. Johnson, "an intercommunion of sensation," that the precise seat of a disease is seldom known. The affections of the bowels and brain furnish many proofs of the truth of this observation.

Errors in theory, seldom fail of producing errors in practice. Nosology has retarded the progress of medicine in the following ways.

1st. It precludes all the advantages which are to be derived from attacking diseases, in their forming state, at which time they are devoid of their nosological characters, and are most easily and certainly prevented or cured.

2d. It has led physicians to prescribe exclusively for the names of diseases, without a due regard to the condition of the system. This practice has done the most extensive mischief, where a malignant or inflammatory constitution of the atmosphere has produced a single or predominating epidemic, which calls for the same class of remedies, under all the modifications which are produced by difference in its seat, and exciting causes.

3d. It multiplies unnecessarily the articles of the materia medica, by employing nearly as many medicines, as there are forms of disease.

I know it has been said, that by rejecting nosology, we establish indolence in medicine, but the reverse of this assertion

---

* Vol. i. p. 184.

is true; for if our prescriptions are to be regulated chiefly by the force of morbid excitement, and if this force be varied in acute diseases by a hundred different circumstances, even by a cloud, according to Dr. Lining, lessening, for a few minutes, the light and heat of the sun, it follows, that the utmost watchfulness and skill will be necessary to accommodate our remedies to the changing state of the system.

I have thus, gentlemen, briefly pointed out the principal causes which have retarded the progress of our science. It remains now, that I mention the means of promoting its certainty and greater usefulness. It will readily occur, that this is to be done, by avoiding all the causes, which have produced its present state of imperfection. I shall select, from those causes, a few that have been hinted at only, and which, from their importance, require further amplification.

1st. Let us strip our profession of every thing that looks like mystery and imposture, and clothe medical knowledge in a dress so simple and intelligible, that it may become a part of academical education in all our seminaries of learning Truth is simple upon all subjects, but upon those which are essential to the general happiness of mankind, it is obvious to the meanest capacities. There is no man so simple, that cannot be taught to cultivate grain, and no woman so devoid of understanding, as to be incapable of learning the art of making that grain into bread. And shall the means of preserving our health by the culture and preparation of aliment, be so intelligible, and yet the means of restoring it, when lost, be so abstruse, as to require years of study to discover and apply them? To suppose this, is to call in question the goodness of the Supreme Being, and to believe that he acts without unity and system in all his works. In no one of the acts of man do we behold more weakness and error, than in our present modes of education. We teach our sons words, at the expense of things. We teach them what was done two thousand years ago, and conceal from them what is doing every day. We instruct them in the heathen mythology, but neglect to teach them the principles of the religion of their country. We teach them to predict eclipses, and the return of comets, from which no physical advantages worth naming, have ever been derived; but we give them no instruction in the signs which precede general and individual diseases. How long shall the human mind bend beneath the usages of ancient and barbarous times? When shall we cease to be mere scholars, and become wise philosophers, well informed citizens, and useful men?

The essential principles of medicine are very few. They are moreover plain. There is not a graduate in the arts, in any of our colleges, who does not learn things of more difficulty, than a system of just principles in medicine.

All the morbid effects of heat and cold, of intemperance in eating and drinking, and in the exercises of the body and mind, might be taught with as much ease as the multiplication table.

All the knowledge which is attainable of diseases by the pulse, might be acquired at a less expense of time and labor, than is spent in committing the contents of the Latin grammar to memory.

The operation of bleeding, might be taught with less trouble than is taken to teach boys to draw, upon paper or slate, the figures in Euclid.

A knowledge of the virtues and doses of the most active and useful medicines, might be acquired with greater facility, and much more pleasure, than the rules for composing syllogisms laid down in our systems of logic.

In support of the truth of the opinions I am now advancing, let us take a view of the effects of the simplicity, which has been introduced into the art of war, by one of the nations of Europe. A few obvious principles have supplied the place of volumes upon tactics; and private citizens have become greater generals, and peasants more irresistible soldiers in a few weeks, than their predecessors in war were, after the instruction and experience of fifteen or twenty years. Could changes equally simple and general be introduced by means of our schools into the practice of medicine, no arithmetic could calculate its advantages. Millions of lives would be saved by it.

In thus recommending the general diffusion of medical knowledge, by making it a part of an academical education, let it not be supposed that I wish to see the exercise of medicine abolished as a regular profession. Casualties which render operations in surgery necessary, and such diseases as occur rarely, will always require professional aid; but the knowledge that is necessary for these purposes may be soon acquired; and two or three persons, separated from other pursuits, would be sufficient to apply it to a city consisting of forty thousand people.

2d. To promote the certainty and greater usefulness of our science, let us study the premonitory signs of diseases, and apply our remedies to them, before they are completely formed. At this time they generally yield to the most simple and common domestic medicines, for there is the same difference between their force, in their forming state, and after they have put forth their strength in the reaction of the system, that there is between the strength of an infant, and of a full grown man. This important truth has been long, and deeply impressed upon my mind, and many of you can witness, that I have often recommended it to your attention. To all physical evils I believe there are certain precursors, which if known and attended to, in due time, would enable us to obviate them. Premonitory signs I am sure occur before all diseases. They are most evident in fevers, in the gout, in apoplexy, epilepsy, melancholy, and madness. They even obtrude themselves upon our notice, as if to demand the remedies which are proper to arrest the impending commotions in the system. This is more obviously the case in those diseases, which, when formed, are difficult to cure. In one of my publications in the year 1793, I asserted, that the yellow fever was as much under the power of medicine as the influenza, or an intermitting fever. This was strictly true in the beginning of the epidemic of that year, and continued to be so, until a belief in the prevalence of a fever of less danger, produced delays in sending for physicians, or negligence in using the simple remedies that were recommended in the forming state of the reigning epidemic. In our lectures upon the practice of physic, I shall mention those remedies, and shall repeat to you the importance of watching the exact time in which they may be exhibited with safety and success.

3d. Let our inquiries be directed with peculiar industry and zeal, to complete the natural and morbid history of the pulse. It is the string which vibrates most readily with discordant motions in every part of the body. Were I allowed to coin a word, I would call the pulse the *nosometer* of the system. There is the same difference in the knowledge of diseases which is obtained by it, and by their other signs, that there is between speech, and inarticulate sounds. The eyes and countenance cannot always be inspected, without exposing sick people to pain and danger from the irritation of light. The tongue cannot be seen in children, nor in the delirium of a fever. Its appearance moreover is liable to be so changed by aliment and drinks as to obliterate the effect of diseases upon it. It is often unsafe to preserve the excretions, and when examined, they afford uncertain marks of the state of the system. None of these objections apply to the pulse. It can be felt in persons of all ages, at all times of the day and night, and in all diseases, and always without any inconvenience to a patient. I shall shortly lay before you the facts and reasonings which have been the result of my observations upon it. They are as yet limited, and very imperfect, but they will serve, I hope, like a distant view of a new and fertile country, to excite your desires to explore it, and to add its products to the treasures of medicine.

The fourth and last means of promoting certainty in medicine, and its more extensive usefulness, is to cherish a belief, that they are both attainable and practicable. "Knowledge" it has been justly said, "is power, and philosophy, the empire of art over nature." By means of the knowledge which has lately been obtained, men now visit the upper regions of the air and the bottom of the ocean, as if they were a part of their original territory. Distance and time have likewise become subject to their power, by the invention of instruments for accelerating the communication of new and important events. Equally great, and far more interesting have been the triumphs of medicine within the last thirty years. Fevers have been deprived of their mortality by attacking them in their forming state; and where this has not been done, they have been made to yield to depleting, or tonic remedies, where they have been properly timed. The smallpox has been disarmed of its remnant of power over human life, by means of vaccine inoculation. But medicine has lately done more. It has discovered those fevers, which have desolated cities and countries, to be derived, in all cases, from putrid and local exhalations, and that they are propagated only by a morbid constitution of the atmosphere. It is true, this discovery has not been generally admitted, but the error, which is opposed to it, has received a blow from the publications of our countrymen, Dr. Mitchell, Dr. Miller and Mr. Webster, from which it cannot recover. Its total destruction will be followed by the same extinction of pestilence, which commerce has produced of famine in Europe, by the level it has introduced of the means of subsistence. The gout, dropsies, hemorrhages, pulmonary consumption, are now cured, when they are treated as symptoms of general fever. Cancers are easily prevented, by the extirpation of tumors in glandular parts of the body. The tetanus has seldom resisted the efficacy of stimulating medicines, where an exclusive reliance has not been had upon any one of them. But modern discoveries have not stopped here. They have taught us to renew the motions of life, where they appeared to be extinguished by death. Hitherto, resuscitation has been confined only to persons, who have been supposed to be dead from drowning, or from other accidents; but the time, I believe, will come, when the labours of science and humanity will be employed in recovering persons, who appear to die from other causes. We are authorized to adopt this opinion by the late discovery of the causes of animal life, and by the light which the external and internal appearances of the body after death from fevers, has thrown upon this subject. Motion, which is one of the operations of life, certainly continues, after persons, who have had fevers, are supposed to be dead. This is evident, in the accumulation of heat in particular parts of the body, in the absorption and diffusion of stagnating fluids, in the change of the countenance from a gloomy, to a placid form, in the occasional appearance of a red colour in one, or in both the cheeks, and in the sudden diffusion of a yellow colour over the whole or a part of the body, in persons who die of malignant bilious fevers. But this motion in the external surface of the body has gone much further. Sweats have been observed to take place for many hours, and in one instance, several days after death, from the maniacal state of fever. The stiffness of the limbs, which so soon succeeds death, is probably, in many cases, the effect of general convulsion, and may hereafter be discovered to be nothing but a chronic spasm of the muscular system. The internal appearances of the body after death, from fevers, still more favour the idea of the possibility of extending the means of resuscitation with success to persons supposed to be dead from those diseases. I shall hereafter teach you, that death from a fever, is induced by one or more of the three following causes.

1st. The disorganization of parts essential to life, by means of great excess of morbid excitement, by congestion, inflammation, or mortification.

2d. By such a change in the fluids, as renders them unfit for the purposes of life.

3d. By the exhausted state of the excitability, and excitement of the system, which renders it incapable of being acted upon by the stimulus of medicine. Death, from the two last causes, rarely occurs in acute fevers, which terminate in less than eleven days. Dissections show some viscus to be in a state of disorganization, nearly in all cases; but this disorganization is often of so partial a nature, as to beget a presumption that it might have been removed by the usual remedies for resuscitation. Where life has appeared to be extinguished by the *sudden* loss of excitement or expenditure of excitability, I believe those remedies might often be employed with success. Such cases probably occur, where patients appear to die in the paroxysm of an intermittent, or under the operation of drastic vomits and purges.

From a review of what has been lately effected by our science, I cannot help admitting with Dr. Hartley, that in that happy period, predicted in the Old and New Testaments, when religion shall combine its influence upon the passions and conduct of men, with fresh discoveries in medicine, Christian Missionaries shall procure the same credit, and kind reception among Pagan and Savage nations, by curing diseases by natural means, which the Apostles obtained by curing them by supernatural power. Yes, the time, I believe, will come, when, from the perfection of our science, men shall be so well acquainted with the method of destroying poisons, that they "shall tread upon scorpions and serpents" without being injured by them.* And mothers, from their knowledge and use of the same antidotes, shall cease to restrain "a sucking child from playing on the hole of the asp, and the weaned child from putting his hand on the cockatrice's den." † Suspended animation, if it should occur in that enlightened state of the world, shall no more expose the subjects of it to premature interment. Pestilential diseases shall then cease to spread terror and death over half the globe; for interest and prejudice shall no longer oppose the removal of the obvious and offensive causes which produce them. Lazarettos shall likewise cease to be the expensive and inhuman monuments of error and folly, in medicine and in government. Hospitals shall be unknown. The groans of pain, the ravings of madness, and the sighs of melancholy shall be heard no more. The cradle and the tomb shall no longer be related; for old age shall then be universal. Long, long before this revolution in the health and happiness of mankind shall arrive, you, and I gentlemen, must sleep with our fathers in the silent grave. But a consolation is still left to us under the pressure of this reflection. If we cannot share in the happiness we have destined for our posterity, we can

---
* Luke, x. xix.
† Isaiah, xi. viii.

contribute to produce it. For this purpose let us attempt a voyage of circumnavigation in medicine, by resurveying all its branches in their connexion with each other. Let no part, nor function of the body, and no law of the animal economy, escape a second investigation. Let all the remote causes of diseases, and above all, let the resources of our profession in the materia medica, be subjected to fresh examinations. It is probable many new remedies remain yet to be discovered; but most of the old ones demand new experiments and observations to determine their doses and efficacy. It is impossible to say how much the certainty of medicine might be promoted, and its usefulness increased, by a more extensive knowledge of the times, place, manner, and means of depletion, by abstracting heat from the body by means of water and ice, as well as air, and applying it by means of vapour, air, oil, salt, sand, and clay, as well as by water; by frictions impregnated with medicinal substances; by the application of stimuli to the skin and lower bowels where they cannot be retained, or after they have been ineffectually administered through the medium of the stomach; by new modes of exercise and labour, and more specific times of using them, by means of rest; by changes of air, climate, and pursuits in life; by diet, by the quality of clothing and forms of dress, by artificial sleep and wakefulness; by pleasure and pain; by simplicity, composition, succession, and rotation, in the use of chronic medicines; and by the extension of the operations of the mind to the cure of diseases. But in vain shall we enlarge our knowledge of all the remedies that have been mentioned; nay more, to no purpose would an antediluvian age be employed in collecting facts upon all the different branches of medicine, unless they can be connected and applied by principles of some kind. Observation without principles is nothing but empiricism: and however much the contradictions and uncertainty of theories may be complained of, I believe much greater uncertainty and contradictions will be found in the controversies among physicians concerning what are said to be facts, and that too upon subjects in which the senses alone are employed to judge between truth and error. It is by means of principles in medicine, that a physician can practise with safety to his patients, and satisfaction to himself. They impart caution and boldness alternately to his prescriptions, and supply the want of experience in all new cases. Between such a physician, and the man who relies exclusively upon experience, there is the same difference that there was between Sir Isaac Newton, after he completed his discoveries in light and colours, and the artist who manufactured the glasses, by which that illustrious philosopher exemplified his principles in optics. After this account of the necessity and advantages of principles in medicine, you will not be surprised, gentlemen, at my declaring, that both duty and inclination unite to determine me to teach them from this chair. I know from experience, the consequences of contending, in this work, with ancient prejudices and popular names in medicine, with abilities greatly inferior to the contest. But I have not laboured in vain. If I have not removed any part of the rubbish which surrounded the fabric of our science, nor suggested any thing better in its place, I feel a consolation in believing, that I have taught many of your predecessors to do both, by exciting in them a spirit of inquiry, and a disposition to controvert old and doubtful opinions, by the test of experiments. I have only to request you to imitate their example. Think, read, and observe. Observe, read, and think, for yourselves.

OBSERVATIONS AND REASONING IN MEDICINE
A Lecture

PHYSICIANS HAVE been divided into empirics and dogmatists. The former pretend to be guided by experience, and the latter by reasoning alone in their prescriptions. I object to both when separately employed. They lead alike to error and danger in the practice of physic. I shall briefly point out the evils which result from an exclusive reliance upon each of them.

1. Empiricism presupposes a correct and perfect knowledge of all the diseases of the human body, however varied they may be in their symptoms, seats, and force, by age, habit, sex, climate, season, and aliment. Now, it is well known, that the longest life is insufficient for the purpose of acquiring that knowledge. This will appear more evident, when we consider that it must be seated, exclusively, in the memory; a faculty which is the most subject to decay, and the least faithful to us of any of the faculties of the mind. Few physicians, I believe, ever recollect, perfectly, the phenomena of any disease more than two years, and, perhaps, for a much shorter time, when they are engaged in extensive business.

2. Neither can the defect of experience, nor the decay, or weakness of the memory in one physician, be supplied by the experience and observations of others. Few men see the same objects through the same medium. How seldom do we find the histories of the same disease, or of the effects of the same medicine to agree, even when they are related by physicians of the

most respectable characters for talents and integrity! An hundred circumstances, from the difference of treatment, produce a difference in the symptoms and issue of similar diseases, and in the operation of the same medicines. The efforts of nature, are, moreover, often mistaken for the effects of a favourite prescription; and, in some instances, the crisis of a disease has been ascribed to medicines which have been thrown out of a window, or emptied behind a fire.

3. If it were possible to obviate all the inconveniences and dangers from solitary experience which have been mentioned, an evil would arise from the nature of the human mind, which would defeat all the advantages that might be expected from it. This evil is a disposition to reason upon all medical subjects, without being qualified by education for that purpose. As well might we attempt to control the motions of the heart by the action of the will, as to suspend, for a moment, that operation of the mind, which consists in drawing inferences from facts. To observe, is to think, and to think, is to reason in medicine. Hence we find theories in the writings of the most celebrated practical physicians, even of those who preface their works by declaiming against idle and visionary speculations in our science; but, I will add, further, that I believe no empiric ever gave a medicine without cherishing a theoretical indication of cure in his mind. Some acrid humour is to be obtunded, some viscid fluid is to be thinned, some spasm is to be resolved, or debility in some part of the body is to be obviated, in all his prescriptions. To an exclusive reliance upon theory in medicine, there are an equal number of objections. I shall only mention a few of them.

1. Our imperfect knowledge of the structure of the human body, and of the laws of the animal economy.

2. The limited extent of the human understanding, which acquires truth too slowly to act with effect, in the numerous and rapid exigencies of diseases.

3. The influence of the imagination and passions, upon the understanding in its researches after truth. An opinion becomes

dear to us by being generated in our imaginations; and contradiction, by inflaming the passions, increases our attachment to error. It is for these reasons, we observe great, and even good men, so zealously devoted to their opinions, and the practice founded upon them, even after they have been exposed and refuted by subsequent discoveries in medicine.

From this view of the comparative insufficiency of experience and theory, in our science, it will be impossible to decide in favour of either of them in their separate states. The empirics and dogmatists have mutually charged each other with the want of successful practice. I believe them both, and will add, further, if an inventory of the mischief that has been done by empirics, within the present century, whether they acted under the cover of a diploma, or imposed upon the public by false and pompous advertisements, could be made out, and compared with the mischief which has been done by a practice in medicine, founded upon a belief in the archeus of Van Helmont, the anima medica of Stahl, the spasm of Hoffman, the morbid acrimonies of Boerhaave, the putrefaction of Cullen, and the debility of Brown, as the proximate causes of diseases, I am satisfied neither sect would have any cause of exultation, or triumph. Both would have more reason to lament the immense additions they have made to pestilence and the sword in their ravages upon the human race.

It is peculiar to man, to divide what was intended by the Author of nature to be indivisible. Religion and morals, government and liberty, nay, even reason and the senses, so happily paired by the Creator of the world, in the order in which they have been mentioned, have each been disunited by the caprice and folly of man. The evils which have arisen from this breach in the symmetry of the divine government cannot now be enumerated. It belongs to our present subject, only to take notice that the same hostile disposition in the human mind, to order and utility, appears in the attempts that have been made to separate experience and reasoning in medicine. They are necessarily united, and it is only by preserving and cultivating their union, that our science can be made to convey extensive and lasting blessings to mankind.

The necessity of combining theory and practice in medicine, may be illustrated, by the advantages which other sciences have derived from the union of principles and facts. The numerous benefits and pleasures we enjoy from the glasses which have been made use of to extend our vision to distant and minute objects, are the results of a knowledge of the principles of optics. The many useful inventions which are employed to shorten and facilitate labor, are the products of a knowledge of the principles of mechanics and hydraulics. The exploits of mariners in subduing the ocean, and all the benefits that have occurred to the world from the connection of the extremities of our globe by means of commerce, are the fruits of a knowledge in the principles of navigation. Equally great have been the advantages of theory in the science of medicine. It belongs to theory to accumulate facts, and hence we find the greatest stock of them is always possessed by speculative physicians. While simple observation may be compared to a power which creates an alphabet, theory resembles a power which arranges all its component parts in such a manner, as to produce words and ideas. But theory does more. It supplies in a great degree the place of experience, and thereby places youth and old age nearly upon a footing in the profession of medicine; for, with just principles, it is no more necessary for a young physician to see all the diseases of the human body before he prescribes for them, than it is for a mariner, who knows the principles of navigation, to visit all the ports in the world, in order to conduct his vessel in safety to them.

To illustrate still further the benefits of theory, I shall take notice of its influence upon the use of several celebrated and popular remedies.

Accident probably first suggested the use of cool air in the cure of fevers. For many years it was prescribed indiscriminately in every form and grade of those diseases, during which time it did as much harm as good. It was not until chemistry taught us that its good effects depended wholly upon its abstracting the heat of the body, that its application was limited to those fevers only, which are accompanied with preternatural heat, and excessive action in the blood-vessels. Since the use of cool air has been regulated by this principle, its effects have been uniformly salutary in inflammatory fevers.

While the Peruvian bark was believed to act as a specific in the cure of intermittents, it was often an ineffectual, and sometimes a destructive medicine, but since its tonic and astringent virtues have been ascertained, its injurious effects have been restrained, and its salutary operation extended to all those fevers, whether intermitting, remitting, or continual, in which a feeble morbid action takes place in the sanguiferous system.

Opium was formerly used only as an antidote to wakefulness and pain, during which time it often increased the danger and mortality of diseases; but since its stimulating virtues have been discovered, its exhibition has been regulated by the degree of excitement in the system, and hence it is now administered with uniform safety, or success.

Mercury was prescribed empirically for many years in the cure of several diseases, in which it often did great mischief, but since it has been discovered to act as a general stimulant and evacuant, such a ratio has been established between it, and the state of diseases, as to render it a safe and nearly an universal medicine.

In answer to what has been delivered in favor of the union of experience and reasoning in medicine, it has been said, that the most celebrated physicians, in all ages, have been empirics, among whom they class Hippocrates and Sydenham. This charge against the illustrious fathers of ancient and modern medicine is not just, for they both reasoned upon the causes, symptoms, and cure of diseases; and their works contain more theory, than is to be met with in many of the most popular systems of medicine. Their theories, it is true, are in many instances erroneous; but they were restrained from perverting their judgments, and impairing the success of their practice, by their great experience, and singular talents for extensive and accurate observation. This defence of Hippocrates and Sydenham does not apply to common empirics. They cure only by chance, for, by false reasoning, they detract from the advantages of their solitary experience. It is true, they often acquire reputation and wealth, but this must be ascribed to the credulity of their patients, and to the zeal with which they justify their preference of such physicians, by multiplying and exaggerating their cures, or by palliating, or denying their mistakes. It is for this reason that it has been well said, "Quacks are the greatest liars in the world, except their patients."

We are further told, in favour of empiricism, that physicians of the first character have acknowledged the fallacy of principles in medicine. I cannot assent to the truth of this assertion. It is contradicted by the history of our science in all ages and countries. The complaints of its fallacy, and even of its uncertainty, originate, I believe, in most cases, in ignorance, indolence, or imposture; and therefore were never uttered by men of eminence and integrity in our profession.

In the progress of medicine towards its present state of improvement, different theories or systems have been proposed by different authors. You will find a minute and entertaining account of such of them as have been handed down to us from antiquity in Dr. Black's History of Medicine. They are all necessarily imperfect, inasmuch as none of them embraces the numerous discoveries in anatomy, physiology, chemistry, materia medica, and natural philosophy, which have been made within the two last centuries in Europe. The systems which divide the physicians of the present day, are those of Dr. Stahl, Dr. Boerhaave, Dr. Cullen, and Dr. Brown.

1. Dr. Stahl lived and wrote in a country remarkable for the simplicity of the manners of its inhabitants. Their diseases partook of their temperate mode of living, and were often cured by the operations of nature, without the aid of medicine; hence arose Dr. Stahl's opinion of the vires naturæ medicatrices, or of the existence of an anima medica, whose business it was to watch over the health of the body. We shall show, therefore,

the error of these supposed healing powers in nature, and the extreme danger of trusting to them in the dangerous and complicated diseases, which are produced by the artificial customs of civilized life.

2. Dr. Boerhaave lived and wrote in a country in which a moist atmosphere, and an excessive quantity of unwholesome aliment, had produced an immense number of diseases of the skin. These were supposed to arise from an impure state of the blood, and hence lentor, tenuity, and acrimony in that fluid were supposed to be the proximate causes of all the diseases of the human body.

3. Dr. Cullen lived and wrote in a country in which indolence and luxury had let loose a train of diseases which appeared to be seated chiefly in the nervous system, and hence we find the laws of that system have been investigated and ascertained by him with a success which has no parallel in the annals of medicine. In his concentrated views of the nervous system he has overlooked, or but slightly glanced at the pathology of the bloodvessels, and by adopting the nosology of Sauvage, Linnæus, and Vogel, he has unfortunately led physicians to prescribe for the names of diseases, instead of their proximate cause.

4. In the system of Dr. Brown, we find clear and consistent views of the causes of animal life, also just opinions of the action of heat and cold, of stimulating, and what are called sedative medicines, and of the influence of the passions in the production and cure of diseases. But while he has thus shed light upon some parts of medicine, he has thrown a shade upon others. I shall hereafter take notice of all the errors of his system. At present I shall only say, I shall not admit with him, debility to be a disease. It is only its predisposing cause. Disease consists in morbid excitement, and is always of a partial nature: of course I shall reject his doctrine of equality of excitement in the morbid states of the body, and maintain, that the cure of diseases consists simply in restoring the equal and natural diffusion of excitement throughout every part of the system. If Dr. Cullen did

harm by directing the attention of physicians, by means of his nosology, only to the names of diseases, how much more mischief has been done by Dr. Brown, by reducing them nearly to one class, and accommodating his prescriptions to the reverse state of the body, of that which constitutes their proximate cause.

A perfect system of medicine may be compared to a house, the different stories of which have been erected by different architects. The illustrious physicians who have been named, have a large claim upon our gratitude, for having, by their great, and successive labours, advanced the building to its present height. It belongs to the present and future generations to place a roof upon it, and thereby to complete the fabric of medicine.

In the following course of lectures I shall adopt such principles of Dr. Boerhaave, Dr. Cullen, and Dr. Brown, as I believe to be true, and shall add to them such others, as have been suggested to me, by my own observations and reflections.

If, in delivering new opinions, I should be so unfortunate as to teach any thing, which subsequent reflection or observation should discover to be erroneous, I shall publicly retract it. I am aware how much I shall suffer by this want of stability in error, but I have learned from one of my masters to "esteem truth the only knowledge, and that laboring to defend an error, is only striving to be more ignorant." *

Upon those parts of our course on which I am unable to deliver principles, I shall lay before you a simple detail of facts. Our labor in this business will not be lost, for, however long those facts may appear to lie in a confused and solitary state, they will sooner or later unite in that order and relation to each other which was established at the creation of the world. From this union of prerelated truths, will arise, as some future period, a complete system of principles in medicine.

We live, gentlemen, in a revolutionary age. Our science has caught the spirit of the times, and more improvements have been

---

* The Rev. Dr. Samuel Finley many years master of a large academy in Nottingham in Maryland, and afterwards President of the College of New-Jersey.

made in all its branches, within the last twenty years, than had been made in a century before. From these events, so auspicious to medicine, may we not cherish a hope, that our globe is about to undergo those happy changes, which shall render it a more safe and agreeable abode to man, and thereby prepare it to receive the blessing of universal health and longevity; for premature deaths seem to have arisen from the operation of that infinite goodness which delivers from evils to come.

MEDICINE AMONG THE INDIANS OF NORTH AMERICA

A Discussion

~~~~~~

You will readily anticipate the difficulty of doing justice to this subject. How shall we distinguish between the original diseases of the Indians and those contracted from their intercourse with the Europeans? By what arts shall we persuade them to discover their remedies? And lastly, how shall we come at the knowledge of facts in that cloud of errors, in which the credulity of the Europeans, and the superstition of the Indians have involved both their diseases and remedies? These difficulties serve to increase the importance of our subject. If I should not be able to solve them, perhaps I may lead the way to more successful endeavours for that purpose.

I shall first limit the tribes of Indians who are to be the objects of this inquiry, to those who inhabit that part of North America which extends from the 30th to the 60th degree of latitude. When we exclude the Esquimaux, who inhabit the shores of Hudson's Bay, we shall find a general resemblance in the colour, manners and state of society, among all the tribes of Indians who inhabit the extensive tract of country above-mentioned.

Civilians have divided nations into savage, barbarous, and civilized. The savage, live by fishing and hunting. The barbarous, by pasturage or cattle; and the civilized by agriculture. Each of these is connected together in such a manner, that the whole appear to form different parts of a circle. Even the manners of the most civilized nations partake of those of the savage. It would seem as if liberty and indolence were the highest pursuits of man; and these are enjoyed in their greatest perfection by savages, or in the practice of customs which resemble those of savages.

The Indians of North America partake chiefly of the manner of savages. In the earliest accounts we have of them, we find them cultivating a spot of ground. The maize is an original grain among them. The different dishes of it which are in use among the white people still retain Indian names.

It will be unnecessary to show that the Indians live in a state of society adapted to all the exigencies of their mode of life. Those who look for the simplicity and perfection of the state of nature, must seek it in systems, as absurd in philosophy, as they are delightful in poetry.

Before we attempt to ascertain the number or history of the diseases of the Indians, it will be necessary to inquire into those customs among them which we know influence diseases. For this purpose I shall,

First, mention a few facts which relate to the birth and treatment of their children.

Secondly, I shall speak of their diet.

Thirdly, Of the customs which are peculiar to the sexes, And,

Fourthly, Of those customs which are common to them both.*

---

* Many of the facts contained in the Natural History of Medicine among the Indians in this Inquiry, are taken from La Hontan and Charlevoix's histories of Canada; but the most material of them are taken from persons who had lived, or travelled among the Indians. The author acknowledges' himself indebted in a particular manner to Mr. Edward Hand, surgeon in the 18th regiment, afterwards brigadier general in the army of the United States, who, during several years' residence at Fort Pitt, directed his inquiries into their customs, diseases, and remedies, with a success that does equal honour to his ingenuity and diligence.

I. Of the birth and treatment of their children.

Much of the future health of the body depends upon its original stamina. A child born of healthy parents always brings into the world a system formed by nature to resist the causes of diseases. The treatment of children among the Indians, tends to secure this hereditary firmness of constitution. Their first food is their mother's milk. To harden them against the action of heat and cold (the natural enemies of health and life among the Indians) they are plunged every day in cold water. In order to facilitate their being moved from place to place, and at the same time to preserve their shape they are tied to a board, where they lie on their backs for six, ten, or eighteen months. A child generally sucks its mother till it is two years old, and sometimes longer. It is easy to conceive how much vigour their bodies must acquire from this simple, but wholesome nourishment. The appetite we sometimes observe in children for flesh is altogether artificial. The peculiar irritability of the system in infancy, forbids stimulating aliment of all kinds. Nature never calls for animal food till she has provided the child with those teeth which are necessary to divide it. I shall not undertake to determine how far the wholesome quality of the mother's milk is increased by her refusing the embraces of her husband, during the time of giving suck.

II. The diet of the Indians is of a mixed nature, being partly animal and partly vegetable; their animals are wild, and therefore easy of digestion. As the Indians are naturally more disposed to the indolent employment of fishing than hunting in summer, so we find them living more upon fish than land animals, in that season of the year.—Their vegetables consist of roots and fruits, mild in themselves or capable of being made so by the action of fire. Although the interior parts of our continent abound with salt springs, yet I cannot find that the Indians used salt in their diet, till they were instructed to do so by the Europeans. The small quantity of fixed alkali contained in the ashes on which they roasted their meat, could not add much to its stimulating quality. They preserve their meat from putrefaction, by cutting it into small pieces, and exposing it in summer to the sun, and in winter to the frost. In the one case its moisture is dissipated, and in the other so frozen, that it cannot undergo the putrefactive process. In dressing their meat, they are careful to preserve its juices. They generally prefer it in the form of soups. Hence we find, that among them the use of the spoon preceded that of the knife and fork. They take the same pains to preserve the juice of their meat when they roast it, by turning it often. The efficacy of this animal juice in dissolving meat in the stomach, has not been equalled by any of those sauces or liquors which modern luxury has mixed with it for that purpose.

The Indians have no set time for eating, but obey the gentle appetites of nature as often as they are called by them. After whole days spent in the chase or in war, they often commit those excesses in eating, to which long abstinence cannot fail of prompting them. It is common to see them spend three or four hours in satisfying their hunger. This is occasioned not more by the quantity they eat, than by the pains they take in masticating it. They carefully avoid drinking water in their marches, from an opinion that it lessens their ability to bear fatigue.

III. We now come to speak of those customs which are peculiar to the sexes. And, first, of those which belong to the WOMEN. They are doomed by their husbands to such domestic labour as gives a firmness to their bodies, bordering upon the masculine. Their menses seldom begin to flow before they are eighteen to twenty years of age, and generally cease before they are forty. They have them in small quantities, but at regular intervals. They seldom marry till they are about twenty. The constitution has now acquired a vigour, which enables it the better to support the convulsions of child-bearing. This custom likewise guards against a premature old age. Doctor Bancroft ascribes the haggard looks—the loose hanging breasts—and the prominent bellies of the Indian women at Guiana, entirely to their bearing children too early.* Where marriages are unfruitful (which is seldom the case) a separation is obtained by means of an easy divorce; so that they are unacquainted with the disquietudes which sometimes arise from barrenness. During pregnancy, the women are exempted from the more laborious parts of their duty: hence miscarriages rarely happen among them. Nature is their only midwife. Their labours are short, and accompanied with little pain. Each woman is delivered in a private cabbin, without so much as one of her own sex to attend her. After washing herself in cold water, she returns in a few days to her usual employments; so that she knows nothing of those accidents which proceed from the carelessness or ill management of midwives, or those weaknesses which arise from a month's confinement in a warm room. It is remarkable that there is hardly a period in the interval between the eruption and the ceasing of the menses, in which they are not pregnant or giving suck. This is the most natural state of the constitution during that interval; and hence we often find it connected with the best state of health, in the women of civilized nations.

The customs peculiar to the Indian MEN, consist chiefly in those employments which are necessary to preserve animal life, and to defend their nation. These employments are hunting and war, each of which is conducted in a manner that tends to call forth every fibre into exercise, and to ensure them the possession of the utmost possible health. In times of plenty and peace, we see them sometimes rising from their beloved indolence, and shaking off its influence by the salutary exercises of dancing and swimming. The Indian men seldom marry before they are thirty years of age: They no doubt derive considerable vigour from this custom; for while they are secured by it from the enervating effects of the premature dalliance of love, they may ensure more certain fruitfulness to their wives, and entail more certain health upon their children. Tacitus describes the same custom among the Germans, and attributes to it the same good effects. "Sera juvenum venus, eoque inexhausta pubertas; nec virgines festinan-

---
* Natural History of Guiana.

tur; eadem juventa, similis proceritas, pares validique miscentur; ac robora parentum liberi referunt." *

Among the Indian men, it is deemed a mark of heroism to bear the most exquisite pain without complaining; upon this account they early inure themselves to burning part of their bodies with fire, or cutting them with sharp instruments. No young man can be admitted to the honors of manhood or war, who has not acquitted himself well in these trials of patience and fortitude. It is easy to conceive how much this contributes to give a tone to the nervous system, which renders it less subject to the occasional causes of diseases.

IV. We come now to speak of those customs which are common to both sexes: These are PAINTING, and use of the COLD BATH. The practice of anointing the body with oil is common to the savages of all countries; in warm climates it is said to promote longevity, by checking excessive perspiration. The Indians generally use bear's grease mixed with a clay, which bears the greatest resemblance to the colour of their skins. This pigment serves to lessen the sensibility of the extremities of the nerves, it moreover fortifies them against the action of those exhalations, which we shall mention hereafter, as a considerable source of their diseases. The COLD BATH likewise fortifies the body, and renders it less subject to those diseases which arise from the extremes and vicissitudes of heat and cold. We shall speak hereafter of the Indian manner of using it.

It is a practice among the Indians never to drink before dinner, when they work or travel. Experience teaches, that filling the stomach with cold water in the forenoon, weakens the appetite, and makes the system more sensible of heat and fatigue.

The state of society among the Indians excludes the influence of most of those passions which disorder the body. The

---

* Cæsar, in his history of the Gallic war, gives the same account of the ancient Germans. His words are "Qui diutissimi impuberes permanserunt, maximam inter suos ferunt laudem hoc ali staturam, ali vires, nervasque confirmari putant." Lib. vi. xxi.

turbulent effects of anger are concealed in deep and lasting resentments. Envy and ambition are excluded by their equality of power and property. Nor is it necessary that the perfections of the whole sex should be ascribed to one, to induce them to marry. "The weakness of love (says Dr Adam Smith) which is so much indulged in ages of humanity and politeness, is regarded among savages as the most unpardonable effeminacy. A young man would think himself disgraced for ever, if he shewed the least preference of one woman above another, or did not express the most complete indifference, both about the time when, and the person to whom, he was to be married." * Thus are they exempted from those violent or lasting diseases, which accompany the several stages of such passions in both sexes among civilized nations.

It is remarkable that there are no deformed Indians. Some have suspected from this circumstance, that they put their deformed children to death; but nature here acts the part of an unnatural mother. The severity of the Indian manners destroys them.†

From a review of the customs of the Indians, we need not be surprised at the stateliness, regularity of features, and dignity of aspect by which they are characterised. Where we observe these among ourselves, there is always a presumption of their being accompanied with health, and a strong constitution. The circulation of the blood is more languid in the Indians than in persons who are in the constant exercise of the habits of civilised life. Out of eight Indian men whose pulses I once examined at the wrists, I did not meet with one in whom the artery beat more than sixty-four strokes in a minute.

The marks of old age appear more early among Indian, than among civilized nations.

---

* Theory of Moral Sentiments.
† Since the intercourse of the white people with the Indians, we find some of them deformed in their limbs. This deformity, upon inquiry, appears to be produced by those accidents, quarrels, &c. which have been introduced among them by spirituous liquors.

Having finished our inquiry into the physical customs of the Indians, we shall now proceed to inquire into their diseases.

A celebrated professor of anatomy has asserted, that we could not tell by reasoning *à priori*, that the body was mortal, so intimately woven with its texture are the principles of life. Lord Bacon declares, that the only cause of death which is natural to man, is that from old age; and complains of the imperfection of physic, in not being able to guard the principle of life, until the whole of the oil that feeds it is consumed. We cannot admit of this proposition of our noble philosopher. In the inventory of the grave in every country, we find more of the spoils of youth and manhood than of age. This must be attributed to moral as well as physical causes.

We need only recollect the custom among the Indians, of sleeping in the open air in a variable climate—the alternate action of heat and cold upon their bodies, to which the warmth of their cabins exposes them—their long marches—their excessive exercise—their intemperance in eating, to which their long fasting, and their public feasts naturally prompt them, and, lastly, the vicinity of their habitations to the banks of rivers, in order to discover the empire of diseases among them in every stage of their lives. They have in vain attempted to elude the general laws of mortality, while their mode of life subjects them to these remote, but certain causes of diseases.

From what we know of the action of these potentiæ nocentes upon the human body, it will hardly be necessary to appeal to facts to determine that FEVERS constitute the only diseases among the Indians. These fevers are occasioned by the sensible and insensible qualities of the air. Those which are produced by cold, are of the inflammatory kind, such as pleurisies, peripneumonies, and rheumatisms. Those which are produced by the insensible qualities of the air, or by putrid exhalations, are intermitting, remitting, and inflammatory, according as the exhalations are combined with more or less heat or cold. The DYSENTERY (which is an Indian disease) comes under the class of fevers It appears to be the febris introversa of Dr. Sydenham.

The Indians are subject to ANIMAL and VEGETABLE POISONS. The effects of these upon the body, are in some degree analogous to the exhalations we have mentioned. When they do not bring on sudden death, they produce, according to their malignity, either an inflammatory or putrid fever.

The SMALL POX and the VENEREAL DISEASE were communicated to the Indians in North-America by the Europeans. Nor can I find that they were ever subject to the SCURVY. Whether this was obviated by their method of preserving their flesh, or by their mixing it at all times with vegetables, I shall not undertake to determine. Dr Maclurg ascribes to fresh meat an antiseptic quality.* The peculiar customs and manners of life among the Indians, seem to have exempted them from these, as well as all other diseases of the fluids. The leprosy, elephantiasis, scurvy, and venereal disease, appear to be different modifications of the same primary disorder. The same causes produce them in every age and country. They are diversified like plants by climate and nourishment. They all sprung originally from a moist atmosphere and unwholesome diet, hence we read of their prevailing so much in the middle centuries, when the principal parts of Europe were overflowed with water, and the inhabitants lived entirely on fish, and a few unwholesome vegetables. The abolition of the feudal system in Europe, by introducing freedom, introduced at the same time agriculture; which by multiplying the fruits of the earth lessened the consumption of animal food, and thus put a stop to these disorders. The elephantiasis is almost unknown in Europe. The leprosy is confined chiefly to the low countries of Africa. The plica polonica once so common in Poland, is to be found only in books of medicine. The small pox is no longer a fatal disorder, when the body is prepared for its reception by a vegetable regimen. Even the plague itself is losing its sting. It is hardly dreaded at this time in Turkey; and its very existence is preserved there by the doctrine of fatalism, which prevails among the inhabitants of that country.

---

* Experiments on the Bile, and Reflections on the Biliary Secretion.

It may serve as a new and powerful motive against political slavery to observe, that it is connected with those diseases which most deform and debase the human body. It may likewise serve to enhance the blessings of liberty, to trace its effects, in eradicating such loathsome and destructive disorders.*

I have heard of two or three cases of the GOUT among the Indians, but it was only among those who had learned the use

---

* Muratori, in his Antiquities of Italy in the middle ages, describes the greatest part of Europe as overflowed with water. The writings of the historians of those ages are full of the physical and political miseries which prevailed during those centuries. The whole of the diseases we have mentioned, raged at one time in all the countries of Europe. In the ninth century there were 19,000 hospitals for lepers only, in Christendom. Louis VIII. king of France, in the year 1227, bequeathed legacies to 2000 leprous hospitals in his own kingdom. The same diet, and the same dampness of soil and air, produced the same effects in South-America. The venereal disease probably made its appearance at the same time in South America and Naples. (Precis de l'histoire physique des tems, par M. Raymond.) The leprosy and scurvy still prevail in the northern parts of Europe, where the manner of living, among the inhabitants, still bears some resemblance to that which prevailed in the middle centuries. Pontopiddan's natural history of Norway. Between the years 1006 and 1680, we read of the plague being epidemic fifty-two times throughout all Europe. The situation of Europe is well known during the fourteenth century: every country was in arms, agriculture was neglected; nourishment of all kinds was scanty and unwholesome, no wonder, therefore, that we read of the plague being fourteen times epidemic in Europe during that period. In proportion as the nations of Europe have become civilized, and cultivated the earth, together with the arts of peace, this disorder has gradually mitigated. It prevailed only six times in the sixteenth, and five times in the seventeenth centuries. It made its last general appearance in the year 1680. It has occasionally visited several cities in Europe within the last century, but has raged with much less violence than formerly. It is highly probable its very existence would be destroyed, could the inhabitants of Turkey (where it is at all times endemic) be prevailed upon to use the same precautions to prevent its spreading, which have been found successful in other parts of Europe. The British, and other foreigners, who reside at Constantinople, escape the plague more by avoiding all intercourse with persons, houses, clothes, &c. infected with the disorder, than by any peculiarities in their diet or manners. The use of wine alone does not preserve them from the infection, we learn from the history of the Armenians, who drink large quantities of wine; and yet, from their belief in the doctrine of fatalism, perish in the same **proportion as the Turks.**

of rum from the white people. A question naturally occurs here, and that is, why does not the gout appear more frequently among that class of people, who consume the greatest quantity of rum among ourselves? To this I answer, that the effects of this liquor upon those enfeebled people, are too sudden and violent, to admit of their being thrown upon the extremities; as we know them to be among the Indians. They appear only in visceral obstructions, and a complicated train of chronic diseases. Thus putrid miasmata are sometimes too strong to bring on a fever, but produce instant debility and death. The gout is seldom heard of in Russia, Denmark, or Poland. Is this occasioned by the vigour of constitution peculiar to the inhabitants of those northern countries? or is it caused by their excessive use of spirituous liquors, which produce the same chronic complaints among them, which we said were common among the lower class of people in this country? The familiarity of their diseases makes the last of these suppositions the most probable. The effects of wine, like tyranny in a well formed government, are felt first in the extremities; while spirits, like a bold invader, seize at once upon the vitals of the constitution.

After much inquiry, I have not been able to find a single instance of MADNESS, MELANCHOLY, or FATUITY among the Indians; nor can I find any accounts of *diseases* from WORMS among them. Worms are common to most animals; they produce diseases only in weak, or increase them in strong constitutions.* Hence they have no place in the nosological systems of physic. Nor does DENTITION appear to be a disorder among the Indians. The facility with which the healthy children of healthy parents cut their teeth among civilized nations, gives us reason to conclude that the Indian children never suffer from this quarter.

The Indians appear moreover to be strangers to diseases and pains in the teeth.

---

* Indian children are not exempted from worms. It is common with the Indians, when a fever in their children is ascribed by the white people to worms, (from their being discharged occasionally in their stools) to say, "the fever makes the worms come, and not the worms the fever."

The employments of the Indians subject them to many accidents, hence we sometimes read of WOUNDS, FRACTURES, and LUXATIONS among them.

Having thus pointed out the natural diseases of the Indians, and shewn what disorders are foreign to them, we may venture to conclude, that FEVERS, OLD AGE, CASUALTIES and WAR, are the only natural outlets of human life. War is nothing but a distemper; it is founded in the imperfection of political bodies, just as fevers are founded on the weakness of the animal body.—Providence in these diseases seems to act like a mild legislature which mitigates the severity of death, by inflicting it in a manner the least painful upon the whole to the patient and the survivors.

Let us now inquire into the REMEDIES of the Indians. These, like their diseases, are simple, and few in number.

It will be difficult to find the exact order in which the Indian remedies were suggested by nature or discovered by art; nor will it be easy to arrange them in proper order. I shall however attempt it, by reducing them to NATURAL and ARTIFICIAL.

To the class of NATURAL REMEDIES belongs the Indian practice of abstracting from their patients all kinds of stimulating aliment. The compliance of the Indians with the dictates of nature, in the early stage of a disorder, no doubt, prevents in many cases their being obliged to use any other remedy. They follow nature still closer, in allowing their patients to drink plentifully of cold water; this being the only liquor a patient calls for in the fever.

Sweating is likewise a natural remedy. It was probably suggested by observing fevers to be terminated by it. I shall not inquire how far these sweats are essential to the crisis of a fever. The Indian mode of procuring this evacuation is as follows: the patient is confined in a close tent, or wigwam, over a hole in the earth, in which a red hot stone is placed; a quantity of water is thrown upon this stone, which instantly involves the patient in a cloud of vapour and sweat; in this situation he rushes out, and plunges himself into a river; from whence he retires to his bed. If the remedy has been used with success, he rises from his bed in four and twenty hours, perfectly recovered from his indisposition. This remedy is used not only to cure fevers, but remove that uneasiness which arises from fatigue of body.

A third natural remedy among the Indians, is PURGING. The fruits of the earth, the flesh of birds, and other animals feeding upon particular vegetables, and above all the spontaneous efforts of nature, early led the Indians to perceive the necessity and advantages of this evacuation.

VOMITS constitute their fourth natural remedy. They were probably, like the former, suggested by nature, and accident. The ipecacuanha is one of the many roots they employ for this purpose.

The ARTIFICIAL REMEDIES made use of by the Indians, are BLEEDING, CAUSTICS, and ASTRINGENT medicines. They confine bleeding entirely to the part affected. To know that opening a vein in the arm, or foot, would relieve a pain in the head or side, supposes some knowledge of the animal economy, and therefore marks an advanced period in the history of medicine.

Sharp stones and thorns are the instruments they use to procure a discharge of blood.

We have an account of the Indians using something like a POTENTIAL CAUSTIC, in obstinate pains. It consists of a piece of rotten wood called *punk*, which they place upon the part affected, and afterwards set it on fire; the fire gradually consumes the wood, and its ashes burn a hole in the flesh.

The undue efforts of nature, in those fevers which are connected with a diarrhœa, or dysentery, together with those hemorrhages to which their mode of life exposed them, necessarily led them to an early discovery of some ASTRINGENT VEGETABLES. I am uncertain whether the Indians rely upon astringent, or any other vegetables, for the cure of the intermitting fever. This disease among them probably requires no other remedies than the cold bath, or cold air. Its greater obstinacy, as well as frequency among ourselves, must be sought for in the greater feebleness of our constitutions; and in that change which our country has undergone, from meadows, mill-dams and the cutting down of woods, whereby morbid exhalations have been multiplied, and their passage rendered more free, through every part of country.

This is a short account of the remedies of the Indians. If they are simple, they are, like their eloquence, full of strength, if they are few in number, they are accommodated, as their languages are to their ideas, to the whole of their diseases.

We said, formerly, that the Indians were subject to ACCIDENTS, such as wounds, fractures, and the like. In these cases, nature performs the office of a surgeon. We may judge of her qualifications for this office, by observing the marks of wounds and fractures, which are sometimes discovered on wild animals. But further, what is the practice of our modern surgeons in these cases? Is it not to lay aside plasters and ointments, and trust the whole to nature? Those ulcers which require the assistance of mercury, bark, and a particular regimen are unknown to the Indians.

The HEMORRHAGES which sometimes follow their wounds, are restrained by plunging themselves into cold water, and thereby producing a constriction upon the bleeding vessels.

Their practice of attempting to recover DROWNED PEOPLE, is irrational and unsuccessful. It consists in suspending the patient by the heels, in order that the water may flow from his mouth. This practice is founded on a belief that the patient dies from swallowing an excessive quantity of water. But modern observation teaches us that drowned people die from another cause. This discovery has suggested a method of cure, directly opposite to that in use among the Indians; and has shewn us that the practice of suspending by the heels is hurtful.

I do not find that the Indians ever suffer in their limbs from the action of COLD upon them. Their moccasins, by allowing their feet to move freely, and thereby promoting the circulation of the blood, defend their lower extremities in the daytime, and their practice of sleeping with their feet near a fire, defends them from the morbid effects of cold at night. In those cases where the motion of their feet in their moccasins is not sufficient to keep them warm, they break the ice, and restore their warmth by exposing them for a short time to the stimulus of cold water.†

We have heard much of their specific antidotes to the VENEREAL DISEASE. In the accounts of these antivenereal medicines, some abatement should be made for that love of the marvellous, and of novelty, which are apt to creep into the writings of travellers and physicians. How many medicines which were once thought infallible in this disorder, are now rejected from the materia medica! I have found upon enquiry that the Indians always assist their medicines in this disease, by a regimen which promotes perspiration. Should we allow that mercury acts as a specific in destroying this disorder, it does not follow that it is proof against the efficacy of medicines which act more mechanically upon the body.*

There cannot be a stronger mark of the imperfect state of knowledge in medicine among the Indians, than their method of treating the SMALLPOX. We are told that they plunge themselves in cold water in the beginning of the disorder, and that it generally proves fatal to them.

Travellers speak in high terms of the Indian ANTIDOTES to POISONS. We must remember, that many things have been thought poisonous, which later experience hath proved to possess no unwholesome quality. Moreover, the uncertainty and variety in the operation of poisons, renders it extremely difficult to fix the certainty of the antidotes to them. How many specifics have derived their credit for preventing the hydrophobia, from per-

---

† It was remarked in Canada, in the winter of the year 1759, during the war before last, that none of those soldiers who wore moccasins were frost-bitten, while few of those escaped that were much exposed to the cold who wore shoes.

* I cannot help suspecting the antivenereal qualities of the lobelia, ceanothus and ranunculus, spoken of by Mr Kalm, in the memoirs of the Swedish academy. Mr Hand informed me, that the Indians rely chiefly upon a plentiful use of the decoctions of the pine-trees, against the venereal disease. He added moreover, that he had often known this disease prove fatal to them.

sons being wounded by animals, who were not in a situation to produce that disorder' If we may judge of all the Indian antidotes to poisons, by those which have fallen into our hands, we have little reason to ascribe much to them in any cases whatever.

I have heard of their performing several remarkable cures upon STIFF JOINTS, by an infusion of certain herbs in water. The mixture of several herbs together in this infusion calls in question the specific efficacy of each of them. I cannot help attributing the whole success of this remedy to the great heat of the water in which the herbs were boiled, and to its being applied for a long time to the part affected. We find the same medicine to vary frequently in its success, according to its strength, or to the continuance of its application. De Haen attributes the good effects of electricity, entirely to its being used for several months.

I have met with one case upon record of their aiding nature in PARTURITION. Captain Carver gives us an account of an Indian woman in a difficult labour, being suddenly delivered in consequence of a general convulsion induced upon her system, by stopping, for a short time, her mouth and nose, so as to obstruct her breathing.

We are sometimes amused with accounts of Indian remedies for the DROPSY, EPILEPSY, COLIC, GRAVEL and GOUT If, with all the advantages which modern physicians derive from their knowledge in ANATOMY, CHEMISTRY, BOTANY and PHILOSOPHY; if, with the benefit of discoveries communicated from abroad, as well as handed down from our ancestors, by more certain methods than tradition, we are still ignorant of certain remedies for these diseases; what can we expect from the Indians, who are not only deprived of these advantages, but want our chief motive, the sense of the pain and danger of those disorders to prompt them to seek for such remedies to relieve them? There cannot be a stronger proof of their ignorance of proper remedies for new or difficult diseases, than their having recourse to enchantment. But to be more particular; I have taken pains to inquire into the success of some of these Indian specifics, and have never heard of one well attested case of their efficacy. I believe they derive all their credit from our being ignorant of their composition. The influence of secrecy is well known in establishing the credit of a medicine. The sal seignette was an infallible medicine for the intermitting fever, while the manufactory of it was confined to an apothecary at Rochelle; but it lost its virtues as soon as it was found to be composed of the acid of tartar and the fossil alkali. Dr Ward's famous pill and drop ceased to do wonders in scrophulous cases as soon as he bequeathed to the world his receipts for making them.

I foresee an objection to what has been said concerning the remedies of the Indians, drawn from that knowledge which experience gives to a mind intent upon one subject. We have heard much of the perfection of their senses of seeing and hearing. An Indian, we are told, will discover not only a particular tribe of Indians by their footsteps, but the distance of time in which they were made. In those branches of knowledge which relate to hunting and war, the Indians have acquired a degree of perfection that has not been equalled by civilized nations. But we must remember, that medicine among them does not enjoy the like advantages with the arts of war and hunting, of being the *chief* object of their attention. The physician and the warrior are united in one character; to render him as able in the former as he is in the latter profession, would require an entire abstraction from every other employment, and a familiarity with external objects, which are incompatible with the wandering life of savages.

Thus we have finished our inquiry into the diseases and remedies of the Indians in North-America. We come now to inquire into the diseases and remedies of civilized nations.

Nations differ in their degrees of civilization. We shall select one for the subject of our enquiries which is most familiar to us; I mean the British nation. Here we behold subordination and classes of mankind established by government, commerce, manufactures, and certain customs common to most of the civilized nations of Europe. We shall trace the origin of their diseases through their customs in the same manner as we did those of the Indians.

I. It will be sufficient to name the degrees of heat, the improper aliment, the tight dresses, and the premature studies children are exposed to, in order to show the ample scope for diseases, which is added to the original defect of stamina they derive from their ancestors.

II. Civilization rises in its demands upon the health of women. Their fashions, their dress and diet, their eager pursuits and ardent enjoyment of pleasure, their indolence and undue evacuations in pregnancy, their cordials, hot regimen and neglect or use of art, in child-birth, are all so many inlets to diseases.

Humanity would fain be silent, while philosophy calls upon us to mention the effects of interested marriages, and of disappointments in love, increased by that concealment which the tyranny of custom has imposed upon the sex.* Each of these exaggerates the natural, and increases the number of artificial diseases among women.

III. The diseases introduced by civilization extend themselves through every class and profession among men. How fatal are the effects of idleness and intemperance among the rich, and of hard labor and penury among the poor! What pallid looks are contracted by the votaries of science from hanging over the "sickly taper!" How many diseases are entailed upon manufacturers, by the materials in which they work, and the posture of their bodies! What monkish diseases do we observe from monkish continence and monkish vices! We pass over the increase of accidents from building, sailing, riding, and the like. War, as if too slow in destroying the human species, calls in a

---

* "Married women are more healthy and long-lived than single women. The registers, examined by Mr Muret, confirm this observation, and show particularly, that of equal numbers of single and married women between fifteen and twenty-five years of age, more of the former died than of the latter, in the proportion of two to one the consequence, therefore, of following nature must be favourable to health among the female sex." Supplement to Price's Observations on Reversionary Payments. p. 357.

train of diseases peculiar to civilized nations. What havock have the corruption and monopoly of provisions, a damp soil, and an unwholesome sky, made, in a few days, in an army! The achievements of British valour at the Havannah, in the last war, were obtained at the expence of 9,000 men, 7,000 of whom perished with the West India fever.* Even our modern discoveries in geography, by extending the empire of commerce, have likewise extended the empire of diseases. What desolation have the East and West Indies made of British subjects! It has been found upon a nice calculation, that only ten of an hundred Europeans, live above seven years after they arrive in the island of Jamaica.

IV. It would take up too much of our time to point out all the customs both *physical* and *moral,* which influence diseases among both sexes. The former have engendered the seeds of diseases in the human body itself. hence the origin of catarrhs, jail and miliary fevers, with a long train of contagious disorders, which compose so great a part of our books of medicine. The latter likewise have a large share in producing diseases. I am not one of those modern philosophers, who derive the vices of mankind from the influence of civilization, but I am safe in asserting, that their number and malignity increase with the refinements of polished life. To prove this, we need only survey a scene too familiar to affect us it is a bedlam, which injustice, inhumanity, avarice, pride, vanity, and ambition, have filled with inhabitants.

Thus have we briefly pointed out the customs which influence the diseases of civilized nations. It remains now that we

---

* The modern writers upon the diseases of armies, wonder that the Greek and Roman physicians have left us nothing upon that subject. But may not *most* of the diseases of armies be produced by the different manner in which wars are carried on by the modern nations? The discoveries in geography, by extending the field of war, expose soldiers to many diseases from long voyages, and a *sudden* change of climate, which were unknown to the armies of former ages. Moreover, the form of the weapons, and the variety in the military exercises of the Grecian and Roman armies, gave a vigour to the constitution, which can never be acquired by the use of muskets and artillery.

take notice of their diseases. Without naming the many new fevers, fluxes, hemorrhages, swellings from water, wind, flesh, fat, pus and blood; foulnesses on the skin from cancers, leprosy, yawes, poxes, and itch, and lastly, the gout, the hysteria, and the hypocondriasis, in all their variety of known and unknown shapes; I shall sum up all that is necessary upon this subject, by adding, that the number of diseases which belong to civilized nations, according to Doctor Cullen's nosology, amounts to 1387, the single class of nervous diseases form 612 of this number.

Before we proceed to speak of the remedies of civilized nations, we shall examine into the abilities of NATURE in curing their diseases. We found her active and successful in curing the diseases of the Indians. Is her strength, wisdom, or benignity, equal to the increase of those dangers which threaten her dissolution among civilized nations? In order to answer this question, it will be necessary to explain the meaning of the term nature.

By nature, in the present case, I understand nothing but *physical necessity*. This at once excludes every thing like intelligence from her operations: these are all performed in obedience to the same laws which govern vegetation in plants and the intestine motions of fossils. They are as truly mechanical as the laws of gravitation, electricity or magnetism. A ship when laid on her broadside by a wave, or a sudden blast of wind, rises by the simple laws of her mechanism; but suppose this ship be attacked by fire, or a water-spout, we are not to call in question the skill of the ship-builder, if she be consumed by the one, or sunk by the other. In like manner, the Author of nature hath furnished the body with powers to preserve itself from its natural enemies; but when it is attacked by those civil foes which are bred by the peculiar customs of civilization, it resembles a company of Indians, armed with bows and arrows, against the complicated and deadly machinery of fire-arms. To place this subject in a proper light, we shall deliver a history of the operations of nature in a few of the diseases of civilized nations.

I. There are cases in which nature is still successful in curing diseases.

In fevers she still deprives us of our appetite for animal food, and imparts to us a desire for cool air and cold water.

In hemorrhages she produces a faintness, which occasions a coagulum in the open vessels, so that the further passage of blood through them is obstructed.

In wounds of the flesh and bones she discharges foreign matter by exciting an inflammation, and supplies the waste of both with new flesh and bone.

II. There are cases where the efforts of nature are too feeble to do service, as in putrid and nervous fevers.

III. There are cases where the efforts of nature are over proportioned to the strength of the disease, as in the cholera morbus and dysentery.

IV. There are cases where nature is idle, as in the atonic stages of the gout, the cancer, the epilepsy, the mania, the venereal disease, the apoplexy, and the tetanus.*

V. There are cases in which nature does mischief. She wastes herself with an unnecessary fever, in a dropsy and consumption. She throws a plethora upon the brain and lungs in the apoplexy and peripneumonia notha. She ends a pleurisy and peripneumony in a vomica, or empyema. She creates an unnatural appetite for food in the hypochondriac disorder. And lastly, she drives the melancholy patient to solitude, where, by brooding over the subject of his insanity, he increases his disease.

We are accustomed to hear of the salutary kindness of nature in alarming us with pain, to prompt us to seek for a remedy. But,

VI. There are cases in which she refuses to send this harbinger of the evils which threaten her, as in the aneurism, scirrhus, and stone in the bladder.

VII. There are cases where the pain is not proportioned to the danger, as in the tetanus, consumption, and dropsy of the head. And,

VIII. There are cases where the pain is over-proportioned to the danger, as in the paronychia and tooth-ache.

---

* Hoffmann de hypothesium medicarum damno, sect. xv.

This is a short account of the operations of nature, in the diseases of civilized nations. A lunatic might as well plead against the sequestration of his estate, because he once enjoyed the full exercise of his reason, or because he still had lucid intervals, as nature be exempted from the charges we have brought against her.

But this subject will receive strength from considering the REMEDIES of civilized nations. All the products of the vegetable, fossil, and animal kingdoms, tortured by heat and mixture into an almost infinite variety of forms; bleeding, cupping, artificial drains by setons, issues, and blisters, exercise, active and passive, voyages and journies, baths, warm and cold, waters saline, aërial and mineral, food by weight and measure; the royal touch; enchantment; miracles; in a word, the combined discoveries of natural history and philosophy, united into a system of materia medica, all show, that although physicians are in speculation the servants, yet in practice they are the masters of nature. The whole of their remedies seem contrived on purpose to arouse, assist, restrain, and control her operations.

There are some truths like certain liquors, which require strong heads to bear them. I feel myself protected from the prejudices of vulgar minds, when I reflect that I am delivering these sentiments in a society of philosophers.

Let us now take a COMPARATIVE VIEW of the diseases and remedies of the Indians with those of civilized nations. We shall begin with their diseases.

In our account of the diseases of the Indians we beheld death executing his commission, it is true; but then his dart was hid in a mantle, under which he concealed his shape. But among civilized nations we behold him multiplying his weapons in proportion to the number of organs and functions in the body, and pointing each of them in such a manner, as to render his messengers more terrible than himself.

We said formerly that fevers constituted the chief diseases of the Indians. According to Doctor Sydenham's computation, above 66,000 out of 100,000 died of fevers in London about

100 years ago; but fevers now constitute but a little more than one-tenth part of the diseases of that city. Out of 21,780 persons who died in London between December 1770 and December 1771, only 2273 died of simple fevers. I have more than once heard Doctor Huck complain, that he could find no marks of epidemic fevers in London as described by Dr Sydenham. London has undergone a revolution in its manners and customs since Doctor Sydenham's time. New diseases, the offspring of luxury, have supplanted fevers; and the few that are left, are so complicated with other diseases that their connection can no longer be discovered with an epidemic constitution of the year. The pleurisy and peripneumony those inflammatory fevers of strong constitutions, are now lost in catarrhs, or colds, which instead of challenging the powers of nature or art to a fair combat, insensibly undermine the constitution, and bring on an incurable consumption. Out of 22,434 who died in London between December 1769, and the same month in 1770, 4594 perished with that *British* disorder. Our countryman, Doctor Maclurg, has ventured to foretel that the gout will be lost in a few years, in a train of hypocondriac, hysteric and bilious disorders. In like manner, may we not look for a season when fevers, the natural diseases of the human body, will be lost in an inundation of artificial diseases, brought on by the modish practices of civilization?

It may not be improper to compare the PROGNOSIS of the Indians, in diseases, with that of civilized nations, before we take a comparative view of their remedies.

The Indians are said to be successful in predicting the events of diseases. While diseases are simple, the marks which distinguish them, or characterize their several stages, are generally uniform and obvious to the most indifferent observer. These marks afford so much certainty, that the Indians sometimes kill their physicians for a false prognosis, charging the death of the patient to their carelessness, or ignorance. They estimate the danger of their patients by the degrees of appetite; while an

Indian is able to eat, he is looked upon as free from danger. But when we consider the number and variety in the signs of diseases, among civilized nations, together with the shortness of life, the fallacy of memory, and the uncertainty of observation, where shall we find a physician willing to risk his reputation, much less his life, upon the prediction of the event of our acute diseases? We can derive no advantage from the simple sign, by which the Indians estimate the danger of their patients; for we daily see a want of appetite for food in diseases which are attended with no danger, and we sometimes observe an unusual degree of this appetite to precede the agonies of death. I honour the name of HIPPOCRATES But forgive me ye votaries of antiquity, if I attempt to pluck a few grey hairs from his venerable head. I was once an idolater at his altar, nor did I turn apostate from his worship, till I was taught, that not a tenth part of his prognostics corresponded with modern experience, or observation. The pulse,* urine, and sweats, from which the principle signs of life and death have been taken, are so variable in most of the acute diseases of civilized nations, that the wisest physicians have in some measure excluded the prognosis from being a part of their profession.

I am here insensibly led to make an apology for the instability of the theories and practice of physic. The theory of physic is founded upon the laws of the animal economy. These (unlike the laws of the mind, or the common laws of matter) do not appear at once, but are gradually brought to light by the phænomena of diseases. The success of nature in curing the simple diseases of Saxony, laid the foundation for the ANIMA MEDICA of

---

* Doctor Cullen used to inform his pupils, that after forty years experience, he could find no relation between his own observations on the pulse, and those made by Doctor Solano. The climate and customs of the people in Spain being so different from the climate and customs of the present inhabitants of Britain, may account for the diversity of their observations. Doctor Heberden's remarks upon the pulse, in the second volume of the Medical Transactions, are calculated to show how little the issue of diseases can be learned from it.

Doctor STAHL. The endemics of Holland * led Doctor BOER-HAAVE to seek for the causes of all diseases in the FLUIDS. And the universal prevalence of the disease of the NERVES, in Great-Britain led Doctor CULLEN to discover their peculiar laws, and to found a system upon them; a system, which will probably last till some new diseases are let loose upon the human species, which shall unfold other laws of the animal economy.

It is in consequence of this fluctuation in the principles and practice of physic, being so necessarily connected with the changes in the customs of civilized nations, that old and young physicians so often disagree in their opinions and practices. And it is by attending to the constant changes in these customs of civilized nations, that those physicians have generally become the most eminent, who have soonest emancipated themselves from the tyranny of the schools of physic, and having occasionally accommodated their principles and practice to the changes in diseases.† This variety in diseases, which is produced by the changes in the customs of civilized nations, will enable us to account for many of the contradictions which are to be found in authors of equal candor and abilities, who have written upon the materia medica.

---

* "The scurvy is very frequent in Holland, and draws its origin partly from their strong food, sea-fish, and smoked flesh, and partly from their dense and moist air, together with their bad water." Hoffman on Endemical Distempers.

"We are now in North-Holland, and I have never seen, among so few people, so many infected with the leprosy as here They say the reason is, because they eat so much fish." Howell's Familiar Letters.

† We may learn from these observations, the great impropriety of those Egyptian laws which oblige physicians to adopt, in all cases, the prescriptions which had been collected, and approved of, by the physicians of former ages. Every change in the customs of civilized nations, produces a change in their diseases, which calls for a change in their remedies What havoc would plentiful bleeding, purging, and small beer, formerly used with so much success by Dr Sydenham in the cure of fevers, now make upon the enfeebled citizens of London! The fevers of the same, and of more southern latitudes, still admit of such antiphlogistic remedies In the room of these, bark, wine, and other cordial medicines, are prescribed in London in almost every kind of fever.

ON NATURAL AND MEDICAL SCIENCES

In forming a comparative view of the REMEDIES of the Indians, with those of civilized nations, we shall remark, that the want of success in a medicine is occasioned by one of the following causes.

First, our ignorance of the disorder. Secondly, an ignorance of a suitable remedy. Thirdly, a want of efficacy in the remedy.

Considering the violence of the diseases of the Indians, it is probable their want of success is always occasioned by a want of efficacy in their medicines. But the case is very different among the civilized nations. Dissections daily convince us of our ignorance of the seats of diseases, and cause us to blush at our prescriptions. What certain or equal remedies have we found for the gout, the epilepsy, apoplexy, palsy, dropsy of the brain, cancer and consumption? How often are we disappointed in our expectation from the most certain and powerful of our remedies, by the negligence or obstinacy of our patients! What mischief have we done under the belief of false facts (if I may be allowed the expression) and false theories! We have assisted in multiplying diseases.—We have done more—we have increased their mortality.

I shall not pause to beg pardon of the faculty, for acknowledging in this public manner the weaknesses of our profession. I am pursuing truth, and while I can keep my eye fixed upon my guide, I am indifferent whither I am led, provided she is my leader.

But further, the Indian submits to his disease, without one fearful emotion from his doubtfulness of its event, and at last meets his fate without an anxious wish for futurity; except it is of being admitted to an "equal sky," where

"His faithful dog shall bear him company."

But among civilized nations, the influence of a false religion in good, and of a true religion in bad men, has converted even the fear of death into a disease. It is this original distemper of the imagination which renders the plague most fatal, upon his first appearance in a country.

Under all these disadvantages in the state of medicine, among civilized nations, do more in proportion die of the diseases peculiar to them, than of fevers, casualties and old age, among the Indians? If we take our account from the city of London, we shall find this to be the case. Near a twentieth part of its inhabitants perish one year with another. Nor does the natural increase of inhabitants supply this yearly waste. If we judge from the bills of mortality, the city of London contains fewer inhabitants, by several thousands, than it did forty years ago. It appears from this fact, and many others of a like nature, which might be adduced, that although the difficulty of supporting children, together with some peculiar customs of the Indians, which we mentioned, limit their number, yet they multiply faster, and die in a smaller proportion than civilized nations, under the circumstances we have described. The Indians, we are told, were numerous in this country before the Europeans settled among them. Travellers agree likewise in describing numbers of both sexes who exhibited all the marks of extreme old age. It is remarkable that age seldom impairs the faculties of their minds.

The mortality peculiar to those Indian tribes who have mingled with the white people, must be ascribed to the extensive mischief of spirituous liquors. When these have not acted, they have suffered from having accommodated themselves too suddenly to the European diet, dress, and manners. It does not become us to pry too much into futurity; but if we may judge from the fate of the original natives of Hispaniola, Jamaica, and the provinces on the continent, we may venture to foretell, that, in proportion as the white people multiply, the Indians will diminish; so that in a few centuries they will probably be entirely extirpated.*

---

* Even the influence of CHRISTIAN principles has not been able to put a stop to the mortality introduced among the Indians, by their intercourse with the Europeans. Dr Cotton Mather, in a letter to Sir William Ashurst, printed, in Boston in the year 1705, says "That above five years before, there were about thirty Indian congregations in the southern

It may be said, that health among the Indians, like insensibility to cold and hunger, is proportioned to their need of it; and that the less degrees, or entire want of health, are no interruption to the ordinary business of civilized life.

To obviate this supposition, we shall first attend to the effects of a single distemper in those people who are the principle wheels in the machine of civil society. Justice has stopt its current, victories, have been lost, wars have been prolonged, and embassies delayed, by the principle actors in these departments of government being suddenly laid up by a fit of the gout. How many offences are daily committed against the rules of good breeding, by the tedious histories of our disorders, which compose so great a part of modern conversation! What sums of money have been lavished in foreign countries in pursuit of health! * Families have been ruined by the unavoidable expenses of medicines and watering-places. In a word, the swarms of beggars which infest so many of the European countries, urge their petitions for charity chiefly by arguments derived from real or counterfeit diseases, which render them incapable of supporting themselves.†

But may not civilization, while it abates the violence of natural diseases, increase the lenity of those that are artificial, in the same manner that it lessens the strength of natural vices by multiplying them? To answer this question, it will only be neces-

---

parts of the province of Massachusetts-Bay " The same author, in his history of New-England, says, "That in the islands of Nantucket and Martha's Vineyard, there were 3000 *adult* Indians, 1600 of whom professed the Christian religion " At present there is but *one* Indian congregation in the whole Massachusetts province.

It may serve to extend our knowledge of diseases, to remark, that epidemics were often observed to prevail among the Indians in Nantucket, without affecting the white people.

* It is said, there are seldom less than 20,000 British subjects in France and Italy, one half of whom reside or travel in those countries upon the account of their health.

† Templeman computes, that Scotland contains 1,500,000 inhabitants, 100,000 of whom, according to Mr Fletcher, are supported at the public expence. The proportion of poor people is much greater in England, Ireland, France, and Italy.

sary to ask another: Who should exchange the heat, thirst and uneasiness of a fever, for one fit of the cholic or stone?

The history of the number, combination and fashions of the remedies we have given, may serve to humble the pride of philosophy; and to convince us that with all the advantages of the whole circle of sciences, we are still ignorant of antidotes to many of the diseases of civilized nations. We sometimes soothe our ignorance by reproaching our idleness in not investigating the remedies peculiar to this country. We are taught to believe that every herb that grows in our woods is possessed of some medicinal virtue, and that heaven would be wanting in benignity if our country did not produce remedies for all the different diseases of its inhabitants. It would be arrogating too much to suppose that man was the only creature in our world for whom vegetables grow. The beasts, birds and insects, derive their sustenance either directly or indirectly from them; while many of them were probably intended from their variety in figure, foliage and colour, only to serve as ornaments for our globe. It would seem strange that the Author of nature should furnish every spot of ground with medicines adapted to the diseases of its inhabitants, and at the same time deny it the more necessary articles of food and cloathing. I know not whether heaven has provided every country with antidotes even to the *natural* diseases of its inhabitants. The intermitting fever is common in almost every corner of the globe; but a sovereign remedy for it has been discovered only in South-America. The combination of bitter and astringent substances, which serve as a succedaneum to the Peruvian bark, is as much a preparation of art, as calomel or tartar emetic. Societies stand in need of each other as much as individuals: and the goodness of the Deity remains unimpeached when we suppose, that he intended medicines to serve (with other articles) to promote that knowledge, humanity, and politeness among the inhabitants of the earth, which have been so justly attributed to commerce.

We have no discoveries in the materia medica to hope for from the Indians in North-America. It would be a reproach to our schools of physic, if modern physicians were not more successful than the Indians, even in the treatment of their own diseases.

Do the blessings of civilization compensate for the sacrifice we make of natural health, as well as of natural liberty? This question must be answered under some limitations. When natural liberty is given up for laws which enslave instead of protecting us, we are immense losers by the exchange. Thus, if we arm the whole elements against our health, and render every pore in the body an avenue for a disease, we pay too high a price for the blessings of civilization.

In governments which have departed entirely from their simplicity, partial evils are to be cured by nothing but an entire renovation of their constitution. Let the world bear with the professions of law, physic, and divinity; and let the lawyer, physician and divine yet learn to bear with each other. They are all necessary, in the present state of society. In like manner, let the women of fashion forget the delicacy of her sex, and submit to be delivered by a man-midwife.* Let her snatch her offspring from her breast, and send it to repair the weakness of its stamina, with the milk of a ruddy cottager.† Let art supply

---

* In the enervated age of Athens, a law was passed which confined the practice of midwifery only to the men It was, however, repealed, upon a woman's dying in childbirth, rather than be delivered by a man-midwife It appears from the bills of mortality in London and Dublin, that about one in seventy of those women die in childbirth who are in the hands of midwives, but from the accounts of the lying-in hospitals in those cities which are under the care of man-midwives, only one in an hundred and forty perishes in childbirth.

† There has been much common-place declamation against the custom among the great, of not suckling their children. Nurses were common in Rome, in the declension of the empire· hence we find Cornelia commended as a rare example of maternal virtue, as much for suckling her sons, as for teaching them eloquence That nurses were common in Egypt, is probable from the contract which Pharaoh's daughter made with the unknown mother of Moses, to allow her wages for suckling her own child. The same degrees of civilization require the same customs. A woman whose times for eating, sleeping &c. are constantly interrupted by the calls of enervating pleasures, must always afford milk of an un-

the place of nature in the preparation and digestion of all our aliment. Let our fine ladies keep up their colour with carmine, and their spirits with ratifia; and let our fine gentlemen defend themselves from the excesses of heat and cold, with lavender and hartshorn. These customs have become necessary in the corrupt stages of society. We must imitate, in these cases, the practice of those physicians who consult the appetite only, in diseases which do not admit of a remedy.

The state of a country in point of population, temperance, and industry, is so connected with its diseases, that a tolerable idea may be formed of it, by looking over its bills of mortality. HOSPITALS, with all their boasted advantages, exhibit at the same time monuments of the charity and depravity of a people.* The opulence of physicians, and the divisions of their offices, into those of surgery, pharmacy and midwifery, are likewise proofs of the declining state of a country. In the infancy of the Roman empire, the priest performed the office of a physician; so simple

---

wholesome nature. It may truly be said of a child doomed to live on this aliment, that as soon as it receives
——————"breath,
It sucks in "the lurking principles of death"

* "Aurengezebe, emperor of Persia, being asked Why he did not build hospitals? said, *I will make my empire so rich, that there shall be no need of hospitals*. He ought to have said, I will begin by rendering my subjects rich, and then I will build hospitals.

"At Rome, the hospitals place every one at his ease, except those who labor, those who are industrious, those who have lands, and those who are engaged in trade

"I have observed, that wealthy nations have need of hospitals, because fortune subjects them to a thousand accidents; but it is plain, that transient assistances are better than perpetual foundations The evil is momentary, it is necessary, therefore, that the succor should be of the same nature, and that it be applied to particular accidents." Spirit of laws, b. xxiii ch 29

It was reserved for the present generation to substitute in the room of public hospitals private DISPENSARIES for the relief of the sick. Philosophy and Christianity alike concur in deriving praise and benefit from these excellent institutions. They exhibit something like an application of the mechanical powers to the purposes of benevolence; for in what other charitable institutions do we perceive so great a *quantity* of distress relieved by so small an **expence?**

were the principles and practice of physic. It was only in the declension of the empire that physicians vied with the emperors of Rome in magnificence and splendor.*

I am sorry to add in this place, that the number of patients in the HOSPITAL, and incurables in the ALMSHOUSE of this city, show that we are treading in the enervated steps of our fellow subjects in Britain. Our bills of mortality likewise show the encroachments of British diseases upon us. The NERVOUS FEVER has become so familiar to us, that we look upon it as a natural disease. Dr Sydenham, so faithful in his history of fevers, takes no notice of it. Dr Cadwallader informed me, that it made its first appearance in this city about five and twenty years ago. It will be impossible to name the CONSUMPTION without recalling to our minds the memory of some friend or relation, who has perished within these few years by that disorder. Its rapid progress among us has been unjustly attributed to the growing resemblance of our climate to that of Great-Britain. The HYSTERIC and HYPOCHONDRIAC DISORDERS, once peculiar to the chambers of the great, are now to be found in our kitchens and workshops. All these diseases have been produced by our having deserted the simple diet, and manners, of our ancestors.

The blessings of literature, commerce, and religion were not *originally* purchased at the expense of health. The complete

---

* The first regular practitioners of physic in Rome, were women and slaves. The profession was confined to them above six hundred years. The Romans during this period lived chiefly upon vegetables, particularly upon PULSE; and hence they were called, by their neighbours PULTIFAGI. They were likewise early inured to the healthy employments of war and husbandry. Their diseases, of course, were too few and simple to render the cure of them an object of a liberal profession. When their diseases became more numerous and complicated, their investigation and cure required the aids of philosophy. The profession from this time became liberal; and maintained a rank with the other professions which are founded upon the imperfection and depravity of human institutions. Physicians are as necessary in the advanced stages of society as surgeons, although their office is less ancient and certain. There are many artificial diseases, in which they give certain relief; and even where their art fails, their prescriptions are still necessary, in order to smooth the avenues of death.

enjoyment of health is as compatible with civilization, as the enjoyment of civil liberty. We read of countries, rich in every thing that can form national happiness and national grandeur, the diseases of which are nearly as few and simple as those of the Indians. We hear of no diseases among the Jews, while they were under their democratical form of government, except such as were inflicted by a supernatural power.* We should be tempted to doubt the accounts given of the populousness of that people, did we not see the practice of their simple customs producing nearly the same populousness in Egypt, Rome, and other countries of antiquity. The Empire of China, it is said contains more inhabitants than the whole of Europe. The political institutions of that country have exempted its inhabitants from a large share of the diseases of other civilized nations. The inhabitants of Switzerland, Denmark, Norway † and Sweden, enjoy the chief advantages of civilization without having surrendered

---

* The principal employments of the Jews, like those of the Romans in their simple ages, consisted in war and husbandry. Their diet was plain, consisting chiefly of vegetables. Their only remedies were plasters and ointments, which were calculated for those diseases which are produced by accidents. In proportion as they receded from their simple customs, we find artificial diseases prevail among them. The leprosy made its appearance in their journey through the wilderness. King Asa's pains in his feet, were probably brought on by a fit of the gout. Saul and Nebuchadnezzar were afflicted with a melancholy In the time of our Saviour, we find an account of all those diseases in Judea, which mark the declension of a people, such as, the palsy, epilepsy, mania, blindness, hemorrhagia uterina, &c It is unnecessary to suppose, that they were let loose at this juncture, on purpose to give our Saviour an opportunity of making them the chief subject of his miracles They had been produced from natural causes, by the gradual depravity of their manners. It is remarkable, that our Saviour chose those artificial diseases for the subject of his miracles, in preference to natural diseases. The efforts of nature, and the operation of medicines, are too slow and uncertain in these cases to detract in the least from the validity of the miracle. He cured Peter's mother-in-law, it is true, of a fever; but to shew that the cure was miraculous, the sacred historian adds, (contrary to what is common after a fever) "that she arose *immediately* and ministered unto them."

† In the city of Bergen, which consists of 30,000 inhabitants, there is but one physician; who is supported at the expence of the public. Pontoppidan's Nat. Hist. of Norway.

for them the blessings of natural health. But it is unnecessary to appeal to ancient or remote nations to prove, that health is not incompatible with civilization. The inhabitants of many parts of New England, particularly the province of Connecticut, are strangers to artificial diseases. Some of you may remember the time, and our fathers have told those of us who do not, when the diseases of PENNSYLVANIA were as few and as simple as those of the Indians. The food of the inhabitants was then simple; their only drink was water; their appetites were restrained by labour, religion excluded the influence of sickening passions; private hospitality supplied the want of a public hospital; nature was their only nurse, temperance their principal physician But I must not dwell upon this retrospect of primæval manners; and I am too strongly impressed with a hope of a revival of such happy days, to pronounce them the golden age of our province.

Our esteem for the customs of our savage neighbours will be lessened, when we add, that civilization does not preclude the honours of old age. The proportion of old people is much greater among civilized, than among savage nations. It would be easy to decide this assertion in our favour, by appealing to facts in the natural histories of Britain, Norway, Sweden, North-America,* and several of the West-India Islands.

---

* It has been urged against the state of longevity in America, that the Europeans, who settle among us, generally arrive to a greater age than the Americans. This is not occasioned so much by a peculiar firmness in their stamina, as by an increase of vigour, which the constitution acquires by a change of climate A Frenchman (cæteris paribus) outlives an Englishman in England An Hollander prolongs his life by removing to the Cape of Good Hope A Portuguese gains fifteen or twenty years by removing to Brazil. And there are good reasons to believe, that a North-American would derive the same advantages, in point of health and longevity, by removing to Europe, which an European derives from coming to this country.

From a calculation made by an ingenious foreigner, it appears, that a greater proportion of old-people are to be found in Connecticut, than in any colony in North-America. This colony contains 180,000 inhabitants. They have no public hospitals or poor-houses; nor is a beggar to be seen among them. There cannot be more striking proofs than these facts of the simplicity of their manners.

The laws of decency and nature, are not necessarily abolished by the customs of civilized nations. In many of these, we read of women among whom nature alone still performs the office of a midwife,† and who feel the obligations of suckling their children, to be equally binding with the common obligations of morality.

Civilization does not render us less fit for the necessary hardships of war. We read of armies of civilized nations, who have endured degrees of cold, hunger and fatigue, which have not been exceeded by the savages of any country.*

Civilization does not always multiply the avenues of death. It appears from the bills of mortality, of many countries, that fewer in proportion die among civilized, than among savage nations. Even the charms of beauty are heightened by civilization. We read of stateliness, proportion, and fine teeth ** and

---

† Parturition, in the simple ages of all countries, is performed by nature. The Israelitish women were delivered even without the help of the Egyptian midwives. We read of but two women who died in childbirth in the whole history of the Jews. Dr Bancroft says, that childbearing is attended with so little pain in Guiana, that the women seem to be exempted from the curse inflicted upon Eve. These easy births are not confined to warm climates. They are equally safe and easy in Norway and Iceland, according to Pontoppidan and Anderson's histories of those countries.

* Civilized nations have, in the end, always conquered savages as much by their ability to bear hardships, as by their superior military skill. Soldiers are not to be chosen indiscriminately. The greatest generals have looked upon sound constitutions to be as essential to soldiers, as bravery or military discipline. Count Saxe refused soldiers born and bred in large cities, and sought for such only as were bred in mountainous countries. The King of Prussia calls young soldiers only to the dangers and honors of the field in his elegant poem, Sur l'Art de la Guerre, chant. 1. Old soldiers generally lose the advantages of their veteranism, by their habits of idleness and debauchery. An able general, and experienced officers, will always supply the defects of age in young soldiers.

** Bad teeth are observed chiefly in middle latitudes, which are subject to alternate heats and colds. The inhabitants of Norway and Russia are as remarkable for their fine teeth as the inhabitants of Africa. We observe fine teeth to be universal likewise among the inhabitants of France, who live in a *variable* climate. These have been ascribed to their protecting their heads from the action of the night air by means of

complexions in both sexes, forming the principal outlines of national characters.

The danger of many diseases, is not proportioned to their violence, but to their duration. America has advanced but a few paces in luxury and effeminacy. There is yet strength enough in her vitals to give life to those parts which are decayed. She may recall her steps. For this purpose,

I. Let our children be educated in a manner more agreeable to nature.

II. Let the common people (who constitute the wealth and strength of our country) be preserved from the effects of spirituous liquors. Had I a double portion of all that eloquence which has been employed in describing the political evils that lately threatened our country, it would be too little to set forth the numerous and complicated *physical* and *moral* evils which these liquors have introduced among us. To encounter this *hydra* requires an arm accustomed like that of Hercules to vanquish monsters. Sir William Temple tells us, that in Spain no man can be admitted as an evidence in a court, who has once been convicted of drunkenness. I do not call for so severe a law in this country. Let us first try the force of severe manners. Lycurgus governed more by these, than by his laws. "Boni mores non bonæ leges," according to Tacitus, were the bulwarks of virtue among the ancient Germans.

III. I despair of being able to call the votaries of Bacchus from their bottle, and shall therefore leave them to be roused by the more eloquent twinges of the gout.

IV. Let us be cautious what kind of manufactures we admit among us. The rickets made their first appearance in the manufacturing towns in England. Dr Fothergill informed me, that he had often observed, when a pupil, that the greatest part of the chronic patients in the London Hospital were Spittal-field

---

woollen night-caps, and to the extraordinary attention to the teeth of their children. These precautions secure good teeth; and are absolutely necessary in all variable climates where people do not adopt all the customs of the savage life.

weavers. I would not be understood, from these facts, to discourage those manufacturers which give employment to women these suffer few inconveniences from a sedentary life: nor do I mean to offer the least restraint to those manufactories among men, which admit of free air, and the exercise of all their limbs. Perhaps a pure air and the abstraction of spirituous liquors might render sedentary employments less unhealthy in America, even among men, than in the populous towns of Great-Britain.

The population of a country is not to be accomplished by rewards and punishments. And it is happy for America, that the universal prevalence of the Protestant religion, the checks lately given to Negro slavery, the general unwillingness among us to acknowledge the usurpations of primogeniture, the universal practice of inoculation for the small-pox, and the absence of the plague, render the interposition of government for that purpose unnecessary.

These advantages can only be secured to our country by AGRICULTURE. This is the true basis of national health, riches and populousness. Nations, like individuals, never rise higher than when they are ignorant whither they are tending. It is impossible to tell from history, what will be the effects of agriculture, industry, temperance, and commerce, urged on by the competition of colonies, united in the same general pursuits, in a country, which for extent, variety of soil, climate, and number of navigable rivers, has never been equalled in any quarter of the globe. America is the theatre where human nature will probably receive her last and principal literary, moral and political honors.

But I recall myself from the ages of futurity. The province of Pennsylvania has already shewn to her sister colonies, the influence of agriculture and commerce upon the number and happiness of a people. It is scarcely an hundred years since our illustrious legislator, with an handful of men, landed upon these shores. Although the perfection of our government, the healthiness of our climate, and the fertility of our soil, seemed to insure a rapid settlement of the province; yet it would have required a prescience bordering upon divine, to have foretold, that in such a short space of time, the province would contain above 300,000 inhabitants, and that near 30,000 of this number should compose a city, which should be the third, if not the second in commerce in the British empire. The pursuits of literature require leisure and a total recess from clearing forests, planting, building, and all the common toils of settling a new country· but before these arduous works were accomplished, the SCIENCES, ever fond of the company of liberty and industry, chose this spot for the seat of their empire in this new world. Our COLLEGE, so catholic in its foundation, and extensive in its objects, already sees her sons executing offices in the highest departments of society. I have now the honour of speaking in the presence of a most respectable number of philosophers, physicians, astronomers, botanists, patriots, and legislators, many of whom have already seized the prizes of honour, which their ancestors had allotted to a much later posterity. Our first offering had scarcely found its way into the temple of fame, when the oldest societies in Europe turned their eyes upon us, expecting with impatience to see the mighty fabric of science, which like a well built arch, can only rest upon the whole of its materials, completely finished from the treasures of this unexplored quarter of the globe.

It reflects equal honour upon our society and the honourable assembly of our province, to acknowledge, that we have always found the latter willing to encourage by their patronage, and reward by their liberality, all our schemes for promoting useful knowledge. What may we not expect from this harmony between the sciences and government! Methinks I see canals cut, rivers once impassible rendered navigable, bridges erected, and roads improved, to facilitate the exportation of grain. I see the banks of our rivers vying in fruitfulness with the banks of the river of Egypt. I behold our farmers, nobles; our merchants princes. But I forbear—Imagination cannot swell with the subject.

I beg leave to conclude, by deriving an argument from our

connection with the legislature, to remind my auditors of the duty they owe to the society. Patriotism and literature are here connected together; and a man cannot neglect the one without being destitute of the other. Nature and our ancestors have completed their works among us, and have left us nothing to do, but to enlarge and perpetuate our own happiness.

THE VICES AND VIRTUES OF PHYSICIANS
A Lecture

MAN IS A compound of good and evil. These dispositions appear in different proportions, according to the circumstances in which he is placed. They are much influenced by different states of society, and by different pursuits and occupations in life. Every profession has its peculiar vices and virtues. The business of our present lecture shall be to point out such of them as are attached to the profession of medicine. This investigation I hope will be useful, by teaching you in your outset in life, to avoid the former, and to cherish the latter. By these means, you will at once render the practice of physic, and your own characters, more respectable. You will likewise be enabled thereby, to bear with more composure and fortitude, the vexations and distresses which are connected with a medical life.

The vices of physicians may be divided into three heads.
I. As they relate to the Supreme Being.
II. To their patients, and
III. To their professional brethren.

1st. Under the first head I shall begin by lamenting, that men whose educations necessarily open to them the wisdom and goodness of the Creator, and whose duties lead them constantly to behold his power over human life, and all its comforts, should be so very prone to forget him. This they evidence by their neglect of that worship, which is paid to him in different forms, under true, or false names, in every country. If it be a fact, that physicians are more inclined to infidelity, than any other body of men, it must be ascribed chiefly to this cause. To correct this disposition, it is necessary we should be frequently reminded of the arguments on which Christianity is founded, and of the numerous and powerful motives which enforce a belief of it. It is in places of public worship that these arguments and motives are delivered to the most advantage, and it is by neglecting to hear them, that the natural propensity of the human heart to infidelity, is cherished and promoted. This vice of the understanding has no natural alliance with the practice of physic, for to no secular profession does the Christian religion afford more aid, than to medicine. Our business leads us daily into the abodes of pain and misery. It obliges us likewise, frequently to witness the fears with which our friends leave the world, and the anguish which follows, in their surviving relatives. Here the common resources of our art fail us, but the comfortable views of the divine government, and of a future state, which are laid open by Christianity, more than supply their place. A pious word, dropped from the lips of a physician in such circumstances of his patients, often does more good than a long, and perhaps an ingenious discourse from another person, inasmuch as it falls upon the heart, in the moment of its deepest depression from grief. There is no substitute for this cordial in the materia medica.

2d. An undue confidence in medicine, to the exclusion of a Divine and Superintending Power over the health and lives of men, is another vice among physicians. A Dr. ———, in New York prescribed on an evening, for a sick man. The next day he called and asked him how he was, "Much better (said he) thank God." "Thank God! (said the doctor) thank me, it was I who cured you."

3d. Drunkenness is a medical vice, which offends not only God, but man. It is generally induced by fatigue, and exposure to great heat and cold. But a habit of drinking intemperately is often incurred by a social spirit, leading physicians to accept of offers of wine, or spirits and water, in every house they enter, in the former part of the day. Good men have often been seduced and ruined by this complaisant practice. I shall hereafter mention to you the safety, and advantages of eating a little fruit, or portable aliment, in preference to drinks of any kind before dinner, or when the body is in a languid state from fatigue. Drunkenness is a hideous vice in any person, but peculiarly so in a physician. If it rendered him offensive to his patients only by the smell it imparted to his breath, it should be a sufficient motive to deter him from it, but its evils are much more serious and extensive. It corrupts his manners, impairs his judgment, and renders him unfit to prescribe for the sick. Two instances of death have occurred, within my knowledge, from patients taking excessive doses of liquid laudanum, from the hands of a drunken physician.

4th. The members of our profession have sometimes been charged with an irreverent, and profane use of the name of the Supreme Being, but from the general disrepute in which that vice is now held in genteel life, I am happy in adding that it is less common among physicians, than it was forty years ago.

II. In speaking of the vices of physicians as far as they relate to their patients, I pass over numerous acts of imposture. They are all more or less contrary to good morals. I shall at present only mention the more obvious and positive vices which belong to this head. They are

1st. Falsehood. This vice discovers itself chiefly in the deceptions which are practised by physicians with respect to the cause, nature, and probable issue of diseases. What oceans of falsehoods have issued from the members of our profession, upon the cause of pestilential epidemics, in all ages and countries! How many false names have been given to them to conceal their existence! In England the plague of 1664, was called, for several months, by the less alarming name of a spotted fever. In the United States of America, the yellow fever, is deprived for a while of the terror it ought to produce in order to its being avoided, or cured, by receiving the name of a common remittent, or by being ascribed to intemperance, or to some cause which only excited it into action. Equally criminal is the practice among some physicians of encouraging patients to expect a recovery, in diseases which have arrived at their incurable stage. The mischief done by falsehood in this case, is the more to be deplored, as it often prevents the dying from settling their worldly affairs, and employing their last hours in preparing for their future state.

This vice in physicians sometimes appears in histories, of cases that never existed, and of cures that were never performed. When it assumes this hateful form, its evil consequences become extensive and durable, from the difficulty with which it is detected and exposed.

2d. Inhumanity is a vice which sometimes appears in the conduct of physicians to their patients. It discovers itself in the want of prompt and punctual attendance upon the sick, and in a careless or unfeeling manner in sick rooms. This insensibility to human suffering is very happily exposed in the New Bath Guide; I should have supposed it too highly coloured, had I not heard of similar instances of inhumanity in several members of our profession. A lord of session, once fell from his seat in the court of Edinburgh in an apoplexy. A physician was called in haste to see him. He applied his fingers to his pulse. His brother judges, and a croud of spectators waited with solicitude to know whether he still retained any sign of life. "He is dead," said the physician, and in the same breath, said to a person who stood next to him, "Pray sir, shall we have a Spanish war." It is some consolation to the lovers of the healing art to recollect, that such instances of a want of sympathy and decency in physicians are very rare, and that examples of a contrary disposition, as I hope to prove hereafter, are more common amongst them.

3d. Avarice, in all its forms of meanness, oppression, and cruelty, is a frequent vice among physicians. It discovers itself,

1st. In a denial of services to the poor. I once heard a physician's eminence estimated by the fewness of his bad debts, and by his doing no business, for which he was not paid. We had a trader in medicine of this kind in Philadelphia, many years ago, who constantly refused to attend poor people, and when called upon to visit them, drove them from his door by a name so impious, that I shall not mention it. This sordid conduct is sometimes aggravated by being exercised towards old patients, who have been unfortunate in business, in the evening of their lives. We owe much to the families, who employ us in the infancy of our knowledge and experience. It is an act, therefore, of ingratitude, as well as avarice, to neglect them under the pressure of age and poverty, as well as sickness, or to consign them over to young physicians or quacks, who are ignorant of their constitutions and habits, and strangers to the respect they commanded in their better days.

2d Avarice, in physicians, discovers itself in their extravagant charges, and in the means which are sometimes employed to obtain payment for such debts as are just. I have heard of a surgeon in the British army, who made it a practice to take the swords of the officers, as a security for the future payment of his bills. A physician, in this country, once took, by legal force, a solitary cow from a poor woman, on which she chiefly relied for the subsistence of her family. But it is after the death of the master of a family, that the avarice of physicians appears in its most distressing and cruel forms. Behold one of these harpies enter into the house of a widow, who has just been bereaved of her husband, on whose daily labour she depended for her daily support. Unmoved by her tears, and by the sight of a group of helpless children, calling upon her, perhaps in vain, for their customary articles of food, sternly he demands an immediate settlement of his account. Gracious Father of the human race! touch the heart of this wretch with a sudden sense of thy justice, and cause him to feel the enormity of his crime! But if, by persevering in habits of extortion, he has forfeited thy reclaiming mercy, extend thy pity to the family which thou hast sorely afflicted, and discover to them, by some unexpected act of thy bounty, that thou art indeed a friend to the fatherless, and the widow's God!

3d. To undertake the charge of sick people, and to neglect them afterwards, is a vice of a malignant dye in a physician. Many lives have been lost, by the want of punctual and regular attention to the varying symptoms of diseases; but still more have been sacrificed by the criminal preference, which has been given by physicians to ease, convivial company, or public amusements and pursuits, to the care of their patients. The most important contract that can be made, is that which takes place between a sick man and his doctor. The subject of it is human life. The breach of this contract, by wilful negligence, when followed by death, is murder; and it is because our penal laws are imperfect, that the punishment of that crime is not inflicted upon physicians who are guilty of it.

4th. It is a vice in a physician to study, more, to please, than to cure his patients. Dr. Young calls such preachers, as prefer pleasing their hearers, to instructing and reforming them, "downy doctors." The same epithet may be applied to physicians, who prescribe for the whims of their patients, instead of their diseases. The life of a sick man should be the first object of a physician's solicitude, and he is not prepared to do his duty, until he can sacrifice his interest and reputation to preserve it.

5th. The last vice I shall mention under this head, is, obstinacy in adhering to old and unsuccessful modes of practice, in diseases which have yielded to new remedies. Dr. Chisholm relates several flagrant instances of this vice, in the treatment of the yellow fever, in his late essay upon that pestilential disease in the West Indies. This obstinacy was the more criminal in the physicians alluded to, as they had constantly before their eyes, numerous and irrefragable evidences of the success of a different mode of practice, which the Doctor had introduced into the islands. Many similar instances of this hoary headed indifference to human life, are to be met with in all countries.

III. Agreeably to our order, I should proceed next to mention the vices of physicians towards their professional brethren, but for obvious reasons, I shall pass over this disagreeable part of our subject in silence, and hasten, with pleasure, to speak of the VIRTUES of physicians.

Here a delightful field opens to our view. It will be impossible to mark every part of it with our footsteps. I shall, therefore, only mention those virtues, which are most conspicuous and practical in the members of our profession.

1. Piety towards God has, in many instances, characterized some of the first physicians in ancient and modern times. Hippocrates did homage to the gods of Greece, and Galen vanquished atheism for a while, in Rome, by proving the existence of a god, from the curious structure of the human body. Botallus, the illustrious father of blood-letting, in Europe, in a treatise, "de munere medici et ægri," advises a physician, when called to visit a patient, never to leave his house, without offering up a prayer to God, for the success of his prescriptions. Cheselden, the famous English anatomist, always implored, in the presence of his pupils, the aid and blessing of heaven upon his hand, whenever he laid hold of an instrument, to perform a surgical operation. Sydenham, the great luminary and reformer of medicine, was a religious man. Boerhaave spent an hour in his closet, every morning, in reading the scriptures, before he entered upon the duties of his profession. Hoffman and Stahl were not ashamed of the gospel of Christ, and Dr. Haller has left behind him, an eloquent defence of it in a series of letters to his daughter. Dr. Lobb exhibited daily, for many years, to the citizens of London, his reliance upon divine aid to render his practice successful, by inscribing "Deo adjuvante" upon his family arms, which were painted upon his chariot. Dr. Fothergill's long life resembled an altar, from which, incense of adoration and praise ascended daily to the Supreme Being. Dr. Hartley, whose works will probably perish, only with time itself, was a devout Christian. To the record of these medical worthies, I shall add but one remark, and that is, the weight of their names alone, in favour of revelation, is sufficient to turn the scale against all the infidelity, that has ever dishonoured the science of medicine.

2. Humanity has been a conspicuous virtue among physicians in all ages and countries. It manifests itself,

1st. In their sacrifices and sufferings, in order to acquire a knowledge of all the different branches of medicine For this, they spend months, and years, in dissecting dead bodies, or in the smoke of laboratories, or in visiting foreign, and sometimes uncivilized countries; or in making painful and expensive experiments upon living animals. Many physicians have contracted diseases, and some have perished in these loathsome and dangerous enterprizes, all of which are intended for the benefit of their fellow-creatures.

2d. No sooner do they enter upon the duties of their profession, than they are called upon to exhibit their humanity by sympathy, with pain and distress in persons of all ranks. It is this heaven-born principle, which produces such acts of self-denial of company, pleasure, and sleep, in physicians. It is this, which enables them to sustain the extremes of heat and cold, and the most laborious exertions of body and mind. Hippocrates, who furnished the earliest, has likewise exhibited the most prominent example of this divine form of humanity, of any physician that ever lived. One while we behold him travelling through the cities and provinces of Greece, dispensing health and joy wherever he went. Again, we see him yielding to the solicitations of neighbouring princes, and extending the blessings of his skill to foreign nations. "There was but one sentiment in his soul" says Galen, "and that was the *love of doing good*, and in the course of his long life, but a single act, and that was the *relieving the sick*." It was, from the influence which his humane feelings had upon his judgment, that he has left the following remark upon record, in speaking of the education of a young man, intended for the study of medicine. "Does he suffer" says the venerable man, "with the sufferings of others? does he naturally feel the tenderest commiseration for the woes incident to his fellow mortals? you may reasonably infer that he will be passionately devoted to an art, that will instruct him in what manner to afford them relief." This noble sympathy, in physicians, is sometimes so powerful, as to predominate over the fear of death; hence we observe them to expose, and frequently to sacrifice their lives, in contending with mortal epidemics. The United States have lately furnished numerous instances of death in physicians, from their ardent attachment to their patients. The grave-yards of Philadelphia alone hold the precious relicts of three and twenty members of our profession, who have died martyrs to this affectionate and heroic sympathy, since the year 1793.

3d. Humanity in physicians manifests itself in gratuitous services to the poor. The greatest part of the business of Dr. Sydenham, seems to have been confined to poor people. It is true, he now and then speaks of a noble lady, and of a learned prelate, in the history of cases, but these were accidental patients. The fashionable part of the citizens of London were deterred from consulting him, by the clamours excited against his new practice, by his medical brethren, particularly by Dr. Morton, whom Dr. Haller calls "the rival and adversary" of this excellent man. Dr. Boerhaave did a great deal of business among the poor. In his attendance upon them, he discovered, it is said, more solicitude and punctuality, than in his attendance upon his rich patients. Being asked by a friend his reason for so doing, he answered, "I esteem the poor my *best* patients, for God is their pay-master." Dr. Cullen spent the first years of his long and useful life, in doing business, for which he was never paid, and when he rose to the first rank in his profession, did not forget that humble class of people, from whom he derived his knowledge and reputation. Dr. Fothergill devoted an hour every morning, before he left his house, to prescribing for the poor, and in his annual visit to Leahall, in Cheshire, he spent one day of every week, in the same humane and benevolent business. Public dispensaries were projected, and are still conducted, chiefly by physicians. These excellent institutions mark an æra in the history of human beneficence. They yearly save many thousand lives.

4th. Humanity in physicians discovers itself in *pecuniary* contributions, as well as in advice, for the relief of the poor. I have read an account of a physician in England, who gave all the fees he received on a Sunday, to charitable purposes. Dr. Heberdeen's liberality to the poor was so great, that he was once told by a friend, that he would exhaust his fortune. "No," said he, "after all my charities, I am afraid I shall die *shamefully* rich." Dr. Fothergill once heard of the death of a citizen of London, who had left his family in indigent circumstances. As soon as he was interred, the doctor called upon his widow, and informed her, that he had, some years before, received thirty guineas for as many visits he had paid her husband in the days of his prosperity. "I have since heard," said the doctor "of his reverse of fortune. Take this purse. It contains all that I received from him. It will do thy family more good, than it will do me." A poor curate, who lived in the city of London upon fifty pounds a year, called upon this worthy man for advice for his wife and five children, who were ill of an epidemic disease, then prevalent in that city. The doctor, without being requested, visited them the next day, and attended them daily till they were all cured. The curate, by great exertions, saved a trifling sum of money, which he offered to the doctor, as a compensation for his services. He refused to receive it . . . but this was not all . . . he put ten guineas into his hand, and begged him, at the same time, to apply to him for relief in all his future difficulties.* Similar anecdotes of his liberality might be multiplied without end. It is said, he gave away one half of all the income of his extensive and lucrative business, amounting, in the course of his life, to one hundred thousand pounds. What an immense interest in honour and happiness must this sum produce to him at the general judgment! With what unspeakable gratitude and delight, may we not suppose the many hundred, and perhaps thousand persons, whom he has fed, clothed, and rescued from prison and death by his charities, will gaze upon their benefactor in that solemn day, while the Supreme Judge credits them all, as done to himself, in the presence of an assembled world.

---

* Lettsom's Life of Fothergill.

III. Physicians have been distinguished in many instances, for their patriotism. By this virtue, I mean a disposition to promote all the objects of utility, convenience, and pleasure, and to remove all the evils of the country to which we belong. It embraces all the interests and wants of every class of citizens, and manifests itself in a great variety of forms. I shall briefly enumerate them.

1st. It appears in acts of liberality to promote science, and particularly medicine. The British Museum was the gift of a physician to the British nation. Dr. Radcliff founded a library at Oxford, and bequeathed three hundred pounds to be applied to the maintenance of a constant succession of students of medicine, who should spend three years in foreign countries, in search of medical knowledge. Dr. Fothergill gave one hundred guineas a year to Dr. Priestley, to defray the expenses of his chemical laboratory. But the patronage afforded to science by that great man, was not confined to his own country. The Pennsylvania hospital will preserve, I hope, to the end of time, a testimony of his munificence, in the elegant casts and paintings of the gravid uterus, which compose a part of the museum of that institution.

2d. Patriotism in physicians has discovered itself in attempts and plans to obviate the prevailing diseases of their native country. Hippocrates was once invited by the kings of Illyria and Peonia, to come to the relief of their subjects, who were afflicted by the plague. He inquired of the messenger, into the course of the winds in those countries. Upon being informed of their direction, he concluded the same disease would visit Athens, and declined the honour intended him, that he might devote himself immediately to the means of saving a city of his own country from destruction. A physician delivered Calcutta from an epidemic malignant fever, by pointing out a new and effectual mode of conveying off its filth. The city of Frankfort, in Germany, was saved from an occasional pestilence, by a physician tracing its origin to a number of offensive privies. The physicians of all the cities in the United States (Philadelphia excepted), have, with nearly perfect unanimity, derived our annual bilious plague from domestic sources, and recommended remedies for it, which, if adopted, would ensure a perpetual exemption of our country from it. The many excellent treatises upon the means of preventing diseases, from errors in diet, dress, exercise and the like, that have been published by physicians in all ages and countries, show that self-love is a weaker principle in them, than a regard to the general health and welfare of their fellow-citizens.

3d. Physicians have contributed largely to the prosperity of their respective countries, by recommending and patronizing plans for promoting agriculture, commerce, morals and literature. Dr. Fothergill's garden at Upton, was a kind of hotbed of useful plants, for the whole nation. His active mind was always busy in devising public improvements that were calculated to increase the wealth, the knowledge, the happiness and even the elegance of his country. Dr. Black, Dr. Home and Dr. Hunter, have all benefitted the British empire, by the application of their chemical researches to national purposes, particularly to agriculture and manufactures.

4th. Physicians have in all ages exhibited an attachment to the independence, peace, and liberties of their country. Hippocrates by his influence in forming an alliance with the Thessalians, delivered his native island of Cos from a war with the Athenians. Dr. Fothergill spent years of anxiety in fruitless efforts to prevent the effusion of kindred blood, in the war which separated the United States from Great Britain. He likewise suggested a plan for securing a perpetual peace between the nations of Europe, by the ties of interest, founded upon commerce. There was not a state in our Union, during the late struggle with Great Britain for our independence, which did not furnish instances of this form of patriotism in physicians. Warren and Mercer both turned their backs upon profitable and extensive business, when they led their countrymen into the field, and fell at the head of their troops, bravely fighting for the liberties of their country. Many of the most distinguished characters in medicine, in Europe, are friends to liberty, and a great majority of the physicians in the United States, are warmly attached to the principles, and form of our excellent republican Constitution.

If you feel, gentlemen, in hearing these details of the exploits of the illustrious worthies of our profession, as I do in relating them, you will not regret the day, you devoted yourselves to the study of medicine.

But there are certain minor virtues which have adorned the characters of physicians, that should not pass unnoticed in this place.

1st. They have often discovered the most extraordinary instances of candour, in acknowledging mistakes both of opinion and practice Hippocrates has left a testimony against himself, of the loss of a patient, from his inability to distinguish between a suture, and a fracture of the skull; and Dr. Sydenham tells, that he generally lost several of the first patients whom he visited in a new epidemic. This candour is the more meritorious in physicians, as it seldom fails to lessen their credit with the world.

2d. The most disinterested and exalted acts of generosity, have often been exhibited by physicians to each other. Dr. Friend was once confined for an offensive act against the British government. During this time, Dr. Mead attended his patients. After his liberation, Dr. Mead called upon him, and gave him several thousand guineas. "Take them," said Dr. Mead. "They are not mine. I received them all from your patients." This act was the more meritorious, as they were competitors for business and fame. Similar instances of generosity are common among physicians, though upon a less scale, in all countries.

3d. The most delicate friendships have often subsisted between physicians. Dr. Fothergill and Dr. Russell were contemporaries in the college of Edinburgh. They passed the greatest part of their lives in a constant exchange of kind offices. The eulogium upon Dr. Russell, delivered before the society of physicians, in London, by Dr. Fothergill, does equal honour to the characters of each of them.

4th. Physicians often perform essential services to the families in which they are employed, by directing the education of their children, by preventing, or healing family disputes, and by their advice and influence in the pursuits and management of the common affairs of life.

5th. As sons, brothers, and parents, physicians have often exhibited the most shining examples of domestic virtue. Dr. Tissot was invited to Warsaw, by the late king of Poland, in order to become the physician of his court. He prepared immediately to accept the offer, but upon being told by his aged father, that he would not accompany him, the doctor declined the royal invitation, and ended his days in an obscure situation, in his native country One of the last journeys of Dr Fothergill's life was to pay a tribute of respect to his father's grave in Yorkshire. He was accompanied in this journey by his sister, who had been his companion, and housekeeper for forty years. I shall give an account of this pious excursion in his own words. "To see that our father's sepulchre was not laid open to the beasts of the field, but secured from the ravages of neglect, was to us a pleasing duty. Firmly persuaded that we had not the least cause to mourn upon his account, and nothing left more becoming us, than to call to mind his precepts, and examples, we left the solitary spot with hearts full of reverent thankfulness, that *such* was our father, and that we were *so far* favoured, as to be able to remember him with gratitude and affection."

From a review of what has been said of the vices and virtues of physicians, the following inferences may fairly be deduced.

1st. That their vices are fewer in number, and of less magnitude, than their virtues.

2d. That the profession of medicine, favours the practice of all the religious, moral and social duties. A physician of course who is a bad man, is more inexcusable than a bad man of any other profession, a minister of the gospel excepted.

3d. That the aggregate mass of physical misery that has existed in the world, owes more of its relief to physicians, than to any other body of men.

Let us learn then, gentlemen, duly to appreciate the profession we have chosen, by acting agreeably to the duties it imposes, and the honours it has acquired. With this short application of the subject of our lecture, I bid you welcome to our school of medicine! The door you have entered, and the room you now occupy, are devoted to Science and Humanity. Let nothing incompatible with the time and attention which they claim, ever find a place within these walls. As far as it shall please God to enable me, by the continuance of my health, you may rely upon my seconding your diligence, and that I shall consider my obligations to you, as my chief duty during the winter.

DUTIES OF A PHYSICIAN
A Closing Lecture to Medical Students

I SHALL, *first*, suggest the most probable means of establishing yourselves in business, and of becoming acceptable to your patients, and respectable in life.

Secondly I shall mention a few thoughts which have occurred to me on the mode to be pursued, in the further prosecution of your studies, and for the improvement of medicine.

I. Permit me, in the first place, to recommend to such of you as intend to settle in the country, to establish yourselves as early as possible upon *farms*. My reasons for this advice are as follow.

1. It will reconcile the country people to the liberality and dignity of your profession, by showing them that you assume no superiority over them from your education, and that you intend to share with them in those toils, which were imposed upon man in consequence of the loss of his innocence. This will prevent envy, and render you acceptable to your patients as men, as well as physicians.

2. By living on a farm you may serve your country by promoting improvements in agriculture. Chemistry (which is now an important branch of a medical education) and agriculture are closely allied to each other. Hence some of the most useful books upon agriculture have been written by physicians. Witness the essays of Dr. *Home* of Edinburgh, and of Dr. *Hunter* of Yorkshire in England.

3. The business of a farm will furnish you with employment

in the healthy seasons of the year, and thereby deliver you from the tedium vitæ, or what is worse, from retreating to low or improper company. Perhaps one cause of the prevalence of dram or grog drinking, with which country practitioners are sometimes charged, is owing to their having no regular or profitable business to employ them in the intervals of their attendance upon their patients.

4. The resources of a farm will create such an independence as will enable you to practice with more dignity, and at the same time screen you from the trouble of performing unnecessary services to your patients. It will change the nature of the obligation between you and them. While *money* is the only means of your subsistence, your patients will feel that they are the channels of your daily bread, but while your farm furnishes you with the necessaries of life, your patients will feel more sensibly that the obligation is on their side, for health and life.

5. The exigencies and wants of a farm, in *stock* and *labor* of all kinds, will enable you to obtain from your patients a compensation for your services in those articles. They all possess them; and men part with that of which money is only the sign, much more readily than they do with money itself.

6. The resources of a farm will prevent your cherishing, for a moment, an impious wish for the prevalence of sickness in your neighbourhood. A healthy season will enable you to add to the produce of your farm, while the rewards of an unhealthy season will enable you to repair the inconvenience of your necessary absence from it. By these means your pursuits will be marked by that *variety* and *integrity*, in which true happiness is said to consist.

7. Let your farms be small, and let your *principal* attention be directed to grass and horticulture. These afford most amusement, require only moderate labor, and will interfere least with your duties to your profession.

II. Avoid singularities of every kind in your manners, dress, and general conduct. Sir *Isaac Newton*, it is said, could not be distinguished in company, by any peculiarity, from a common well-bred gentleman. Singularity in any thing, is a substitute for such great or useful qualities as command respect; and hence we find it chiefly in little minds. The profane and indelicate combination of extravagant ideas, improperly called wit, and a formal and pompous manner, whether accompanied by a wig, a cane, or a ring, should all be avoided, as incompatible with the simplicity of science and the real dignity of physic. There is more than one way of playing the quack. It is not necessary, for this purpose, that a man should advertise his skill, or his cures, or that he should mount a phæton and display his dexterity in operating to an ignorant and gaping multitude. A physician acts the same part in a different way, who assumes the character of a madman or a brute in his manners, or who conceals his fallibility by an affected gravity and taciturnity in his intercourse with his patients. Both characters, like the quack, impose upon the public. It is true, they deceive different ranks of people; but we must remember that there are two kinds of vulgar, viz. the rich and the poor, and that the rich vulgar are often below the poor, in ignorance and credulity.

III. It has been objected to our profession, that many eminent physicians have been unfriendly to Christianity. If this be true, I cannot help ascribing it in part to that neglect of public worship with which the duties of our profession are often incompatible; for it has been justly observed, that the neglect of this religious and social duty generally produces a relaxation either in principles or morals. Let this fact lead you, in setting out in business, to acquire such habits of punctuality in visiting your patients, as shall not interfere with acts of public homage to the SUPREME BEING. Dr. *Gregory* has observed, that a cold heart is the most frequent cause of deism. Where this occurs in a physician, it affords a presumption that he is deficient in humanity. But I cannot admit that infidelity is peculiar to our profession. On the contrary, I believe Christianity places among its friends more men of extensive abilities and learning, in medicine, than in any other secular employment. *Stahl, Hoffman, Boerhaave, Sydenham, Haller* and *Fothergill*, were all Christians. These enlightened physicians were considered as the ornaments of the ages in which they lived, and posterity has justly ranked them among the greatest benefactors of mankind.

IV. Permit me to recommend to you a regard to all the interests of your country. The education of a physician gives him a peculiar insight into the principles of many useful arts, and the practice of physic favours his opportunities of doing good, by diffusing knowledge of all kinds. It was in Rome, when medicine was practised only by slaves, that physicians were condemned by their profession "mutam exercere artem." But in modern times, and in free governments, they should disdain an ignoble silence upon public subjects. The history of the American Revolution has rescued physic from its former slavish rank in society. For the honor of our profession it should be recorded, that some of the most intelligent and useful characters, both in the cabinet and the field, during the late war, have been physicians. The illustrious Dr. *Fothergill* opposed faction and tyranny, and took the lead in all public improvements in his native country, without suffering thereby the least diminution of that reputation, or business, in which, for forty years, he flourished almost without a rival in the city of London.

V. Study *simplicity* in the preparation of your medicines. My reasons for this advice are as follow.

1. Active medicines produce the most certain effects in a simple state.

2. Medicines when mixed frequently destroy the efficacy of each other. I do not include chemical medicines alone in this remark. It applies likewise to galenical medicines. Nor do I assert that the virtues of all these medicines are impaired by mixture; but we can only determine when they are not, by actual experiments and observation.

3. When medicines of the same class, or even of different classes, are given together, the *strongest* only produces an effect. But what are we to say to a compound of two medicines which gives exactly the same degrees of impression to the system? The effect of them will probably be such, if we may judge from

analogy, as would have been produced by neither in a simple state.

4. By observing simplicity in your prescriptions, you will always have the command of a greater number of medicines of the same class, which may be used in succession to each other, in proportion as habit renders the system insensible of their action.

5. By using medicines in a simple state, you will arrive at an exact knowledge of their virtues and doses, and thereby be able to decide upon the numerous and contradictory accounts, which exist in our books, of the characters of the same medicines.

Under this head I cannot help adding two more directions.

1. Avoid sacrificing *too much* to the taste of your patients, in the composition of your medicines. The nature of a medicine may, in some instances, be wholly changed, by being mixed with sweet substances. The Author of nature seems to have had a design in making medicines unpalatable. Had they been more agreeable to the taste, they would long ago have yielded to the unbounded appetites of man, and by becoming articles of diet or condiments, have lost their efficacy in diseases.

2. Give as few medicines as possible in tinctures made with distilled spirits. Perhaps there are but few cases in which it is safe to exhibit medicines prepared in spirits, in any other form than in *drops*. Many people have been innocently seduced into a love of *strong drink*, from taking large or frequent doses of bitters infused in spirits. Let not our profession in a single instance be charged with adding to the calamities which have been entailed upon mankind by this dreadful species of intemperance.

V. Let me advise you, in your visits to the sick, *never* to appear in a hurry, nor to talk of indifferent matters before you have made the necessary inquiries into the symptoms of your patient's disease.

VII. Avoid making light of any case; "respice finem" should be the motto of every indisposition. There is scarcely a disorder so trifling, that has not, directly or indirectly, proved an outlet to human life. This consideration should make you anxious and punctual in your attendance upon every acute disease, and keep you from risking your reputation by an improper or hasty prognosis.

VIII. Do not condemn, or oppose, unnecessarily, the simple prescriptions of your patients Yield to them in matters of little consequence, but maintain an inflexible authority over them in matters that are essential to life.

IX. Preserve, upon all occasions, a composed or cheerful countenance in the room of your patients, and inspire as much hope of a recovery as you can, consistent with truth, especially in acute diseases. The extent of the influence of the will over the human body, has not yet been fully ascertained. I reject the futile pretensions of Mr. Mesmer to the cure of diseases, by what he has absurdly called animal magnetism, but I am willing to derive the same advantages from his deceptions, which the chemists have derived from the delusions of the alchemists. The facts which he has established, clearly prove the influence of the imagination and will upon diseases. Let us avail ourselves of the aid which these powers of the mind present to us, in the strife between life and death. I have frequently prescribed remedies of doubtful efficacy in the critical stage of acute diseases, but never till I had worked up my patients into a confidence, bordering upon certainty, of their probable good effects. The success of this measure has much oftener answered, than disappointed my expectations, and while my patients have commended the vomit, the purge, or the blister which was prescribed, I have been disposed to attribute their recovery to the vigorous concurrence of the *will* in the action of the medicine. Does the will beget insensibility to cold, heat, hunger, and danger? Does it suspend pain, and raise the body above feeling the pangs of Indian tortures? Let us not then be surprised that it should enable the system to resolve a spasm, to open an obstruction, or to discharge an offending humor. I have only time to hint at this subject. Perhaps it would lead us, if we could trace it fully, to some very important discoveries in the cure of diseases.

X. Permit me to advise you to attend to that principle in the human mind, which constitutes the association of ideas, in your intercourse with your patients. A chamber, a chair, a curtain, or even a cup, all belong to the means of life or death, accordingly as they are associated with cheerful or distressing ideas, in the mind of a patient. But this principle is of more immediate application in those chronic diseases which affect the mind. Nothing can be accomplished here, till we produce a new association of ideas. For this purpose, a change of place and company are absolutely necessary. But we must sometimes proceed much further. I have heard of a gentleman in South-Carolina, who cured his fits of low spirits by changing his clothes. The remedy was a rational one. It produced at once a new train of ideas, and thus removed the paroxysm of his disease.

XI. A physician in sickness is always a welcome visitor in a family hence he is solicited to partake of the usual sign of hospitality in this country, by taking a draught of some strong drink every time he enters into the house of a patient. Let me charge you to lay an early restraint upon yourselves, by refusing to yield to this practice, especially in the forenoon. Many physicians have been led by it into habits of drunkenness. You will be in the more danger of falling into this vice, from the fatigue and inclemency of weather to which you will be exposed in country practice. But you have been taught that strong drink affords only a temporary relief from those evils, and that it tends afterwards to render the body more sensible of them.

XII. Make it a rule never to be angry at any thing a sick man says or does to you. Sickness often adds to the natural impatience and irritability of the temper. We are, therefore, to submit to the severe and unnecessary toils that are sometimes exacted from us, and to bear even the reproaches of our patients with meekness and silence. It is folly to resent injuries at any time, but it is cowardice to resent an injury from a sick man; since, from his weakness and dependence upon us, he is unable to contend with us upon equal terms. You will find it difficult to attach your patients to you by the obligation of friendship or gratitude. You will sometimes have the mortification of being deserted by those patients who owe most to your skill and humanity. This led Dr. *Turner* to advise physicians never to choose their friends from among their patients. But this advice can never be followed by a heart that has been taught to love true excellency, wherever it finds it. I would rather advise you to give the benevolent feelings of your hearts full scope, and to forget the unkind returns they will often meet with, by giving to human nature— a tear. Let us not despair. From the increasing influence of reason and religion in our world, the time must soon come, when even physicians, and the brute creation, shall become the objects of the justice and humanity of mankind.

XIII. Avoid giving a patient over in an acute disease. It is impossible to tell, in such cases, where life ends and where death begins. Hundreds of patients have recovered who have been pronounced incurable, to the great disgrace of our profession. I know that the practice of predicting danger and death upon every occasion, is sometimes made use of by physicians, in order to enhance the credit of their prescriptions, if their patients recover, and to secure a retreat from blame, if they should die. But this mode of acting is mean and illiberal. It is not necessary that we should decide with confidence at any time, upon the issue of a disease.

XIV. Cases will frequently occur in which you will be exposed to a struggle between a regard for your own reputation, and for the life of a patient. In such cases, let Christianity determine what is to be done. That new commandment which directs us to make the measure of our love to our fellow-creatures, the same as the love of the Author of our religion was to the human race, certainly requires that we should at all times risk, and even sacrifice reputation, to preserve the life of a fellow-creature. The pusillanimous, or, as he is commonly called, the *safe* physician, who, absorbed wholly in the care of his own reputation, views without exertion the last conflict between life and death in a patient, in my opinion will be found hereafter to have been guilty of a breach of the Sixth Commandment; while the conscientious, or, as he is commonly called, the *bold* physician, who loses sight of his character, and even of the means of his subsistence, and by the use of a remedy of doubtful efficacy turns the scale in favour of life, performs an act that borders upon divine benevolence. A physician who has only once in his life enjoyed the godlike pleasure that is connected with such an act of philanthropy, will never require any other consideration to reconcile him to the toils and duties of his profession.

. XV. I shall now give some directions with respect to the method of charging for your services to your patients.

When we consider the expence of a medical education, and the sacrifices a physician is obliged to make of ease, society, and even health, to his profession, and when we add to these, the constant and painful anxiety which is connected with the important charge of the lives of our fellow-creatures, and above all, the inestimable value of that blessing which is the object of his services, I hardly know how it is possible for a patient sufficiently and justly to reward his physician. But when we consider, on the other hand, that sickness deprives men of the means of acquiring money; that it increases all the expenses of living; and that high charges often drive patients from regular-bred physicians to quacks; I say, when we attend to these considerations, we should make our charges as moderate as possible, and conform them to the following state of things.

Avoid measuring your services to your patients by scruples, drachms, and ounces. It is an illiberal mode of charging. On the contrary, let the number and the *time* of your visits, the nature of your patient's disease, and his rank in his family or society, determine the figures in your accounts. It is certainly just to charge more for curing an apoplexy, than an intermitting fever. It is equally just to demand more for risking your life by visiting a patient in a contagious fever, than for curing a pleurisy. You have a right likewise to be paid for your anxiety. Charge the same services, therefore, higher to the master or mistress of a family, or to an only son or daughter, who call forth all your feelings and industry, than to less important members of a family and of society. If a rich man demands more frequent visits than are necessary, and if he imposes the restraints of keeping to hours by calling in other physicians to consult with you upon every trifling occasion, it will be just to make him pay accordingly for it. As this mode of charging is strictly agreeable to reason and equity, it seldom fails of according with the reason and sense of equity of our patients. Accounts made out upon these principles, are seldom complained of by them. I shall only remark further upon this subject, that the sooner you send in your accounts after your patients recover, the better. It is the duty of a physician to inform his patient of the amount of his obligation to him at least *once* a year. But there are times when a departure from this rule may be necessary. An unexpected misfortune in business, and a variety of other accidents, may deprive a patient of the money he had allotted to pay his physician. In this case, delicacy and humanity require, that he should not know the amount of his debt to his physician, till time has bettered his circumstances.

I shall only add, under this head, that the poor of every description should be the objects of your peculiar care. Dr. Boerhaave used to say, "they were his best patients, because God was their paymaster." The first physicians that I have known, have found the poor the steps by which they ascended to business and reputation. Diseases among the lower class of people are generally simple, and exhibit to a physician the best cases of all epidemics, which cannot fail of adding to his ability of curing the complicated diseases of the rich and intemperate. There is an inseparable connection between a man's duty and his interest. Whenever you are called, therefore, to visit a poor patient, imagine you hear the voice of the good Samaritan sounding in your ears, "Take care of him, and I will repay thee."

I come now to the second part of this address, which was to point out the best mode to be pursued, in the further prosecution of your studies, and the improvement of medicine.

I. Give me leave to recommend to you, to open all the dead bodies you can, without doing violence to the feelings of your patients, or the prejudices of the common people. Preserve a register of the weather, and of its influence upon the vegetable productions of the year. Above all, record the epidemics of every season, their times of appearing, and disappearing, and the connection of the weather with each of them. Such records, if published, will be useful to foreigners, and a treasure to posterity. Preserve, likewise, an account of chronic cases. Record the name, age and occupation of your patient, describe his disease accurately, and the changes produced in it by your remedies; mention the doses of every medicine you administer to him. It is impossible to tell how much improvement and facility in practice you will derive from following these directions. It has been remarked, that physicians seldom remember more than the two or three last years of their practice. The records which have been mentioned, will supply this deficiency of memory, especially in that advanced stage of life when the advice of physicians is supposed to be most valuable.

II. Permit me to recommend to you further, the study of the anatomy (if I may be allowed the expression) of the human mind, commonly called metaphysics. The reciprocal influence of the body and mind upon each other, can only be ascertained by an accurate knowledge of the faculties of the mind, and of their various modes of combination and action. It is the duty of physicians to assert their prerogative, and to rescue the mental science from the usurpations of schoolmen and divines. It can only be perfected by the aid and discoveries of medicine. The authors I would recommend to you upon metaphysics, are, Butler, Locke, Hartly, Reid, and Beattie. These ingenious writers have cleared this sublime science of its technical rubbish, and rendered it both intelligible and useful.

III. Do not confine your studies and attention only to *extraordinary* cases. The most frequent outlets of human life are through the channels of *common* diseases. A late professor in the college of Glasgow, when a student in one of the London hospitals, was observed to be busy in examining the pulse of a patient in a fever, while all his fellow students were employed in examining with uncommon attention the case of a child with two heads that had just been brought into the hospital. Upon being condemned by his companions for neglecting to profit by the examination of so new a case, he answered, "I never expect in the whole course of my life to see, or hear, of another child with two heads; but I expect to meet with fevers in my practice, every day of my life." This sensible answer admits of extensive application to the advancement of medicine. Could we eradicate fevers only from our bills of mortality, how much more should we add to the population and happiness of our country, than by discovering remedies for swollen membrane and abnormal dilation of blood vessels?

IV. Let me remind you, that improvement in medicine is not to be derived, only from colleges and universities. Systems of physic are the productions of men of genius and learning; but those facts which constitute real knowledge, are to be met with in every walk of life. Remember how many of our most useful remedies have been discovered by quacks. Do not be afraid, therefore, of conversing with them, and of profiting by their ignorance and temerity in the practice of physic. Medicine has its Pharisees, as well as religion. But the spirit of this sect is as unfriendly to the advancement of medicine, as it is to Christian charity. By conversing with quacks, we may convey instruction to them, and thereby lessen the mischief they might otherwise do to society. But further. In the pursuit of medical knowledge, let me advise you to converse with nurses and old women. They will often suggest facts in the history and cure of diseases which have escaped the most sagacious observers of nature. Even Negroes and Indians have sometimes stumbled upon discoveries in medicine. Be not ashamed to inquire into them. There is yet one more means of information in medicine which should not be neglected, and that is, to converse with persons who have recovered from indispositions without the aid of physicians. Examine the strength and exertions of nature in these cases, and mark the plain and home-made remedy to which they ascribe their recovery. I have found this to be a fruitful source of instruction, and have been led to conclude, that if every man in a city, or a district, could be called upon to relate to persons appointed to receive and publish his narrative, an exact account of the effects of those remedies which accident or whim has suggested to him, it would furnish a very useful book in medicine. To preserve the facts thus obtained, let me advise you to record them in a book to be kept for that purpose. There is one more advantage that will probably attend the inquiries that have been mentioned; you may discover diseases, or symptoms of diseases, or even laws of the animal economy, which have no place in our systems of nosology, or in our theories of physic.

V. In dangerous cases that are *plain* and *common*, let me caution you against having recourse to consultations. They relax exertion, suspend enterprise, and lessen responsibility in a physician. They moreover add, unnecessarily, to the expenses of a patient. But in *difficult* and *obscure* cases let me advise you to anticipate the fears of your patients, by *requesting* assistance. Such candor begets subsequent confidence and business, for truth is the universal interest of mankind. There are few instances in which any solid advantages have been derived from more than *two* physicians consulting together. Where a greater number are employed, the prescriptions are generally the result of neutralized opinions, and are of course often unsuccessful. The epitaph of Pliny, viz. "Se turba medicorum peruisse," might be inscribed upon the tombstones of many persons, whose sick beds had been surrounded by a crowd of physicians.

VI. Let me recommend to your particular attention, the indigenous medicines of our country. Cultivate or prepare as many of them as possible, and endeavour to enlarge the materia medica, by exploring the untrodden fields and forests of the United States. The ipecacuana, the Seneca and Virginia snake roots, the Carolina pink-root, the spice-wood, the sassafras, the butter-nut, the thoroughwort, the poke, and the strammonium, are but a small part of the medicinal productions of America. I have no doubt but there are many hundred other plants which now exhale invaluable medicinal virtues in the desert air. Examine, likewise, the mineral waters, which are so various in their impregnation, and so common in all parts of our country. Let not the properties of the insects of America escape your investigation. We have already discovered among some of them, a fly equal in its blistering qualities to the famous fly of Spain. Who knows but it may be reserved for America to furnish the world, from her productions, with cures for some of those diseases which now elude the power of medicine? Who knows but what, at the foot of the Alleghany mountain there blooms a flower that is an infallible cure for the epilepsy? Perhaps on the Monongahela, or the Potomac, there may grow a root that shall supply, by its tonic powers, the invigorating effects of the savage or military life in the cure of consumptions. Human misery of every kind is evidently on the decline. Happiness, like truth, is a unit. While the world, from the progress of intellectual, moral and political truth, is becoming a more safe and agreeable abode for man, the votaries of medicine should not be idle. All the doors and windows of the temple of nature have been thrown open by the convulsions of the late American Revolution. This is the time, therefore, to press upon her altars. We have already drawn from them discoveries in morals, philosophy, and government, all of which have human happiness for their object. Let us preserve the unity of truth and happiness, by drawing from the same source, in the present critical moment, a knowledge of antidotes to those diseases which are supposed to be incurable.

ON MISCELLANEOUS THINGS

INFLUENCE OF THE AMERICAN REVOLUTION

October 1, 1788.

THERE WERE several circumstances peculiar to the American Revolution, which should be mentioned previously to an account of the influence of the events which accompanied it, upon the human body.

1. The revolution interested every inhabitant of the country of both sexes, and of every rank and age that was capable of reflection. An indifferent, or neutral spectator of the controversy, was scarcely to be found in any of the states.

2. The scenes of war and government which it introduced, were new to the greatest part of the inhabitants of the United States, and operated with all the force of *novelty* upon the human mind.

3. The controversy was conceived to be the most important of any that had ever engaged the attention of mankind. It was generally believed by the friends of the Revolution, that the very existence of *freedom* upon our globe, was involved in the issue of the contest in favor of the United States.

4. The American Revolution included in it the cares of government, as well as the toils and dangers of war. The American mind was, therefore, frequently occupied at the *same time*, by the difficult and complicated duties of political and military life.

5. The revolution was conducted by men who had been born *free*, and whose sense of the blessings of liberty was of course

more exquisite than if they had just emerged from a state of slavery.

6. The greatest part of the soldiers in the armies of the United States had family connections and property in the country.

7. The war was carried on by the Americans against a nation, to whom they had long been tied by the numerous obligations of consanguinity, laws, religion, commerce, language, interest, and a mutual sense of national glory. The resentments of the Americans of course rose, as is usual in all disputes, in proportion to the number and force of these ancient bonds of affection and union.

8. A predilection to a limited monarchy, as an essential part of a free and safe government, and an attachment to the reigning king of Great Britain, (with a very few exceptions) were universal in every part of the United States.

9. There was at one time a sudden dissolution of civil government in *all*, and of ecclesiastical establishments in several of the states.

10. The expences of the war were supported by means of a paper currency, which was continually depreciating.

From the action of each of these causes, and frequently from their combination in the same persons, effects might reasonably be expected, both upon the mind and body, which have seldom occurred; or if they have, I believe were never fully recorded in any age or country.

It might afford some useful instruction, to point out the influence of the military and political events of the revolution upon the understandings, passions, and morals of the citizens of the United States; but my business in the present inquiry, is only to take notice of the influence of these events upon the human body, through the medium of the mind.

I shall first mention the effects of the military, and secondly, of the political events of the revolution. The last must be considered in a two-fold view, accordingly as they affected the friends or the enemies of the revolution.

I. In treating of the effects of the military events, I shall take notice, first, of the influence of *actual* war, and, secondly, of the influence of the military life.

In the beginning of a battle, I have observed *thirst* to be a very common sensation among both officers and soldiers. It occurred where no exercise, or action of the body, could have excited it.

Many officers have informed me, that after the first onset in a battle, they felt a glow of heat, so universal as to be perceptible in both their ears. This was the case in a particular manner, in the battle of Princeton, on the third of January in the year 1777, on which day the weather was remarkable cold.

A veteran colonel of a New England regiment, whom I visited at Princeton, and who was wounded in the hand at the battle of Monmouth, on the 28th of June, 1778, (a day in which the mercury stood at 90° of Fahrenheit's thermometer) after describing his situation at the time he received his wound, concluded his story by remarking, that "fighting was hot work on a cold day, but much more so on a warm day." The many instances which appeared after that memorable battle, of soldiers who were found among the slain without any marks of wounds or violence upon their bodies, were probably occasioned by the heat excited in the body by the emotions of the mind, being added to that of the atmosphere.

Soldiers bore operations of every kind immediately *after* a battle, with much more fortitude than they did at any time afterwards.

The effects of the military life upon the human body come next to be considered under this head.

In another place I have mentioned three cases of pulmonary consumption being perfectly cured by the diet and hardships of a camp life.

Doctor Blane, in his valuable observations on the diseases incident to seamen, ascribes the extraordinary healthiness of the British fleet in the month of April 1782, to the effects produced on the spirit of the soldiers and seamen, by the victory obtained over the French fleet on the 12th of that month; and relates, upon the authority of Mr. Ives, an instance in the war between Great Britain and the combined powers of France and Spain in 1744, in which the scurvy, as well as other diseases, were checked by the prospect of a naval engagement.

The American army furnished an instance of the effects of victory upon the human mind, which may serve to establish the inferences from the facts related by Doctor Blane. The Philadelphia militia who joined the remains of General Washington's army, in December 1776, and shared with them a few days afterwards in the capture of a large body of Hessians at Trenton, consisted of 1500 men, most of whom had been accustomed to the habits of a city life. These men slept in tents and barns, and sometimes in the open air during the usual colds of December and January; and yet there were only two instances of sickness, and only one of death, in that body of men in the course of nearly six weeks, in those winter months. This extraordinary healthiness of so great a number of men under such trying circumstances, can only be ascribed to the vigour infused into the human body by the victory of Trenton having produced insensibility to all the usual remote causes of diseases.

Militia officers and soldiers, who enjoyed good health during a campaign, were often affected by fevers and other disorders, as soon as they returned to their respective homes. I knew one instance of a militia captain, who was seized with convulsions the first night he lay on a feather bed, after sleeping several months on a mattress, or upon the ground. These affections of the body appeared to be produced only by the sudden abstraction of that tone in the system which was excited by a sense of danger, and the other invigorating objects of a military life.

The NOSTALGIA of Doctor Cullen, or the *home-sickness*, was a frequent disease in the American army, more especially among the soldiers of the New England states. But this disease was suspended by the superior action of the mind under the influence of the principles which governed common soldiers in the

American army. Of this General Gates furnished me with a remarkable instance in 1776, soon after his return from the command of a large body of regular troops and militia at Ticonderoga. From the effects of the nostalgia, and the feebleness of the discipline, which was exercised over the militia, desertions were very frequent and numerous in his army, in the latter part of the campaign, and yet during the *three weeks* in which the general expected every hour an attack to be made upon him by General Burgoyne, there was not a single desertion from his army, which consisted at that time of 10,000 men

The patience, firmness, and magnanimity with which the officers and soldiers of the American army endured the complicated evils of hunger, cold, and nakedness, can only be ascribed to an insensibility of body produced by an uncommon tone of mind excited by the love of liberty and their country.

Before I proceed to the second general division of this subject, I shall take notice, that more instances of apoplexies occurred in the city of Philadelphia, in the winter of 1774–5, than had been known in former years. I should have hesitated in recording this fact, had I not found the observation supported by a fact of the same kind, and produced by a nearly similar cause, in the appendix to the practical works of Doctor Baglivi, professor of physic and anatomy at Rome. After a very wet season in the winter of 1694–5, he informs us, that "apoplexies displayed their rage, and perhaps (adds our author) that some part of this epidemic illness was owing to the universal grief and domestic care, occasioned by all Europe being engaged in a war. All commerce was disturbed, and all the avenues of peace blocked up, so that the strongest heart could scarcely bear the thoughts of it." The winter of 1774–5, was a period of uncommon anxiety among the citizens of America. Every countenance wore the marks of painful solicitude, for the event of a petition to the throne of Britain, which was to determine whether reconciliation, or a civil war, with all its terrible and distressing consequences, were to take place. The apoplectic fit, which deprived the world of the talents and virtues of Peyton Randolph, while he filled the chair of Congress in 1775, appeared to be occasioned in part by the pressure of the uncertainty of those great events upon his mind. To the name of this illustrious patriot, several others might be added, who were affected by the apoplexy in the same memorable year. At this time a difference of opinion upon the subject of the contest with Great Britain, had scarcely taken place among the citizens of America.

II. The political events of the revolution produced different effects upon the human body, through the medium of the mind, accordingly as they acted upon the friends or enemies of the revolution.

I shall first describe its effects upon the former class of citizens of the United States.

Many persons of infirm and delicate habits, were restored to perfect health, by the change of place, or occupation, to which the war exposed them. This was the case in a more especial manner with hysterical women, who were much interested in the successful issue of the contest. The same effects of a civil war upon the hysteria, were observed by Doctor Cullen in Scotland, in the years 1745 and 1746. It may perhaps help to extend our ideas of the influence of the passions upon diseases, to add, that when either love, jealousy, grief, or even devotion, wholly engross the female mind, they seldom fail, in like manner, to cure or to suspend hysterical complaints.

An uncommon cheerfulness prevailed everywhere, among the friends of the Revolution. Defeats, and even the loss of relations and property, were soon forgotten in the great objects of the war.

The population in the United States was more rapid from births during the war, than it had ever been in the same number of years since the settlement of the country.

I am disposed to ascribe this increase of births *chiefly* to the quantity and extensive circulation of money, and to the facility of procuring the means of subsistence during the war, which favored marriages among the laboring part of the people.* But I have sufficient documents to prove, that marriages were more fruitful than in former years, and that a considerable number of unfruitful marriages became fruitful during the war. In 1783, the year of the peace, there were several children born of parents who had lived many years together without issue.

Mr. Hume informs us, in his History of England, that some old people upon hearing the news of the restoration of Charles the II. died suddenly of joy. There was a time when I doubted the truth of this assertion; but I am now disposed to believe it, from having heard of a similar effect from an agreeable political event, in the course of the American Revolution. The doorkeeper of Congress, an aged man, died suddenly, immediately after hearing of the capture of Lord Cornwallis's army. His death was universally ascribed to a violent emotion of political joy. This species of joy appears to be one of the strongest emotions that can agitate the human mind.

Perhaps the influence of that ardor in trade and speculation, which seized many of the friends of the Revolution, and which was excited by the fallacious nominal amount of the paper money, should rather be considered as a disease than as a passion. It unhinged the judgment, deposed the moral faculty, and filled the imagination, in many people, with airy and impracticable schemes of wealth and grandeur. Desultory manners, and a peculiar species of extempore conduct, were among its characteristic symptoms. It produced insensibility to cold, hunger, and danger. The trading towns, and in some instances the extremities of the United States, were frequently visited in a few hours or days by persons affected by this disease; and hence "to travel with the speed of a speculator," became a common saying in many parts of the country. This species of insanity (if I may

---

* Wheat which was sold before the war for seven shillings and sixpence, was sold for several years *during* the war for four, and in some places for two and sixpence Pennsylvania currency per bushel. Beggars of every description disappeared in the year 1776, and were seldom seen till near the close of the war.

be allowed to call it by that name) did not require the confinement of a bedlam to cure it, like the South Sea madness described by Doctor Mead. Its remedies were the depreciation of the paper money, and the events of the peace.

The political events of the Revolution produced upon its enemies very different effects from those which have been mentioned.

The hypochondriasis of Doctor Cullen, occurred in many instances in persons of this description. In some of them, the terror and distress of the Revolution brought on a true melancholia.* The causes which produced these diseases, may be reduced to four heads. 1. The loss of former power or influence in government. 2. The destruction of the hierarchy of the English Church in America. 3. The change in the habits of diet, and company and manners, produced by the annihilation of just debts by means of depreciated paper money. And, 4. The neglect, insults, and oppression, to which the Loyalists were exposed, from individuals, and in several instances, from the laws of some of the states.

It was observed in South Carolina, that several gentlemen who had protected their estates by swearing allegiance to the British government, died soon after the evacuation of Charleston by the British army. Their deaths were ascribed to the neglect with which they were treated by their ancient friends, who had adhered to the government of the United States. The disease was called, by the common people, the *Protection fever.*

From the causes which produced this hypochondriasis, I have taken the liberty of distinguishing it by the specific name of *Revolutiana.*

In some cases, this disease was rendered fatal by exile and confinement; and, in others, by those persons who were afflicted with it, seeking relief from spirituous liquors.

The termination of the war by the peace in 1783, did not terminate the American Revolution. The minds of the citizens

---

* Insania partialis sine dyspepsia, of Doctor Cullen.

of the United States were wholly unprepared for their new situation. The excess of the passion for liberty, inflamed by the successful issue of the war, produced, in many people, opinions and conduct which could not be removed by reason nor restrained by government. For a while, they threatened to render abortive the goodness of heaven to the United States, in delivering them from the evils of slavery and war. The extensive influence which these opinions had upon the understandings, passions and morals of many of the citizens of the United States, constituted a species of insanity, which I shall take the liberty of distinguishing by the name of *Anarchia*.

I hope no offence will be given by the freedom of any of these remarks. An inquirer after philosophical truth, should consider the passions of men in the same light that he does the laws of matter or motion. The friends and enemies of the American Revolution must have been more or less than men, if they could have sustained the magnitude and rapidity of the events that characterised it, without discovering some marks of human weakness, both in body and mind. Perhaps these weaknesses were permitted, that human nature might receive fresh honours in America, by the contending parties (whether produced by the controversies about independence or the national government) mutually forgiving each other, and uniting in plans of general order, and happiness.

THE EFFECTS OF ARDENT SPIRITS UPON MAN

By ARDENT spirits, I mean those liquors only which are obtained by distillation from fermented substances of any kind. To their effects upon the bodies and minds of men, the following inquiry shall be exclusively confined. Fermented liquors contain so little spirit, and that so intimately combined with other matters, that they can seldom be drunken in sufficient quantities to produce intoxication and its subsequent effects without exciting a disrelish to their taste, or pain, from their distending the stomach. They are, moreover, when taken in a moderate quantity, generally innocent, and often have a friendly influence upon health and life.

The effects of ardent spirits divide themselves into such as are of a prompt, and such as are of a chronic nature. The former discover themselves in drunkenness; and the latter, in a numerous train of diseases and vices of the body and mind.

I. I shall begin by briefly describing their prompt or immediate effects, in a fit of drunkenness.

This odious disease (for by that name it should be called) appears with more or less of the following symptoms, and most commonly in the order in which I shall enumerate them.

1. Unusual garrulity.
2. Unusual silence.
3. Captiousness, and a disposition to quarrel.
4. Uncommon good humor, and an insipid simpering, or laugh.
5. Profane swearing and cursing.

ON MISCELLANEOUS THINGS

6. A disclosure of their own or other people's secrets.

7. A rude disposition to tell those persons in company, whom they know, their faults.

8. Certain immodest actions. I am sorry to say this sign of the first stage of drunkenness sometimes appears in women, who, when sober are uniformly remarkable for chaste and decent manners.

9. A clipping of words.

10. Fighting; a black eye, or a swelled nose, often mark this grade of drunkenness.

11. Certain extravagant acts which indicate a temporary fit of madness. These are singing, hallooing, roaring, imitating the noises of brute animals, jumping, tearing off clothes, dancing naked, breaking glasses and china, and dashing other articles of household furniture upon the ground or floor. After a while the paroxysm of drunkenness is completely formed. The face now becomes flushed, the eyes project, and are somewhat watery, winking is less frequent than is natural; the under lip is protruded—the head inclines a little to one shoulder—the jaw falls—belchings and hickup take place—the limbs totter—the whole body staggers. The unfortunate subject of this history next falls on his seat—he looks around him with a vacant countenance, and mutters inarticulate sounds to himself—he attempts to rise and walk: in this attempt he falls upon his side, from which he gradually turns upon his back: he now closes his eyes and falls into a profound sleep, frequently attended with snoring, and profuse sweats, and sometimes with such a relaxation of the muscles which confine the bladder and the lower bowels, as to produce a symptom which delicacy forbids me to mention. In this condition he often lies from ten, twelve, and twenty-four hours, to two, three, four, and five days, an object of pity and disgust to his family and friends. His recovery from this fit of intoxication is marked with several peculiar appearances. He opens his eyes and closes them again—he gapes and stretches his limbs—he then coughs and pukes—his voice is hoarse—he rises with difficulty, and staggers to a chair—his eyes resemble balls

of fire—his hands tremble—he loathes the sight of food—he calls for a glass of spirits to compose his stomach—now and then he emits a deep-fetched sigh, or groan, from a transient twinge of conscience, but he more frequently scolds, and curses every thing around him. In this state of languor and stupidity he remains for two or three days before he is able to resume his former habits of business and conversation.

Pythagoras, we are told, maintained that the souls of men after death expiated the crimes committed by them in this world by animating certain brute animals; and that the souls of those animals, in their turns, entered into men, and carried with them all their peculiar qualities and vices. This doctrine of one of the wisest and best of the Greek philosophers, was probably intended only to convey a lively idea of the changes which are induced in the body and mind of man by a fit of drunkenness. In folly, it causes him to resemble a calf—in stupidity, an ass—in roaring, a mad bull—in quarrelling and fighting, a dog—in cruelty, a tiger—in fetor, a skunk—in filthiness, a hog—and in obscenity, a he-goat.

It belongs to the history of drunkenness to remark, that its paroxysms occur, like the paroxysms of many diseases, at certain periods, and after longer or shorter intervals. They often begin with annual, and gradually increase in their frequency, until they appear in quarterly, monthly, weekly, and quotidian, or daily periods. Finally they afford scarcely any marks of remission either during the day or the night. There was a citizen of Philadelphia, many years ago, in whom drunkenness appeared in this protracted form. In speaking of him to one of his neighbors, I said, "Does he not *sometimes* get drunk?" "You mean," said his neighbor, "is he not *sometimes* sober?"

It is further remarkable, that drunkenness resembles certain hereditary, family, and contagious diseases. I have once known it to descend from a father to four out of five of his children. I have seen three, and once four brothers, who were born of sober ancestors, affected by it; and I have heard of its spreading through a whole family composed of members not originally related to each other. These facts are important, and should not be overlooked by parents, in deciding upon the matrimonial connexions of their children.

II. Let us next attend to the chronic effects of ardent spirits upon the body and mind. In the body they dispose to every form of acute disease; they moreover *excite* fevers in persons predisposed to them from other causes. This has been remarked in all the yellow fevers which have visited the cities of the United States. Hard drinkers seldom escape, and rarely recover from them. The following diseases are the usual consequences of the habitual use of ardent spirits, viz.

1. A decay of appetite, sickness at stomach, and a puking of bile, or a discharge of a frothy and viscid phlegm, by hawking, in the morning.

2. Obstructions of the liver. The fable of Prometheus, on whose liver a vulture was said to prey constantly as a punishment for his stealing fire from heaven, was intended to illustrate the painful effects of ardent spirits upon that organ of the body.

3. Jaundice, and dropsy of the belly and limbs, and finally of every cavity in the body. A swelling in the feet and legs is so characteristic a mark of habits of intemperance, that the merchants in Charleston, I have been told, cease to trust the planters of South Carolina as soon as they perceive it. They very naturally conclude industry and virtue to be extinct in that man, in whom that symptom of disease has been produced by the intemperate use of distilled spirits.

4. Hoarseness, and a husky cough, which often terminate in consumption, and sometimes in an acute and fatal disease of the lungs.

5. Diabetes, that is, a frequent and weakening discharge of pale or sweetish urine.

6. Redness, and eruptions on different parts of the body. They generally begin on the nose, and after gradually extending all over the face, sometimes descend to the limbs in the form of leprosy. They have been called "Rum buds," when they appear in the face. In persons who have occasionally survived

these effects of ardent spirits on the skin, the face after a while becomes bloated, and its redness is succeeded by a death-like paleness. Thus, the same fire which produces a red color in iron, when urged to a more intense degree, produces what has been called a white heat.

7. A fetid breath, composed of every thing that is offensive in putrid animal matter.

8. Frequent and disgusting belchings.

9. Epilepsy.

10. Gout, in all its various forms of swelled limbs, colic, palsy, and apoplexy.

11. Lastly, madness. The late Dr. Waters, while he acted as house pupil and apothecary of the Pennsylvania Hospital, assured me, that in one-third of the patients confined by this terrible disease, it had been induced by ardent spirits.

Most of the diseases which have been enumerated are of a mortal nature. They are more certainly induced, and terminate more speedily in death, when spirits are taken in such quantities, and at such times, as to produce frequent intoxication, but it may serve to remove an error with which some intemperate people console themselves, to remark, that ardent spirits often bring on fatal diseases without producing drunkenness. I have known many persons destroyed by them who were never completely intoxicated during the whole course of their lives. The solitary instances of longevity which are now and then met with in hard drinkers, no more disprove the deadly effects of ardent spirits than the solitary instances of recoveries from apparent death by drowning, prove that there is no danger to life from a human body lying an hour or two under water.

The body, after its death, from the use of distilled spirits, exhibits, by dissection, certain appearances which are of a peculiar nature. The fibres of the stomach and bowels are contracted—abscesses, gangrene, and scar tissue are found in the viscera.

Not less destructive are the effects of ardent spirits upon the human mind. They impair the memory, debilitate the understanding, and pervert the moral faculties. It was probably from observing these effects of intemperance in drinking upon the mind, that a law was formerly passed in Spain which excluded drunkards from being witnesses in a court of justice. But the demoralizing effects of distilled spirits do not stop here. They produce not only falsehood, but fraud, theft, uncleanliness, and murder. Like the demoniac mentioned in the New Testament, their name is "Legion," for they convey into the soul a host of vices and crimes.

A more affecting spectacle cannot be exhibited than a person into whom this infernal spirit, generated by habits of intemperance, has entered: it is more or less affecting, according to the station the person fills in a family, or in society, who is possessed by it. Is he a husband? How deep the anguish which rends the bosom of his wife! Is she a wife? Who can measure the shame and aversion which she excites in her husband? Is he the father, or is she the mother of a family of children? See their averted looks from their parent, and their blushing looks at each other! Is he a magistrate? or has he been chosen to fill a high and respectable station in the councils of his country? What humiliating fears of corruption in the administration of the laws, and of the subversion of public order and happiness, appear in the countenances of all who see him! Is he a minister of the Gospel? Here language fails me. If angels weep—it is at such a sight.

In pointing out the evils produced by ardent spirits, let us not pass by their effects upon the estates of the persons who are addicted to them. Are they inhabitants of cities? Behold! their houses stripped gradually of their furniture, and pawned, or sold by a constable, to pay tavern debts. See! their names upon record in the dockets of every court, and whole pages of newspapers filled with advertisements of their estates for public sale. Are they inhabitants of country places? Behold! their houses with shattered windows—their barns with leaky roofs—their gardens overrun with weeds—their fields with broken fences—their hogs without yokes—their sheep without wool—their cattle and horses without fat—and their children, filthy and half clad, without manners, principles and morals. This picture of agricultural wretchedness is seldom of long duration. The farms and property thus neglected and depreciated are seized and sold for the benefit of a group of creditors. The children that were born with the prospect of inheriting them are bound out to service in the neighborhood; while their parents, the unworthy authors of their misfortunes, ramble into new and distant settlements, alternately fed on their way by the hand of charity, or a little casual labor.

Thus we see poverty and misery, crimes and infamy, diseases and death, are all the natural and usual consequences of the intemperate use of ardent spirits.

I have classed death among the consequences of hard drinking. But it is not death from the immediate hand of the Deity, nor from any of the instruments of it which were created by him: it is death from *suicide*. Yes—thou poor degraded creature who art daily lifting the poisoned bowl to thy lips—cease to avoid the unhallowed ground in which the self-murderer is interred, and wonder no longer that the sun should shine, and the rain fall, and the grass look green upon his grave. Thou art perpetuating, gradually, by the use of ardent spirits, what he has effected suddenly by opium or a halter. Considering how many circumstances from surprise, or derangement, may palliate his guilt, or that (unlike yours) it was not preceded and accompanied by any other crime, it is probable his condemnation will be less than yours at the day of judgment.

I shall now take notice of the occasions and circumstances which are supposed to render the use of ardent spirits necessary, and endeavor to show that the arguments in favor of their use in such cases, are founded in error, and that in each of them ardent spirits, instead of affording strength to the body, increase the evils they are intended to relieve.

1. They are said to be necessary in very cold weather. This is far from being true, for the temporary warmth they produce is always succeeded by a greater disposition in the body to be

affected by cold. Warm dresses, a plentiful meal just before exposure to the cold, and eating occasionally a little gingerbread, or any other cordial food, is a much more durable method of preserving the heat of the body in cold weather.

2. They are said to be necessary in very warm weather. Experience proves that they increase instead of lessening the effects of heat upon the body, and thereby dispose to diseases of all kinds. Even in the warm climate of the West Indies, Dr. Bell asserts this to be true. "Rum," says this author, "whether used habitually, moderately, or in excessive quantities in the West Indies, always diminishes the strength of the body, and renders men more susceptible of disease, and unfit for any service in which vigor or activity is required." As well might we throw oil into a house, the roof of which was on fire, in order to prevent the flames from extending to its inside, as pour ardent spirits into the stomach to lessen the effects of a hot sun upon the skin.

3. Nor do ardent spirits lessen the effects of hard labor upon the body. Look at the horse, with every muscle of his body swelled from morning till night in the plough, or a team; does he make signs for a draught of toddy, or a glass of spirits, to enable him to cleave the ground, or to climb a hill? No—he requires nothing but cool water and substantial food. There is no nourishment in ardent spirits. The strength they produce in labor is of a transient nature, and is always followed by a sense of weakness and fatigue.

ON OLD AGE

Most of the facts which I shall deliver upon this subject, are the result of observations made during the last five years, upon persons of both sexes, who had passed the 80th year of their lives I intended to have given a detail of the names—manner of life—occupations—and other circumstances of each of them, but, upon a review of my notes, I found so great a sameness in the history of most of them, that I despaired, by detailing them, of answering the intention which I have purposed in the following essay. I shall, therefore, only deliver the facts and principles which are the result of the inquiries and observations I have made upon this subject.

I. I shall mention the circumstances which favor the attainment of longevity.

II. I shall mention the phænomena of body and mind which attend it and,

III. I shall enumerate its peculiar diseases, and the remedies which are most proper to remove, or moderate them.

I. The circumstances which favor longevity, are,

1. *Descent from long-lived Ancestors.* I have not found a single instance of a person, who has lived to be 80 years old, in whom this was not the case. In some instances I found the descent was only from one, but in general, it was from both parents. The knowledge of this fact may serve, not only to assist in calculating what are called the chances of lives, but it may be made useful to a physician. He may learn from it to cherish

hopes of his patients in chronic, and in some acute diseases, in proportion to the capacity of life they have derived from their ancestors.*

2. *Temperance in Eating and Drinking.* To this remark I found several exceptions. I met with one man of 84 years of age, who had been intemperate in eating, and four or five persons who had been intemperate in drinking ardent spirits. They had all been day-labourers, or had deferred drinking until they began to feel the languor of old age. I did not meet with a single person who had not, for the last forty or fifty years of their lives, used tea, coffee, and bread and butter twice a day as part of their diet. I am disposed to believe that those articles of diet do not materially affect the duration of human life, although they evidently impair the strength of the system. The duration of life does not appear to depend so much upon the strength of the body, or upon the quantity of its excitability, as upon an exact accommodation of stimuli to each of them. A watch spring will last as long as an anchor, provided the forces which are capable of destroying both, are always in an exact ratio to their strength. The use of tea and coffee in diet seems to be happily suited to the change which has taken place in the human body, by sedentary occupations, by which means less nourishment and stimulus are required than formerly, to support animal life.

3. The *moderate exercise of the Understanding* It has long been an established truth, that literary men (other circumstances being equal) are longer lived than other people. But it is not necessary that the understanding should be employed upon philosophical subjects to produce this influence upon human life. Business, politics, and religion, which are the objects of attention

---

* Dr. Franklin, who died in his 84th year, was descended from long-lived parents. His father died at 89, and his mother at 87. His father had 17 children by two wives. The Doctor informed me that he once sat down as one of 11 adult sons and daughters at his father's table. In an excursion he once made to that part of England from whence his family migrated to America, he discovered in a grave-yard, the tomb-stones of several persons of his name, who had lived to be very old. These persons he supposed to have been his ancestors.

of men of all classes, impart a vigour to the understanding, which, by being conveyed to every part of the body, tends to produce health and long life.

4. *Equanimity of temper*. The violent and irregular action of the passions tends to wear away the springs of life.

Persons who live upon annuities in Europe have been observed to be longer lived, in equal circumstances, than other people. This is probably occasioned by their being exempted, by the certainty of their subsistence from those fears of want which so frequently distract the minds, and thereby weaken the bodies of old people. Life-rents have been supposed to have the same influence in prolonging life. Perhaps the *desire of life,* in order to enjoy for as long a time as possible, that property which cannot be enjoyed a second time by a child or relation, may be another cause of the longevity of persons who live upon certain incomes. It is a fact, that the desire of life is a very powerful stimulus in prolonging it, especially when that desire is supported by hope. This is obvious to physicians every day. Despair of recovery is the beginning of death in all diseases.

But obvious and reasonable as the effects of equanimity of temper are upon human life, there are some exceptions in favour of passionate men and women having attained to a great age. The morbid stimulus of anger, in these cases, was probably obviated by less degrees, or less active exercises of the understanding, or by the defect or weakness of some of the other stimuli which keep up the motions of life.

5. *Matrimony*. In the course of my inquiries, I met with only one person beyond eighty years of age who had never been married.——I met with several women who had borne from ten to twenty children, and suckled them all. I met with one woman, a native of Herefordshire in England, who is now in the 100th year of her age, who bore a child at 60, menstruated till 80, and frequently suckled two of her children (though born in succession to each other) at the same time. She had passed the greatest part of her life over a washing-tub.

ON MISCELLANEOUS THINGS

6. *Emigration.* I have observed many instances of Europeans who have arrived in America in the decline of life, who have acquired fresh vigour from the impression of our climate, and of new objects upon their bodies and minds, and whose lives, in consequence thereof, appeared to have been prolonged for many years.

7. I have not found *Sedentary Employments* to prevent long life, where they are not accompanied by intemperance in eating or drinking. This observation is not confined to literary men, nor to women only, in whom longevity, without much exercise of body, has been frequently observed. I met with one instance of a weaver; a second of a silver-smith, and a third of a shoe-maker, among the number of old people, whose histories have suggested these observations.

8. I have not found that *acute*, nor that all *chronic* diseases shorten human life. Dr. Franklin had two successive cavities in his lungs before he was 40 years old. I met with one man beyond 80, who had survived a most violent attack of the yellow fever; a second who had several of his bones fractured by falls, and in frays; and many who had been frequently affected by inter-mittent fever. I met with one man of 86, who had all his life been subject to fainting; another who had for 50 years been occasionally affected by a cough, * and two instances of men who had been afflicted for forty years with obstinate head-aches †. I met with only one person beyond 80, who had ever been affected by a disorder in the *stomach*; and in him, it arose from an occasional rupture. Mr. John Strangeways Hutton, of this city, who died last year, in the 109th year of his age, informed me, that he had never vomited in his life. This circumstance is the more remarkable, as he passed several years at sea when

---

* This man's only remedy for his cough was the fine powder of dry Indian turnip and honey.

† Dr. Thiery says, That he did not find the itch, or slight degrees of the leprosy, to prevent longevity. Observations de Physique, et de Medi-cine faites en differens lieux de L'Espagne. Vol. II. p 171.

a young man.† These facts may serve to extend our ideas of the importance of a healthy state of the stomach in the animal economy; and thereby to add to our knowledge in the prognosis of diseases, and in the chances of human life.

9. I have not found the *loss of teeth* to affect the duration of human life, so much as might be expected. Edward Drinker, who lived to be 103 years old, lost his teeth thirty years before he died from drawing the hot smoke of tobacco into his mouth through a short pipe.

Dr. Sayre, of New Jersey, to whom I am indebted for several very valuable histories of old persons, mentions one man aged 81, whose teeth began to decay at 16, and another of 90, who lost his teeth thirty years before he saw him. The gums, by becoming hard, perform, in part, the office of teeth. But may not the gastric juice of the stomach, like the tears and urine, become acrid by age, and thereby supply, by a more dissolving power, the defect of mastication from the loss of teeth? Analogies might easily be adduced from several operations of nature, which go forward in the animal economy, which render this supposition highly probable.

10. I have not observed *Baldness*, or *Grey Hairs*, occurring in early or middle life, to prevent old age. In one of the histories furnished me by Dr. Sayre, I find an account of a man of 81,

---

‡ The venerable old man, whose history first suggested this remark, was born in New-York in the year 1684— His grandfather lived to be 101, but was unable to walk for thirty years before he died, from an excessive quantity of fat. His mother died at 91. His constant drinks were water, beer, and cider He had a fixed dislike of spirits of all kinds. His appetite was good, and he ate plentifully during the last years of his life. He seldom drank any thing between his meals. He was never intoxicated but twice in his life, and that was when a boy, and at sea, where he remembers perfectly well to have celebrated by a feu de joye the birthday of Queen Anne. He was formerly afflicted with the head-ache and giddiness, but never had a fever, except from the small-pox, in the course of his life. His pulse was slow, but regular. He had been twice married. By his first wife he had eight, and by his second seventeen children. One of them lived to be 83 years of age. He was about five feet nine inches in height, of a slender make, and carried an erect head to the last year of his life.

ON MISCELLANEOUS THINGS 347

whose hair began to assume a silver colour when he was only one-and-twenty years of age.

I shall conclude this head by the following remark:

Notwithstanding there appears in the human body a certain capacity of long life, which seems to dispose it to preserve its existence in every situation; yet this capacity does not always protect it from premature destruction; for among the old people whom I examined, I scarcely met with one who had not lost brothers or sisters, in early and middle life, and who were born under circumstances equally favourable to longevity with themselves.

II. I come now to mention some of the phenomena of the body and mind which occur in old age.

1. There is a great sensibility to *cold* in all old people. I met with an old woman of 84, who slept constantly under three blankets and a coverlet during the hottest summer months. The servant of Prince de Beaufremont, who came from Mount Jura to Paris at the age of 121, to pay his respects to the first National Assembly of France, shivered with cold in the middle of the dog days, when he was not near a good fire. The National Assembly directed him to sit with his hat on, in order to defend his head from the cold.

2. Impressions made upon the *ears* of old people, excite sensation and reflection much quicker than when they are made upon their eyes. Mr. Hutton informed me, that he had frequently met his sons in the street without knowing them until they had spoken to him. Dr. Franklin informed me that he recognized his friends, after a long absence from them, first by their voices. This fact does not contradict the common opinion, upon the subject of memory, for the recollection in these instances, is the effect of what is called reminiscence, which differs from memory in being excited only by the renewal of the impression which at first produced the idea which is revived.

2. The *appetite* for food is generally increased in old age. The famous Parr, who died at 152, ate heartily in the last week of his life. The kindness of nature, in providing this last portion

of earthly enjoyments for old people, deserves to be noticed. It is remarkable, that they have, like children, a frequent recurrence of appetite, and sustain with great uneasiness the intervals of regular meals. The observation, therefore, made by Hippocrates, that middle aged people are more affected by abstinence than those who are old, is not true. This might easily be proved by many appeals to the records of medicine; but old people differ from children, in preferring *solid* to liquid aliment. From inattention to this fact, Dr. Mead has done great mischief by advising old people, as their teeth decayed or perished, to lessen the quantity of their solid, and to increase the quantity of their liquid food. This advice is contrary to nature and experience, and I have heard of two old persons who destroyed themselves by following it. The circulation of the blood is supported in old people chiefly by the stimulus of aliment. The action of liquids of all kinds upon the system is weak, and of short continuance, compared with the durable stimulus of solid food. There is a gradation in the action of this food upon the body. Animal matters are preferred to vegetable; the fat of meat, to the lean, and salted meat to fresh, by most old people. I have met with but few old people who retained an appetite for milk. It is remarkable, that a less quantity of *strong drink* produces intoxication in old people than in persons in the middle of life. This depends upon the recurrence of the same state of the system, with respect to excitability, which takes place in childhood. Many old people, from an ignorance of this fact, have made shipwreck of characters which have commanded respect in every previous stage of their lives. From the same recurrence of the excitability of childhood in their systems, they commonly drink their tea and coffee much weaker than in early or middle life.

3. The *pulse* is generally full, and frequently affected by pauses in its pulsations when felt in the wrists of old people. A regular pulse in such persons indicates a disease, as it shews the system to be under the impression of a preternatural stimulus of some kind. This observation was suggested to me above

twenty years ago by Morgagni, and I have often profited by it in attending old people. The pulse in such patients is an uncertain mark of the nature or degree of an acute disease. It seldom partakes of the quickness or convulsive action of the arterial system, which attends fever in young or middle-aged people. I once attended a man of 77 in a fever of the bilious kind, which confined him for eight days to his bed, in whom I could not perceive the least quickness or morbid action in his pulse until four-and-twenty hours before he died.

4. The marks of old age appear earlier, and are more numerous in persons who have combined with hard labour, a vegetable or scanty diet, than in persons who have lived under opposite circumstances. I think I have observed these marks of old age to occur sooner, and to be more numerous in the German, than in the English or Irish citizens of Pennsylvania. They are likewise more common among the inhabitants of country places, than of cities and still more so among the Indians of North America, than among the inhabitants of civilized countries

5. Old men tread upon the *whole base* of their feet at once in *walking*. This is perhaps one reason why they wear out fewer shoes, under the same circumstances of constant use, than young people, who, by treading on the posterior, and rising on the anterior part of their feet, expose their shoes to more unequal pressure and friction. The advantage derived to old people from this mode of walking is very obvious. It lessens that disposition to totter, which is always connected with weakness:—hence we find the same mode of walking is adopted by habitual drunkards, and is sometimes from habit practiced by them, when they are not under the influence of strong drink.

6. The *memory* is the first faculty of the mind which fails in the decline of life. While recent events pass through the mind without leaving an impression upon it, it is remarkable that the long forgotten events of childhood and youth are recalled and distinctly remembered.

I met with a singular instance of a German woman, who had learned to speak the language of our country after she was forty years of age, who had forgotten every word of it after she had passed her 80th year, but spoke the German language as fluently as ever she had done. The memory decays soonest in hard drinkers. I have observed some studious men to suffer a decay of their memories, but never of their understandings. Among these, was the late Anthony Benezet of this city. But even this infirmity did not abate the cheerfulness, or lessen the happiness of this pious philosopher, for he once told me, when I was a young man, that he had a consolation in the decay of his memory, which gave him a great advantage over me. "You can read a good book (said he) with pleasure but *once*, but when I read a good book, I so soon forget the contents of it, that I have the pleasure of reading it over and over, and every time I read it, it is alike new and delightful to me."—The celebrated Dr. Swift was one of those few studious men, who have exhibited marks of a decay of understanding in old age; but it is judiciously ascribed by Dr. Johnson to two causes which rescue books, and the exercise of the thinking powers, from having had any share in inducing that disease upon his mind. These causes were, a rash vow which he made when a young man, never to use spectacles, and a sordid seclusion of himself from company, by which means he was cut off from the use of books, and the benefits of conversation, the absence of which left his mind without its usual stimulus—hence it collapsed into a state of fatuity. It is probably owing to the constant exercise of the understanding, that literary men possess that faculty of the mind in a vigorous state in extreme old age. The same cause accounts for old people preserving their intellects longer in cities, than in country places. They enjoy society upon such easy terms in the former situation, that their minds are kept more constantly in an excited state by the acquisition of new, or the renovation of old ideas, by means of conversation.

7. I did not meet with a single instance in which the moral or religious faculties were impaired in old people. I do not believe, that these faculties of the mind are preserved by any supernatural power, but wholly by the constant and increasing exer-

cise of them in the evening of life. In the course of my inquiries, I heard of a man of 101 years of age, who declared that he had forgotten every thing he had ever known, except his God. I found the moral faculty, or a disposition to do kind offices, to be exquisitely sensible in several old people, in whom there was scarcely a trace left of memory or understanding.

8. Dreaming is universal among old people. It appears to be brought on by their imperfect sleep, of which I shall say more hereafter.

9. I mentioned formerly the sign of a *second childhood* in the state of the appetite in old people. It appears further,—1. In the marks which slight contusions or impressions leave upon their skins. 2. In their being soon fatigued by walking or exercise, and in being as soon refreshed by rest. 3. In their disposition, like children, to detail immediately every thing they see and hear. And, 4. In their aptitude to shed tears; hence they are unable to tell a story that is in any degree distressing without weeping. Dr. Moore takes notice of this peculiarity in Voltaire, after he had passed his 80th year. He wept constantly at the recital of his own tragedies. This feature in old age did not escape Homer Old Menelaus wept ten years after he returned from the destruction of Troy, when he spoke of the death of the heroes who perished before that city.

10 It would be sufficiently humbling to human nature, if our bodies exhibited in old age the marks only of a second childhood; but human weakness descends still lower. I met with an instance of a woman between 80 and 90, who exhibited the marks of a *second infancy*, by such a total decay of her mental faculties as to lose all consciousness in discharging her alvine and urinary excretions. In this state of the body, a disposition to sleep, succeeds the wakefulness of the first stages of old age. Dr. Haller mentions an instance of a very old man who slept twenty, out of every twenty-four hours during the few last years of his life.

11. The disposition in the system to *renew* certain parts in extreme old age, has been mentioned by several authors. Many instances are to be met with in the records of medicine of the,

sight * and hearing having been restored, and even of the teeth having been renewed in old people a few years before death. These phenomena have led me to suspect, that the antediluvian age was attained by the frequent renovation of different parts of the body, and that when they occur, they are an effort of the causes which support animal life, to produce antediluvian longevity, by acting upon the revived excitability of the system.

12. The *fear* of death appears to be much less in old age, than in early, or middle life I met with many old people who spoke of their dissolution with composure, and with some who expressed earnest desires to lie down in the grave. This indifference to life, and desire for death (whether they arise from satiety in worldly pursuits and pleasures, or from a desire of being relieved from pain) appear to be a wise law in the animal economy, and worthy of being classed with those laws which accommodate the body and mind of man to all the natural evils, to which, in the common order of things, they are necessarily exposed.

III. I come now briefly to enumerate the diseases of old age, and the remedies which are most proper to remove, or to mitigate them.

The diseases are chronic and acute. The CHRONIC are,

1. *Weakness* of the *knees* and *ankles*, a lessened ability to walk, and tremors in the head and limbs.

---

* There is a remarkable instance of the sight having been restored after it had been totally destroyed in an old man near Reading in Pennsylvania. My brother, Jacob Rush, furnished me with the following account of him in a letter from Reading, dated June 23, 1792.——

"An old man of 84 years of age, of the name of Adam Riffle, near this town, gradually lost his sight in the 68th year of his age, and continued entirely blind for the space of twelve years. About four years ago his sight returned, without making use of any means for the purpose, and without any visible change in the appearance of the eyes, and he now sees as well as ever he did. I have seen the man, and have no doubt of the fact. He is at this time so hearty, as to be able to walk from his house to Reading, (about three miles) which he frequently does in order to attend church. I should observe, that during both the gradual loss, and recovery of his sight, he was no ways affected by sickness, but on the contrary enjoyed his usual health. I have this account from his daughter and son-in-law, who live within a few doors of me."

2. *Pains in the bones,* known among nosological writers by the name of rheumatalgia.

3. *Involuntary flow of tears,* and of mucus from the nose.

4. *Difficulty of breathing,* and a short *cough,* with copious expectoration. A weak, or hoarse voice generally attends this cough.

5. *Constipation.*

6. An *inability to retain the urine* as long as in early or middle life. Few persons beyond 60 pass a whole night without being obliged to discharge their urine.* Perhaps the stimulus of this liquor in the bladder may be one cause of the universality of dreaming among old people. It is certainly a frequent cause of dreaming in persons in early and middle life: this I infer, from its occurring chiefly in the morning when the bladder is most distended with urine. There is likewise an inability in old people to discharge their urine as quickly as in early life. I think I have observed this to be among the first symptoms of the declension of the strength of the body by age.

7. *Wakefulness.* This is probably produced in part by the action of the urine upon the bladder, but such is the excitability of the system in the first stages of old age, that there is no pain so light, no anxiety so trifling, and no sound so small, as not to produce wakefulness in old people. It is owing to their imperfect sleep, that they are sometimes as unconscious of the moment of their passing from a sleeping to a waking state, as young and middle aged people are of the moment in which they pass from the waking to a sleeping state. Hence we so often hear them complain of passing sleepless nights. This is no doubt frequently the case, but I am satisfied, from the result of an inquiry made upon this subject, that they often sleep without knowing it, and that their complaints in the morning, of the want of sleep, arise from ignorance, without the least intention to deceive.

---

* I met with an old man who informed me, that if from any accident he retained his urine after he felt an inclination to discharge it, he was affected by a numbness, accompanied by an uneasy sensation in the palms of his hands.

8. *Giddiness.*
9. *Deafness.*
10. *Imperfect vision.*

The acute diseases most common among old people, are
1. *Inflammation of the eyes.*
2. The *pneumonia notha,* or bastard peripneumony.
3. The *colic.*
4. *Palsy* and *apoplexy.*
5. The *piles.*
6. A *difficulty* in *making water.*
7. *Intermittent fever.*

All the diseases of old people, both chronic and acute, originate in predisposing debility. The remedies for the former, where a feeble morbid action takes place in the system, are stimulants. The first of these is,

1. HEAT. The ancient Romans prolonged life by retiring to Naples, as soon as they felt the infirmities of age coming upon them. The aged Portuguese imitate them, by approaching the mild sun of Brazil, in South America But heat may be applied to the torpid bodies of old people artificially—1st. By means of the *warm bath.* Dr. Franklin owed much of the cheerfulness and general vigour of body and mind which characterized his old age, to his regular use of this remedy. It disposed him to sleep, and even produced a respite from the pain of the stone, with which he was afflicted during the last years of his life.

2. Heat may be applied to the bodies of old people by means of *stove rooms.* The late Dr. Dewit of Germantown, who lived to be near an 100 years of age, seldom breathed an air below 72°, after he became an old man. He lived constantly in a stove room.

3. *Warm clothing,* more especially warm bedclothes, are proper to preserve or increase the heat of old people. From the neglect of the latter, they are often found dead in their beds in the morning, after a cold night, in all cold countries. The late Dr. Chovet, of this city, who lived to be 85 slept in a baize night gown, under eight blankets, and a coverlet, in a stove room, many

years before he died. The head should be defended in old people by means of woollen, or fur caps, in the night, and by wigs and hats during the day, in cold weather. These artificial coverings will be the more necessary, where the head has been deprived of its natural covering. Great pains should be taken likewise to keep the feet dry and warm, by means of thick shoes.* To these modes of applying and confining heat to the bodies of old people, a young bed-fellow has been added; but I conceive the three artificial modes which have been recommended, will be sufficient without the use of one, which cannot be successfully employed without a breach of delicacy or humanity.

II. To keep up the action of the system, *generous diet* and *drinks* should be given to old people. For a reason mentioned formerly, they should be indulged in eating between the ordinary meals of families. Wine should be given to them in moderation. It has been emphatically called the milk of old age.

III. YOUNG COMPANY should be preferred by old people to the company of persons of their own age. I think I have observed old people to enjoy better health and spirits, when they have passed the evening of their lives in the families of their children, where they have been surrounded by grand children, than when they lived by themselves. Even the solicitude they feel for the welfare of their descendants contributes to invigorate the circulation of the blood, and thereby to add fuel to the lamp of life.

IV. GENTLE EXERCISE. This is of great consequence in pro-

---

* I met with one man above 80, who defended his feet from moisture by covering his shoes in wet weather with melted wax; and another who, for the same purpose, covered his shoes every morning with a mixture composed of the following ingredients melted together—Linseed oil a pound, mutton suet eight ounces, bees-wax six ounces, and rosin four ounces. The mixture should be moderately warmed, and then applied not only to the upper leather, but to the soles of the shoes. This composition, the old gentleman informed me, was extracted from a book entitled "The complete Fisherman," published in England in the reign of Queen Elizabeth. He had used it for twenty years in cold and wet weather, with great benefit, and several of his friends who had tried it, spoke of its efficacy in keeping the feet dry, in high terms.

moting the health of old people. It should be moderate, regular, and always in fair weather.

V. CLEANLINESS This should by no means be neglected. The dress of old people should not only be clean, but more elegant than in youth or middle life. It serves to divert the eye of spectators from observing the decay and deformity of the body, to view and admire that which is always agreeable to it.

VI. To abate the pains of the chronic rheumatism, and the uneasiness of the old man's cough (as it is called); also to remove wakefulness, and to restrain during the night, a troublesome inclination to make water, OPIUM may be given with great advantage. Chardin informs us, that this medicine is frequently used in the eastern countries to abate the pains and weaknesses of old age, by those people who are debarred the use of wine by the religion of Mahomet.

I have nothing to say upon the acute diseases of old people, but what is to be found in most of our books of medicine, except to recommend BLEEDING in those of them which are attended with an excess of blood in the body, and an inflammatory action in the pulse. The degrees of appetite which belong to old age, the quality of the food taken, and the sedentary life which is generally connected with it, all concur to produce that state of the system, which requires the above evacuation. I am sure that I have seen many of the chronic complaints of old people mitigated by it, and I have more than once seen it used with obvious advantage in their inflammatory diseases. These affections I have observed to be more fatal among old people than is generally supposed. An inflammation of the lungs, which terminated in an abscess, deprived the world of Dr. Franklin. Dr. Chovet died of an inflammation in his liver. The blood drawn from him a few days before his death was sizy, and such was the heat of his body, produced by his fever, that he could not bear more covering, (notwithstanding his former habits of warm clothing) than a sheet in the month of January.

Death from old age is the effect of a gradual palsy. It shews itself first in the eyes and ears in the decay of sight and hearing—

it appears next in the urinary bladder, in the limbs and trunk of the body, then in the sphincters of the bladder, and rectum, and finally in the nerves and brain, destroying in the last, the exercise of all the faculties of the mind.

Few persons appear to die of old age. Some one of the diseases which have been mentioned, generally cuts the last thread of life.

SERMON ON EXERCISE

How long wilt thou sleep, O sluggard? when wilt thou arise out of thy sleep?—Yet a little sleep—a little slumber—a little folding of the hands to sleep.—So shall thy poverty come as one that travelleth, and thy want as an armed man.
PROVERBS VI. 9, 10, 11.

MAN was formed to be active. The vigour of his mind, and the health of his body can be fully preserved by no other means, than by labour of some sort. Hence, when we read the sentence which was pronounced upon man after the fall, "That in the sweat of his brow he should eat bread all the days of his life." We cannot help admiring the goodness of the Supreme Being, in connecting his punishment with what had now become the necessary means of preserving his health. Had God abandoned him to idleness, he would have entailed tenfold misery upon him. The solid parts of his body, particularly the nerves, would have lose their tone—the muscles would have lost their feeling and moving powers—and the fluids in consequence of this, would have lost their original or native qualities, and have stagnated in every part of his body. But, instead of inflicting this complicated punishment upon him, he bids him be ACTIVE, and implants a principle within him which impels him to it. Civil society and agriculture began together. The latter has always been looked upon among the first employments of mankind.—It calls forth every individual of the human race into action.—It employs the body in a manner the most conducive to its health.—It preserves and increases the species most;—and lastly, it is most friendly to the practice of virtue. For these reasons, therefore, it is natural to conclude that it is most agreeable to the Supreme Being that man should be supported by it. The earth is a skilful as well as a kind mother to her children. Instead of pouring her treasures in lapfuls upon them at once, and consigning them to idleness ever afterwards, she bestows her gifts with a sparing hand, and ceases to yield them any thing, as soon as they cease to cultivate her. Thus by entailing constant labour, she meant to entail constant health upon them.

But these employments were too innocent for the restless spirit of man. He soon deserted his fields—and his flocks—and sought for some more speedy methods of acquiring fortune—independence—and a superiority over his fellow creatures. These have been obtained by commerce—war—rapine—and lastly, to the reproach of the American colonies, and of humanity, be it spoken, by the perpetration of a crime, compared with which, every other breach of the laws of nature or nations, deserves the name of holiness, I mean, by slavery. But in exchange for these, he hath given up that greatest of all blessings, health. He hath had recourse to medicine as a succedaneum for labour but this hath proved ineffectual, for the fossil—vegetable—and those parts of the animal kingdom which are employed in medicine, have not yet learned, like man, to rise in rebellion against the will of their Creator. Solomon seems to have been aware of this in the words of our text, and hence we hear him calling upon him to awake from his unhealthy "slumber"—to rise from his enervating bed —to unfold his "arms," and employ them in some useful labour, lest sickness, with its companion "poverty," should come upon him like "travail upon a woman with child," or like an "armed man," neither of which can be avoided or resisted. But Solomon, and all the preachers from his time to the present day, who have addressed him upon this subject, have used their eloquence in vain. Since therefore we cannot bring man back again to his implements of husbandry, we must attempt to find out some kinds of exercise as substitutes for them. The most healthy and long-lived people are found among the labouring part of mankind— Would the rich then enjoy health and long life, they must do that of choice which these people do of necessity. They must by exercise, subject themselves to a kind of voluntary labour.

As this discourse is addressed chiefly to the rich and the luxurious, who are the most given to idleness, I shall confine myself to Exercise only; and, in order to handle the subject in the most extensive manner, I shall consider

I. The different modes of exercise.

II. The proper time for using it; and then I shall conclude with an Application.

I. All Exercise may be divided into Active and Passive.

Active exercise includes walking—running—dancing—fencing—swimming, and the like.

Passive exercise includes sailing—riding in a carriage, and on horseback. The last of these is of a mixed nature, and is in some measure active as well as passive. We shall treat of each of them in order.

OF ACTIVE EXERCISE

Walking is the most gentle species of it we are acquainted with. It promotes perspiration, and if not continued too long, invigorates and strengthens the system. As the most simple and wholesome drink, namely water, is within every body's reach, so this species of simple and wholesome exercise is in every body's power, who has the use of his limbs. It is to be lamented, that carriages are substituted too often in the room of it. In Peking in China, we are told, that none but the Emperor, and a few of the first officers of state, are suffered to use chariots. Although the intention of this law was to suppress the number of horses, in order to make room for the increase and support of the human species, in the number of which the riches of all countries consist, yet we find it attended with good effects otherwise; for the rich and the great, by being obliged to walk in common with the poor people, enjoy with them the common blessing of health, more than people of the same rank in other countries. To such as can bear it, I would recommend walking frequently up a hill.

The inhabitants of mountainous countries are generally healthy and long lived. This is commonly attributed to the purity of the air in such places. Although this has a *chief* share in it, yet I cannot help thinking, that the frequent and necessary exercise of climbing mountains, which these people are obliged to undergo, adds much to their health and lives. Every body knows how much walking up a hill tends to create an appetite. This depends upon its increasing the insensible perspiration—a secretion with which the appetite, and the state of the stomach in general, are much connected.

Running is too violent to be used often, or continued for any length of time. The running footmen in all countries are short-lived—Few of them escape consumptions before they arrive at their thirty-fifth year.

Dancing is a most salutary exercise. Future ages will be surprised to hear, that rational creatures should, at any time, have looked upon it as a criminal amusement. To reason against it, from its abuse, concludes equally strong against the lawfulness of every thing we hold sacred and valuable in life.—It was a part of the Jewish worship. By its mechanical effects on the body, it inspires the mind with cheerfulness, and this, when well founded, and properly restrained, is another name for religion. It is common among the Indians, and the savage nations of all countries, upon public and festive occasions.—They have their war—their love—and their religious dances. The music, which always accompanies this exercise, hath a pleasing and salutary effect upon the body as well as the mind. It is addressed through the avenue of the ears to the brain, the common centre of life and motion, from whence its oscillations are communicated to every part of the system, imparting to each, that equable and uniform vigour and action, upon which the healthy state of all the functions depends. It would lead us to a long digression, or I might here mention many remarkable cures which have been performed, particularly of those disorders, which are much connected with the nervous system, by the magic power of music. Dancing should not be used more than once or twice a week. It should never be continued 'till weariness comes on, nor should we expose ourselves to the cold air too soon after it.

Fencing calls forth most of the muscles into exercise, particularly those which move the limbs. The brain is likewise roused by it, through the avenue of the eyes, and its action, as in the case of music, is propagated to the whole system. It has long been a subject of complaint, that the human species has been degenerating for these several centuries. When we see the coats of mail of our ancestors, who fought under the Edwards and Henries of former ages, we wonder how they moved, much more how they achieved such great exploits, beneath the weight of such massy coverings. We grant that rum—tobacco—tea—and some other luxuries of modern invention, have had a large share in weakening the stamina of our constitutions, and thus producing a more feeble race of men; yet we must attribute much of our great inferiority in strength, size and agility to our forefathers, to the disuse which the invention of gun-powder and fire arms hath introduced of those athletic exercises, which were so much practised in former ages, as a part of military discipline.

Too much cannot be said in praise of swimming, or as the poet of Avon expresses it—"buffeting the waves with lusty sinews." Besides exercising the limbs, it serves to wash away the dust, which is apt to mix itself with the sweat of our bodies in warm weather. Washing frequently in water, we find, was enjoined upon the Jews and Mahometans, as a part of their religious ceremonies. The Hollanders are cleanly in their houses and streets, without remembering, or perhaps knowing, that cleanliness was absolutely necessary at first, to guard against the effects of those inundations of mire, to which their country is always exposed—so a Jew and a Mussulman contend for, and practise their ablutions, without remembering that they were instituted only to guard them against those cutaneous diseases, to which the constant accumulation of scales upon their skins in a warm climate, naturally exposed them. For the same reason, I would strongly recommend the practice of bathing, and swimming, frequently in the summer season. But remember, you should not stay too long in the water at one time, lest you lessen instead of increasing the vigour of the constitution.

To all these species of exercise which we have mentioned, I would add, skeating, jumping, also, the active plays of tennis, bowles, quoits, golf,* and the like. The manner in which each of these operate, may be understood from what we said under the former particulars.

Active exercise includes, in the last place, talking—reading with an audible voice—singing and laughing. They all promote the circulation of the blood thro' the lungs, and tend to strengthen those important organs, when used in moderation. The last has the advantage over them all, inasmuch as the mind co-operates with it. May unfading laurels bloom to the latest ages upon the grave of him ** who said, "That every time a man laughs, he adds something to his life."

I would remark here, that all these species of exercise which we have described, should be varied according to age—sex—temperament—climate—and season. Young people stand in less need of exercise than old.—Women less than men. The natural vigour of their constitutions is such, that they suffer *least* from the want of it. This will explain the meaning, and show the propriety of an opinion of a modern Philosopher † that "Women only should follow those mechanical arts which require a sedentary life." But again, a man who is phlegmatic, requires more frequent and violent exercise than he who is of a bilious constitution: And lastly, people in warm climates and seasons, require less than those who live in cold. As Providence, by supply-

---

* Golf is an exercise which is much used by the Gentlemen in Scotland. A large common in which there are several little holes is chosen for the purpose. It is played with little leather balls stuffed with feathers; and sticks made somewhat in the form of a bandy-wicker. He who puts a ball into a given number of holes, with the fewest strokes, gets the game. The late Dr. M'Kenzie, Author of the Essay on Health and Long Life, used to say, that a man would live ten years the longer for using this exercise once or twice a week.

** Dr. Sterne.
† Rousseau.

ing the inhabitants of warm climates with so many of the spontaneous fruits of the earth, seems to have intended they should labour less than the inhabitants of cold climates, so we may infer from this, that less exercise, which is only a substitute for labour, is necessary for them. The heat of such climates is sufficient of itself to keep up a regular and due perspiration. We said in a former discourse, that the longest lived people were to be found in warm climates, and we gave one conjecture into the cause of it. It may not be improper here to add another. The coldness of northern climates, from the vigour it gives to the constitution, prompts to all kinds of exercise, which are not always restrained within proper bounds. These, when used to excess, wear out the body. Thus, blowing a fire, may cause it to burn the brighter, but it consumes it the sooner. The inhabitants of warm climates being less prompted to these things, their bodies continue longer unimpaired. I confine this observation, as in the former instance, to the improved parts of Asia and Africa only. The inhabitants of the West-Indian islands are so mixed, and partake so much of the European manners, that we cannot as yet include them in any general remarks which are made upon this subject.

I come to speak of those exercises which are of a Passive Nature. These are proper chiefly for valetudinarians: But, as I intend these sermons should be of use to them as well as the healthy, I shall make a few remarks upon each of them.

The life of a Sailor is environed with so many dangers, that Heaven has in compensation for them connected with it an exemption from many diseases. In vain do the angry elements assault him. His body, like some huge promontory, is proof against them all. Notwithstanding the dangers from shipwreck—fire—falling overboard—and famine, to which sailors are exposed, I believe, that if we were to count an hundred sailors, and the same number of people on land, in a place that was ordinarily healthy, we should find more of the former alive at the end of ten years than the latter. The exercise of Sailing is constant. Every muscle is occasionally brought into exercise from the efforts we make to keep ourselves from falling. These efforts continue to be exerted by the oldest sailors, although the consciousness of the mind in these, as well as in many other actions we perform, is not observed from the influence of habit. By means of this regular and gentle exercise, the blood is moved in those small capillaries, where it is most apt to stagnate, and perspiration is increased, which is carried off as fast as it is discharged from the body, by the constant change of atmosphere in a ship under sail. I say nothing here of the benefit of the sea air, it being entirely negative. Its virtue both at sea and on the sea-shore, consists in nothing but its being freed from those noxious animal and vegetable effluvia, which abound in the air, which comes across land. From what has been said, you will no longer be surprised at the uncommon appetite which some people feel at sea. It is owing to the great and constant discharge of the aliment (after it has undergone its usual changes) by means of perspiration. I would recommend this species of exercise to consumptive people, especially to such as labour under a spitting of blood. Dr. Lind tells us,* "That out of 5741 sailors who were admitted into the naval hospital at Haslar, near Portsmouth, in two years, only 360 of them had consumptions, and in one fourth of these, (he says,) it was brought on by bruises or falls." In the same number of hospital patients, in this or any other country, I am persuaded six times that number would have been consumptive—so much does the gentle exercise of sailing fortify the lungs against all accidents, and determine the quantity and force of the fluids towards the surface of the body.

Riding in a chariot has but few advantages, inasmuch as we are excluded from the benefit of fresh air; an article, upon which the success of all kinds of exercise in a great measure depends. It should be used only by such persons as are unable to walk or to ride on horseback. We cannot help lamenting here, that those people use this mode of exercise the most, who stand in the greatest need of a more violent species of it.

Riding on horseback is the most manly and useful species of

---

* Essay on the means of preserving the health of seamen.

exercise for gentlemen. Bishop Burnet expresses his surprise at the lawyers of his own time, being so much more long-lived (*cacteris paribus*) than other people, considering how much those of them who become eminent in their profession, are obliged to devote themselves to constant and intense study. He attributes it entirely to their riding the circuits so frequently, to attend the different courts in every part of the kingdom. This no doubt has a chief share in it: But we shall hereafter mention another cause which concurs with this, to protract their lives. It may be varied according to our strength, or the nature of our disorder, by walking—pacing—trotting—or cantering our horse All those diseases which are attended with a weakness of the nerves, such as the hysteric and hypochondriac disorders, which show themselves in a weakness of the stomach and bowels—indigestion—low spirits, &c. require this exercise. It should be used with caution in the consumption, as it is generally too violent, except in the early stage of that disorder. In riding, to preserve health, eight or ten miles a day are sufficient to answer all the purposes we would wish for. But in riding, to restore health, these little excursions will avail nothing. The mind as well as the body must be roused from its languor. In *taking an airing*, as it is called, we ride over the same ground for the most part every day. We see no new objects to divert us, and the very consideration of our riding for health sinks our spirits so much, that we receive more harm than good from it. Upon this account I would recommend long journeys to such people, in order, by the variety or novelty of the journey to awaken and divert the mind. Many people have by these means been surprised into health. Persons who labour under hysteric or epileptic' disorders, should be sent to cold; those who labour under hypochondriac or consumptive complaints should visit warm climates.

Before I finish this head of our discourse, I shall add a few words concerning the exercise of the faculties of the soul. The mind and body have a reciprocal action upon each other. Are our passions inflamed with desire or aversion? Or does our reason trace out relations in those things which are the objects of our understanding?—The body we find is brought into sympathy. The pulse and the circulation of the blood are immediately quickened. Perspiration and the other secretions are promoted, and the body is sensibly invigorated afterwards. The body partakes therefore of the torpor which the mind contracts by its neglecting to exercise its faculties. He must be but little acquainted with biography, who has not remarked, that such as have distinguished themselves in the literary world, have generally been long-lived. Addison, Swift, Locke, Newton, Franklin, with many others whom we might mention, all found a retreat in the evening of their lives under the shade of laurels which they had planted in their youth. Perhaps in most cases, they might promise themselves an exemption from diseases, and a death from mere old age, could they be persuaded to relinquish their midnight lamp before the oil which feeds it was consumed. Great care should be taken, however, to avoid too great application of the mind to study. The most powerful medicines in nature are the most certain poisons. Many promising geniuses have sacrificed themselves, before they arrived at the altar in the Temple of Fame. Such as are in danger of suffering from this cause, will do well in consulting the ingenious and humane Dr. Tissot's excellent treatise upon the diseases of literary people. The passions as well as our reason, should always be exercised as much as possible. We shall walk—run—dance—swim—fence—sail—and ride to little purpose, unless we make choice of an agreeable friend to accompany us. Solitude is the bane of man, insomuch, that it is difficult to tell which suffers most, the soul in its qualities, or the body in its temperament, from being alone. Too great a concourse of people breeds diseases. Too much company is destructive to cheerfulness. For the sake of both mind and body, therefore, we should move in a little circle, and let heaven circumscribe it for us. Let our wives and children be always around us, or if we are not blessed with these, let a few cheerful friends be our constant companions. It is remarked, that more single people die among those who are come to manhood than married, and all physicians agree, that single men and women, compose by far the greatest number of their chronic patients among adults. Some men may talk against the cares of a family. They are unavoidable, it is true, but they are necessary. Stagnating waters are never sweet. Thus, these little cares, by keeping the tenderer passions always agitated, prevent that uniformity in life, which is so foreign and disagreeable both to the body and mind. After all, I believe, I shall have the suffrages of most of my hearers, when I add, that they are at least balanced by the sweets of domestic friendship.

We come now to the next head of our discourse, namely,

II. To enquire into the proper Time for Exercise—Sanctorius informs us,* that "exercise, from the seventh to the eleventh hour after eating, wastes more insensibly in one hour, than in three at any other time." If this be true, then (supposing you sup at eight o'clock in the evening) that exercise which is used from five 'till seven o'clock in the morning, will promote the greatest discharge in a given time, by insensible perspiration. Such as make dinner their principal meal, are excluded from the benefit of this aphorism; as the interval, between the seventh and the eleventh hour, with them (supposing they dine at two o'clock in the afternoon) is from nine in the evening 'till one o'clock in the morning—a time, in which darkness, and the unwholesome night air, forbid walking—riding—and almost every other species of manly exercise we have described.

I know it will be objected here, that we often see labourers return, after a full meal, to their work, without feeling any inconvenience from it. This is like the argument of those who recommend raw flesh to the human species, because the strongest and fiercest animals in nature eat it. It is because they are so fierce and so strong, that they are able to digest raw flesh. In like manner it is, because these men are naturally so strong, that labour immediately after eating does not hurt them.† But let me ask, whether you have not observed such people leave their tables with reluctance—How slowly do they return,—and how

---
* Sect. V. Aphorism vii.
† *O! dura messorum ilia.* Hor. Epod. III.

many excuses do they form to loiter away a little time, before they renew their work.

But further—there is another reason why I would recommend this practice of eating the chief meal in the evening, which is indeed a little foreign to our present subject.—In a country like this, where the constant labour of every individual is so very necessary, the general use of this custom would add several hours to every day, and thus have the most beneficial effects upon the agriculture—commerce—and manufactures of the country, exclusive of its influence upon the health of the inhabitants.

After what has been said, I need hardly add, that exercise should never be used with a full stomach. Persons who exercise either to preserve, or restore health immediately after eating a hearty meal, resemble the man "who fled from a lion, and a bear met him, and who went into the house, and leaned his hand upon the wall, and a serpent bit him."

I come now to the application of this discourse.

I have endeavoured in every part of it, to lay before you the most powerful arguments, to excite you to exercise, and have addressed them chiefly to that main spring of human actions—Self Preservation. I have taught you the true art of alchemy, and furnished you with the genuine Philosopher's stone, but with this difference from that which has been sought for, by the deluded pretenders to philosophy in all ages, that instead of converting, like Midas, every thing you touch into gold—every thing which touches you shall—not convert you into gold—but impart health to you—compared with which, even the gold of Ophir loses its weight. In a word—I have showed you an harbour where I have anchored safely for many years; for, from my youth upwards, I have followed the mode of living I have recommended to you, as far as my connections or intercourse with the world would admit; and although I received from nature a weakly constitution, yet—I speak it with a grateful heart!—few men enjoy better health—none better spirits than myself; and was I now about to leave the world, surrounded with a family of children, I would charge them, among the most important lessons I should give them, to bind these things as "a sign upon their hands, or as frontlets between their eyes"—to think of them "when they sat in their houses, and when they walked by the way—when they lay down, and when they rose up—that their days might be multiplied, and that the days of their children, might be as the days of Heaven upon the earth."

I shall conclude this discourse with a story, which I hope, will not be looked upon as foreign to what has been delivered upon this subject.

In the island of Ceylon, in the Indian Ocean, a number of invalids were assembled together, who were afflicted with most of the chronic diseases, to which the human body is subject. In the midst of them sat several venerable figures, who amused them with encomiums upon some medicines, which they assured them would afford infallible relief in all cases. One boasted of an elixir—another of a powder, brought from America—a third, of a medicine, invented and prepared in Germany—all of which they said were certain antidotes to the gout—a fourth, cried up a nostrum for the vapours—a fifth, drops for the gravel—a sixth, a balsam, prepared from honey, as a sovereign remedy for a consumption—a seventh, a pill for cutaneous eruptions—while an eighth cried down the whole, and extolled a mineral water, which lay a few miles from the place where they were assembled. The credulous multitude partook eagerly of these medicines, but without any relief of their respective complaints. Several of those who made use of the German preparation, were hurried suddenly out of the world. Some said their medicines were adulterated—others that the Doctors had mistaken their disorders—while most of them agreed that they were much worse than ever. While they were all, with one accord, giving vent in this manner, to the transports of disappointment and vexation, a clap of thunder was heard over their heads. Upon looking up, a light was seen in the sky.—In the midst of this appeared the figure of something more than human—she was tall and comely—her skin was fair as the driven snow—a rosy hue tinged her cheeks—

her hair hung loose upon her shoulders—her flowing robes disclosed a shape which would have cast a shade upon the statue of Venus of Medicis—In her right hand she held a bough of an evergreen—in her left hand she had a scroll of parchment—she descended slowly, and stood erect upon the earth—she fixed her eyes, which sparkled with life, upon the deluded and afflicted company—there was a mixture of pity and indignation in her countenance—she stretched forth her right arm, and with a voice which was sweeter than melody itself, she addressed them in the following language. "Ye children of men, listen for a while to the voice of instruction. Ye seek health where it is not to be found. The boasted specifics you have been using, have no virtues. Even the persons who gave them, labour under many of the disorders they attempt to cure. My name is Hygiæa. I preside over the health of mankind. Descard all your medicines, and seek relief from Temperance and Exercise alone. Every thing you see is active around you. All the brute animals in nature are active in their instinctive pursuits. Inanimate nature is active too—air—fire—and water are always in motion. Unless this were the case, they would soon be unfit for the purposes they were designed, to serve in the economy of nature. Shun sloth. This unhinges all the springs of life—fly from your diseases—they will not—they cannot pursue you." Here she ended —she dropped the parchment upon the earth—a cloud received her, and she immediately ascended, and disappeared from their sight—a silence ensued—more expressive of approbation, than the loudest peals of applause. One of them approached with reverence to the spot where she stood—took up the scroll, and read the contents of it to his companions. It contained directions to each of them, what they should do to restore their health. They all prepared themselves to obey the advice of the heavenly vision. The gouty man broke his vial of elixir, threw his powders into the fire, and walked four or five miles every day before breakfast. The man afflicted with the gravel threw aside his drops, and began to work in his garden, or to play two or three hours every day at bowles. The hypochondriac and hysteric patients discharged their boxes of assafœtida, and took a journey on horseback to distant and opposite ends of the island. The melancholic threw aside his gloomy systems of philosophy, and sent for a dancing master. The studious man shut up his folios, and sought amusement from the sports of children. The leper threw away his mercurial pills, and swam every day in a neighbouring river. The consumptive man threw his balsam out of his window, and took a voyage to a distant country. After some months, they all returned to the place they were wont to assemble in. Joy appeared in each of their countenances. One had renewed his youth—another had recovered the use of his limbs—a third, who had been half bent for many years, now walked upright—a fourth began to sing some jovial song, without being asked—a fifth could talk for hours together, without being interrupted with a cough—in a word, they all enjoyed now a complete recovery of their health. They joined in offering sacrifices to Hygiæa. Temples were erected to her memory; and she continues, to this day, to be worshipped by all the inhabitants of that island.

ON MANNERS

Excerpts from a Diary Traveling Through France

NATIONAL PREJUDICES are of such a nature that it is seldom they are entirely overcome. We are very apt to imagine everything we see in our own country to be the standard of what is right in taste, politeness, customs, languages et cetera, and therefore we condemn everything which differs from us. This is a fruitful source of error in the opinions we form of different nations. Thus much I thought necessary to introduce an account of a journey made to a country and among people whose manners are so very opposite to our own that it is no wonder we are led (considering the great partiality we have for ourselves) to condemn them above most nations in the world. We shall perhaps find upon enquiry that they have many excellent things among them, and that they deserve to be as much the envy as the jest of each neighboring state.

I set off from London February 16, 1769, and reached Dover the same evening. I crossed the Channel in the night and arrived next morn at Calais. From hence I travelled in company with two young gentlemen by land to Paris. There was little variety in this journey except quarrelling with tavern keepers about their bills, crowds of beggars in every village (all of which is extremely common in France) can be called variety. The country of France is extremely beautiful and even at this early season of the year, in many places, it was covered with verdure. Few counties in England exceed Picardy (the only province over which I travelled), yet I am informed it is one of the poorest in France. It wants nothing but a greater plenty of water to afford the richest prospect in nature. The finest landscapes in the world without this capital beauty of nature become insipid and in a short time satiate the eyes. There and there indeed I saw fields covered with water by the hands of art, in order to heighten the beauty of several country scenes. But this was but a poor substitute for Rivers or Brooks, since the thirst cannot be duly entertained with it unless it appears to be always in motion.

Paris is generally supposed to be $\frac{1}{3}$ less than London both in size and in the number of its inhabitants. I cannot for my part agree in this calculation, considering the more oval figure of Paris, it appears to cover as much ground as London, which is rather of an elliptical form and considering the greater height and compactness of their houses, together with the narrowness of their streets, I am apt to think it contains as many inhabitants as London (about 800,000) especially when you excluded from the latter the vast number of seamen that daily crowd the streets, who belong to other countries, and who are by no means to be ranked among the inhabitants of London. I shall begin my account of this city by making a few remarks upon the state of the fine arts among them and first I shall take notice of their architecture.

Architecture is carried to much greater perfection here than in England. Their palaces are more in number, and more magnificent in their appearance than any building perhaps in the whole world. Their churches impress the mind, with a sublime kind of solemnity, which is easier to be conceived than described. The richness of their altars, the grandeur of their images, and the beauty of their paintings makes a stranger imagine he is walking into the Temple of Solomon itself. The outside of several of their most celebrated palaces are notwithstanding very faulty, in being rather too uniform, insomuch that no one part of them strikes the mind more than another. In painting as well as poetry, the attention should always be directed to some one object, to which every other part of the work should be subservient, Virgil's Aenead would cease to please us, unless our eyes were kept constantly fixed upon the illustrious hero of the poem, nor would Milton's Paradise Lost be in the least entertaining if our attention was not perpetually kept up to the fate of Adam.

The same rule applies to architecture, some one pillar or piece of statuary should always strike the mind at first sight and every other part of the building should be inferior to it both in beauty and size.

The *paintings* in and about Paris, afford the highest entertainment to a man of taste. Here is everything that is instructing in portraiture, history, poetry, and religion represented to the very life. I could dwell with pleasure upon eight or ten of them, which detained me for hours in viewing them. In a church dedicated to the Virgin Mary, is a representation of a woman dying with the plague, raised up in her bed to receive the sacrament from the hands of a priest; you imagine you see the very sweat of death upon her face, and you cannot help sympathizing in some measure with her husband and children, who are weeping around her bed.

In the palace of the Duke of Orleans is to be seen painted in the most masterly manner, everything remarkable in the History of Aeneas, from the destruction of Troy to his arrival in Italy. Nothing struck me more than the moving story of his leaving Dido at Carthage. You behold grief mixed with resentment in the countenance of the queen, while Aeneas expresses in every feature of his face all the passionate fondness of a lover, mingled at the same time with all that manly heroism which the prospect of establishing a kingdom and being the author of an illustrious race of heroes, in a distant country naturally fired his soul. Besides this I was much struck with several admirable pieces of Scriptural history.

In the Palace of Luxembourg is a gallery representing most of the memorable events in the history of Henry the Fourth and Louis the Thirteenth. The birth of the latter is expressed to the very life. The little prince is brought and presented to his royal mother, Marie de Medici, who receives him with an air of joy mingled with a degree of pain which nothing but the pencil of a Rubens would have captured, for this whole gallery was filled by that illustrious painter.

Statuary is another fine art, which is cultivated with great success in Paris. This art is superior to the former in resisting better the strokes of time. 'Tis owing to this that Rome even to this day allures strangers from all parts of the world, there as the poet expressed it:

> "Heroes in animated marble shoen,
> And Legislators seem to think in stone."
> POPE

There Trajan, Pompey and most of the illustrious genii of Rome appear in all their wonted glory, and seem to tell the traveller in every feature of their faces, the history of their lives and illustrious actions. I have received great pleasure from viewing the statues of some of the most celebrated men in France, which are to be seen in most of their public buildings. One piece of sculpture particularly struck me very much. It was that of Cardinal Richelieu, which stands by a large church founded by himself, called the Church de Sorbonne. He is represented in a dying posture, with his right hand upon his breast, and in his left he holds all his works which he is offering to the Savior. Religion in the form of a beautiful maid supports his head, while Science in the form of another sits with her robes ruffled around her face and appears to be inconsolable for the loss she was about to sustain by his death.

But even this useful art has been prostitute in France. In many places you see some of the most absurd fictions of Ovid's Metamorphoses, such as women transformed into fishes and other animals, and then into trees represented in as striking a manner as if they were facts of yesterday and believed by all the world. Besides this many of them want that chastity which we would wish to find in all civilized, but more especially in all Christian countries. Who would expect to find the Rape of Orythia, by Borreau, in one of the most public walks of the city?

Paris, like London, abounds with a number of charitable institutions for the relief of the sick and poor; the most remarkable of these is what is called the Hotel Dieu or the Hospital of God, into which all distressed persons of all religions and from all countries are received and provided for. At some seasons it contains 8,000 souls. The Foundling Hospital is another admirable institution founded upon the same plan as that in London. The day before I saw it, 18 or 20 little children were received into it; it is supposed one eighth of the children born in Paris are brought up here. One reason why it is so much crowded is, that if a woman brings forth a dead child without first declaring her pregnancy, she is burnt alive; this puts an entire stop to child murder, and every poor child of course that is born in Paris is naturally sent to this hospital; the motto over the door is very a propos to the condition of the children. It is "Mon père, et ma mère m'ont abandonné, mais le Signeur a pris soin de moi." (My father and my mother have abandoned me, but the Lord hath taken care of me.)

In a country like France, where the belles lettres are cultivated with so much success, we might naturally expect to find oratory much studied by everybody, that is called upon to appear in a public character. Rhetoricians divide oratory into four kinds —1st that of the pulpit; 2nd that of the bar, 3rd that of the popular assemblies and 4th that of the stage. The first of these deserves the particular notice of strangers. The preachers in general here are much more animated than in any other country. Their sermons abound with the boldest strokes of rhetoric, as frequent apostrophes or addresses to the Deity, or to particular virtues, and in some cases the very walls of the churches in which they are preaching. The subjects of all the sermons I heard were chiefly moral. One reason why the French preachers excell the English is that they almost always commit their sermons to memory and never carry a written word into the pulpit with them.

It is impossible for a man to speak well or use the least graceful action, who is closely confined to his notes. As to the eloquence of the bar, I can say nothing from my own observation, having never been able to gain admittance into any of their courts of justice. All criminal trials are heard in private, and it is in these chiefly that an orator has an opportunity of showing his abilities. As to the eloquence of their popular assemblies, I believe there is scarcely any remains of it to be found amongst them. The parliaments of France are mere courts of justice, and have no power of any kind as a legislative body. It is in free countries only that this species of eloquence appears with all its advantages. Demosthenes and Cicero lived in ages that have ever since been celebrated as the most favorable to the liberties of mankind. If a man dares in the least to oppose the King's *Arrettes* or proclamations, he is immediately secluded from his seat in Parliament, and banished from Paris during the King's pleasure. May we never live to see this the case in Great Britain. There was a time when the Parliaments of France were as free and independent as our own, but what will not bribery and corruption accomplish.

The last species of eloquence, namely that of the stage, has been much celebrated throughout all Europe but in my opinion it is much inferior to that of the English stage in everything. Their tragedies are all written in rhyme. How very ridiculous must it appear, to hear a husband lamenting the death of a wife in all the harmony of verse? Besides this, so fond are the French of humor in all their dramatic performances that I once saw a woman after having taken leave of her children, with an intention to destroy herself after weeping in so pathetic a manner as to oblige the whole audience to weep with her suddenly dissipate all their tears and raise a universal laughter by a piece of low wit which had no connection with the subject of the tragedy. Their comedies, in general, are much better than the English. All kinds of buffoonery are excluded from them. They abound in more sentiments and are for the most part designed only to expose living vices and not living characters. I never read a French comedy in my life that had even a double entendre in it, very different is the character of most of our English comedies. A foreigner once said of them, that the "Conscious Lovers" was the only English comedy he had ever seen, that was not much fitter to be acted in a brothel than upon an English stage.

The ladies in Paris in general are very beautiful. Their easiness of behavior, their sprightliness and apparent good humor, give additional charm to their persons. Much however of their beauty is borrowed from art; I mean painting. This fashion prevails so much in Paris, that the ladies take no pains to conceal it. It is very common to see them take out a little box of paint which they always carry in their pockets, together with a small looking-glass, and a fine pencil, and daub their cheeks over in their coaches, when they are going out to an Assembly or any public entertainment. This practice of painting however is far from being general as some have reported, being confined chiefly to ladies of quality.

Much has been said of the want of delicacy in the French ladies. The freedom of their behavior, their using certain expressions in conversation which are looked upon as indelicate in other countries, and above all their admitting gentlemen to pay them morning visits in their bed chambers have all been urged as arguments to support the justness of the censure. For my part I am far from agreeing in the common opinion, which is entertained of the propriety or impropriety of these things. What is looked upon as decent in one country, is often condemned as highly indecent in another.

I have heard some Scotch ladies (who are remarkable for their delicacy in most things) make use of expressions in public companies which I should blush to have repeated. Had I expressed the same ideas they did, in the language I had always been used to in my own country, it is probable they would have blushed much more, to have heard them and perhaps, have condemned me for a want of delicacy in their company. In Turkey, no woman is ever looked upon as virtuous, who has been seen dancing with a man. In England and in many other countries we see this custom practised without detracting in the least from the character of a lady.

I am far from thinking a lady's virtue should be called in question, who receives a gentleman in her bed-chamber, nor can I see wherein the difference consists, between seeing a lady in her ordinary dress and under a pile of bed clothes—much more of the body is exposed in the former case (even by our most delicate English ladies) than in the latter. Upon the whole I cannot help concluding that there is as much real virtue among the ladies of France as among the women of any other country in the world. Too much cannot be made of their accomplishments of other kinds: a well-bred woman here is one of the most entertaining companions in the world.

'Tis not enough for her to understand the duties of domestic life, she extends her enquiries much further, and never thinks her education complete till she has acquired some general knowledge of the principles of geography, philosophy, and belles lettres, etc. In spite of all the commonplace declamation against women's reading and women's learning, I cannot help thinking that some of the above accomplishments add much to the native charms of a woman, and render her in every respect a more agreeable companion to a man of sense. If a sympathy of affections only gives such a degree of happiness in the married state, how much greater might it be were there always a sympathy of understanding going with it? A common objection to learning in women is, that it makes them vain, but were their education more attended to, and a little knowledge in the fine arts more common among them, it would in a short time destroy that preeminence in a few which is the chief cause of their vanity.

It remains now that I say a few words concerning the religion of France. Everybody knows that popery is established here by law. The number of Protestants or Hugonots, as they were called at the reformation, were supposed to compose ⅓ of the inhabitants of France but since the great massacre in the year 1572, and since the Revocation of the Edict of Nantes, by Louis XIV their number is very much diminished. The men of learning and taste (who are too apt to take the Church of

Rome, with all its absurdities, for the true Christian Church) in general profess themselves Deists. This must always be the case in those countries where all freedom of enquiry in religious matters is checked by law. The many artful attacks which have been made upon Christianity by the Deistical writers in England instead of lessening its credibility have tended rather to establish it by drawing forth some of the most learned publications in its defense which have ever appeared upon any subjects whatever.

Were the clergy in France less numerous, less powerful and less rich, we might hope that the rapid progress in learning and those arts which enlarge and unfetter the human mind have made among them would alone be sufficient to overthrow the established religion. But this never can be the case, while a city like Paris contains 10,000 priests, while they are the first and constant companions of each succeeding prince, and while they have ⅓ of all the land in the kingdom in their possession.

I was led once to visit a monastery at a place called St. Dennis (about 6 miles from Paris). There several hundred monks were shut up and lived together under one roof. I went to their chapel which adjoined their monastery, and heard them say mass. Some of them were grey-headed, others bald with age. There was something melancholy in seeing such a number of them alone at their devotions. I followed them from the chapel after mass was over into the monastery. Instead of sitting down and eating and drinking or talking together, they parted in a large hall, where each one went into his own private apartment. I could hardly bear to think of the gloomy manner in which each of them passed the remaining part of the evening. Heavens! thought I—such a religion must be unworthy of God, and unfit for men, which dissolves his ties with society, and obliges him to pass through the world a stranger to the tender names of husband-father-friend. Religion does not forbid us the enjoyment of any of the good things in life. It only teaches us to enjoy them in the devotion, and in subordination to better things.

I left this solitary asylum of indolent and cowardly piety, if it deserves the name of piety, with a heart filled with pity and disgust, and could not help repeating to myself that inimitable passage in one of Dr. Stern's Sermons upon Mortification in which he says, A good heart wants something to be kind to. Let the torpid monk seek heaven comfortless and alone. God speed him! I fancy I never should so find the way. Let me have a companion in my journey be it only to remark to—how are shadows lengthening as the sun goes down—to whom I may say— How fresh is the face of nature? How sweet the flowers of the field? How delicious are these fruits?

The nunneries, where young women only are confined, are never visited by the men, so I could only view them at a distance, or at best peep through the gates of their apartments, while they were at worship. The number of nuns in and around Paris is very great, those who retire into nunneries for the sake of religion compose by far the smaller share of them. Men with small fortunes generally contrive to get their daughters off their hands, by persuading them to take the veil. . . . If they are unable to do this, their eldest sons, when they come to take possession of their fathers' estates, seldom fail of accomplishing it, in order to free the estate from the incumbrance of a small jointure, which is allowed them. This unnatural practice is not peculiar to France, but is common to all Roman Catholic countries, especially where the civil law (which provides so carefully for eldest sons) is in force.

What shall I say of the politeness of the French nation? Politeness has its seat in the heart only, and if an assemblage of good qualities, are necessary to constitute it, then the French people possess no more of it than many other nations of Europe. But if it consists in giving as little pain and as much pleasure as possible, to everybody around us as well as in saying and doing everything with a graceful manner, then the French have a right to lay claim to that character, above all the nations of the world. It is true that many of their expressions of civility and respect are counterfeit, such as "I am transported to see you"—"I am charmed with the company" and "I have the honor to be your very humble servant." But even these expressions serve to keep up a little ceremony in company, which is absolutely necessary, to make conversation agreeable and instructing. Although they have no value in themselves, yet they serve as pieces of money in trade, as a medium of intellectual commerce among mankind.

Where men mix much together, as they are obliged to do in all large towns a familiarity would be produced which would soon destroy all good manners, were they not to keep one another at a little distance by these formal and seemingly unmeaning modes of addressing each other. They lay a restraint upon their passions, or at least they teach them to vent them in such a manner that they seldom give much uneasiness or offence. Where men meet together often, and neglect these little formalities, however diversified by education or religion they may be, we generally find they degenerate into rudeness, which seldom fails of ending in disputes, quarrels and the like.

Much contempt and ridicule have been thrown upon the French nation upon the account of the singularity of their dress. To suppose that the whole nation was composed of nothing but fops and coxcombs, would be to allow them too large a proportion of the follies of the rest of the world, and to suppose that every man who carries a sword or umbrella or wears a muff feels a pride in these useless appendages to his dress, would be to admit of a union between pride and poverty in some cases, between pride and good sense which is rarely to be met with in other countries. We shall in a little time trace the origin of this singularity in the dress of a Frenchman, and shall find perhaps, that pride and vanity have but a very inconsiderable share in producing it.

There is nothing the French nation is more to be envied for than the knightliness of their manners, or their knowledge in what they call L'art de vivre, or the art of living. With a much smaller share of ordinary blessings of life, than many of their neighbors possesss, they appear always cheerful and happy. Poverty and slavery to a Frenchman are but imaginary evils. They cultivate the Social Principle and household arts to which Englishmen are strangers.

Everything which tends to bring the sexes together, tends at the same time to increase all the pleasures of society. Men when they associate much with each other become rough and unpolished; women from the same practice become trifling or disagreeable, but by mingling together they mutually polish and improve one another. In England the sexes meet only at assemblies, plays and other places of public entertainment. Here everything is conducted with ceremony which forbids conversation, or if this is laid aside, it is only for the sake of introducing cards, which will more effectively put a stop to all kinds of improvement of conversation. In France the sexes besides meeting at the above places have frequent select meetings which they call *coteries*. Here ladies and gentlemen meet only to talk upon subjects in science. Here they forget their little domestic cares and amuse one another with their remarks upon the news, politics, witty sayings, books and events of the past day or week. There is nothing stiff or reserved in these companies. Sometimes they all listen to one person speaking; at other times they all form themselves into little parties. Some of them sit, some stand and walk up and down without any restraint.

I had the pleasure of belonging to a society of this kind, which met at Marquis de Mirabeau's, a nobleman of great merit, who has lately distinguished himself by writing some excellent pieces, upon the finances, agriculture, commerce and politics of France. He calls himself in this work *L'ami des hommes* or "A friend of mankind."

Nothing pleased me more in this society than the behavior of the ladies. They were the umpires of all disputes. To them all the conversation was addressed, and a gentleman was listened to with more or less pleasure, according as he seemed to entertain them. The many judicious remarks and answers they gave to what was said and the very agreeable manner in which they interested themselves in everything carried on showed how well they were qualified for the part, and entitled to the respect which was shown them in this society.

It is here a proper place to enquire into the causes which constitute the differences between the manners of a Frenchman and an Englishman. For the most part the vivacity of the French nation has been attributed to their climate and manner of living. But this in my opinion has but a small share in forming their characters. This may be easily proved. 1st from their differing widely from the ancient Gauls who lived in the same climate, and 2nd from their retaining their own peculiar manners in all countries, more especially in the warm climates of the East and West Indies. Further, if their manners were entirely formed by their climate or manner of living we should always find the same manners in parallel latitudes, and where the same methods of living took place. But this we know is far from being the case. The peculiarity of their manners must therefore be resolved into imitation. This we prove from the great facility with which Englishmen contract their manners when in Paris. Chance at first probably gave a sanction to them, and this has through time operated with all the force of a law, insomuch that at present to deviate from them is to be singular and of consequence to be ridiculous.

Before I conclude the account of manners of the French nation, I shall make a little digression and point out a striking resemblance in many things between the manners and customs of the French and of most savage nations, particularly the Indians, in North America. Civilians divide mankind into 3 classes; savage, barbarous and civilized. The Savage lives by fishing and hunting; the Barbarous by pasturage and the spontaneous fruits of the earth, and the civilized by agriculture. There is a certain chain which connects each of these classes together, so that they appear to be different parts of one circle.

All extremes meet in a point. The highest degrees of civilization border a good deal upon savage life. This we shall illustrate by mentioning a few of those customs in which the French nation, perhaps the most civilized in the whole world, resembles

Indians or savages. First they possess the most perfect freedom in their behavior and like the savages are strangers to every thing which looks like restraint in their intercourse with each other. This is the case in a more especial manner in that intercourse which subsists between the sexes. We before reconciled the seeming indelicacy of the modes of expression and behavior of the French ladies in the company of gentlemen with the strictest regard to virtue. The Women among savage nations know nothing of the arts of concealing those wants and necessities to which their sex has subjected them, from my knowledge of them, nor are they acquainted with any mode of expressing them, and yet no one has ever pretended, from these circumstances alone, to call their modesty or virtue in question.—There are instances of some savage nations, among whom these things, are looked upon as innocent, who never fail to punish adultery and other cases of a want of chastity in the severest manner.

Secondly. The French Nation, are particularly fond of *Painting* (their faces). This is a question which prevails chiefly among Savages. Among these it was introduced partly to defend the Race from the inclemency of the weather, and partly to add to its Beauty. It is used among the French People chiefly to answer the latter Purpose. I know it is condemned by most of the civilized nations in Europe. But I am far from thinking that common objections made to it, have any weight. No one will pretend to say that the works of Nature, are so perfect, as to be incapable of receiving any Improvements from Art. Flowers, Fields, Forrests and Prospects of all Kinds, all receive new Beauties from the Hand of Cultivation. No one thinks it a crime to improve the air, and figure of the human body by dancing, dress and the like. Why should it be thought criminal then, to attempt to improve its Beauty in Painting? A mixture of red and white forms the most beautiful contrast of colours in the world. The face was formed with this beautiful mixture of colours, originally by nature. We see it even yet in those who have not lost it by sickness or exposure to the air.

Painting of cheeks therefore with vermillion is only imitating

Nature, and notwithstanding all that has been said against it, adds much to its beauty. If an inseparable connection is established in Nature, between such a mixture of colours, and a pleasure in the imagination, I see no harm in giving or increasing this pleasure by every innocent means, which lies in our power.

Thirdly, the French people eat their principal meal at night. A family is seldom convened for this purpose until the evening. They go to their closets as often as they are impelled by hunger, and eat and drink some light matter, which satisfy them till 8 or 9 o'clock at night. This is in some measure the custom among the Indians. They take but one principal meal in the 24 hours, which is for the most part at night, after the fatigue of hunting, fishing, or marching in time of War are over. This practice however much it may be condemned by some is an appeal among civilized nations, from the tyranny of custom to the unerring law of Nature. It is always most wholesome to sleep after eating. This is the practice of all the brute animals, we are acquainted with. Nature recoils from business of all kinds, after a hearty meal, nor is this to be wondered at, when we consider that the digestion of the food in the stomach, is carried on chiefly by fermentation, to which *Rest* we know contributes so much, that no fermentation can be compleat without it.

Fourthly, The People of Rank and Fortune among the French, are particularly fond of *Fishing* and *Hunting*. Those are their principal amusements. Everybody knows that it is by means of these, that all savage nations support themselves As the greatest part of Mankind have been or are still savage, Nature has implanted in them a love for these employments, and however much it may be restrained, there are few who have not at some time of their lives felt the force of this Passion. The Nobleman who drives the boar from his den, or chases the stag across his woods, or draws the fish from his ponds differs from the Indian only in doing these things for his pleasure, while the latter is obliged to follow them for his support. There is no life so agreeable as that of the savage. It is free and independent, and in this consists the highest happiness of Man. When he is removed from it he is perpetually striving to get back to it again.

The stages in society are like those in human life. A man is to be "once a man and twice a child." So it is with him in respect to Society. He is once civilized and when left to follow the bent of his inclination will never fail of becoming twice a Savage.

Fifthly. There is one more custom, in which I observed the French People to resemble the Savage and that is, they seldom address one another by their proper names, but for the most part by the titles of "Madame" or "Monsieur." It is no uncommon thing for a Frenchman, when called by his name in company to say "Sir I am much obliged to you for putting me in mind of my name, but I assure you, I had not forgot it." I must here add to this remark, that I have observed the best people in all parts of the World, call one another by their names as seldom as possible in company. I am at a loss to point out the foundation of this custom in Nature.

We observe however something like it in the Indians of North America. They call one another so seldom by their names, that some have supposed they have none, as they are all divided into little tribes, which marry within themselves, they become in time related in such a manner to each other, that they call one another for the most part, by a name which is expressive of some of their relations, such as *Father, Mother, Sister, Brother* and *Cousin*. The last of these is a term, which they use in general to those whose relationship is too distant to be traced. This custom among the Indians, I know has been urged (with many other arguments) to prove that the Indians are descended from one of the *Jewish Tribes*. The Jews we find were fond of addressing each other in this manner. Hence we find *Abraham* say to *Lot*, We are *Brethren* whereas he was only his nephew. So *Jacob* tells *Rachel*, that he was her *Fathers Brother*, when we are sure no such relationship, (in the common acceptation of that word) subsisted between them.

But this custom is far from being confined to the Indians

in *North America*. It prevails among many of the Savage Negroes in Africa. It must therefore have some foundation in Nature. We naturally call those whom we love, by some name expressive of that love or respect. A man calls his wife his *dear* and his children his little *darlings* and the like. A countryman brought up at a distance from those places, where the forms of politeness are kept up, naturally accosts a Person whom he thinks his superior, or who fills some office by a Title which supposes him to possess some quality above himself, such as *Honour, Excellency, Grace, Highness* and the like.

These little things, however trifling they appear to some, tend to preserve an harmony and good order among the different Ranks of Mankind, which are absolutely necessary to keep up the happiness and well being of Society.

As my time was closely employed all the while I was in Paris, I had but little leisure to make excursions in the Country. *Versailles* was the most remarkable place near Paris, that I went to see. I found the gardens, palaces, painting and statuary. To answer the description I *had* of them, it would take up a volume to give a particular account of every thing I saw here, that was beautiful or grand. I shall confine myself only to an account of the *Royal Family*, who reside chiefly in this Palace.

I arrived at Versailles about 11 o'clock in the forenoon in company with several English gentlemen. I went immediately into the *Royall Chapel* which adjoins the Palace where we had a full view of his Majesty at his Devotion. He is between 59 and 60 years of age, but looks so well that no one would take him to be above 45. His behaviour during the whole service was serious, and respectful. After Mass was over we went to see the *Dauphin* and the rest of the Royal Family dine in Public. The *Dauphin* is between 15 and 16 years of age, and tho' so young is arrived at his full growth.

We generally watch with impatience, the openings of the minds of those persons, who are born to fill important stations in Life. We admire every prelude they give us of Genius, and this in some measure from their early behaviour, draw the character they will sustain thru' life. Was I to judge from the appearance of the *Dauphin of France*, I should declare, that he was formed on purpose to show the world of how little value Crowns, and Kingdoms are in the sight of Heaven, or he would never have a right to succeed to either of them. He is remarkably coarse featured—stoops in his shoulders, has a brown skin, and is very awkward in every respect. When he first came out to Dinner, he sat down without speaking to anybody. Several gentlemen and ladies who came occasionally into the room went up and bowed to him, but he took no notice of them.

But this was far from being the most brutish part of his behaviour. During the time of dinner, he took a piece of meat from his mouth, which he had been chewing and after looking at it for some time in the presence of near 100 spectators, threw it under the table. I found upon inquiry, that he had never given the least proofs of forwardness in anything, and that by his preceptions and the people around him, and is regarded only as a prodigy of dullness—for all Princes according to Dean Swift, are prodigies of some sort. Very different is the character of the *Count D'Artois*, his youngest brother who sat at his left hand. He is about 12 years of age, but has already, the behaviour of a man. I think he is the handsomest form, I ever saw in my life. Everybody is charmed with him. Everybody speaks with admiration of the pregnancy of his genius, of his great love for every thing that is noble or princely. So much was I pleased with his appearance, that I could not help saying to one of my companions, who stood by me, that I should not be surprised to hear hereafter, that this little Prince directed the Counsels, or led the Armies of France all over the World. The *King's Daughters* dined in a private apartment by themselves, to which I was likewise admitted. They had nothing remarkable about them, except it was a prodigious quantity of paint upon their cheeks, which was still insufficient to conceal their ages, or to supply the want of that Beauty which Nature had denied them.

I have nothing particular to say of the *King of France*. He appears to be alike incapable of doing either good or harm. Most of his time is spent in Hunting, or with his mistress. Let such as maintain the Divine Right of Kings come and behold this Monarch, setting on a couch with a common prostitute, picked up a few years ago from the streets of Paris, or let them follow him in his Forrests and there behold him sporting with the death of a fox or stag, and then let them declare if they can, that they believe him to be the *Lord Anointed*: It is Blasphemy itself to suppose that God ever gave an absolute command over 18 millions of his creatures, for this is the number of the inhabitants of France, to a man like Louis the 15th.

Before I finish my remarks upon the French Nation, I shall only add, that there is one circumstance which bears a very favourable aspect upon the liberties of this country and that is, that *Agriculture*, begins to flourish more here than formerly. Few countries in the world equal France, for all the varieties of soil, climate, manners and situation of every kind, and yet, notwithstanding this, so great has been the neglect of cultivation here, that an acre of ground in the most fruitful parts of France is computed to be worth no more than $\frac{1}{8}$ of an acre in most parts of England. Many causes have concurred to prevent the cultivation of their lands, the chief of these are, first, the extreme contempt, in which Agriculture and Farmers, have always been held in France. Secondly, the vast number of Parks for hunting which are to be found in all parts of the Kingdom. Thirdly. The shortness of leases granted to farmers, by the proprietors of lands. Fourthly. The want of enclosure for their fields. Fifthly. The want of encouragement from the Crown. It is easy to see in what manner each of these act, so as to prevent the encouragement of agriculture. But at present it begins to wear a very different appearance.

Several of the principal men in the Nation have lately written very largely upon this subject. Societies for granting premiums are now instituting all over the Kingdom, in imitation of those formed in England and Scotland. From this it seems probable, that the Crown before long will view it in the important light it deserves and give proper encouragement to it. It is surprising that so ancient and useful an employment as *Agriculture* should ever fall into disrepute in any country. The Civilization of Mankind and Agriculture began together; all notions of property were unknown, while men continued to live by fishing—hunting, pasturage. As soon as they began to cultivate the Earth, they sought for the protection of laws, to secure to them, those spots of ground which they had cultivated. *Agriculture* is the only valid basis of the riches of any county. In *Rome* when that empire flourished most, we find agriculture was held in the highest estimation. Even Emperors themselves have exchanged the pleasures of a Court, for the more innocent enjoyments of *Husbandry* and those hands which had been accustomed to wield a Sceptre, and to handle a crown, became voluntarily familiar with the plough, the spade, the sickle and the pruning hook. The riches of Britain are derived from this source alone. Her manufactures, her fleets, her armies and her Empire over the Deep, will always keep pace, with her improvements in Agriculture.

It is owing to this that the American Colonies have in so short a space of time arisen to such a pitch of grandeur and riches. Where this is neglected, there can be neither riches nor grandeur. *Spain* we find is poor in the midst of all her treasures of gold and silver, from the want of industry among her inhabitants. The poverty of the greatest part of *Germany*, *Sweden* and *Denmark*, is more owing to the neglect of Agriculture, than to the Northern situation or natural barrenness of their soil. In a word, where agriculture is encouraged, there will be riches, where there are riches, there will be Power, and where there is Power, there will be Freedom and Independence.

I might here add a particular account of the names and characters of *Physicians, Chemists, Philosophers* and *Academicians,* to whom I was recommended, and among whom, I spent my time in the most agreeable manner during my stay in Paris. There is no difficulty of getting acquainted with men of this Character in France. They seem to acquire knowledge only for the sake of communicating it. Besides this, they are extremely polite and hospitable, and have none of those formalities which so much distinguish Men of Science in other countries. I cannot help mentioning the name of one gentleman of this character, to whom I was introduced by a letter from Dr. Franklin.

As he honoured me with many civilities whilst I was in Paris, and has since favoured me with his correspondence, I desire this little history of him to stand as a monument of the high esteem, I entertain for his merit and virtues. The name is *John Barew Dubourg*. When I first went into his house, I found him employed in translating the *Farmers Letters* into French. The first question he asked me was, whether I knew the author of them? I told him that I had that Honour. He then broke out into a great many fine encomiums upon them and said "that in his opinion the Roman Orator Cicero, was less eloquent than the Pennsylvania Farmer." Here I beheld (to borrow an allusion from the Farmers Letters) "The Fire of Liberty, still blazing in a country, after the altar upon which it was kindled, was burned to the ground."

In a little time I forgot that he was a stranger, I forgot that he was a Frenchman, I forgot that he was once the enemy of my country. I took him into my arms, nay more. I took him into my very Heart. From that moment he became my friend, and should I gain no other advantage by going to France, than the benefit of his friendship, and correspondence, I shall esteem my visit well bestowed. His wife is one of the most amiable women in the world. He has lately written a treatise upon *Botany*, calculated for the use of ladies only, which he has dedicated to his wife. This dedication he designed as a monument of their conjugal happiness. They have never had any children.

When I consider myself in the character of a Physician, that one design I had in view, in going to France, was to improve myself in knowledge. I cannot avoid adding in this place that little improvement in that way is to be acquired in any part of this country. Medicine is not cultivated here by men of rank and fortune, nor is the profession looked upon so liberal in this country, as it is in England or America. I visited most of their hospitals and conversed with several of the principal physicians in Paris, and was sorry to find them at least 50 years behind the Physicians in England and Scotland in medical knowledge.

After having satisfied my curiosity with regard to everything that was remarkable, or worthy of a stranger's notice in Paris, I set off March 21st for London. On my return I passed thro' several considerable villages, which seemed to be crowded with inhabitants—*Amiens* in particular, is said to contain 30,000 inhabitants. There is a large and most magnificent Church, built by Henry the 3rd, King of England, in memory of some Victory gained over the French. The floor and most of the Pillars of the Church are of fine marble, the paintings, the ornaments round the Altar exceed all description, none of them however struck me so much as the Figure of a venerable *Abbe*, whom I saw walking up and down the Church. He appeared to be about 40 years of age. His complexion was dark, his countenance grave inclining a little to the melancholy. His eyes were fixed so intently upon the floor, that all the noise that was made by those who passed and repassed, (some of whom talked pretty loud) did not cause him once to lift them up or look up at them. I approached him as near as possible, and put myself in his way, but it was to no purpose. I could not disturb him.

Had I given way to the prejudices of my education with regard to the opinions, which are entertained in most Protestant countries, concerning the Popish Religion, I should have concluded that this venerable man, this Son of the Roman Catholic Church, was plotting some schemes to subvert the State, or to eradicate the Tenets of the Heretics. But I was far from cherishing a thought of this kind. This Holy Man (said I to myself) has betook himself this morning to this Sanctuary, in order to offer up his Morning Oblations to Heaven.

The flame of devotion can burn notwithstanding it is kindled upon the Altar of Superstition. The Deity pays no regard to those little ceremonies, in Worship, which divide most of the Christian Churches. He will always worship acceptably, who worships him in Spirit and in Truth. The perfume of flowers is the same on whatsoever soil they grow and there is no Church I believe so corrupt, that does not contain within its bosom many individuals whose devotion (tho' mingled with superstition and enthusiasm) does not rise like grateful incense to the Throne of Heaven.

I arrived at Calais March 25th and sailed next day in the Packet Boat for Dover, was 23 hours on the water, altho' the distance was but 21 miles. I set out from Dover March 27th and arrived at a Village called *Dartford* the same day. The next morning I set off for *London* which was within 15 miles of Dartford. With this I finish my account of my journey to *Paris*.

DIRECTIONS FOR CONDUCTING A NEWSPAPER

Addressed to Mr. Brown, editor of the Federal Gazette

1. CONSIDER that we live three thousand miles from the nations of Europe, and that we have but little interest in their domestic parties, or national quarrels. The less therefore you publish of them, the better.

2. Avoid filling your paper with anecdotes of British vices and follies. What have the citizens of the United States to do with the duels, the elopements, the crim. cons, the kept mistresses, the murders, the suicides, the thefts, the forgeries, the boxing matches, the wagers for eating, drinking, and walking, &c. &c. of the people of Great Britain? such stuff, when circulated through our country, by means of a newspaper, is calculated to destroy that delicacy in the mind, which is one of the safeguards of the virtue of a young country.

3. If any of the above-named vices should ever be committed in the United States, the less that is said about it the better. What have the citizens of Philadelphia to do with the criminal amours of Mr. M——, of Boston?—the frequent and minute histories of such gross vices, take off from the horror they would otherwise excite in the mind.

4. Never suffer your paper to be a vehicle of private scandal, or of personal disputes. If the faults of public officers are exposed, let it be done with decency. No man has a right to attack

the vices or follies of private citizens, in a newspaper. Should you under a false idea of preserving the liberty of the press, lay open the secrets of families, and thereby wound female honour and delicacy, I hope our legislature will repeal the law that relates to assault and battery, and that the liberty of the bludgeon will be as sacred and universal in Pennsylvania, as your liberty of the press.

5. Never publish an article in your paper, that you would not wish your wife or daughter (if you have any) should read or understand.

6. The less you publish about yourself the better. What have your readers to do with the neglects or insults that are offered to you by your fellow citizens? if a printer offends you, attack him in your paper, because he can defend himself with the same weapons with which you wound him; type against type is fair play; but to attack a man who has no types nor printing press, or who does not know any thing about the manual of using them, is cowardly in the highest degree. If you had been in twenty Bunkers-hill battles, instead of one, and had fought forty duels into the bargain, and were afterwards to revenge an affront, upon a man who was not a printer, in your newspaper, I would not believe that you possessed a particle of true courage. If such a person injures you, if you are a Christian, you may forgive him, or sue him—if you are a savage, you may challenge him to fight a duel—and if you are a wild beast, you may tear him to pieces with your claws, or kick him into the gutter.

7. Publish, as often as you can obtain them, an exact but short account of all the laws that are passed in all the states in the Union.

8. Furnish your customers if possible with the future debates of the Senate and House of Representatives of the United States.

9. Let the advancement of agriculture—manufactures—and commerce, be the principal objects of your paper. A receipt to destroy the insects that feed upon turnips, or to prevent the rot in sheep, will be more useful in America, than all the inventions

for destroying the human species, which so often fill the columns of European newspapers.

10 Publish a price-current, and a state of the weather, once a week; and once a month, publish a list of all the deaths in the city—and if possible, the names of the diseases which occasioned them.

11. Do not neglect to insert a good essay, or paragraph, because it has been published in another newspaper. Extracts from modern publications upon useful subjects, will at all times be acceptable to your readers.

THE BENEFITS OF CHARITY
A Dream

OVERCOME with the heat and business of a warm day, I threw myself down in the afternoon of the 6th of this month, upon a sopha, where I had not remained long, before I dropped asleep. In the course of my nap, the following train of singular events were presented to my imagination. They made so strong an impression upon my mind that I could not help committing them to paper, and have since yielded to the importunities of several of my friends, to whom I showed them, by consenting to make them public, through the medium of the magazine.

I thought that I was conveyed, suddenly into the kingdom of Heaven, where I was first struck with the appearance of a large book, lettered on the back "the Judgements and Mercies of God"—On each side of the book stood an angel with a large breast plate, suspended from each of their necks, on one of them was engraved in flaming characters, The Destroying Angel,—on the other was engraved, in letters of gold, The Angel of Mercy.—The title of the latter engaged my attention and confidence, and I took the liberty of asking him the meaning of the book, and the nature of the offices which he and his companion held in the heavenly mansions. With a smile of benignity he told me, that the large book contained a particular account of all the judgments of God, which had ever been inflicted upon the nations and inhabitants of the earth, as well as the deliverances and mercies which had been conferred upon them. "My friend on the right hand, said he, is the minister of the former. I have the happiness of being the minister of the latter—War—fire—pestilence—famine—and earthquakes sue to him for employment, whenever he visits the earth—while peace—plenty and joy always follow my footsteps." After this he gave me an account of the steps which preceded all the great and terrible calamities which had destroyed cities and countries in different ages of the world. As I still retained an affection for the city of Philadelphia, I expressed a desire to know something of the past and future dispensations of Providence towards it. "You shall be gratified (said the angel of mercy.) In this book is an exact detail of these dispensations." Upon this he opened the book, which was of a folio size, and begged me to read the contents of half a page, which I accordingly did, and which, as nearly as I can recollect, contained the following history.

"In the month of June 1778 an order was issued to destroy the city of Philadelphia by fire. The destroying angel, had already winged his flight with a flaming torch in his hand, to lay that beautiful city in ashes.——When, suddenly, the angel of mercy pointed to the Pennsylvania Hospital, which stands in the neighbourhood of the city. Instantly the destroying angel extinguished his torch in the river Delaware, and returned to his usual post in the kingdom of heaven.

In the year 1786 an edict was issued to punish the city of Philadelphia for its wickedness by famine. The destroying angel appeared with blights—and mill-dew, and insects of various kinds, which feed on all manner of vegetable aliment, in his hand.—The angel of mercy appeared, and with his right hand and eyes uplifted to heaven, pointed to a small building in Strawberry Alley, called the Dispensary, and offered up at the same time the prayers and praises of upwards of 1800 patients who had been relieved by it from sickness and death. Instantly the destroying angel disappeared, the autumn was crowned with plenty, and the inhabitants enjoyed their usual profusion of the good things of life.

In the month of March 1787, the wickedness of Philadelphia increased to such a degree, as to awaken the divine vengeance a third time, and the destroying angel was commanded to let loose upon it the calamities of sickness and death. He appeared with a box in his hand, in which was confined the contagion of a malignant fever. The angel of mercy followed close upon his heels, and pointed to the Society for the Gradual Abolition of Slavery, and the Relief of Free Negroes, unlawfully held in Bondage. The destroying angel buried his box, and retired again to heaven.

In the month of May, of the same year, the wickedness of Philadelphia again provoked the wrath of heaven; and the destroying angel was sent to excite among her citizens a civil war. Already he waved in the air all the terrible instruments of death. The angel of mercy wept over the calamities which threatened the children of men,—but he soon wiped away his tears upon contemplating the German Lutheran school house. "Behold! here, (said he to the destroying angel) a Society for Alleviating the Miseries of Public Prisons.—See in the chair of the society the Bishop of Pennsylvania, and at his right hand the minister of the Lutheran church.—See! the chains fall from the prisoner, and hunger—nakedness—and vice fly before them."—Instantly the destroying angel broke his military instruments into a thousand pieces, and winged his way to the regions of peace and happiness.

In the month of July of the same year, the cry of the wickedness of the citizens of Philadelphia once more reached the heavens. The divine wrath was kindled in a more especial manner at the profanation of the Sabbath day, and at the impious and indecent language, which was to be heard from the children in the streets in every part of the city. The destroying angel was commissioned to overwhelm the city by an earthquake.—Though habituated to the business of destruction, he hesitated in the execution of his order. At last he appeared with a mixture of sulphur—air—water and fire (the ingredients of earthquakes) in his hand. The angel of mercy looked around him, for a pious and charitable institution, to plead with heaven in favour of the city.—Having heard of a proposal—he cried out free-schools.

"But where are they"—said the destroying angel?—In vain he sought for them in every part of the city.—But "hold (said the angel of mercy)—allow the citizens of Philadelphia only a few months more, and they will establish them. Hear in the mean time the following prayer." *May we be accepted, also concerning one thing more, O God! our spirit is stirred up with compassion for the multitudes of children in this great city, who stroll about unheeded and untaught. Lord of Mercy!—Make speed to save them, by putting it into the hearts of the humane, and affluent to gather these destitute ones, in some kindly folds of instruction, that they likewise may become useful and happy.*

The destroying angel was moved with the language of this prayer. He retired a few minutes from the sight of the angel of mercy, and upon returning addressed him in the following words. "I am commanded to suspend the execution of the last sentence, denounced against the city of Philadelphia, upon a certain condition.—If the inhabitants shall unite and establish free schools in which human learning shall be accompanied, and corrected with religious instruction, at any time before the first of May 1788, the city shall not be destroyed by an earthquake, nor shall the righteous indignation of heaven, again be awakened against it; for the diffusion of knowledge and religion among the poor shall protect it against every evil, and render this city the delight and admiration of the world."—

Here I closed the book, and was suddenly conveyed back to my native city. Anxious to preserve it from destruction, I flew immediately to the State House, where I was introduced to the presence of the General Assembly. My countenance, I suppose, bespoke distress and impatience, for the speaker interrupted the business of the house, and called upon me to know whether I had any thing to communicate to the assembly. After a low bow at the bar of the house, I began to address them, as nearly as I can remember, in the following language. "Legislators

---

* This excellent petition is part of a sublime and devout prayer, delivered by Dr. Magaw, at the close of the quarterly examination, on the 28th of July, at Mr. Brown's Female Academy.

of Pennsylvania, permit me to call your attention a few minutes from the present subject of your deliberations, to the salvation of the city of Philadelphia. It is in your power to save it from being destroyed by an earthquake. It is in vain to enact laws to suppress, or to punish vice and immorality. It is of much more consequence, and infinitely more easy, to *prevent* them, by providing for the education of the children of poor people. Have compassion upon yourselves.—Let not human nature be degraded any longer in Pennsylvania by the crimes and punishments which follow ignorance and vice.—Hear—ye guardians of the lives of your fellow citizens, the dreadful catastrophe which awaits the capital of your state. Nothing can prevent it but the immediate establishment of free schools in your city.— On the 1st day of May, in the year of our Lord 1788."—In pronouncing these words, my voice faltered, and I attempted in vain to finish the sentence. The agitation of my mind and body attracted the sympathy of a gentleman who sat near me, who, in offering me the support of his hand, suddenly awaked me from my dream.

THE YELLOW FEVER
Some Family Letters

PHILAD^A: Aug: 21. 1793.

MY DEAR JULIA,—To prevent your being deceived by reports respecting the sickliness of our city, I sit down at a late hour, and much fatigued, to inform you that a malignant fever has broken out in Water Street between Arch and Race Streets which has already carried off twelve persons within the space which has been mentioned. It is supposed to have been produced by some damaged coffee which had putrified on one of the wharves near the middle of the above district. The disease is violent and of short duration. In one case it killed in twelve hours, and in no case has it lasted more than four days. Among its victims is Mrs. LeMaigre. I have attended three of the persons who have died with it, and seven or eight who have survived, or who are I hope recovering from it.

As yet it has not spread thro' any parts of the city which are beyond the reach of the putrid exhalation which first produced it. If it should, I shall give you notice, that you may remain where you are till you receive further advice and information from me. The influenza continues to spread, and with more violent symptoms than when it made its first appearance. I did more business in 1780 than I do at present, but with much less anxiety, for few of the diseases of that year were attended with any danger, whereas *now*, most of the cases I attend are acute and alarming, and require an uncommon degree of vigilance and attention.

Aug: 22.

Marcus has been ill with the influenza, but is now better. Rich'd: Ben, and all the rest of the family are in good health.

I have just rec'd: a letter from Dr. * * * in which he has the following paragraph: "I have just seen Mr. Woolstonecraft. He does not like your lands, and that for the most childish reasons. He says that he saw but *one* flight of pheasants, *three* fishy ducks and *not one* woodcock on the whole creek, and that he will never settle anywhere where he cannot support himself by his *gun*."

So much the better! I have received since you left town conveyances for nearly all the lands I sold to the New Eng'd. men. They *adjoin* the lands sold by Rob't. Morris to the French Company who are about to improve them in the most extensive manner next Spring. *All* is for the best and *all will end well*.

A son of Dr. Priestley has just arrived in this city from France. He gives a most distressing account of the affairs of that country. But let us not despair. Chaos existed before the order and beauty of the universe. The devil who is the present tenant of our world, will not quit his hold of it till he has done the premises all the mischief that lies in his power, but go he must sooner or later, with all his family of nobles and kings.

Adieu: with love as usual I am my dear Julia,

Yours affect'y,
BENJ^N RUSH.

P.S.—John should come home as soon as his vacation expires.

PHILADELPHIA, AUG: 25. 1793.

MY DEAR JULIA,—Since my letter to you of Friday, the fever has assumed a most alarming appearance. It not only mocks in most instances the power of medicine, but it has spread thro' several parts of the city remote from the spot where it originated. Water Street between Arch and Race Streets is nearly desolated by it. This morning I witnessed a scene there, which reminded me of the histories I had read of the plague. In one house I lost two patients last night, a respectable young merchant and his only child. His wife is frantic this evening with grief. Five other persons died in the neighbourhood yesterday afternoon and four more last night at Kensington. The College of Physicians met this afternoon to consult upon the means of checking the progress of this dreadful disease. They appointed a Committee to draw up directions for that purpose. The Committee imposed this business upon me, and I have just finished them. They will be handed to the Mayor when adopted by the College and published by him in a day or two. I hope, and believe that they will be useful.

After this detail of the state of the fever, I need hardly request you to remain for a while with all the children where you are. Many people are flying from the city, and some by my advice. Continue to commit me by your prayers to the protection of that Being who has so often manifested his goodness to our family by the preservation of my life, and I hope I shall do well. I endeavour to have no will of my own. I enjoy good health and uncommon tranquility of mind. While I depend upon divine protection, and feel that at present I live, move, and have my being in a more especial manner in God alone, I do not neglect to use every precaution that experience has discovered, to prevent taking the infection. I even strive to subdue my sympathy for my patients, otherwise I should sink under the accumulated loads of misery I am obliged to contemplate. You can recollect how much the loss of a single patient once in a month used to affect me. Judge then how I must feel, in hearing every morning of the death of three or four!

I shall confine John and Richard to the house, and oblige them to use precautions against the disorder. My mother and sister are so kind and attentive as to prevent all our wants and wishes.

My love to your uncle and aunt and all the children. I am afraid you will burden our good relations, No—this cannot be.

They love you, and they love to do offices of kindness and humanity.

    Adieu, from your
     sincere and affectionate
         Benjn Rush.

       Philad^a Aug: 29th 1793.

My dear Julia,—Your letter dated yesterday came safe to hand.

I am pleased with your situation at your good aunts. Be assured that I will send for you, if I should be seized with the disorder, for I conceive that it would be as much your duty not to desert me in that situation, as it is now mine not to desert my patients. I have sent Becky with Ben to Mr. Bradford's farm this afternoon. They were most affectionately received by Betsey Johnson. Mrs. Wallace furnished them with tea, coffee, sugar and sundry other things to render them less burdensome to our good friends. The disease has raged with great virulence this day. Among the dead are Woodruf Sims, and Mr. Stiles the stone cutter. The last exhibited signs of the plague before he died. I have seen the same symptoms in the hospital fever during the late war. They have however greatly increased the terror of our citizens, and have excited an apprehension that it is in reality the Plague, but this I am sure is not the case, altho' it comes nearer to it in violence and mortality than any disease we have ever before had in this country. Its symptoms are very different in different people. Sometimes it comes on with a chilly fit, and a high fever, but more frequently it steals on with headache, languor and sick stomach. These symptoms are followed by stupor, delirium, vomiting, a dry skin, cool or cold hands and feet, a feeble slow pulse, sometimes below in frequency the pulse of health. The eyes are at first suffused with blood, they afterwards become yellow, and in most cases a yellowness covers the whole skin on the 3rd. or 4th. day. Few survive the 5th day, but more die on the 2nd. and 3rd. days. In some cases the patients possess their reason to the last, and discover much less weakness than in the last stage of common fevers. One of my patients stood up and shaved himself on the morning of the day he died. Livid spots on the body, a bleeding at the nose, from the gums and from the bowels, and a vomiting of black matter in some instances close the scenes of life. The common remedies for malignant fevers have all failed. Bark, wine and blisters make no impression upon it. Baths of hot vinegar applied by means of blankets, and the cold bath have relieved and saved some. Mrs. Chalmer owes her life to the former remedy. She caught it from her husband, who caught it in Water Street near the place where it originated. He too is upon the recovery. This day I have given mercury, and I think with some advantage. Dr. . . . and myself consult much together, and I derive great support and assistance from him in all my attempts to stop the progress of this terrible malady. He is an excellent man, and rises in his humanity and activity with the danger and distress of his fellow citizens. I have advised all the families that I attend, that can move, to quit the city. There is but one preventative of it that is certain, and that is "to fly from it."

Johnny Stall sleeps and eats with us, and thereby relieves me very much. My mother and sister are a part of the means that providence employs to preserve me from the infection. They are very kind. Mrs. Wallace has contrived a small mattress on some chairs on which I rest myself by lying down every time I come into the house. Adieu, with love to your Mama, your aunts, the children, and all friends, I am my Dear Julia

Your faithful and affectionate

BENJ[N] RUSH.

Aug. 30th. Another night and morning have been added to my life. I am preparing to set off for my daily round of duty, and feel heartily disposed to say with Jabez, "O that the hand of the Lord may be with me" not only to preserve my life, but to heal my poor patients. Betsey's relations are all well.

PHILAD^A Septem: 1. 1793.

MY DEAR JULIA,—In the language of good old Dr. Sproats prayer I am enabled yet to thank God "that I am alive, while others are dead" Two persons have died at Mrs. Lewis', next door to Peter Bayntons with the malignant fever, viz: Two of the Misses Mifflins. A woman has died with the same disorder in Dock Street near ——— and her husband will probably follow her before tomorrow morning. Thirty-eight persons have died in eleven families in nine days in Water Street, and many more in different parts of the city. Funerals are conducted agreeably to the advice of the College of Physicians.

BENJ^N RUSH.

Wed. Sept. 4. 1793.

MY DEAR JULIA,—The post is on the wing. I can only inform you that I put a letter into the post office for you directed to Princeton—this morning. I shall, if well, write to you again this evening. After a busy morning, I am, thank God, still in good health. Dr. . . . is not dead, but in great danger. The disease spreads, but its mortality is much less in proportion to the number who are affected. The jalap and mercury cures 9 out of 10, of all who take it on the day of the attack. Adieu.

BENJ^N RUSH

PHILAD^A Septem: 5: 1793.

MY DEAR JULIA,—*Still alive* and in *good health*, after having visited and prescribed for nearly one hundred patients. The disease continues to spread, but with no more mortality than a common bilious fever in the hands of those physicians who use the mercurial antidote. I now save 29 out of 30 of all to whom I am called on the first day, and many to whom I am called after it. Fewer deaths have occurred I believe this day than on several days last week, and yet many hundred people have the fever now than had it last week. Some of my brethren rail at my new remedy, but they have seen little of the disease, and some of them not a single patient. Most of the publications in the papers come from those gentlemen. They abound in absurdities and falsehoods. This night will probably end the busy life of Dr. . . . He continued to object to taking my medicine and was supported in his obstinacy by two young Doctors who had obtruded themselves upon him. Dr. . . . is better. Dr. . . . is well, and my invaluable friend . . . is out of danger. Poor Bill Bache was almost heart broken during his masters indisposition. Pet. Baynton is infected, Mrs. Baynton, Kitty and Mrs. Bullock are all in a safe way. I have had 12 new calls today, and have not lost a single patient since the night before last. I have found lately I hope a preventative of the disease, as well as a cure. It consists [not in drenching the stomach with wine, bark and bitters] but in keeping the bowels gently open, for in them the disease first fixes its poison. I owe these discoveries, as well as my preservation, to the prayers of my friends.

Septem. 6th.—6 o'clock in the morning. Blessed be God, my life, health and reason are still preserved to me. I forgot to mention that one of my pupils Washington has got the disease. He lies at Mrs. ——— a mile from town, where he is so much ashamed of being visited by me, that I heard of his illness by accident only from Johnny Stall. I shall try to see him, tho' I fear from the violence of his symptoms, and the progress of the disease that he will not recover. John Cox has become active and useful to me. He is very intelligent on the subject of the disorder, and knows no fear. Dr. . . . has taken charge of all Dr. . . . public patients, and is to divide the profits of attending them equally. If the Dr. survives, the partnership is to be perpetual. But this is improbable, for tho' I have just heard that he is still alive, yet I hear that he has a symptom which none [at least of my patients] have survived. Adieu. The box of clothes, with a letter from my sister were sent this morning by the stage committed to the care of Mr. Sayre. I paid the freight of the box here. Adieu; my love to all the family at Morven. Do oblige the boys to read systematically, and to avoid cold, fatigue and heat, also intemperance in eating, for each of those existing causes has produced the disease when the body has been infected. There is no certainty that they did not carry the infection from town. It lies from 1 to 16 days in the body, and the fever may be excited at any time within those days.

Adieu, again; yours, yrs—yrs

BENJ^N RUSH.

PHILADELPHIA Septem^r 15, 1793.

MY DEAR JULIA,—Life and health become every day more and more a miracle in persons who are constantly exposed to it. The disease spreads. Scarcely a family escape it. I have this day visited above twenty families which have all from two to six persons in it confined to their beds, and many which have one. Poor Mr. ————! After dismissing me and sending for a French physician, sent for me again this morning; but alas! it was too late to help him. He was yellow, cold and puking blood. "O Doctor" said he wringing his hands, "I was persuaded by my friends to employ the French physician. But help me, help me." I told him I would do my utmost for him, and with a heart wrung with anguish I hurried from his room. Many, many such scenes do I witness daily. For several days past I have sent 50 and 60 patients to other doctors. My old patients are constantly preferred by me. . . .'s publication has done immense mischief. Many doctors still follow him, and scores are daily sacrificed to bark and wine. My method is too simple for them. They forget that a stone from the sling of David effected what the whole armoury of Saul could not do. Many hundreds of my patients now walk the streets and follow their ordinary business. Could our physicians be persuaded to adopt the new mode of treating the disorder, the contagion might be eradicated from our city in a few weeks. But they not only refuse to adopt it but they persecute and slander the author of it. Sep. 16. Since writing the above I have had an attack of the disorder, but in consequence of losing blood and taking one of my purges I am now perfectly well—so much so that I rested better last night

than I have done for a week past. Thus you see that I have proved upon my own body that the yellow fever when treated in the new way, is no more than a common cold. I tho't it proper to give you this information to prevent your being alarmed by reports concerning me. Dont think of coming to see me. Our city is a great mass of contagion. The very air in it is now offensive to the smell. If I should relapse you shall hear from me. Mr. Stall and Mr. Cox are doing wonders in our city. They visit and cure all my patients. Adieu. Continue not only to pray for, but to give thanks for my dear Julia your
ever affectionate
BENJ^N RUSH.

PHILADELPHIA Octob^r 28. 1793.

MY DEAR JULIA,—I have great pleasure in informing you that Dr. . . . is much better. He was bled five times. After the 3rd bleeding an old patient of Dr. . . .'s went down to Gloucester and begged Mrs. . . . in the most pathetic terms not to consent to his being bled again. Mrs. . . . acted with firmness and propriety, and submitted to the subsequent bleedings with full confidence of their being proper, tho' advised only by Mr. Coxe. In this way have I been opposed and frequently defeated, from the commencement of the disorder, by the interference of the friends and followers of Dr. . . .

The disease visibly and universally declines. But some worthy people still have it, among whom is our cousin Parry Hall who is in great danger. Dr. . . . and Mr. Fisher attend him.

Tomorrow we expect to move into the front parlour. Our little back parlour has resembled for two months past the cabin of a ship. It has been shop, library, council chamber, dining room, and at night a bed chamber for one of the servants. My mother has hired Betsey Correy at 7/6 a week to take charge of the kitchen, which will enable Marcus to clean and white-wash the house, and to purify all the infected articles of furniture in it.

A new clamor has been excited against me in which many citizens take a part. I have asserted that the yellow fever was generated in our city. This assertion they say will destroy the character of Philad. for healthiness, and drive Congress from it. Truth in science as in morals never did any harm. If I prove my assertion, which I can most easily do, I shall at the same time point out the means of preventing its ever being generated among us again. I am urged to bring forward my proofs immediately. To this I have objected, until I am able to call upon a number of persons for the priviledge of using their names. To a gentleman who pressed the matter upon me this day, I said that the good opinion of the citizens of Philad was now of little consequence to me, for that I thought it probable from present appearances, that I should begin to seek a retreat and subsistance in some other part of the United States.

"Do all the good you can [said Mr. Westly to Mr. Pilmore when he entered into the ministry], expect to be persecuted for doing good, and learn to *rejoice* in persecution,"—a hard lesson to flesh and blood! but I hope it will please my divine Master to teach it to me.

Octobr 29th. We are all well—thank God! Adieu from yours with usual love and sincerity.

BENJ{N} RUSH.

Octobr 29. 1793.

MY DEAR SISTER,—Your affectionate letters drew tears from our eyes. Never did a brother feel more for the loss of a sister than I felt for ours. She was my friend and councillor in the difficult and distressing duties I was called upon to perform to my fellow citizens. She was my nurse in sickness. In short she gave her life to save mine, for when she was advised to go out of town to escape the fever, she calmly said "no, I will stay and take care of my brother, though I were sure I should die with the disorder, for my life is of no consequence to anybody compared with his." During the prevalence of the fever she was active, intelligent and useful among the patients who crowded my house at every hour of the day, and at most of the hours of the night. No person ever wept in our parlour or entry [and many, many tears were shed in both] with whom she did not weep. Her whole soul was made up of sympathy and kindness. In her last illness she was composed, and patient as an angel. She repeated several passages from the psalms expressive of the love and goodness of God, the day before she died. Her last words to me were "A thousand and a thousand thanks to you my dear brother for all your kindness to me."

BENJ^N RUSH.

PHILADELPHIA Novr 8th 1793.

MY DEAR JULIA,—I have this day received by Capt. Josiah from London, a letter to you from Dr. . . . accompanied with your silk gown which you committed to his care to be dyed. I have sent the letter by the post. I received a long and interesting letter from him at the same time, also a valuable medical book from Dr. Proudfit.

The disease has declined again since the last rain. I have had no calls to patients in the yellow fever for two days past, but several to patients indisposed with other diseases. My applications for advice in my house have been considerable likewise, but from no person affected with our late epidemic.

That my letters may contain a faithful narrative of all that related to myself during the late calamities of our city, I may now venture to inform you that in the morning of Octob^r 10th at one o'clock, I was attacked in a most violent manner with all the symptoms of the fever. Seldom have I endured more pain. My mind sympathized with my body. You, and my seven dear children rushed upon my imagination, and tore my heart strings in a manner I had not experienced in my former illness. A recovery in my weak and exhausted state, seemed hardly probable. At 2 o'clock I called up Marcus and Mr. Fisher who slept in the adjoining room. Mr. Fisher bled me which instantly removed my pains, and then gave me a dose and an half of the mercurial medicine. It puked me several times during the night, and brought off a good deal of bile from my stomach. The next morning it operated downwards, and relieved me so much, that I was able to sit up long eno' to finish my letter to you. In the afternoon, my fever returned, attended with a sleepiness, which is always considered as an alarming symptom. Mr. Fisher bled me again, which immediately removed it. I slept pretty well, the next night, was very weak, but free of pain the next day; but the night following, I fell into just such a fainting fit, as I had about the crisis of my pleurisy in the year 1788. I called upon Marcus who slept in the room with me for something to drink, and afterwards for some nourishment, which revived me in a few minutes, so that I slept well the remaining part of the night. One or two nights afterwards he gave me something to eat, which prevented a return of the fainting fits. It was not till the 15th of the month I was able to sit up, nor did I leave my room for many days afterwards. Mr. Fisher says he has seen no person more violently seized than I was. My recovery was under God owing to the *speedy* use of the new remedies.

This second attack of the fever, I now see was sent in mercy to me and my family. Had I not been arrested by it in my labors, my poor frame would probably have sunk before this time, under nothing but weakness, and fatigue.

I used to wish when called to more patients than I could attend, that I had an hundred hands, and an hundred feet. I now wish that I had an hundred hearts and an hundred tongues to praise the power, goodness and mercy of my gracious Deliverer, to whom alone belong the issues from sickness, and the grave.

Strike out from the list of deaths in your letters Jos. Harrison, and Jonth Penrose. Many people walk the streets now, who were said to be dead, during the prevalence of the disorder. Adieu. Love as usual.

                                    Yrs. sincerely
                                        BENJ^N RUSH.

APPENDIX

LIST

of the writings of Benjamin Rush published during his lifetime.

An inquiry into the natural history of medicine among the Indians of North America, and a comparative view of their diseases and remedies, with those of civilized nations.

An account of the climate of Pennsylvania, and its influence upon the human body.

An account of the bilious remitting fever, as it appeared in Philadelphia in the summer and autumn of the year 1780.

An account of the *scarlatina anginosa*, as it appeared in Philadelphia in the years 1783 and 1784.

An inquiry into the cause and cure of the cholera infantum.

Observations on the cynanche trachealis.

An account of the efficacy of blisters and bleeding in the cure of obstinate intermitting fevers.

An account of the disease occasioned by drinking cold water in warm weather, and the method of curing it.

An account of the efficacy of common salt in the cure of hæmoptysis.

Thoughts on the cause and cure of pulmonary consumption.

Observations upon worms in the alimentary canal, and upon anthelmintic medicines.

An account of the external use of arsenic in the cure of cancers.

Observations on the tetanus.

The result of observations made upon the diseases which occurred in the military hospitals of the United States, during the Revolutionary War.

An account of the influence of the military and political events of the American Revolution upon the human body.

An inquiry into the relations of tastes and aliments to each other, and upon the influence of this relation upon health and pleasure.

The new method of inoculating for the small-pox.

An inquiry into the effects of ardent spirits upon the human body and mind, with an account of the means of preventing, and the remedies for curing them.

Observations on the duties of a physician, and the methods of improving medicine; accommodated to the present state of society and manners in the United States.

An inquiry into the causes and cure of sore legs.

An account of the state of the body and mind in old age, with observations on its diseases and their remedies.

An inquiry into the influence of physical causes upon the moral faculty.

Observations upon the cause and cure of pulmonary consumption.

Observations upon the symptoms and cure of dropsies.

Inquiry into the cause and cure of the gout.

Observations on the nature and cure of the hydrophobia.

An account of the measles as they appeared in Philadelphia in the spring of 1789.

An account of the influenza, as it appeared in Philadelphia in the years 1790 and 1791.

An inquiry into the cause of animal life.

Outlines of a theory of fever.

An account of the bilious yellow fever, as it appeared in Philadelphia in 1793, and of each successive year till 1805.

An inquiry into the various sources of the usual forms of the summer and autumnal diseases in the United States, and the means of preventing them.

Facts, intended to prove the yellow fever not to be contagious.

APPENDIX

Defence of blood-letting, as a remedy in certain diseases.

An inquiry into the comparative states of medicine in Philadelphia, between the years 1760 and 1766, and 1805.

A volume of essays, literary, moral and philosophical, in which the following subjects are discussed:

A plan for establishing public schools in Pennsylvania, and for conducting education agreeably to a republican form of government. Addressed to the legislature, and citizens of Pennsylvania, in the year 1786.

Of the mode of education proper in a republic.

Observations upon the study of the Latin and Greek languages, as a branch of liberal education; with hints of a plan of liberal instruction without them, accommodated to the present state of society, manners, and government, in the United States.

Thoughts upon the amusements and punishments which are proper for schools.

Thoughts upon female education, accommodated to the present state of society, manners and government, in the United States of America.

A defence of the Bible as a school book.

An address to the ministers of the gospel of every denomination in the United States, upon subjects interesting to morals.

An inquiry into the consistency of the punishment of murder by death, with reason and revelation.

A plan of a peace-office for the United States.

Information to Europeans who are disposed to migrate to the United States of America.

An account of the progress of population, agriculture, manners and government, in Pennsylvania.

An account of the manners of the German inhabitants of Pennsylvania.

Thoughts on common sense.

An account of the vices peculiar to the Indians of North America.

Observations upon the influence of the habitual use of tobacco, upon health, morals, and property.

An account of the sugar maple tree of the United States.
An account of the life and death of Edward Drinker, who died on the 17th of November, 1782, in the one hundred and third year of his age.
Remarkable circumstances in the constitution and life of Ann Woods, an old woman of ninety-six years of age.
Biographical anecdotes of Benjamin Lay.
Biographical anecdotes of Anthony Benezet.
Paradise of negro slaves—a dream.
Eulogium upon Dr. William Cullen.
Eulogium upon David Rittenhouse.
A volume of lectures, most of which were introductory to his annual courses of lectures on the institutes and practice of medicine.
Medical inquiries and observations on the diseases of the mind.

SELECTED BIBLIOGRAPHY

"A Memorial containing Travels Through Life, or Sundry Incidents in the Life of Dr. Benjamin Rush. Written by Himself. Also Extracts from His Commonplace Book as well as A Short History of the Rush Family in Pennsylvania " Edited by Louis Alexander Biddle. Lanoraie, 1905.

"An Account of the Bilious Remitting Yellow Fever as It Appeared in the City of Philadelphia in the Year 1793 " Philadelphia, 1794.

"Old Family Letters Relating to the Yellow Fever." Series B. Edited by Alexander Biddle Philadelphia, J B. Lippincott, 1892.

"Rush Papers" in the Ridgway Branch of the Library Company of Philadelphia, the Pennsylvania Historical Society, the American Philosophical Society, the Pierpont Morgan Library, the University of Pennsylvania, the Philadelphia College of Physicians, the Girard Estate, the New York Academy of Medicine, the New York Historical Society, the Library of Congress. Also in the following collections: Dreer, Gratz, Cadwalader, Conarroe, Etting, Irvine, Logan, Pemberton, Peters, Sprague, Watson, Wayne and Wilson Papers.

"Rush Letters" in the Library Company of Philadelphia, Yale University Library, Franklin Collection; Historical Society of Pennsylvania, Gratz Collection.

"Journal of Rush's Trip to Paris" in the Pierpont Morgan Library, New York.

"Letters of Members of the Continental Congress." Edited by E C. Burnett, Washington, D. C., 1921-36. Volumes I to III, Volume VII.

Index Catalogue of the Library of the Surgeon-General's Office, U S.A., Volume XII. Washington, D. C, 1891.

Ramsay, David. "An Eulogium upon Benjamin Rush, M.D." 1813.

Robinson, Victor. "The Myth of Benjamin Rush." *Medical Life*, September 1929, Volume XXXVI.

Cobbett, William. *Porcupine's Gazette*. Philadelphia, files for 1797. *The Rush Light*. New York, 1800.

Eve, Sarah. "Extracts from the Journal of Miss Sarah Eve While Living near the City of Philadelphia in 1772-3." *Pennsylvania Magazine of History and Biography*, Volume V. Philadelphia, 1881.

Ford, Paul Leicester. "Dr. Rush and General Washington." *Atlantic Monthly*, Volume LXXV. Boston, 1895.
Mitchell, Silas Weir. "Historical Notes of Dr. Benjamin Rush." *Pennsylvania Magazine of History and Biography*, Philadelphia, 1903.
Ramsay, David. "A Report of an Action for Libel Brought by Benjamin Rush against William Cobbett." Philadelphia, 1800.
Butterfield, L. H. "Report of Progress." American Philosophical Society Year Book. 1945.
Mills, Charles K. "Benjamin Rush and American Psychiatry." *Medico Legal Journal*, 1886.
Shryock, Richard H. "The Psychiatry of Benjamin Rush." *American Journal of Psychiatry*, Volume IV. 1945.
Galdston, Iago "Diagnosis in Historical Perspective" *Bulletin of the History of Medicine*. 1941.
Butterfield, L. H. "Benjamin Rush: a Physician as Seen in His Letters." *Bulletin of the History of Medicine*, Volume XX, No. 2. 1946.
Wittels, Fritz. "The Contribution of Benjamin Rush to Psychiatry." *Bulletin of the History of Medicine*, Volume XX, No. 2. 1946.
Butterfield, L. H. "A Survey of Benjamin Rush Papers." *The Pennsylvania Magazine of History and Biography*, Volume LXX, No. 1. 1946.

Carey, Matthew. "A Short Account of the Malignant Fever Lately Prevalent in Philadelphia." Philadelphia, 1793.
Good, Harry G. "Benjamin Rush and His Services to American Education." Berne, Indiana, Witness Press, 1918.
Goodman, Nathan G. "Benjamin Rush, Physician and Citizen." Philadelphia, University of Pennsylvania Press, 1934.
Lettsom, John Coakley. "Recollections of Dr. Rush." London, 1815.
Shippen, Nancy. "Nancy Shippen, Her Journal Book." Compiled and edited by Ethel Armes, Philadelphia, J. B. Lippincott, 1935.
Flexner, James Thomas. "Doctors on Horseback." New York, 1937.
Gross, D. Samuel, editor. "Lives of Eminent American Physicians and Surgeons in the Nineteenth Century." Philadelphia, 1861.
Burrage, W. L. and Kelly, H. A., editors. "Dictionary of American Medical Biography." 1928.
Fitzpatrick, John C., editor. "The Writings of George Washington from the Original Manuscript Sources, 1745-1799." U. S. Government Printing Office, Washington, D. C.
Caldwell, Charles. "Autobiography." Edited by Harriet W. Warner, Philadelphia, 1855.

INDEX

Adam, 41, 375
Adams, John, 57
Addison, 59, 367
Aenead, 374
Aeneas, 192, 375
African Church of Philadelphia, 24, 25
African Company, 13
Agriculture,
 books on, 308
 in France, 391, 392
 livelihood for physicians, 308, 309
 national health, 290
Aiken, Dr., 195
Alchemical mania, 216
Amentia, 183
"American Museum," 35
American Revolution,
 events of, 325, 326
 influences on human body and mind, 326–333
American Stamp Act, 13
Amhurst, Sir William, 280
Amnesia, 183
Amusements proper for schools,
 associated with future employment, 106–109
 exclusion of gunnery, 107, 108
"Anarchia," 333
Anatomy, 133, 134
Animal electricity, 177
Animal life,
 infancy, 152, 153
 lectures on, 133
 middle stage, 155
 old age, 155

Animal magnetism, 313
Anomia, 192
Anthony, 183
Appetite, indicative of disease, 277, 284
Aræteus, 228
Architecture,
 English, 374
 French, 374
Ardent spirits,
 effects upon man, 334–341
Arnold, Dr, 162
Art of Living, French, 383
Assembly,
 annual elections, 65
 disadvantages of single legislative group, 58, 76, 77
 open meetings, 64
Association, influence on morals, 204, 205
Atheism, 170, 171, 179
Aurengezebe, Emperor of Persia, 284
Avarice, vice of physicians, 297

Bacon, Lord, 122, 261
Baglivi, Dr., 235, 329
Baldness, 346
Ballonius, 229
Bancroft, Dr., 257, 288
Barnevelt, 66
Barton, Dr, 174
Beattie, Dr., 182, 318
Bell, Dr., 241
Belknap, Rev. Jeremy, letter to, 117
Benezet, Anthony, 196, 210, 350

INDEX

Bible, 7, 21
  as a school book, 117-130
  Doctrine of Love, 125
  early aptitude for learning its tenets, 117, 118
  on capital punishment, 48, 49
  teaches Truth, 119
  value to medical science, 123
Bill of Rights, 32, 54, 77
  natural and civil rights, 55
Black, Dr.,
  "History of Medicine," 250
  research work, 304
Blacklock, 158
Blane, Dr., 327
Bleeding, in old age, 356
Blood phobia, 223
Boerhaave, Dr., 133, 134, 148, 228, 229, 250, 251, 252, 278, 299
  humanity of, 301
  piety of, 310
Bolingbroke, 59, 128
Borreau, 376
Botallus, 299
Boyle, 122, 158, 159
Brambilla, Dr., 151
Brissot, 168
Brown, Dr, 136, 137, 145, 147, 148, 228, 247, 250, 251, 252
Brown, editor of "Federal Gazette," 396
Bruce, 123, 153
Brydone, 200
Burgoyne, General, 82, 329
Burnet, Bishop, 366
Butler, 318

Cadwallader, Dr, 285
Cæsar, 183, 259
Cain, 41
Capital punishment,
  punishing murder by death, 35-53
  revision of penal code, 20
Carver, Captain, 169
Cassius, 183
Cat phobia, 220
Cavendish, 228
Chardin, 356
Charity, benefits of, 399-403
Charlevoix, 255
Chatham, Lord, 217

Cheselden, 299
Child bearing, 288
Chisholm, Dr., 234, 298
Chovet, Dr., 354, 356
Christ, 9, 10, 37
  "Golden Rule," 9
  miraculous cures, 286
Christianity,
  declares war unlawful, 51
  human understanding, 211
  incompatible with slavery, 9
  influenced abolishment of capital punishment, 51
  religious conversion of slaves, 10
Church de Sorbonne, 376
Church phobia, 224
Cicero, 378
  moral faculty, 181
  orator, 393
Cleanliness, 197, 198
  in old age, 356
Cleghorn, Dr., "Account of Diseases of Minorca," 229, 230
Clergy, French, 381, 382
Climate,
  effects on diseases, 271, 272
  effects on moral faculty, 192, 193
Clymer, George,
  letter to, 106-116
  representative from Pennsylvania, 114
Cochin-China, 5
College of Physicians, 406, 409
Confederation,
  defects, 27, 28
  need for two houses, 27
Conscience, 181, 182, 185, 186
"Conscious Lovers," 379
Constantine, 9
Constitution,
  free government, 54
  of Pennsylvania, 55-84
  of Massachusetts Bay, 82, 83
  revision needed, 79-82
Convention of New York, 81
Convention of Pennsylvania, 74, 75, 76, 77
Council of Censors, 64, 74, 75, 76, 78
  a check on the assembly, 66
Count D'Artois of France, 390
Cook, Captain, 198

Cornelia, 283
Cornwallis, Lord, 331
Creighton, Dr., 162
Cretins, 144, 158
Cullen, Dr., 136, 137, 174, 187, 228, 234, 247, 250, 251, 252, 301, 330
  nerves, disease of, 278
  nosology, 273
  nostalgia, 328
  on hydrophobia, 220
  on madness, 212, 332
  pulse, 277
Cyrus, 208

Darwin, Dr, 145, 151
Dauphin of France, 389, 390
David, 201
Death, 175, 176
  due to intemperance, 340
  fear of, 351
  resuscitation, 241, 242
Death phobia, 225
De Haen, 269
Deists, 49, 118
  in France, 381
Demosthenes, 378
Desdemona, 200
Dewit, Dr., 354
Diabetes, 337
Dido, 375
Diet,
  effect on moral faculty, 193
  influence on health, 285, 286, 287
  in old age, 355
Dirt phobia, 221
Diseases,
  definition, 251
  effect on intellect, 195
  effect on longevity, 345
  effect on moral faculty, 195
  in old age, 352-354
  nervous, 278
  of civilized nations, 271
  of North American Indians, 261-270
Dispensary, in Philadelphia, 400
Doctor phobia, 223
Dolabella, 183
Donation mania, 214
Dreams, 164
  effect on moral faculty, 188
  of children, 154

Dreams—*cont'd*
  of old people, 156, 351
Dress, in France, 383
Dress mania, 217
Drink, effect on moral faculty, 193, 194
Drunkenness, 334-340
  medical vice 294
Drinker, Edward, 346
Dubourg, John Barew, 393
Duelling mania, 215
Duke of Orleans, palace of, 375
Duke of Sully, 46, 89
  memoirs, 184, 185
Duke of Tuscany, 36
Dysentery, among North American Indians, 261, 266

Eating habits,
  effect on health, 164
  in old age, 348
Ecclesiastical mania, 217
Edict of Nantes, 380
Education,
  advantages of learning, 97
  arts, 94
  for women, 95, 96
  free schools, 19, 20, 98
  government, 95
  history and chronology, 94
  languages, 93
  "liberal education," 93
  mathematics, 93
  moral teachings, 90
  political instruction, 91, 92, 93
  religion the foundation, 88
  sciences, 94
  vocal music, 92
Elizabeth, Queen of England, 211
Emotions, effect on the body, 144, 145
Empress of Russia, 36
  abolishes capital punishment, 44
Engelbrecht, apparent death and return to life, 163, 164
English Constitution, 16
Epicurean philosophy, 179
Epilepsy, 338
Excitement, state of, necessary for good health, 146, 251
Executive powers of a free government, 69, 70

INDEX

Exercise,
  active, 360-364
  in old age, 355
  passive, 364-367
  time for, 368

Faction phobia, 222
Family letters, written during the yellow fever epidemic, 404-415
Fasting, 159
Federal Constitution, 19, 32
"Federal Gazette," 396
Federal University, 29
  degree requisite for civil or public office, 104
  plans for, 101
  preparation for civil and public careers, 102
  subjects taught, 102, 103
Fevers,
  among civilized nations,
  among North American Indians, 261
  nervous fever, 285
Fothergill, Dr., 198, 289
  humanity of, 301, 302, 305
  piety of, 299, 310
  promotes science, 303, 304
  tribute to family, 306
Foundling Hospital, 377
Franklin, Dr. Benjamin, 67, 144, 367
  longevity, 343, 345, 347, 356
Free government, 54
  dangers of a single legislature, 60-68
  double or compound legislature, 68, 69
French women,
  impropriety of, 379, 380
  lack of delicacy, 379
  painting, 379, 386
  virtue of, 380

Galen, 228, 299
  on humanity, 300
Gaming mania, 215
Gates, General, 329
German Lutheran School, 401
Ghost phobia, 224, 255
Gibbon, 102
Girtanner, Dr., 136

God, 9
  His exclusive power to give life and destroy it, 38, 39
  love for Him to be taught in schools, 120
Goldsmith, Dr., 219
Goodwin, Dr., 140
Gout,
  among Indians of North America, 263, 264
  due to intemperance, 338
Gregory, Dr., 197, 310

Habit, effect on morals, 203, 204
Hales, Dr., 169
Haller, Dr., 151, 167, 301, 351
  on corporal punishment, 111
  on religion, 299, 310
Haman, 217
Hamilton, Sir Wm., 168
Hamlet, 204
Hand, Edward, 255, 268
Harrington, 58, 78
Hartley, Dr., 135, 242, 318
  on piety, 299
Hazard, 40
Heberden, Dr., 277
Henry III of England, 394
Henry III of France, 200
Henry IV, 89, 211, 375
Hippocrates, 228, 230, 277
  on humanity, 300
  patriotism of, 303
Hoffman, Dr., 247, 274, 299
Holland, endemics, 278
Home, Dr., 304, 308
Home phobia, 224
Homer, 158
Horace, 119
Horse mania, 213
Hospital of God, 377
Hospitals, 284
  in France, 377
  in Philadelphia, 400
House of Commons, 61
House of Lords, 61
House of Representatives, state, 57
Howard, 195, 196, 197
Howell, "Familiar Letters," 278
Howe, General, 78
Huck, Dr., 276

INDEX 429

Humane mania, 218
Humanity, in physicians, 300, 301, 302
Hume, "History of England," 331
Hunter, Dr., 133, 134, 304, 308
Hunter, John, 152 161, 173, 174
Hunting, in France, 387
Hunting mania, 215
Husbandry, 392
Hutchison, Dr., 182
Hutton, John S., 345, 347
Huxham, 229
Hydrophobia, 220
Hygiæa, 371, 372
Hypochondria, 285, 332
   "Protection Fever," 332
   "Revolutiana," 332
Hysteric disorders, 285
   in wartime, 330

Idleness, 195, 196
   cause of disease, 271
Imagination,
   affected by disease, 186
   moral faculty, 188
Impeachment of state officers, 73
Insect phobia, 220, 221
Intellectual faculty, 188, 189
Intemperance, cause of disease, 271, 337, 338

Jaundice, 337
Jews, 7, 8
   health, 286
   knowledge of the Scriptures, 120, 121
Johnson, Dr., 102, 235, 350
   on corporal punishment, 111
   death phobia, 225
   ecclesiastical mania, 217
Josiah, 121
Josiah, Capt., 414
Judgment, affected by disease, 186
Judicial body of free government, 71, 72
Junius, 102

Kalm, 268
King of Prussia,
   death phobia, 225
   ghost phobia, 225
   poetry of, 288

King of Sweden, 36

La Hontan, 255
Land mania, 213
Laughing and crying, promote human life, 153
Lavoisier, 138, 228
Laws, executive part of Constitution, 54
Laws of Barbadoes, 18
Lay, Benj., 145
Legislation,
   against slavery, 16
   benefitting Negroes, 17
Le Poivre, 5, 6
Leprosy,
   among civilized nations, 277
   among Indians of North America, 262
Levitical law,
   cleanliness, 197
   punishment of murderers, 39
Liberty mania, 213, 214
Life,
   desire to live, 168, 344
   properties of *motion, sensation, thought*, 135
   suspended, 160, 161
Light, effect on behaviour, 200
Lind, Dr., 365
Linnæus, on madness, 219
Linning, Dr., 236
Lobb, Dr., 299
Locke, 33, 78, 146, 367
   Essay on Human Understanding, 189
   on metaphysics, 318,
Louis VIII, 263
Louis XIII, 375
Louis XIV, 380
Louis XV, 390, 391
Love mania, 217

Machine mania, 215
Maclurg, Dr., 262, 276
Madness,
   definition, 212
   due to intemperance, 338
   species of, 212–219
Magau, Dr., 402
Manassah, 121

Mania, 183
  definition, 212
  species of, 212-219
Manners and customs, French, 382, 383, 385-389
Marie de Medici, 376
Marius, vices of, 182
Marquis of Beccaria, 46
Materia Medica, 177
Mathematical mania, 219
Mather, Dr. Cotton, 280
Mead, Dr., 8, 169
  humanity of, 305
  South Sea madness, 332
Medicine,
  observations on, 245-292
  practice of, in America, 248, 249
  practice of, in France, 393, 394
  principles of, 237-253
  progress of, 227-244
  theory of, 248, 249
Medicine Among the Indians of North America, 254-292
  anointing body with oil, 259
  antidotes to poisons, 268, 269
  childbirth, 256, 258
  cold baths, 259
  death, 261
  diet, 256, 257
  diseases, 261-270
  dysentery, 261, 266
  fevers, 261
  leprosy, 262
  natural and artificial remedies, 265-270
  pulse rate, 260
  scurvy, 262
  smallpox, 262, 268
  venereal diseases, 262, 268
Medicines,
  discovering new, 319, 320, 321
  effect on moral faculty, 201
  prescribing, 311, 314
Megapolensis, Rev., 40
Melancholia, 183
Memory,
  affected by disease, 186
  in old age, 349, 350
Mercury, in curing yellow fever, 408
Mesmer, 313
Metaphysics, 227, 318

Methodists, morals, 208
Michaelis, Dr., 120, 158
Micronomia, 192
Military mania, 214
Militia law, 56, 72
  Delaware's amendments, 68
Miller, Dr, 240
Milton, 59, 158, 208
  "Paradise Lost," 185, 375
Mitchell, Dr., 240
Mithridates, 208
M'Kenzie, Dr., "Essay on Health and Long Life," 363
Monarchial mania, 214
Montesquieu, 4, 58, 78
  "Spirit of Laws," 4, 12, 17
Moral faculty, 181-211
Mordecai, 217
More, Sir Thomas, 115
Morgani, 349
Morton, Dr, 301
Mosaic law, with regard to murder, 39
Moses, 37, 124
Moyse, Dr, 158
Muratori, "Antiquities of Italy," 263
Musical mania, 219

National mania, 217
National prejudices, 373
Natural history, 228
Nature, cures diseases, 273, 274
Nebuchadnezzar, 201, 286
Negro mania, 212, 213
Nerves, diseases of, 278
  nervous fever, 285
Nervous system, 177
Newspaper, directions for conducting, 396-398
New Testament, 18
  cure of diseases, 242
  moral faculty, 199, 201
  on vice and crime, 339
Newton, Sir Isaac, 78, 144, 208, 244, 309, 367
  knowledge of Bible, 122
Noah, 37, 38
North, Lord, 78
Nosology, 234
  retarded progress of medicine, 235, 236

INDEX

Nostalgia, 328
Nunneries, French, 382

Odor phobia, 221
Odours, 200
Old Testament, 8, 18, 120–128
  Aaron, 124
  Abraham, 7
  Amos, 18
  cure of diseases, 242
  Ezra, 8, 121
  historical record, 119
  Jacob, 18
  Joshua, 7
  Leviticus, 8
  moral faculty, 199, 201
  Proverbs, 8
  Rahab, 7
Old age,
  attainment of, 342–357
  mental changes, 349
  phenomena of, 347
  physical changes, 345–349
Onesimus, 10
Oratory, French, 377
Othello, 200
Ovid, Metamorphoses, 376

Pain, effect on moral faculty, 197
Paintings, in Paris, 375, 376
Palace of Luxembourg, 375
Palsy, cause of death, 356, 357
Parliament, 13
  in France, 378
Parr, 347
Pascal, 226
Passions,
  as remedies in cure of diseases, 231
  opposed to longevity, 344
Patriotism, virtue of physicians, 303, 304, 305
"Peace Office," 19, 20, 21, 22
Pennsylvania Hospital, 400
"Pennsylvania Mercury," 42
Philemon, 10
Philochoras,
  favouring punishment of murder by death, 42
  Rush's argument against it, 43
Phobia,
  definition, 220

Phobia—*cont'd*
  species of, 220–226
Physicians,
  advice to, 311–321
  Christian behavior of, 310, 311
  duties of, 308–321
  fees for service, 316, 317
  vices of, 293–298
  virtues of, 298–306
Physiology, 133
Piety, in physicians, 299, 310
Pilmore, Rev. Mr., 25
Pleasure mania, 218
Pliny, 320
Poetical mania, 219
Pompey, 376
Pontoppiddan, "Natural History of Norway," 263, 286, 288
Pope, 376
Post office, 29, 30
Power phobia, 222
Prescriptions, 311, 314
Price, 59
Pride mania, 217
Priestly, Dr., 228, 303
Prince de Beaufremont, 347
Pringle, Sir John, 120, 197, 198
Prognosis of disease, 276, 277
Prometheus, 337
Protestants (Hugonots), in France, 380
Pulpit,
  eloquence of, and effect on moral faculty, 199
Pulse, 239, 277
  in old age, 348
  of Indians, 260
Punishments proper for schools, 109, 113
  arguments against corporal punishment, 110–113
Pythagoras, 336

Quakers, 122
  morals, 208

Radcliff, Dr., 303
Rambling mania, 216
Ramsay, Dr., letter to, 32–35
Randolph, Peyton, 330
Ranks of mankind, 389

"Rape of Orythia," 376
Rat phobia, 220
Raynal, Abbé, 29
Reason, effect on moral faculty, 190
Reid, Dr., 318
Relief of Free Negroes, 401
Remedies,
  advice on, 319, 320, 321
  among civilized nations, 275, 276, 279, 282
  among North American Indians, 265-270, 279
  Nature's, 274
Republican mania, 214
Respiration, 153
Resuscitation, 161, 163, 240, 241, 242
Richelieu, Cardinal, 376
Rittenhouse, 67, 137
Riverius, 229
Robertson, Dr., 10
Rogue mania, 218
Rousseau, 164, 363
  "Moral instinct," 182, 190
Royal Family of France, 389, 390, 391
Rubens, 376
Rum phobia, 222
Rush, Jacob, 352
Rush, Julia, letters to, 404-415
Russel, Dr. Patrick, 195
  friendships of, 305

St. Anthony, 214
St. John, 182
St. Paul, 10, 39, 47
  moral faculty, 181, 182, 191, 201, 202
Sanctorius, 368
Sanderson, 158
Saul, 201, 286
Sauvage, Dr., 251
Sayre, Dr., 346, 410
Schoolmasters, duties of, 114
Schools,
  amusements proper for, 106-109
  punishments proper for, 109-113
Scurvy,
  among civilized nations, 277
  among Indians of North America, 262
Second childhood, 351
Sedatives, 177

Sensation,
  excitability to motion, 136
  vital, 167
Senses, lack of sight, hearing, speech, 158, 159
Servin, 184, 185, 208
Shaftesbury, Lord, 119, 190
Shakespeare, 200, 208
Sharp, Granville, 14
  letter to, 24, 25
Silence, 198, 199
Slave-keeping, 3, 5, 6, 7
  education for Negroes, 14, 24
  end of domestic slavery in Pennsylvania, 24
  inconsistent with Christian behavior, 11, 12, 17
  liberty, 6, 17
  manumission, 10
  punishment of slaves, 16
  unlawful, 13, 16, 17
Sleep, 147-151
  excessive, 196
Smallpox,
  among Indians of North America, 262, 268
  inoculation against, 290
Smith, 123
Smith, Dr. Adam, 182, 233, 260
Society,
  in England, 384
  in France, 384, 389
Society for the Gradual Abolition of Slavery, 401
Socinians, 49
Socrates, 66
Solano, Dr., 277
Solitude, 198, 367
Solo phobia, 222
Solomon,
  labour, 359
  moral training, 202
"Song of Solomon," 5
Soul,
  faculties of, 366, 367, 368
  immortality of, 191
Sovereignty, federal, not state power, 28
"Spectator," 3
Spirituous liquors,
  in prescriptions, 312

INDEX

Spirituous liquors—*cont'd*
  physical and moral evils, 289
Sproats, Dr., 409
Stage plays, in France, 378, 379
Stahl, Dr., 174, 247, 250
  "Anima Medica," 277
  on religion, 299, 310
Stamp and Revenue Acts, 18
State colleges, 98
State University, 98
Statuary, in Paris, 376
Stern, Dr., Sermons Upon Mortification, 382
Sterne, Dr., 363
Stewart, 138
Stimulants, 177
  use in old age, 354
Stimuli,
  external, 137-141
  internal, 141
  mental, 168
Supreme Being, 178, 179
Suspended animation, 161, 242
Swift, Dr., 350, 367
Sydenham, Dr., 229, 230, 261, 275, 276, 285
  humanity of, 301, 305
  piety of, 310

Tacitus, 8, 258, 289
Taste, effect on morals, 190
Teeth,
  care of, 288, 289
  loss of, 345
Temple, Sir William, 289
Temple of Solomon, 374
Thiery, Dr., 345
Thunder phobia, 224
Tissot, Dr., 306, 367
Trajan, 182
  statuary, 376
Travels through France, 373-395
"Tristam Shandy,"
  military mania, 214
  want phobia, 223
Turner, Dr., 315
Turner, Rev. Mr., 37

Umfreville, 152
University of Cambridge, 105

"Utopian scheme," 115

Van Helmont, 247
Valli, 177
Venereal diseases, among Indians of North America, 262, 268
Verulam, Lord, 208
Vice, 181, 182
Vices of physicians, 293-298
Virgil, 5, 374
Virgin Mary, 128
  church dedicated to, 375
Virginia Assembly, 13
Virtue, 181, 182
Virtues of physicians, 298-306
Virtuoso mania, 216
Vogel, Dr., 251
Volney, 165, 166
Voltaire, 8, 128
  belief in religious tolerance, 46
  Bible as source of knowledge of justice, 118

Want phobia, 223
War,
  diseases caused by 327-333
  education to prevent, 108
  evils of, 22
  hardships of, 288
  repeal of militia laws, 21
Ward, Dr., 270
Washington, George, 410
Water phobia, 222
Waters, Dr., 338
Webster, 240
Whitehurst, 123
Whytt, Dr., 143, 174
Wintringham, 229
Worms, among Indians of North America, 264

Yellow fever, 229, 238
  effect of intemperance on, 337
  epidemic of, 404-415
  letters to family during epidemic, 404-415
  remedies and cures, 408, 409
  symptoms of, 407, 414, 415
Young, Dr., 221, 298

CPSIA information can be obtained
at www.ICGtesting.com
Printed in the USA
BVHW041931220719
554080BV00006B/99/P